The African National Congress and the negotiated settlement in South Africa

Johannes Mutshutshu Rantete

J. L. van Schaik

ACADEMIC

Published by J.L. van Schaik Publishers
1064 Arcadia Street, Hatfield, Pretoria

First edition 1998

ISBN 0 627 02329 0

Typeset in 10,5/12,5 pt Meridian by Iskova Image Setting CC, Johannesburg
Diagrams by Iskova Image Setting CC, Johannesburg
Printed and bound by National Book Printers, Drukkery Street, Goodwood, Western Cape

Foreword by the National Chairperson of the African National Congress

The African National Congress and the negotiated settlement in South Africa represents a comprehensive documentation of the ANC's recent history. It unravels the complex dynamics leading to the conclusion of the negotiated political settlement and the formation of a unique democratic Government based on the principles of National Unity. This book is not an ANC mouthpiece but a critical piece of work written by a youthful author, courageous enough to confront and scrutinise difficult topics facing us today. His critical postulations and points of argument advanced both in the theoretical text and the empirical sections of the book are very interesting and may serve as a point of departure for strategic and academic debate.

Although the book is presented in themes, it provides a comprehensive coverage of the ANC's organisational and political development, including its momentous advances towards assuming state power. Topics are diligently organised and analysed. Thus, from the ANC's condition of exile at the beginning of the 1990s, the book unfolds the organisation's transition into a home-based movement, its creation of a head office, regions and branches. It proceeds to analyse the ANC's political development, in particular its relations with allied organisations such as the SACP, COSATU and the civic movement. It also scrutinises internal democratic practices, crises and tensions, including policy development and the effects of violence. The second part of the book analyses the factors behind the ANC's movement towards negotiations. It looks at initiatives taken by the ANC in advancing this course, including an analysis of CODESA negotiations, the election campaign and the installation of the new government.

The issues dealt with in the book may not be new, but the manner in which they are analysed and the rigour with which topics such as violence, negotiations, theory and strategy are scrutinised make this book a distinctive masterpiece. This publication provides the basis from which some of these topics and themes may be pursued comprehensively on their own. It may also serve as a springboard to further analyses of the ANC government.

Finally, I commend the author for work well done and hope that this book will inspire similar efforts by others.

MGP Lekota
ANC National Chairperson

Contents

Foreword – Patrick Lekota v

Preface ix

List of abbreviations xii

Introduction xv

Section A: From an exile and underground liberation movement to an open legal organisation inside South Africa 1

1 The ANC's organisational development 3

Formation of the ANC 3

State of exile 3

The unbanning and the building of an organisational structure –
head office, regions and branches 6

Mass membership recruitment and the consolidation of branches 17

Organisational reconstruction and finance 23

2 The ANC's political development 31

Relations with allied organisations 31

Internal tensions, crises and democratic practice 56

3 The ANC and policy development 83

Policy development and *Ready to govern* 83

The Reconstruction and Development Programme 88

4 The ANC and the challenges posed by violence 98

Section B: The African National Congress and the negotiated trajectory to power in the 1990s 113

5 Factors behind the ANC's decision to negotiate 115

The armed struggle – from propaganda warfare to people's war 115

The Mandela factor – setting the stage for negotiations 128

Internal mass struggles including political and diplomatic
achievements of the organisation 130

Pressure exerted on the organisation by the Soviet Union and
the front-line states 132
Internal debates within the ANC on the questions of theory,
strategy and tactics for attaining power through negotiations 135

6 The ANC – taking the initiative in negotiations 143

The ANC's 1987 Negotiation Statement and the
1989 Harare Declaration 143
P.W. Botha's political dilemma and the crisis of stalemate 150
The De Klerk era: the normalisation of hostilities and the building of a
peaceful climate conducive to negotiations 153
The release of Nelson Mandela from prison 158

7 The ANC and substantive negotiations 161

Preliminary negotiations and the removal of obstacles to substantive
negotiations 161
The demand for transitional mechanisms: interim government and a
constituent assembly 165
The Convention for a Democratic South Africa (CODESA) and the
beginning of substantive negotiations 173
The fall of CODESA and resultant mass mobilisation 183
Putting a tap on mass mobilisation: whither the armed struggle and the
sanctions campaign? 185
Back to negotiations and the Record of Understanding 197
Strategic self-analysis, the "sunset clause" and the new strategic
perspective to power 198
From Strategic perspective to the Negotiating Council and the passing
of the transitional mechanisms bills 204
The interim constitution and the birth of South Africa's democratic
dispensation 214
The conclusion of an inclusive settlement: popular uprising in
Bophuthatswana, the fall of the Freedom Alliance and the
succumbing of KwaZulu 216

8 Ke nako: the ANC's election campaign and victory of the elections 229

Preparations for democratic elections 229
The ANC election manifesto 233
Nomination of election candidates 235
The election campaign and the road to victory 238
Voting, the election results, victory celebrations and the installation
of the Government of National Unity 244

9 Power positioning, negotiations and the making of South Africa's transition from apartheid 254

10 Conclusion 262

From apartheid to democracy: the ANC's road to power 262

Photo section 269

Appendices

Appendix A: Members of the National Executive Committee of the African National Congress as at July 1991 287

Appendix B: Summary of the 1993 interim constitution 288

Appendix C: The ANC's nominations list for the national assembly 293

Appendix D: SACP members in the ANC nominations list for the April 1994 elections 295

Appendix E: Results of South Africa's first democratic elections, 26–29 April 1994 296

Appendix F: The cabinet of South Africa's Government of National Unity, 1994 299

Bibliography 301

Index of persons, organisations and other bodies 315

Preface

This book is an edited version of a thesis submitted by the author to the University of the Witwatersrand for a Master of Arts Degree. Although it does provide historical traces to previous decades, the book is primarily about the African National Congress (ANC) between 1990 and 1994. It analyses the ANC's organisational reconstruction inside South Africa and its negotiated road to power. Apart from the introduction and the conclusion, the book is divided into two sections, one dealing with the ANC's organisational reconstruction and the other dealing with the ANC and negotiations. The introduction locates the ANC's experiences within two comparative theoretical frameworks, transition to democracy theory and the decolonisation paradigm. The weaknesses of these theoretical approaches in relation to the South African transition process are pointed out. In spite of these weaknesses it is argued in the introduction that these two paradigms are jointly useful in providing a broad framework within which the ANC and the South African transition process can be understood.

Section A analyses the transition of the ANC from being an exile and underground liberation movement to an open legal organisation inside South Africa. This section contains four chapters:

- Chapter 1 deals with the ANC's organisational development. It analyses the state of the ANC's organisation in exile, its return home, the building of its organisational structures, mass membership recruitment and the consolidation of its branches. It also analyses the ANC's organisational reconstruction and finance.

- Chapter 2 discusses the ANC's political development. It focuses on the ANC's relations with its youth and women's organisations as well as its relations with the Congress of South African Trade Unions (COSATU), the South African Communist Party (SACP) and the civics. Internal tensions and democratic practice are also examined.

- Chapter 3 deals with the ANC and policy development. It traces the processes behind the ANC's "Ready to govern" policy document and its Reconstruction and Development Programme. It demonstrates that while the organisation was engaged in meeting two major challenges of building its organisational structures and negotiating a political settlement, the interjection of violence made a significant impact on the speedy realisation of these objectives.

- Chapter 4 analyses the ANC and violence.

Section B covers the ANC and negotiations, including elections and the installation of the Government of National Unity:

- Chapter 5 analyses factors behind the ANC's decision to negotiate. It traces problems experienced with armed revolutionary politics, the role of Nelson Mandela in setting the stage for negotiations, and the political and diplomatic achievements of the movement against the state. It also probes the pressure put on the organisation to negotiate as well as the organisation's internal debate on negotiations.

- Chapter 6 deals with various initiatives that laid the ground for serious negotiations. It begins with the ANC's 1987 Negotiation Statement and proceeds to the Harare Declaration. It also analyses the government's attempts to come to terms with the challenges of negotiations by focusing on P.W. Botha's crisis of stalemate and De Klerk's bold liberalisation initiatives, which ended with the release of Nelson Mandela.

- Chapter 7 investigates the ANC and the negotiation process. It looks at the evolution of the negotiation process, beginning with the ANC's decision to negotiate and ending with the conclusion of an inclusive settlement.

- Chapter 8 focuses on the ANC's preparations for elections, its election manifesto, its election campaign as well as its election victory and the installation of the Government of National Unity.

- Chapter 9 concludes Section B, with an observation of the simultaneous processes of power positioning and negotiating followed by the ANC and the National Party in the making of South Africa's transition from apartheid.

The conclusion summarises the major findings of the book. Here the successes of the ANC's organisational reconstruction and the conclusion of a negotiated settlement are measured against important weaknesses and problems.

It is important to emphasise that the book is broadly presented in themes and the deployment of information is informed by this. This means that, despite a coherent arrangement of chapters, the presentation of information is not necessarily logical (e.g. the history of the ANC's formation is referred to more broadly in Chapter 5 than at the beginning of the book, where it should logically be), and certain developments are described in more than one chapter. For example, the revelation of the Inkathagate scandal appears in both Chapter 4 (where violence is discussed) and 7 (negotiations). While the question of violence is fully discussed in Chapter 4, its impact on the ANC's organisational reconstruction is briefly referred to in Chapter 2. Moreover, the question of the ANC's military camps in Angola, which ought to be discussed with the ANC's armed struggle, is analysed separately in Chapter 2.

I was inspired to write this book by my own interest in the organisation. This interest dates back to 1989 when I wrote an Honours Dissertation on the ANC entitled ''The ANC: from revolutionary armed seizure to a negotiated transfer of power''. This dissertation was submitted to the Faculty of Arts at the University of the Witwatersrand. The unbanning of the ANC in

1990 presented me with an opportunity to further my studies on the organisation. While my proposal for the MA thesis was based on conjecture, since most of what I was to write about had not happened, subsequent developments constantly required changes in the writing of the thesis. Analysing an organisation of such magnitude was not an easy task. It meant dealing with a flow of information almost on a daily basis and keeping abreast of information inside and outside the ANC. The enormity of the task taught me the serious demerits of studies based on contemporaneity. Although this was finally overcome, managing information and discerning emerging patterns for analysis always appeared threatening. During the course of undertaking research some parts of the book or thoughts originating from this work were published in journals and books as articles. These include:

- A chapter written together with Mark Swilling entitled 'Organisation and strategies of the major resistance movements in the negotiation era', which appears in the Centre for Policy Studies book, *Transition to democracy – policy perspectives, 1991.*

- *Room for compromise: the ANC and transitional mechanisms.* Centre for Policy Studies Transition Series, Johannesburg, February 1992.

- *Liberation and negotiation: the PAC in the South African transition.* Centre for Policy Studies Transition Series, 5(2), 1992.

- The non-CODESA wing of the Patriotic Front: the PAC and AZAPO. *South Africa Foundation Review,* December 1992.

- 'Transition to democracy through transaction? Bilateral negotiations between the ANC and the National Party in South Africa'. *African Affairs,* 1992. This article was written together with Prof. Herman Giliomee.

In the case of co-written articles, care has been taken to ensure that the contents of this book do not reflect the contribution to these articles by the co-authors. I am greatly indebted to a number of people for the final production of this book. These include my supervisor Doctor Sheila Meintjes and Professor Tom Lodge who have been more than helpful in ensuring the completion of the book when it was still a thesis. I am also grateful to Mark Swilling, Steven Friedman, Lawrence Schlemmer and Khehla Shubane for their comments on my initial drafts on the ANC and negotiations. Raymond Suttner has also been helpful with his critical comments. I am also deeply indebted to the many ANC members and leaders who were more than generous to grant interviews and avail me of useful information for my research. In particular, I would like to thank Saki Macozoma, Carl Niehaus, Titus Maleka, Siziwe, Philisiwe, Mandla Nkomfe and the many others who were generous in offering their time and insights. Finally, I would like to thank my family for exercising patience during the four years of my research.

List of abbreviations

ACDP	African Christian Democratic Party
ACHIB	African Council of Hawkers and Information Business
AIDS	Acquired Immune Deficiency Syndrome
AMC	African Moderates Congress
ANC	African National Congress
ANCWL	African National Congress Women's League
ANCYL	African National Congress Youth League
APLA	Azanian People's Liberation Army
AVU	Afrikaner Volksunie
AWB	Afrikaner Weerstandbeweging
AZAPO	Azanian People's Organisation
AZASO	Azanian Student Organisation
BC	Black Consciousness
CAST	Civic Association of Southern Transvaal
CBDO	community-based development organisation
CBO	community-based organisation
CIB	Campaign for Independent Broadcasting
CMB	Constitution-making Body
CODESA	Convention for a Democratic South Africa
CONTRALESA	Congress of Traditional Leaders of South Africa
COSAG	Concerned South Africa Group
COSAS	Congress of South African Students
COSATU	Congress of South African Trade Unions
CP	Conservative Party
CST	Colonialism of a Special Type
CWIU	Chemical Workers Industrial Union
DBSA	Development Bank of Southern Africa
DIP	Department of Information and Publicity
DP	Democratic Party
EEC	European Economic Community
EPG	Eminent People's Group
FA	Freedom Alliance
FABCOS	Foundation for African Business and Consumer Services
FAPLA	People's Armed Forces for the Liberation of Angola
FAWO	Film and Allied Workers Union
FAWU	Food and Allied Workers Union
FEDSAW	Federation of South African Women
FEDTRAW	Federation of Transvaal Women
FIDA	Federal Independent Democratic Alliance
FLN	Front de Libération Nationale

FNLA	National Liberation Front of Angola
FRELIMO	Front for the Liberation of Mozambique
GAC	Gender Advisory Committee
GNU	Government of National Unity
IDASA	Institute for a Democratic Alternative in South Africa
IDT	Independent Development Trust
IEC	Independent Electoral Commission
IFP	Inkatha Freedom Party
ILC	Internal Leadership Core
ILG	Interim Leadership Group
LDRC	Local Dispute Resolution Committee
MDM	Mass Democratic Movement
MK	Umkhonto we Sizwe
MPLA	Movemento Popular de Libertaçao de Angola (Popular Movement for the Liberation of Angola)
NACTU	National Council of Trade Unions
NAYO	National Youth Organisation
NCEW	National Commission for the Emancipation of Women
NDF	National Defence Force
NEC	National Executive Committee
NECC	National Education Coordination Committee
NGDO	non-government development organisation
NGO	non-government organisation
NHF	National Housing Forum
NP	National Party
NPA	National Peace Accord
NRC	National Reception Committee
NSC	National Steering Committee
NUM	National Union of Mineworkers
NUMSA	National Union of Metalworkers of South Africa
NUSAS	National Union of South African Students
NWC	National Working Committee
OAU	Organisation of African Unity
OFS	Orange Free State
OTG	Office of the Treasurer-General
PAC	Pan Africanist Congress
PF	Patriotic Front
PLO	Palestine Liberation Organisation
PNYS	Provisional National Youth Secretariat
PRYC	Provisional Regional Youth Committees
PWV	Pretoria-Witwatersrand-Vaal Triangle
R	rand
RDP	Reconstruction and Development Programme
RDRC	Regional Dispute Resolution Committee
REC	Regional Executive Committee
RENAMO	Mozambican National Resistance Movement
SABC	South African Broadcasting Corporation

SACC	South African Council of Churches
SACCAWU	South African Commercial Catering and Allied Workers Union
SACP	South African Communist Party
SACTU	South African Congress of Trade Unions
SACTWU	South African Clothing and Textile Workers Union
SADF	South African Defence Force
SADTU	South African Democratic Teachers Union
SANCO	South African National Civic Organisation
SANSCO	South African National Student Congress
SAP	South African Police
SARHWU	South African Railways and Harbour Workers Union
SASCO	South African Student Congress
SASM	South African Student Movement
SASO	South African Student Organisation
SAYCO	South African Youth Congress
SDU	self-defence unit
SIDA	Swedish Internal Development Agency
SOMAFCO	Solomon Mahlangu Freedom College
SUCA	Students United for Christian Action
SWAPO	South West African People's Organisation
TBVC	Transkei, Bophuthatswana, Venda and Ciskei
TEC	Transitional Executive Council
TIC	Thebe Investment Corporation
Tripartite Alliance	ANC, SACP, and COSATU
UDF	United Democratic Front
UN	United Nations
UNITA	National Union for the Total Independence of Angola
UPC	Union des Populations du Cameroun
UWUSA	United Workers Union of South Africa
VAT	value added tax
WNC	Women's National Coalition
WOSA	Workers Organisation for Socialist Action
YCS	Youth Christian Students
ZANU	Zimbabwe African National Union
ZAPU	Zimbabwe African People's Union

Introduction

Liberation movements[1] and negotiated transitions to power: The case of the African National Congress (ANC) in the South African transition

The decision by South Africa's major political parties to engage in dialogue over the future post-apartheid polity in early 1990 brought with it an interesting academic debate over the nature of transition the country was traversing. A majority of South African analysts dismissed the analogy of South Africa's transition to the decolonisation model followed by many African states.[2] In their view, South Africa was not a colony with a distinct colonial power ready to relinquish its power to govern. The ruling party was not an expatriate colonial force ready to leave the country, nor was it intending to hand over power to indigenous claimants, but to negotiate with them to reach an inclusive political settlement. This perceived irrelevance of the decolonisation model made analysts apply the transition to democracy theoretical model to the South African transition. Drawn from O'Donnell, Schmitter & Whitehead's comparative analyses,[3] the transition to democracy paradigm sees societal transformations as moving away from authoritarian rule to democracy through peaceful processes. It sees transitions from authoritarian rule normally beginning when the authoritarian incumbents, for whatever reason, begin to modify their own rules and open the political system to other groups.[4] It emphasises the importance of civil society organisations in challenging authoritarian rules. In an introduction to Southern European transitions, Schmitter argues that

> ... for an effective and enduring challenge to authoritarian rule to be mounted, and for political democracy to become and remain an alternative mode of political domination, a country must possess a civil society in which certain community and group identities exist independent of the state and in which certain types of self-constituted units are capable of acting autonomously in defense of their own interests and ideals.[5]

Moreover, the transition to democracy theory contends that, despite the influence of international factors, parochial and domestic national factors and conditions are crucial in conditioning transitions from authoritarian rule. According to O'Donnell et al., national conditions

> ... demonstrate the importance of institutions, of mediating procedures and forums that help make the rules of political discourse legitimate and

credible in a period of change. They illustrate the vital significance of political leadership and judgement, of the role of single individuals in complex historical processes. They point out, again and again, the importance of timing, the complexity of interactive processes carried out over extensive periods, the various ways in which transitions produce surprises, and some of the ironies and paradoxes that result.[6]

This theoretical paradigm was amply applied by local analysts to the South African case. Peter Berger and Bobby Godsell, Frederik van Zyl Slabbert and Andre du Toit have in varying degrees of emphasis characterised South Africa's transition as a democratisation process similar to the transition to democracy in Latin America and Southern Europe.[7] They contend that, like the states in Latin America and Southern Europe, South Africa is moving away from an authoritarian regime through the forces of struggle in which civil society organisations play a crucial role in challenging the incumbent regime. According to Du Toit, the power of civil society

> . . . amounts to a populist mobilisation, an intense politicisation of large numbers of people, in which the emergent popular fronts literally take to the streets to exploit and expand the limits of mere liberalisation and the partial "reforms" initiated by the "soft-liners" in the regime. The popular upsurge is a euphoric moment when "the people" rediscover their own freedom and power, and believe they are able to challenge and take over the state itself. This moment of popular upsurge is critical to the transitional process as a whole.[8]

While the transition to democracy framework is helpful in understanding the broad evolution of transition processes, it is weak in accounting cases in which a liberation movement like the ANC is one of the important main players. Broad generalisations which regard the ANC as simply one of the political parties involved in the transition process have limitations in that they do not provide a comprehensive understanding of liberation politics in the process of transition. They do not give insight into the revolutionary dynamics of the struggle pursued by the organisation. They tell us little about how it manages to adapt its revolutionary strategies to a radically different discourse of negotiations, and how a successful transition eventually emerges under these conditions. In particular, they fail to raise pertinent critical questions about the organisation. For example, what do the challenges of legality present to the organisation's transition from an exile liberation movement into a home-based mass membership movement? To what extent does its insistence to remain a liberation movement during the period of transition impact upon its attempts to negotiate a settlement? Is the decolonisation model helpful in explaining its experiences?

Despite the contention by transition analysts that the decolonisation model is inappropriate to South Africa, to reject this model entirely is to ignore the specific reality of the country's history. Liberation politics have played a significant role during the transition process. Despite its choice of a democratic undoing of apartheid, the ANC's approach to the transition process and its struggle for political power has been informed by a liberation paradigm which envisages a far more fundamental transformation of the South African society than its liberalisation and democratisation. This is a version of African decolonisation which has as its central features an insistence on the "transfer of power", the installation of an interim government, the election of a constituent assembly to write the constitution and the insistence to remain a liberation movement (which would complement its negotiation strategy with liberation strategies such as mass action) to fulfil the historic mission of liberating all the people of South Africa.[9]

However, the ANC's adherence to the decolonisation paradigm, and the added comparative value of this paradigm, do not imply its complete relevance to South Africa. By comparison, commonalties between the ANC and other liberation movements in Africa are balanced by significant differences. While the struggle for power in African colonies dominated by intransigent European powers and despotic neocolonial settlers gave birth to violent armed struggles and the rise of national liberation movements, the tempo of their struggles, the intensity of the conflict they initiated and the speed within which independence was realised depended neither on the will of their leaders nor on the laws of logic found within theories of armed liberation, but rather on the prevailing conditions in each separate case.

Except for the Union des Populations du Cameroun (UPC) which failed to come to power with the official granting of independence to the Cameroon in 1960,[10] the war of liberation in the French and Portuguese colonies of Algeria, Angola and Mozambique saw the Front de Libération Nationale (FLN), the Movemento Popular de Libertaçao de Angola (MPLA) and the Front for the Liberation of Mozambique (FRELIMO) respectively fighting their way to power in the wake of the collapsing colonial power.[11] In spite of the interjection of negotiations, the intensification of the conflict in Zimbabwe and Namibia also produced independence for the two countries.[12]

Notwithstanding the ANC's involvement in armed insurgency since the 1960s, the prospect of negotiations in South Africa at the beginning of the 1990s did not signify the beginning of a process of the transfer of power to the country's liberation movement. Rather, it meant the beginning of a new mode of political life that was to pose critical challenges for the ANC. Not only did it have to grapple with its organisational transition from exile and underground operation to an internally based legal mass membership organisation, it also had to negotiate with the incumbent regime under unfavourable conditions of heightened violence.

The two processes were by no means easily traversable. The ANC's brother organisations in Africa did not have to go through a tortuous period of rebuilding their organisations while at the same time negotiating with the incumbent regimes once the colonial powers decided to hand over power. Despite the fact that negotiations were held between colonial powers and nationalist movements in most cases of African decolonisation, the latter did not have to spend enormous amounts of energy in seeking to revitalise their organisational strength. This was the case with the Zimbabwe African

National Union (ZANU) in Zimbabwe which, despite negotiations, did not have to start afresh to organise its structures for the purposes of elections. The fresh memories of the freedom struggle in the minds of the people simply swept it into power.

Some movements obtained independence while already in control of legislative power, as in the cases of the French colonies of Guinea, the Ivory Coast, Mali and Senegal.[13] Other movements attained power without having to prove their popularity in elections. In Angola, a revolutionary government (the Independent People's Republic of Angola) was proclaimed by the MPLA, which ultimately took over the reigns of power when the Portuguese regime collapsed.[14] The liberation struggle in Algeria also saw the creation of a government in exile (the Gouvernement Provisoire de la République Algérienne), which after being internationally recognised paved the way to negotiations and the coming to power of the FLN.[15] In instances where liberation movements were compelled to hold elections, it was not so much organisational strength and viability which ensured the triumph of the parties. The symbolic identification of Zimbabwe's ZANU with the people's committees that had developed in the rural areas of Mazvingo, Manicaland, Mashonaland, Mashonaland West, East and Central Provinces, Midlands and even some parts of Matebeleland South, gave the party a walkover in the 1980 elections.[16]

Exile liberation movements which encountered problems in establishing themselves in the communities once they returned home, merely reorganised their organisational structures after independence, and most often in circumstances where the leadership had committed itself to party vanguardism. This was the case with FRELIMO in Mozambique and the MPLA in Angola. These parties did not have to embark on massive membership campaigns. Rather, given their inclination towards building socialist cadre parties, their methods of recruitment were selective, seeking only to draw in experienced and politically mature activists.[17] These experiences were dramatically different from that which the ANC was to encounter after its unbanning in 1990. Despite the refusal by the leadership to transform the organisation from a liberation movement into a political party, the ANC which re-emerged inside the country in early 1990 was thrust into a complex and challenging milieu. Unlike other African liberation movements, the organisation had to deal with a regime which was not intent on transferring power. In spite of the fact that ZANU in Zimbabwe also went through a process of negotiations, the existence and intervention of the original colonial power (Britain) in forcing the Zimbabwean parties to honour their obligations, served – despite its problems – to hasten the "transfer of power" in a way quite unparalleled in South Africa.

While both decolonisation and transition to democracy paradigms have limitations and cannot separately give a comprehensive account for the South African transition, they are jointly useful in providing a broad theoretical framework within which both the process of transition and the liberation politics of the ANC can be understood. By focusing on the ANC in the South African transition, this book seeks to make a specific contribution to the epistemology of transition politics, particularly with regard to how exile liberation movements reconstitute themselves in their home countries and negotiate constitutional settlements. This case-orientated study is primarily empirical.

The book focuses on two broad themes of the ANC's political life in the early 1990s: its organisational adaptation to legality and its strategic approach to a negotiated settlement. It will analyse in the first section the ANC's metamorphosis from being an exile liberation movement to becoming a main organisation inside South Africa. This will cover the dynamics of its organisational reconstruction, membership recruitment, relationship with allied organisations, internal tensions and democratic exercise including policy development. Violence, and how the ANC sought to address it, will also be analysed in this section. In the second section, the book will analyse factors behind the ANC's decision to negotiate and the organisation's approach to negotiations. It will also analyse the movement towards the conclusion of a negotiated settlement, the election campaign and the installation of the Government of National Unity.

ENDNOTES

1. The term "liberation movements" is used to describe those organisations that have challenged colonial regimes in their home countries. Unlike conventional political parties which normally represent sectoral interests, liberation movements often claim to represent the whole society with one clearly stated objective of liberating the people.
2. Berger, P. & Godsell, B. (Eds). *A future South Africa: vision, strategies and realities*. Cape Town: Human & Rousseau/Tafelberg, 1988, 267; Nedcor/Old Mutual. *South Africa: prospects for successful transition*. Cape Town: Juta, 1992, 12; Van Zyl Slabbert, F. *The quest for democracy*. London: Penguin, 1992, 98.
3. O'Donnell, G., Schmitter, P. & Whitehead, L. (Eds). *Transitions from authoritarian rule: Latin America*. Baltimore/London: John Hopkins University Press, 1986; O'Donnell, G., Schmitter, P. & Whitehead, L. (Eds). *Transitions from authoritarian rule: Southern Europe*. Baltimore/London: John Hopkins University Press, 1986; O'Donnell, G. & Schmitter, P. *Transitions from authoritarian rule: tentative conclusions about uncertain democracies*. Baltimore/London: John Hopkins University Press, 1986.
4. O'Donnell & Schmitter, op cit., 6.
5. O'Donnell et al., op cit. [Europe], 6.
6. O'Donnell et al., op cit. [Latin America], ix–x.
7. Berger & Godsell, op cit.; Van Zyl Slabbert, op cit.; Du Toit, A. (Ed.) *Towards democracy: building a culture of accountability in South Africa*. Cape Town: IDASA, 1991. See also Friedman, S. *The shapers of things to come? National Party choices in the South African transition*. Centre for Policy Studies Transition Series, February 1992; Tjonneland, E.N. *Negotiating apartheid away? Constitution-making, transition politics and conditions for democracy in South Africa*. International Peace Research Institute, Oslo, 1990; Schlemmer, L. Between polarisation and pacts: what kind of transition does South Africa have? *Indicator South Africa*, 7(4), Spring, 1990; Van Zyl Slabbert, F. *South Africa: beginning at the end of the road* (no name of publisher), March 1990; Booysen, S. Transition, the state and relations of political power in South Africa. *Politikon*, 17(2), December 1990; Pierce, D. *Post-apartheid South Africa: lessons from Brazil's 'Nova Republica'*. Centre for Policy Studies Comparative Perspectives, February 1992; Ottoway, M. Liberation movements and transition to democracy: the case of the ANC. *Journal of Modern African Studies*, 29(1), 1991; Giliomee, H. & Rantete, J. Transition to democracy through transaction? Bilateral negotiations between the ANC and NP in South Africa. *African Affairs*, 91, 1992.
8. Du Toit, op cit., 13.

9. Giliomee & Rantete, op cit., 525. It is important to note that, despite the fact that the ANC ultimately made compromises in its approach and strategies, elements of its decolonisation/power transfer approach continued to play an important part in its thinking and behaviour during the period of transition. This cannot be fully accounted for by the neoliberal transition to democracy paradigm, whose pro-democracy bias and predetermination of what should constitute appropriate role-players to successful transitions have excluded revolutionary transitions (which presumably include liberation movements) from analysis (see Guillermo O'Donnell's "Introduction" in *Transition from authoritarian rule: Latin America*, op cit., 10). The presumption that revolutionary transitions often revert to authoritarian rule has produced scepticism about South Africa's chances of success, simply because the ANC refused to transform itself into a political party and continues to harbour liberation politics. In the view of Marina Ottoway (op cit., 81), liberation movements, as demonstrated in many cases in Africa, often produce authoritarian regimes and for South Africa to have a successful transition to democracy the ANC has to transform itself into a political party. This theoretical prescription of appropriate role-players constitutes an indulgence in a priori judgement and violates one fundamental principle of the transition to democracy paradigm, which is to subject theory to an analysis of concrete processes, complex factors and conditions obtainable in a given case.

10. Gibson, R. *African liberation movements: contemporary struggles against white minority rule.* London: Oxford University Press, 1972, 6.

11. Gifford, P. & Louis, R. (Eds). *Decolonisation and African independence: the transfers of power, 1960–1980.* New Haven/London: Yale University Press, 1988, see "Introduction", xxiv–xxv. On FRELIMO see Aquino de Bragança's article 'Independence without decolonisation: Mozambique, 1974–1975' in the same book. On the MPLA see Marcum, J.A *The Angolan revolution: exile politics and guerrilla warfare.* Cambridge: MIT, 1978. On the Front National de Libération see Rubin, L. & Weinstein, B. *Introduction to African politics: a continental approach.* New York: Praeger, 1974.

12. For Zimbabwean independence see Hudson, M. *Triumph or tragedy: Rhodesia to Zimbabwe.* London: Hamish Hamilton, 1981.

13. Tordoff, W. *Government and politics in Africa.* Macmillan Education, 1984. See Chapter 3: Nationalism and the transfer of power, 74.

14. Marcum, op cit., 225. This move emulated the Provisional Revolutionary Government formed by the National Liberation Front in South Vietnam in 1969. See Tang, N.T. *A Vietcong memoir.* New York: Vintage, 1985, 254.

15. Rubin & Weinstein, op cit., 98.

16. Stoneman, C. & Cliffe, L. *Zimbabwe: politics, economics and society.* Marxist Regimes Series. London: Printer Publishers, 1989, 79. It should also be added that the people's committees that developed in many parts of Zimbabwe and which were most often activated by Zimbabwean National Liberation Army forces also contributed to the party's victory.

17. Egero, B. People's power: the case of Mozambique. In Munslow, B. (Ed.), *Africa: problems in the transition to socialism.* London: Zed, 1986, 127.

Section A

From an exile and underground liberation movement to an open legal organisation inside South Africa

This section will analyse the organisational and political development of the African National Congress during the early 1990s. It will pay particular attention to its bid to establish an organisational presence inside the country, to transform mass popular following into card-carrying membership and to integrate its varying political components into a coherent organisation. Internal tensions, democratic practice, policy development as well as attempts to address violence will also be analysed.

The ANC's organisational development

Formation of the ANC

The African National Congress (ANC) was formed on 8 January 1912 in Bloemfontein.[1] This took place against the background of the formation of the Union of South Africa in 1910 which expressly excluded black people from the political system. For a number of years after its formation the ANC adopted non-violent strategies in an attempt to persuade the government to accommodate black political aspirations. In later years, however, economic development and rapid industrialisation in particular led to the emergence of nascent forms of militant resistance to white rule.

The strikes in the mining sector influenced a change in class composition of the ANC's leadership, with the scale being tilted in favour of the workers. The repression of workers' demands during strikes and the rise in political consciousness further accounted for the formation of the Women's League and the ANC Youth League in the 1940s, and led to the ANC's adoption of a militant programme of action in the beginning of the 1950s. In political terms the 1950s were characterised by mass defiance campaigns, the drafting of the Freedom Charter at Kliptown in 1955, the anti-pass law demonstrations and the treason trial of anti-apartheid activists.

Instead of responding to the people's demands, the government responded with more repression and with dedication to the entrenchment of apartheid rule. The 1960s not only marked an era of violent confrontation with the Sharpeville shooting in 1960. The government also adopted a new constitution, homelands were created, black political organisations were banned and their leaders arrested and prosecuted, thus ending an era of peaceful resistance to apartheid. Consequently the ANC as an organisation was forced into exile.

State of exile

After its banning in 1960 and the imprisonment of its leadership following the Rivonia trial, the ANC went underground and reconstituted itself in

3

exile under the leadership of Oliver Tambo. After years of intense campaigning to mobilise the international community, it finally succeeded in winning world recognition as a representative liberation movement and voice of the people of South Africa. This world recognition was to be reflected in the spread of its diplomatic empire, it being granted observer status by the United Nations and the Organisation of African Unity, as well as the decision by some African states to host its organisational infrastructures.

By 1990 the ANC had a bureaucratic network which was worth millions of rands across the globe. In Lusaka, Zambia, where it had established its headquarters, the combined value of its property amounted to R13 570 700.[2] This sum was made up of office blocks, residences and an industrial infrastructure. There was also a factory, Star Furniture Manufacturers Ltd, developed in 1967 and established on a 1200 sq. metre property. The factory, with twelve stationary woodwork machines and two trucks, was created to generate funds for the movement and provide household and office furniture, as well as to train ANC cadres. The Alpha Mechanical Workshop, established in 1984, was used to repair a fleet of ANC vehicles and to provide training for ANC members, as well as generate funds for the organisation.

Chongela Farm, bought in 1978, was used to grow maize, sorghum, sunflower, soybeans and sugar beans. A vegetable garden was also developed to provide the community with cabbages, potatoes, carrots, pumpkins, onions, tomatoes, etcetera. Another farm, Makeni, was also used for growing vegetables. Other parts of the land in Chongela were left for grazing for a total of 1011 head of cattle, which by 1990 were producing 3500 litres of milk. A poultry section was also built with a total capacity of six laying pens with 3900 birds, which by 1990 were producing 2800 units of eggs. Stocks of pigs, sheep and goats were also maintained on the farm. By 1990 Chongela Farm covered 1344 ha and was worth R2 456 700. Makeni, covering 405 ha, was valued at R638 200 while other farms like Alpha and Constantinos were worth R876 200 and R226 700 respectively.

In Tanzania, the combined value of ANC properties in Morogoro and Dar-es-Salaam amounted to R575 800 000. In 1990 the Dakawa and Mazimbu settlements had a total value of R70 million and R250 million respectively. The Mazimbu settlement, granted to the ANC by the Tanzanian government in 1978, mainly comprised the Solomon Mahlangu Freedom College (SOMAFCO).[3]

Mazimbu had started as a transit and training camp for young men and women who fled South Africa in the wake of the 1976 Soweto uprising.[4] At first the ANC's Department of Personnel rented houses in the town of Morogoro to accommodate these people before deciding whether to send them for further education or for military training in Angolan camps. The department moved to Mazimbu immediately after the setting up of college blocks. The Department of Education and Culture was subsequently formed, which constituted a complex pyramid of committees linking leading office-bearers in the ANC, the South African Congress of Trade Unions (SACTU), Youth and Women's sections to the administration of the school.[5]

SOMAFCO was made up of three huge secondary classroom blocks, a science, a technical and six dormitory blocks, as well as a covered school square, a library, recreational and sports facilities. There were also primary and pre-school divisions, a clinic, youth centre, children's centre, maternity centre, a cemetery and over 300 residences. Small-scale industries, offices, services and a huge farm were also established. Seen as one of the most advanced farms in Tanzania, the Mazimbu Farm was able to provide the local community with up to 45 % of its food. Maize, sorghum, sunflower, beans and a range of vegetables and fruits were grown. Dairy cattle, goats, pigs and poultry were also kept.

The Dakawa settlement was established in 1983, after the ANC was donated a 2800 ha tract of land by the Tanzanian government 60 km north-west of Morogoro, as Mazimbu was no longer able to cope with the number of people coming in from South Africa. Dakawa was used to assess new arrivals and to determine their placement. It was also used as an orientation centre. By 1990 Dakawa was a self-reliant community of between 5000 and 8000 people. It was made up of ten villages with an Intervillage Centre consisting of a health post, nursery school and a day care facility. There were also schools and vocational training centres, an Education Orientation Centre (the Ruth First Centre) to house youth from South Africa and a Rehabilitation Centre for victims of torture, alcohol and drugs.

Angola, which was regarded by the ANC as a war zone, housed a spread of ANC camps accommodating thousands of ANC Umkhonto we Sizwe (MK) cadres. Established after 1976, these camps were Cama Lundi, Vianna, Malange, Pango, Quibaxe, Nova Catengue, Fazenda, Caxito and Quadro. Vianna served as a transit site from which cadres were moved to other camps. Quadro, which was established towards the end of 1979, was used exclusively as a detention and rehabilitation centre. Apart from these camps there was the Moses Kotane Self-Reliance Centre established in Vianna in 1984. The centre had a mechanical workshop for the maintenance and repair of ANC vehicles, a medical health training centre, a poultry farm and a tailoring workshop. A printing shop was also established in Labutsibeni. In 1989 Lilie's Farm, situated 42 km south of Luanda and covering 1600 ha of land, was donated to the ANC by the Angolan government. The farm was used for growing vegetables, bananas and paw-paw. Angolan camps were, however, closed down after the New York Accord between South Africa, Cuba, the United States and the Soviet Union, which paved the way for the independence of Namibia in 1990. In Zimbabwe, the ANC had 31 houses in Harare and Bulawayo to the value of R3 million. It also acquired the Vukani Cooperative Farm of 10 ha near Bulawayo, which produced vegetables and eggs to generate income.

The ANC had huge assets in its 40 diplomatic missions around the world, the most important of which were buildings and facilities in London (worth R2 875 300), Brussels (R258 400), Bonn (R881 300), the Norwegian capital, Oslo (R327 700), the Swedish capital, Stockholm (R1 332 900) and in Toronto in Canada (R403 900). By 1990 it had a fleet of 269 vehicles in these cities to the value of R4 162 072.[6] The organisation had thousands of members spread over the front-line states and abroad. Apart from the concentration in Zambia and Tanzania of National Executive Committee (NEC) and personnel staff members, many also served in foreign diplomatic missions scattered around the globe. There was also a complex military bureaucracy of Regional Political Military Committees in the front-line states and inside South Africa.

Although towards the end of the 1980s the ANC was prepared for negotiations with the South African government on the political future of the country, it was taken by surprise by the turn of events in early 1990. Despite the rapid reform initiatives introduced by De Klerk the liberation movement had not expected a sudden unconditional unbanning. Thus, when this happened in February 1990 and the date of Mandela's release was announced, the organisation had not made preparations for its return home. Much of the groundwork for the return of the ANC was consequently laid by structures within the allied Mass Democratic Movement (MDM) – the Congress of South African Trade Unions (COSATU), the United Democratic Front (UDF) and civic, student, women, church and sports organisations.

An added challenge brought about by the unbanning was that the ANC had to abandon liberation politics. It had to jettison violence, reconsider the role of its military wing, MK, and transform itself into a conventional political party. This option was strongly resisted by the organisation, which reasoned that transforming itself into a political party would imply abandoning its historic mission to liberate the people of South Africa. Until apartheid was destroyed and a new democratic government installed, the organisation argued, there would always be the need for a liberation movement. Opting to remain a liberation movement was strategically important: it created room for the ANC to pursue other strategies, such as mass action outside negotiations with the government. It also allowed the organisation to participate in negotiations without ruling out the alternative of an armed struggle. Insistence on remaining a liberation movement did not, however, imply a complete rejection of political party practices. The building of ANC organisational structures inside South Africa since 1990, membership recruitment and the movement's behaviour, all resemble conventional political party practices.

The unbanning and the building of an organisational structure – head office, regions and branches

While the rebuilding of the structures of the ANC inside South Africa was undertaken by activists who had long identified with the movement, the process through which this was done was both complex and challenging. The ANC that emerged was not simply a transplantation of structures that had existed in exile.[7] Rather, it was a new organisational entity, forged out of an amalgamation of different segments of the movement that had developed during the previous decade.[8] For those involved, the process of uniting exiles, ex-prisoners and former MDM leaders, together with rank and file members into an homogeneous structure was exciting and enriched with a diversity of experience. It was also, however, fraught with tensions and problems that sometimes retarded the progress of development.

Despite the uncertainty that characterised the aftermath of its unbanning in February 1990, foundations had already been laid inside the country that eased the formal return of the ANC. During the weeks preceding the release of Walter Sisulu and other Rivonia prisoners in 1989, a National Reception Committee (NRC) had been formed, comprising leaders from the MDM, such as Cyril Ramaphosa, Mohammed Valli Moosa and Murphy Morobe, to prepare for the reintegration of ex-prisoners into their families and the existing political situation.[9] A few days after their release, a new structure, the Internal Leadership Core (ILC) of the ANC, was formed comprising five core leaders: Nelson Mandela (in Pollsmoor), Walter Sisulu (Chairperson of the ILC and the Internal Head of the ANC), Govan Mbeki, Raymond Mhlaba, as well as Mac Maharaj, who operated from underground.

Sanctioned by the exile leadership, the main task of the ILC was to establish the legal structures of the ANC inside the country – particularly the headquarters, regions and branches. The euphoria born of the unbanning of the ANC and the release of Mandela had already led to some activists taking it upon themselves to establish ANC structures well before the leadership could release its organisational plan. This was the case in Natal, where ex-Robben Islander Steven Mpanza had already opened his first legal "ANC offices" at Stanger in February 1990.[10]

As the ILC was formed before the legal unbanning of the ANC, departmental structures were created to deal with the various day-to-day matters facing the organisation.[11] However, most of these structures duplicated those existing in Lusaka, and in some cases were established without consultation with the members in exile. The Department of Information and Publicity (DIP) was established and headed by Ahmed Kathrada, Transport came under Mlangeni, Organising under Wilton Mkwayi, Finance under Vusi Khanyile, Political Education under Raymond Suttner, with Mohammed Valli Moosa as the Secretary of the ILC. The ILC operated until the middle of June 1990, by which time most NEC members had established a permanent presence inside the country following the official unbanning of the organisation.[12] A special meeting of the NEC was subsequently held, which extended its membership to include ILC leaders. The position of deputy president was also created to accommodate Nelson Mandela.

Although Jacob Zuma, Head of the Department of Intelligence and Security, was the first among the exiles to return to South Africa, his department was not the first to be re-established. The DIP was the first department to create its presence inside the country, formally reconstituted in June 1990 through the efforts of Pallo Jordan, Gill Marcus and Joel Netshitenzhe (alias Peter Mayibuye). Established to deal with media and information which were becoming so crucial with the unbanning of the ANC, the DIP grew steadily with the employment of Saki Macozoma from the media section of the South African Council of Churches (SACC), Obar Omar, Terry Matlala, Carl Niehaus and Patrick Lekota. The second department to be set up was the Organising Department under Steve Tshwete, which was entrusted with the task of recruiting people into the ANC. This included the drawing up of membership lists, production of cards and information materials, as well as the development of a sound organisational strategy. Other departments subsequently established included the Department of Political Education under Raymond Suttner, Economic Planning under Max Sisulu, Legal and Constitutional Affairs under Zola Skweyiya, Transport under Mlangeni, Special Projects (Military) under Joe Modise, Social Welfare under Winnie Mandela, Arts and Culture, initially under Barbara Masekela and after her resignation, Wole Serote, and International Affairs under Thabo Mbeki.

The return of the NEC and the heads of departments previously based in Lusaka sparked tensions within the emerging departmental structures inside the country. This was the case with the DIP which for a while had two heads – Pallo Jordan from Lusaka and Ahmed Kathrada from the ILC. However, problems like these were resolved with the weaker parties giving way to the stronger ones.[13] While in this case, Kathrada decided to give way to Jordan as head of the department, other departments, still in exile by the middle of 1990, were effectively replaced by the new ones inside the country. The appointment of Raymond Suttner as Head of the Department of Political Education completely nullified the structure which existed in Lusaka.

By July 1990 the ANC had all its departments operating in South Africa. Before finally locating its headquarters in Shell House, Plein Street, Johannesburg, these departments were housed in eight buildings in central Johannesburg and Braamfontein.[14] The headquarters were in Munich Re House in Sauer Street, housing the offices of the deputy president, secretary-general and treasurer-general, as well as the Departments of Legal Affairs, Administration, Security and International Affairs.[15] The Social Welfare Department was housed in the Southern Life Building, the Women's League at the Bank of Lisbon, and the Department of Arts and Culture at the Market Theatre. The Youth League was housed in the Devonshire Building in Braamfontein and the Department of Manpower Development in the Old Mutual Building, also in Braamfontein. The National Planning Committee was based at His Majesty's in Eloff Street. The Departments of Finance, Political Education, Information and Publicity, Information and Communication, Economics and Planning, as well as Land Commission, Special Projects and Movement Enterprise (the ANC's marketing agency) were housed in Frederick Street. At its meeting on 31 July 1991 the NEC decided to restructure the departments into three main categories, namely political, policy and service:[16]

- The political departments comprised the Negotiation Commission, convened by Cyril Ramaphosa. Other members of the commission were Thabo Mbeki, Joe Slovo, Mohammed Valli Moosa and Jacob Zuma. As Deputy Secretary-General, Zuma was made responsible for the running of the affairs of the organisation. The Organising Department was convened by Steve Tshwete and comprised John Nkadimeng, Ronnie

Kasrils, Sydney Mufamadi, Popo Molefe, Joel Netshitenzhe and Ebrahim Ismail Ebrahim. The Army was convened by Joe Modise, the Department of International Affairs by Thabo Mbeki, and the Department of Security and Intelligence was headed by Joe Nhlanhla and included Patrick Lekota.

- The policy departments comprised Economic Planning convened by Trevor Manuel, Constitutional Development headed by Zola Skweyiya, and Health, Welfare and Human Resources convened by Cheryl Carolus.

- The service departments comprised the Legal Department convened by Zola Skweyiya and an Evaluation Commission convened by the National Chairman, Oliver Tambo, which included Alfred Nzo and Barbara Masekela.

The ANC's organisational structures (in exile and after 1990) are depicted in Figures 1 and 2. It is important to note that MK's complex military structures were no longer operational. MK was represented within the ANC as a department, the Army. This was a new development, as MK was a much more autonomous organisation during the period of exile.

As important as the setting up of ANC headquarters and departments was the election of a new leadership at the July 1991 national conference in Durban. During the ANC's unbanning, a leadership crisis had emerged as a result of Oliver Tambo's illness. Despite widespread rumours of Mandela's release and possible assumption of the ANC's leadership, ANC officials were very cautious about this eventuality. Statements were issued to the effect that the leadership of the ANC was a collective responsibility and not a matter of one individual – a position which was stressed by Mandela himself after his release. In most of his speeches Mandela used the plural "we", even when expressing his own opinions. However, despite the attempts by ANC leaders to project a collective leadership, Mandela's stature was such that his person overshadowed the organisation. In fact, he assumed effective leadership of the organisation immediately after his release, when an NEC meeting created the position of deputy president specially for him. In July 1991 his candidacy for president of the organisation was unopposed.

However, the contest for other senior positions was very intense. The position of secretary-general held by Alfred Nzo was lost to a young enthusiastic trade unionist, Cyril Ramaphosa, while the treasury went to the incumbent Thomas Nkobi. Jacob Zuma was elected deputy secretary-general. Walter Sisulu was elected deputy president to avert what was becoming a tense contest between Chris Hani and Thabo Mbeki. In the final showdown, Hani won more votes than any other member elected onto the NEC. All in all a total of 56 NEC members were elected.[17] In addition to elected members, the NEC also comprised unelected members from the regions and representations of its women and youth organisations. The ANC leadership was a mixture which, to a certain degree and unlike other South African parties, reflected South African society: it consisted of Africans, Indians, coloureds and some whites. It had a significant representation

Figure 1 The ANC'S organisational structure in exile before 1990

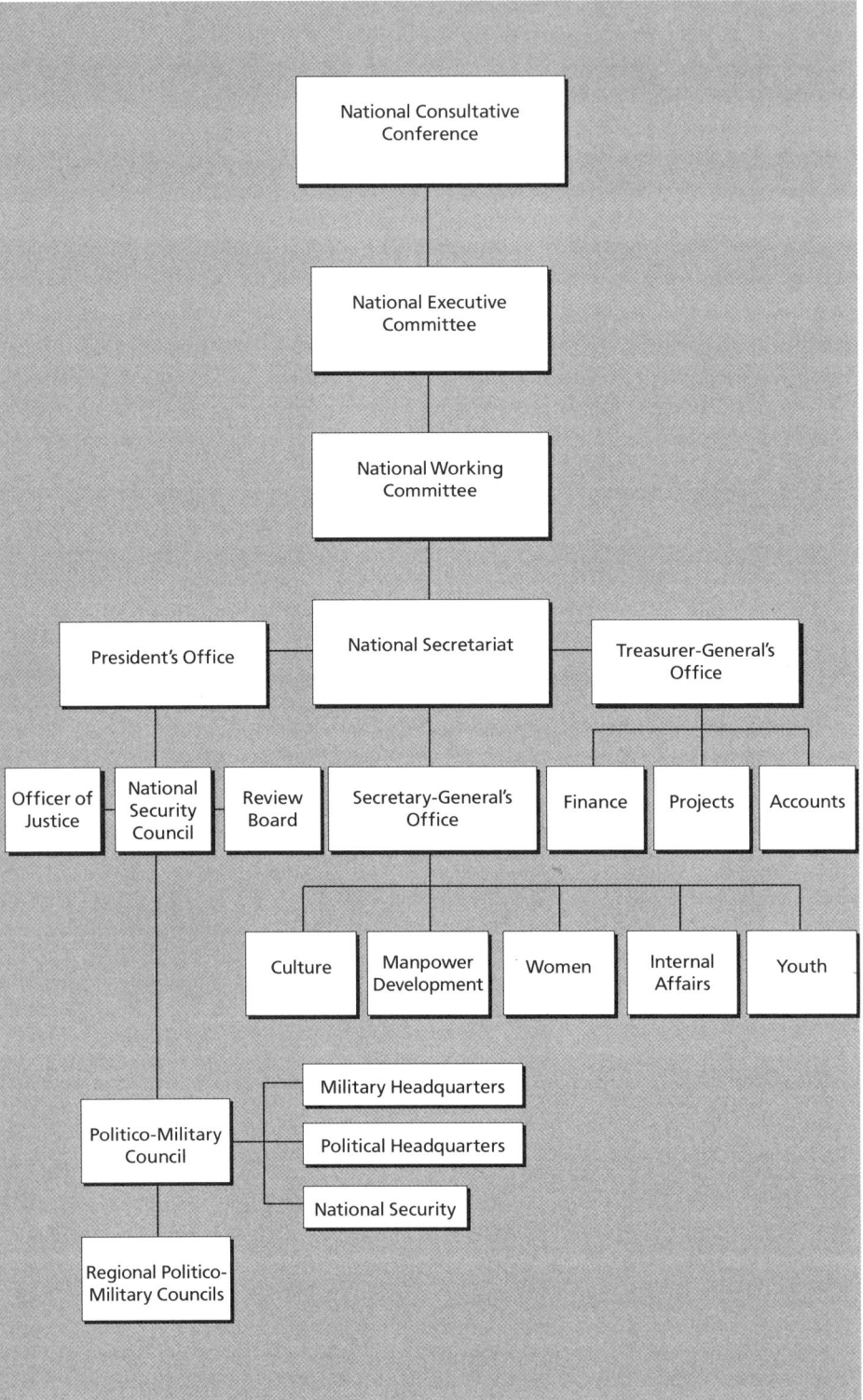

Figure 2 The ANC's organisational structure as at July 1991

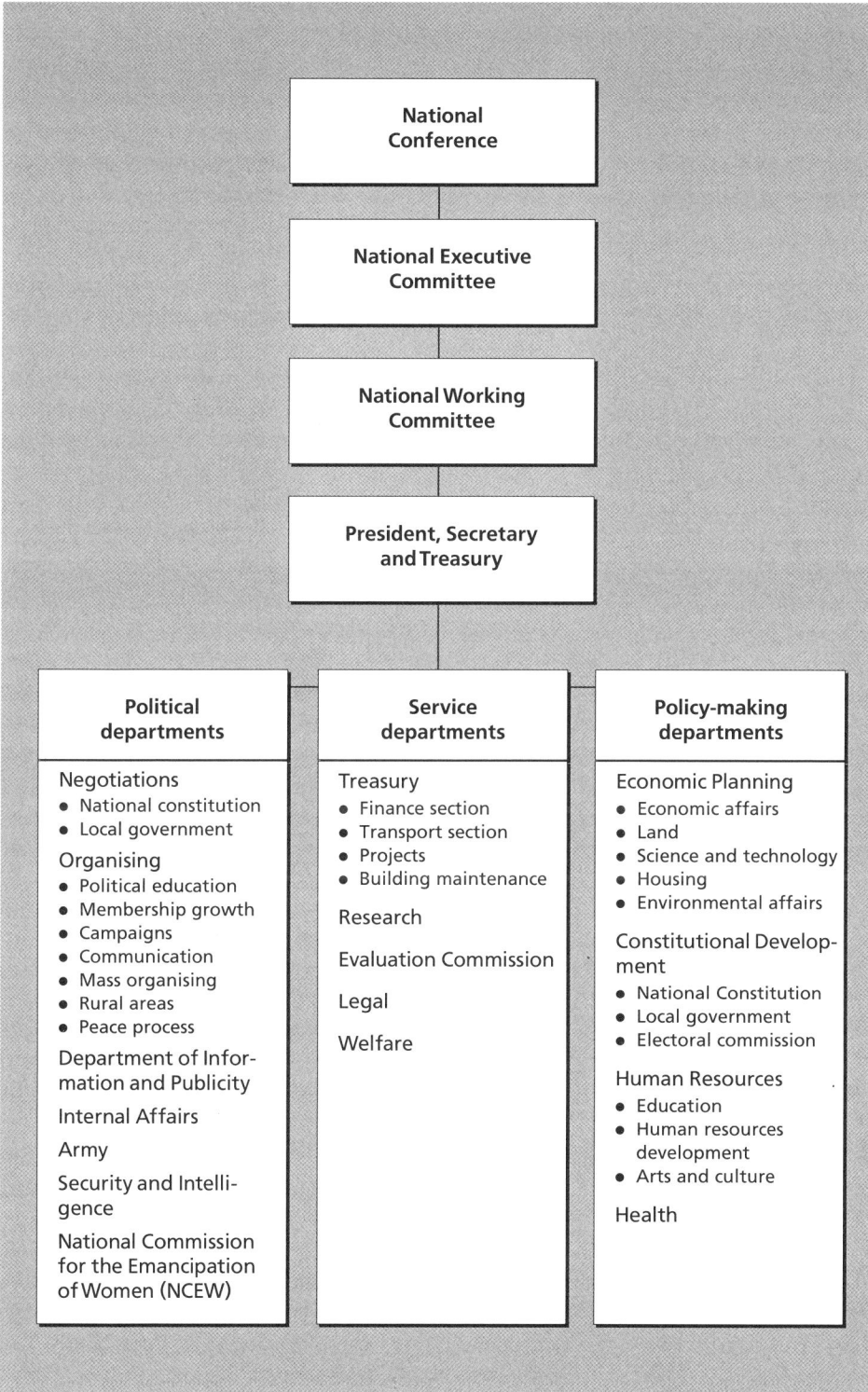

```
                    ┌─────────────────────┐
                    │     National        │
                    │    Conference       │
                    └─────────────────────┘
                    ┌─────────────────────┐
                    │ National Executive  │
                    │    Committee        │
                    └─────────────────────┘
                    ┌─────────────────────┐
                    │ National Working    │
                    │    Committee        │
                    └─────────────────────┘
                    ┌─────────────────────┐
                    │ President, Secretary│
                    │   and Treasury      │
                    └─────────────────────┘
```

Political departments	Service departments	Policy-making departments
Negotiations • National constitution • Local government Organising • Political education • Membership growth • Campaigns • Communication • Mass organising • Rural areas • Peace process Department of Information and Publicity Internal Affairs Army Security and Intelligence National Commission for the Emancipation of Women (NCEW)	Treasury • Finance section • Transport section • Projects • Building maintenance Research Evaluation Commission Legal Welfare	Economic Planning • Economic affairs • Land • Science and technology • Housing • Environmental affairs Constitutional Development • National Constitution • Local government • Electoral commission Human Resources • Education • Human resources development • Arts and culture Health

of women. It mixed the older generation with the cream of young leadership. Ethnically, it had Xhosas, who comprised the majority, as well as Zulus, Tswanas, Sothos, Pedis, Shangaans and Vendas. Because of the size of the NEC the day-to-day running of the organisation was undertaken by a smaller executive, the National Working Committee, which reported to the larger executive.[18]

While the process of setting up departments and electing leaders was relatively easy, the more daunting task lay in the establishment of branches. In March 1990 the ILC was given a mandate by the organisation to establish regional structures in the 14 regions it had demarcated. The ILC appointed the following people to facilitate the establishment of such structures, which would in turn facilitate the creation of branches: Kgalema Motlante for the Pretoria-Witwatersrand-Vaal Triangle (PWV) region, Ntombi Shope for Eastern Transvaal, Thabo Makunyane for Northern Transvaal, Zakes Molekane for Western Transvaal, Caleb Motshabi for Southern Orange Free State (OFS), Vincent Motsepe for Northern Orange Free State, Patrick Lekota for Southern Natal, Willis Mchunu for Northern Natal, Harry Gwala for Natal Midlands, Arnold Stofile for the Border region, Benson Fihla for Eastern Cape, Jomo Kashu for Northern Cape, Trevor Manuel for Western Cape and Alfred Xobololo for Transkei. These convenors, who were also made part of the ILC,[19] appointed regional interim committees, which divided regions into smaller geographical units for the purpose of establishing branches. The ANC's national and regional organisational structures are depicted in Figure 3.

The task of overall coordination of recruitment, however, lay with the Department of National Organising. Other departments provided relevant publicity material. The Department of Political Education provided two booklets, *Joining the ANC: An introductory handbook to the ANC* (1990) and *The road to peace* (1990), which detailed the history of the ANC, outlined its principles and explained the procedure for applying for membership. The Department of Legal and Constitutional Affairs issued an interim constitution which, among other things, stated that only individuals above the age of 18 were allowed to be members and that a branch could only be established after it had enlisted 100 members.

A target number of one million members by December 1990 was set by the organisation to encourage activists involved in the process of recruitment. This target number was subdivided among the regions according to their perceived strength. The recruitment campaign started in earnest on 9 May 1990 and by September 315 branches had already been established. At the end of December 1990, eight out of 14 regions had held their founding conferences to establish regional executive committees, and the ANC could boast 200 000 registered members.

- The Border regional conference was held on 13 October 1990 and was attended by 700 delegates from 66 branches representing 28 000 members.

- The Southern Natal regional conference was attended by 400 delegates from 62 branches.[20]

Figure 3 The ANC's national and regional organisational structure

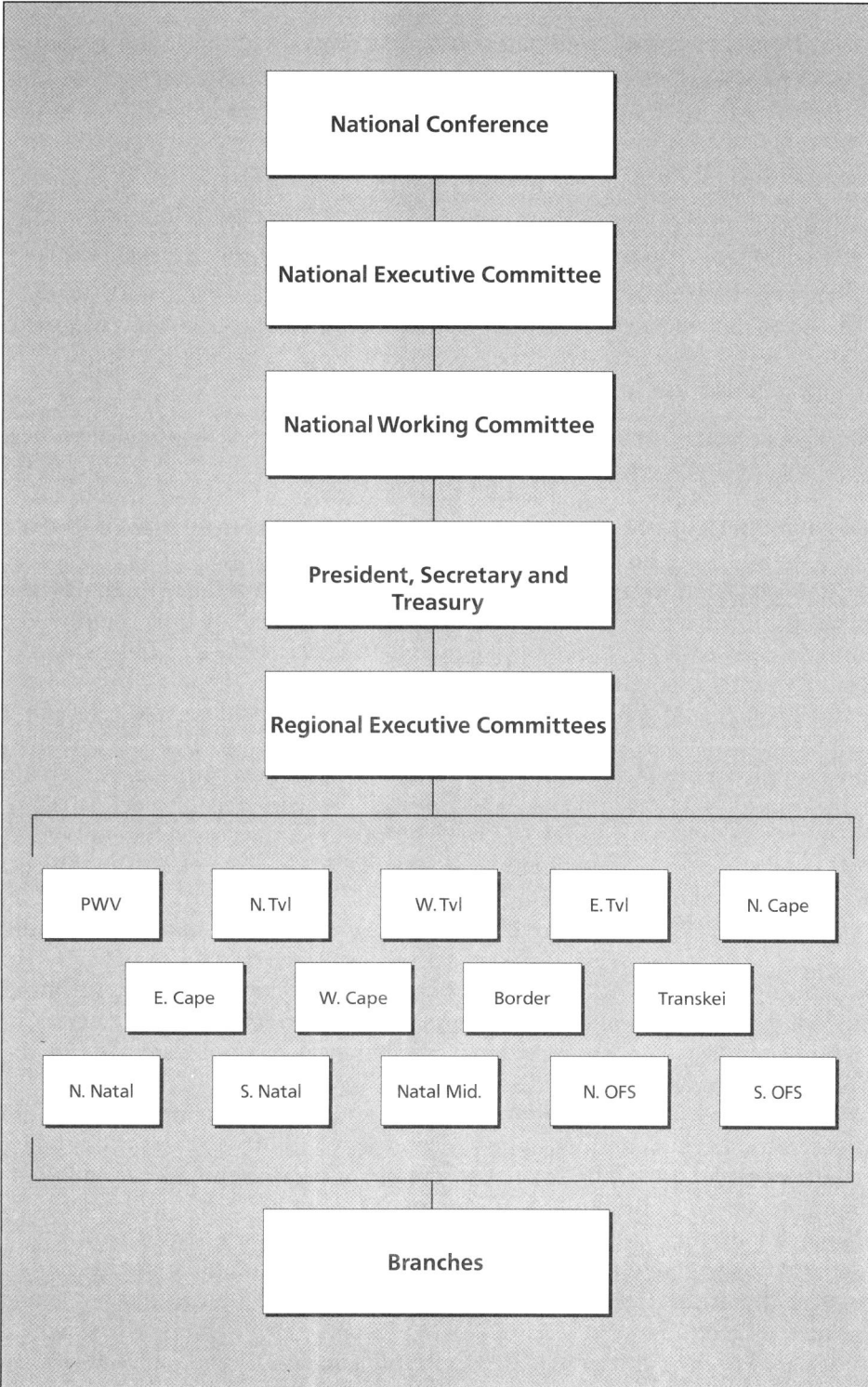

```
                    ┌──────────────────────────┐
                    │   National Conference    │
                    └──────────────────────────┘
                                 │
                    ┌──────────────────────────┐
                    │National Executive Committee│
                    └──────────────────────────┘
                                 │
                    ┌──────────────────────────┐
                    │National Working Committee │
                    └──────────────────────────┘
                                 │
                    ┌──────────────────────────┐
                    │ President, Secretary and  │
                    │         Treasury          │
                    └──────────────────────────┘
                                 │
                    ┌──────────────────────────┐
                    │Regional Executive Committees│
                    └──────────────────────────┘
                                 │
```

PWV	N. Tvl	W. Tvl	E. Tvl	N. Cape

E. Cape	W. Cape	Border	Transkei

N. Natal	S. Natal	Natal Mid.	N. OFS	S. OFS

```
                    ┌──────────────────────────┐
                    │        Branches          │
                    └──────────────────────────┘
```

- The Eastern Transvaal regional conference drew 82 branches representing 37 000 members.[21]

- Northern Transvaal regional conference was held with 39 branches representing 19 845 members.

- Natal Midlands drew 49 branches representing a membership of up to 17 000.

- The Transkei regional conference, held at the University of Transkei in Umtata, was attended by 28 branches representing 10 500 members.[22]

- Eastern Cape regional conference, held in Port Elizabeth, was attended by 51 branches representing 20 000 members.

- Regions that did not hold their conferences in 1990 and only did so in 1991 were Western Transvaal, Northern Cape, Northern Orange Free State and Northern Natal.

The PWV region, which was the largest in all ANC regions, can best illustrate the trend of membership recruitment and the broad performance of the organisation in its reconstruction efforts. Appointed by the ILC, Kgalema Motlante, assisted by Titus Mofolo, Barbara Hogan and Lala Chiba, created an Interim Regional Executive Committee, which brought in activists from the UDF and COSATU. The committee held its first meeting in the second week of April, leading to the first press conference announcing the launch of the region on 9 May 1990. The offices of the region were subsequently opened at Essanby House, Jeppe Street, Johannesburg on 11 May. In its regional consultative conference held on 2 September 1990 to prepare for the regional conference of 29 September, the committee announced that a total of 53 branches with a membership figure of up to 25 000 had been established. Soweto accounted for half of the membership, with approximately 10 000 members making up its 22 branches.[23] With a membership of 804 Orlando East was the biggest branch in Soweto, as against other branches which had an average of 500 members. The Pretoria subregion accounted for 3000 members in nine branches, while the West Rand and the East Rand accounted for 480 in two branches and 3500 in nine branches respectively. Johannesburg (including Alexandra and the coloured townships) had 3337 members in 11 branches. The Vaal subregion had launched no branches because of the violence in the area.

While overall the ANC had not achieved its one million membership target when it convened its national conference in June 1991, there were, nevertheless, as shown in Table 1, dramatic improvements in the membership numbers of some regions, if one compares their performance between February and June 1991. According to the Secretary-General's report presented to the conference, the ANC's membership doubled in the period between December 1990 and June 1991. Even if the figures did not reach the new targeted figure of 776 000 by April 1991, they nevertheless swelled from 289 320 in February to 521 181 in June 1991, with a total of 936 launched branches.[24] Some regions even went beyond the targeted figures set for them. Northern Transvaal recruited 22 160 members to the target figure of 15 000; Eastern Transvaal, 65 000 to 60 000; Western Transvaal, 11 262 to 10 000; Northern Cape, 15 260 to 10 000 and Northern Orange Free State 20 554 to 15 000.

The PWV region, despite the fact that it was ravaged by violence and fell short of its target of 186 000, was able to increase its membership figure from 62 202 in February 1991 to 77 429 in June 1991. In this context where one would have expected the region to record a steady decline in its recruitment campaign because of violence, there were remarkable improvements, if one looks at the region between 1990 and 1992. From a total of 34 209 paid-up members in August 1990, membership had increased to 85 156 (including 2488 members from unlaunched branches) in August 1991, and to 116 104 (including 3527 members from unlaunched branches) in August 1992.[25] By its third regional conference on 17–18 October 1992, the region had increased its branches from 89 in June 1991 to 93, excluding 46 branches which still had to be launched.

Table 1 ANC regional membership between February and June 1991

Region	Membership February 1991	Target figures April 1991	Membership June 1991	Branches
1. PWV	62 202	186 000	77 429	89
2. N. Tvl	5 736	15 000	22 160	56
3. E. Tvl	42 164	60 000	65 000	126
4. W. Tvl	3 750	10 000	11 262	25
5. N. Cape	2 138	10 000	15 250	56
6. E. Cape	24 633	80 000	57 854	53
7. W. Cape	30 000	80 000	53 000	111
8. Border	35 689	80 000	65 228	116
9. Transkei	18 031	40 000	36 937	63
10. N. Natal	–	5 000	2 500	3
11. Natal Midlands	20 051	40 000	26 401	57
12. S. Natal	27 720	75 000	50 596	96
13. N. OFS	5 507	15 000	20 554	24
14. S. OFS	11 699	40 000	15 000	61
Total	289 320	776 000	521 181	936

This excluded 534 members from seven unlaunched branches. Its subregions had since 1990 tripled in growth. Of its six subregions, Soweto remained the largest with a membership number of 36 735 from 31 launched branches. Its members accounted for 37 % of the entire PWV membership record. Soweto was followed by the East Rand with 25 641 members from 13 launched branches. This excluded 513 members from six unlaunched branches. The subregion also played host to the largest ANC branch in the country, Katlehong, with a total membership of 10 693. Pretoria, which had been the third largest subregion with a membership of 7126 in 1990, was replaced by Johannesburg-Midrand in 1992 with a total membership of 22 770 drawn from 14 launched branches. This dramatic growth was accounted for by the transfer of the Tembisa branch with 7683 members from the East Rand subregion.

The success in the speedy establishment of branches immediately after the ANC's unbanning needs explaining. The profile which the ANC enjoyed and the euphoria surrounding Mandela's release from prison paved the way for easy recruitment, particularly within the black community. The efforts of MDM organisations and individual activists also played a crucial role in the setting up of branch structures. The youth and women's organisations, the Congress of Traditional Leaders of South Africa (CONTRALESA) in the rural areas, and underground MK operatives all contributed to building ANC branches.[26]

While the euphoria of new-found freedom seemed to underline the initial efforts in the establishment of branches, the success and failure of some initiatives lay in the different approaches to, and techniques and styles of recruitment adopted by activists. The system adopted by the Katlehong branch, established on 19 August 1990 and the most successful of all the ANC branches in the country, is instructive.[27] Organisers and branch officials encouraged the chain-reaction method of recruitment, whereby each new member recruited other members. House meetings where ANC policies were discussed also boosted membership to the branch. Women were most effective in this regard. Many branch organisers were union shop stewards and often attended weekly workshops to discuss progress. Branch meetings were organised in such a way as to encourage membership participation. The branch also enjoyed the presence of ANC stalwarts in the area, who served as an inspiration to the younger generation, and efforts by the branch to involve itself directly in community issues established a sense of identity with the ANC. Finally, the participation of leaders in discussions and workshops not only deepened membership understanding of ANC policies, but also attracted new members. Other factors also accounted for large branches in other regions: the size of the Welkom branch in Northern Orange Free State was due to the presence of the 99 000 members of the National Union of Mineworkers (NUM) who were potential ANC supporters. The Butterworth branch was the biggest branch in the Transkei, primarily because the town was in an industrial area, with a large workforce well disposed to the ANC.

While attaining the target of one million was probably unrealistic, the ANC's recruitment campaign and the consolidation of branches were, to some extent, undermined by a diversity of factors. Despite the success in setting up its organisational bureaucracy (head office, regional structures and branches), the simultaneous outbreak of violence and internal organisational problems critically affected its mass recruitment campaign and the effective functioning of its branches.

Mass membership recruitment and the consolidation of branches

The effects of violence

Despite the ANC's success in recruiting 500 000 members within 16 months of its legality – a dramatic achievement if one compares this with the 100 000 members the organisation enlisted in the 1950s – the outbreak of violence complicated the recruitment campaign and diverted ANC leaders' attention from organisational reconstruction to addressing its effects. The outbreak of violence in areas such as Natal and the PWV undermined the creation of branches and made attendance at meetings virtually impossible. Widespread harassment was prevalent in homelands such as KwaZulu, Bophuthatswana and Ciskei, where ANC members were denied access to public facilities such as community halls and stadiums. Repression in Bophuthatswana forced branches in Odi and Moretele to use facilities in Hammanskraal (the St Peters seminars), Medunsa or the Soshanguve stadium outside the borders of the homeland. In some instances ANC activists were detained and tortured, as was the case in Modderspruit and Mabopane.[28] The fact that a majority of town councils in Eastern Transvaal were dominated by the Conservative Party (CP) created serious problems for ANC recruiters in the region. The Black Cats murder squad, which targeted activists for harassment, and the alleged collusion of the police in violence undermined recruitment efforts by ANC organisers.[29] The Western Transvaal region which covered most of Bophuthatswana and neighbouring right-wing-dominated towns faced severe repression by Bophuthatswana police. Conservative town councils also refused ANC members access to public amenities and freedom of political activity.[30] In Natal ANC membership forms were confiscated from recruiters, thus forcing them to adopt semi-clandestine methods of organising. Such was the case with branches in the Enseleni, Esikhawini and Ngwelezane areas.[31] Organising members in hostels ravaged by violence could also prove a hazardous undertaking, as residents were either forced to join the Inkatha Freedom Party (IFP) or chose to do so for the sake of their lives.

As mentioned above, the spiralling wave of violence inevitably forced ANC leaders into exhaustive efforts to cool down explosive situations in many confrontational instances, thus turning the organisation into a quasi crisis management committee on violence. Violence also ushered in a cloud of doom and undermined people's confidence in the organisation, leading to apathy and resentment within certain sections of the population. Government accusations that the ANC was responsible for the unrest further convinced these sections that the organisation was essentially violence-orientated and hence to be shunned. This development, which became prevalent within the white community, was further strengthened by the ANC's position on sanctions and nationalisation – policies which were perceived by some as anachronistic and not worth pursuing. In the end, while the ANC tried earnestly to contribute towards ending violence,[32] this issue remained the biggest stumbling block, both to its organisational development and the speedy transition to democracy.

Organisational problems

Besides the destabilising effects of violence, other factors also contributed to undermining the progress of organisational reconstruction. These factors ranged from the recruitment strategy to diverse internal political problems.

The recruitment campaign

While regions such as the PWV were densely populated and could be relatively easily managed, the most critical challenge facing the campaign was organising and coordinating recruitment in vast but sparsely populated regions with branches located many kilometres apart.[33] For example, the Eastern Transvaal region, with only four organisers, had to cover areas stretching from Ogies through Leandra, Standerton, Ermelo, Piet Retief, Kangwane, Inkomazi, Lydenburg and Belfast, to Witbank.[34] This entailed serious communication and transport problems that impinged on the regions' ability to organise and effectively mobilise their constituencies.

While the PWV region was fairly manageable through a combination of advanced communication technology and a wide transport system,[35] the size of some of its branches created its own problems. The results were over-stretched agendas and a general inability to exhaust agenda issues to allow for broader participation in discussions at branch level. It was against this background that suggestions were made for the subdivision of branches which had grown unwieldy, and the creation of zonal structures to coordinate branches and facilitate links with the regions.

While ANC branches adopted different recruitment strategies, they were nonetheless confronted by common problems and difficulties. The year 1990, in particular, saw many branches embarking on mass recruitment without a clear plan. Despite the fact that the National Organising Department eventually intervened to correct and invigorate the recruitment campaign, the general belief held by many activists that people would simply join the organisation because of its popularity negated prompt efforts at devising such a plan. This resulted in campaigners often ignoring members of civic, trade union, church, youth, student, and women's organisations well disposed to the ANC. Alternatively, some activists who belonged to ANC-allied organisations felt that they were already members of the ANC and did not have to "rejoin" the organisation. To them, the question of filling in forms was "bureaucratic" and "harassing".[36] In some instances, activists who joined the organisation refused to pay membership fees, quoting their innumerable sufferings for the movement. That a majority of regions had too few organising officials also hindered recruitment. Furthermore, few of these officials had organising experience and were appointed only because they had suffered prison, exile or police detention.[37] The Southern Orange Free State region, which covered an area which stretched from Bloemfontein to Botshabelo, Ficksburg, Edenburg, Brandfort and Ladybrand, was serviced by only two organisers.[38] But a more serious drawback was that, except for regions located around major metropolitan areas, the branches had inadequate resources and finances to realise their objectives.

The diverse and often ineffective approaches by branches were a product of a highly administrative recruitment campaign, which had few links to ongoing political activities.[39] The failure to adopt the UDF and COSATU's strategies on mobilisation and organisation, which had worked effectively during the 1980s, was symptomatic of the rise of bureaucratic forms of organisation. Even with the launch of mass campaigns such as the demand for an elected constituent assembly, an interim government, the signature campaign (to endorse these demands), and the holding of mass rallies, no clear connection with the recruitment campaign was successfully effected.[40] Despite awareness of this shortcoming and attempts towards its rectification, branches continued to have difficulty in mobilising membership around these issues. Persuading people to join the ANC because it was fighting for a democratic constituent assembly or, alternatively, asking people to join the ANC, when it apparently lacked an effective remedy for the spiralling violence, was often extremely difficult. It would appear that the lack of political direction on membership recruitment and on consolidating branches lay equally with the regions, in so far as they were entrusted with the responsibility of coordinating and guiding branches. Often lines of communication between regions and branches were reed thin as a consequence of being hardly ever utilised. There were insufficient periodic visits by regional and national leaders to branches to help boost the work on the ground, and not all leaders responded when invited by branches.[41]

The decision by the organisation to limit membership to those over the age of 18 denied the ANC access to the potentially solid support of a committed youth movement. The lack of clarity on the role of the youth and women's leagues in ANC branches had its own negative repercussions. That the two saw themselves as autonomous entities effectively deprived the mother organisation of important tools for membership recruitment. The youth, in particular, showed a lack of enthusiasm to channel their militancy into the branches. In some regions their claim to autonomy also caused tensions during the waging of campaigns. The Women's League, too, did not make the maximum contribution to the ANC, probably because of the league's efforts on the question of women's representation in ANC structures and the drawing up of a women's charter.

On the administrative side, the initial ANC membership forms drawn up by the National Office created problems that hampered the progress of the entire campaign, particularly the consolidation of branch structures. Insufficient details were required of new members, thus making it subsequently impossible to locate them. For example, the new members were not asked to fill in their telephone numbers; in some cases, people from as far afield as Venda would join the ANC in Johannesburg whenever they came across ANC recruitment tables in the streets, but were not asked to supply their place of residence or current address. When meetings were called the result was poor attendance.

Organising in the rural areas presented challenges of its own. The location of villages kilometres apart created serious transport and communication problems. Despite the fact that most of these areas, particularly Northern

Transvaal, Orange Free State, Natal and parts of the Cape, were already politicised, it was difficult for activists to actually organise people in these areas into strong ANC branches. The question of illiteracy and the belief by some that it was still illegal to join the ANC further complicated matters.[42]

In white, coloured and Indian areas the organising and recruiting problems were of a very different nature. Despite the fact that these communities had a significant number of activists and sympathisers, who had made their mark within the democratic movement and other anti-apartheid organisations during the repressive epoch of the Botha regime, ANC branches were not able to successfully recruit them. The wave of criticism and fierce questioning of ANC policies and actions bred apathy and demoralised campaigners in these constituencies. As noted in the Secretary-General's report to the national conference, the question of an alliance with the South African Communist Party (SACP), the ANC's position on nationalisation, its befriending of the Palestine Liberation Organisation (PLO), its depiction by Inkatha and certain sectors within the state system as being responsible for township violence, and other factors, served to create a general feeling of antipathy towards the organisation. In some circles, the notion of the ANC as an activist, "toyi-toyi" organisation was pervasive. This led to reservations in the minds of potential members with liberal inclinations. The consequent lack of a strong white participation in ANC branches meant that the principle of non-racialism was not translated into practice, except within the confines of activists at national, regional and branch executive structures.

It was only after Mandela's concerted efforts in 1992, particularly in the Cape, that the coloured community responded with more enthusiasm to ANC initiatives, and efforts were now also made to woo the white community into the ANC. Branches were established in the suburbs of Johannesburg – Hillbrow, Berea, Mayfair, Brixton, Parktown, Melville, Yeoville, Bellevue, Randburg and others;[43] in central Pretoria,[44] Benoni and Springs,[45] as well as in the remote areas of Northern Transvaal and the Orange Free State. In some of the conservative Afrikaner-dominated towns, a significant number of whites joined the ANC. However, most of them preferred not to disclose their identity for fear of harassment. In the Free State the "house call" initiative, introduced by the ANC and aimed at allowing discussion of its policies and recruitment, helped to stimulate white interest in the organisation.[46] The ANC also succeeded in establishing branch structures in the almost forgotten and barren lands of Namaqualand.[47] Notwithstanding these efforts, the ANC remained a mainly black organisation.

In some areas, tensions within the ANC weakened organisational reconstruction. The welding together of three different types of ANC members – exiles, former prisoners and those from the democratic formations inside the country – had an impact on the process of mobilisation and organisation. In many cases these people had a different understanding of and approach to issues.[48] In the Transkei, for example, tensions crystallised between branch recruiters and ANC underground operatives, with the former accusing the latter of having taken over local structures without consulting the existing UDF formations. The regional office also developed a tendency to send recently released prisoners or returning exiles to preside over the launch of local branches, a move that was met with suspicion by local activists. This feeling of tension was conspicuous, for example, during the establishment of branches in Butterworth and Buzana.[49] Although the differences in political style were successfully reconciled in this region, particularly after the intervention of Chris Hani and Steve Tshwete, they nevertheless remained a problem that permeated the entire organisation.[50]

Tensions also occurred in ANC structures that accommodated diverse groups which were historically hostile to the organisation.[51] This was most prevalent in Northern Transvaal, where ANC activists drawn from the South African Youth Congress (SAYCO) and the UDF, had to share a political bed with their arch-enemies – homeland leaders, policemen and chiefs. Furthermore, a majority of the civil servants in the four bantustans to the north (Lebowa, Venda, Gazankulu and Kwandebele), black entrepreneurs and teachers also sought a home in the emerging ANC structures, thus posing a critical challenge to the ANC's ability to reconcile their interests. This challenge was not always successfully met, as demonstrated by the strife that occurred in Kwandebele (between the local Ekangala branch and the ruling Intando Ye Sizwe), caused by the leadership's failure to reconcile its strategy of wooing bantustan leaders with the interests of its local structures.[52]

Internal organisational problems

Similar factors appeared to be responsible for the ineffective functioning of a majority of ANC branches. Most of them lacked offices and meeting venues, making adequate communication between members difficult. In some branches there was a lack of competence; some members took branch positions while holding full-time jobs or belonging to fraternal organisations such as COSATU, the SACP and civics, as was apparent in the Kagiso branch (West Rand) and the Eersterus/Hammanskraal branch (Pretoria subregion). The tendency of certain executive members to work alone deprived branches of organisational skills when these individuals left: the Weppenaar branch in Southern Orange Free State had to be suspended, because it had effectively become a one-man branch.[53] Opportunism and fraud were rife in some areas, with people collecting membership fees that never reached the regional offices. Sello Morake, a former candidate in community council elections, caused havoc in the Sebokeng hostels when he continued to collect twenty rand notes from the local residents for ANC activities which never took place.[54] Without consulting the community, Mr Morake also signed a controversial agreement with the Sebokeng Administrator, Mr Johan Kilian, to provide housing for the homeless in a new transit camp in the area.[55] Branches such as Morokolong/Mandelaville completely failed to account for membership fees. Some branches, such as Bekkersdal, were crippled because branch executive members failed to attend meetings, as was the case with the suspension of the Orlando West branch chairperson. Factionalism in branches such as those in the Vaal bred gangsterism and criminality, paralysing their ability to function. The creation of two executive committees within the Toekomsrus branch in the West Rand because of differences rendered the structure moribund, while the misuse of branch money in Bekkersdal led to tensions that ultimately bred factions. In some instances the style of operation by activists, in which crucial information was limited to a few individuals, persisted even after the ANC was legalised, much to the detriment of fledgling branches.[56] Maladministration, cliquism and in-fighting in the Western Transvaal region resulted in the dissolution of the Regional Executive Committee and the appointment of a caretaking committee.[57]

A significant number of branches had since their launch come close to collapsing and had to be resuscitated by the intervention of the regions. This was the case with branches in the PWV such as Ratanda, Kwa-Thema, Atteridgeville, Themba, Eersterus/Mamelodi and Orlando West (the home of ANC Deputy President Walter Sisulu). Some branches failed to survive because of insufficient resources, while others became totally dependent on the regions for logistical assistance. Branches such as Delmas and Tladi Camp effectively died.

A majority of branches in squatter settlements, such as Sweetwaters in Lenasia, were paralysed by undemocratic practices. In most cases, decisions were arrived at through emotions and fiery speeches, without rational and sober analysis of the issues in hand. Some branches even developed an element of tribalism. Significant tensions arose between these structures and the more established ANC branches in the townships. This was the case in Shoshanguve and Lenasia, for example.[58] Tensions between these structures stemmed either from a lack of representation of squatter interests in the main branches or the scramble for the allocation of sites in the settlement areas. While squatters accused the main branches of ignoring their interests and the conditions in the squatter settlements, township branches often regarded the creation of "alternative" branches as an act of disloyalty, and confrontational. Branches that had substructures in the hostels (e.g. Tembisa and Sebokeng) always found themselves having to contend with a lack of discipline and the propensity in these structures to either act independently or challenge incumbent branch officials. Hostile relations also developed between ANC branches and civic structures in Weilersfarm (Vaal subregion) and Delmas (East Rand), due to either personality differences of activists or to a complete misunderstanding of the demarcation of functions between these structures.

However, despite these myriad factors which marred the ANC's organisational reconstruction, the organisation made an important leap in establishing itself as a mass-based liberation movement inside South Africa. From its vast departmental structures and huge fixed assets in exile, from its diplomatic missions around the world, from its military bureaucracy and its tributary underground structures both inside the country and in neighbouring countries, the ANC synthesised a new mass-based organisational structure that drastically departed from the highly hierarchic, authoritarian and militaristic structure that had existed in exile.

Organisational reconstruction and finance

During its life in exile the ANC relied heavily on foreign funding for most of its activities. Not only was finance secured for developmental projects and the legal defence of apartheid victims in South Africa,[59] it was also secured for the building of ANC organisational structures around the world.

However, the unbanning of the ANC in 1990 brought with it new challenges in its relationship with foreign donors. Spearheaded by the media, a flurry of criticism was launched against this relationship, with particular focus on the rationale for the world's continued support of one political party against others. Two clear arguments were advanced, one urging foreign donors to discontinue their support for the ANC, and the other calling for the organisation to transform itself into a political party. But donors refused to jettison their old-time ally and the ANC resisted transforming itself from a liberation movement into a political party.

While donors did not cease their financial support to the ANC as a result of the changing political developments,[60] it was clear that the ANC's access to foreign funding during the period of transition had more strings attached than was the case before its unbanning. Media scrutiny and the ANC's straddling of the world political spectrum – from America to Libya and China to Taiwan[61] – for financial support, awakened donor sensitivity and concern about financial accountability. A new sense also developed within the ANC of encouraging financial self-sufficiency by exploring alternative sources of funding. Nkobi, the ANC's Treasurer-General, put it bluntly to the 1991 national conference that ''as the national liberation movement, preparing our people to govern themselves, we must see to it that a political culture of self-reliance and funding of our struggle by ourselves takes a firm root among our people''.[62]

However, developing financial self-sufficiency for the organisation against the backdrop of its heavy reliance on foreign grants was to prove a daunting challenge. According to the report of the Treasurer-General, the ANC's income in December 1990, as depicted in Figure 4 was comprised of 86 % grants, 5,3 % membership fees, 3,8 % other income, 3,7 % donations and 0,5 % sales. This meant that out of a total of R11 341 598, R9 824 569 came from grants, R598 420 from membership fees, R422 307 from donations, R240 089 from other income, R191 799 from interest and R64 414 from sales. The greater part of its expenditure fell into three categories: salaries (16,82 %), travelling, particularly by air (14,95 %) and the women and youth leagues (9,74 %).

This financial dependency prompted a new strategy, emphasising a departure from welfarism to self-reliance. But existing challenges of organisational reconstruction and financial support to returning exiles[63] dictated the need for continued foreign funding, hence Mandela's fund raising world tours[64] and direct pleadings with former donors to continue their support.

Sweden, through the Swedish Internal Development Agency (SIDA), contributed a total of SEK120 million for 1991/92. It also contributed R1 521 793,13 towards the ANC's national conference. The Norwegian government, which had financed the Mazimbu/Dakawa settlements, also contributed R520 000 to the ANC conference; the Finnish government allocated FIM7 million to the ANC for 1991; the Australian government allocated A$15 million for the period 1990–1993, while Denmark and Italy pledged support for the ANC's development projects. Non-governmental organisations, such as the World University Services and the World Council of Churches, were also approached for financial support. However, while donors continued their support, clear signals were given to the ANC indicating the trimming of such support in the future.[65]

The move towards laying the basis for financial self-reliance began with the reorganisation of the Office of the Treasurer-General (OTG) and the reorientation of its financial strategy. During its existence in exile, the OTG had been composed of the following departments: Finance, Projects, Logistics, Transport, and Economics and Planning. After the unbanning of the ANC, the Department of Economics and Planning reconstituted itself as the Department of Economic Policy and was placed under the Office of the Secretary-General. The Department of Social Welfare was created and placed under the OTG to cater for the social welfare of ANC members, and to formulate a social welfare policy for the new South Africa. Another department, the Information System Department, was also formed in January 1991 to deal with the general computerisation and telecomputing of ANC structures, and to develop an information technology strategy and telecommunications strategy for South Africa.

The task of devising a new finance strategy, however, remained with the Department of Finance. While the brief for this department was to produce a financial strategy for the ANC, the varied pressures on the ANC by its members and people outside its ambit compelled a broader financial strategy, that not only looked at income generation for the organisation, but also at development projects that could alleviate the living conditions of both ANC members and the community in general. Thus while the Finance Department focused on income generation, the Projects Department, also within the OTG, devised a broader developmental strategy.

In consultation with existing development agencies inside the country, the Projects Department started a series of meetings beginning in October 1990, which resulted in the production of a draft development strategy document. Initiatives were also taken to set up and coordinate regional development forums. Meetings with the Development Bank of South Africa (DBSA), the Independent Development Trust (IDT) and other donors were held to secure funding for projects. Consequently, a number of projects were initiated, such as the Transkei Pilot Housing Project, the skills-training Khuphuka Project in Durban, Project Capricorn in Venda, and the Association of Ex-Political Prisoners. These projects were innovative and potentially important, aimed as they were at addressing the acute unemployment crisis affecting the ANC and which was especially severe within the ranks of MK.[66]

Figure 4 The ANC's income, 1990 (Rand million)

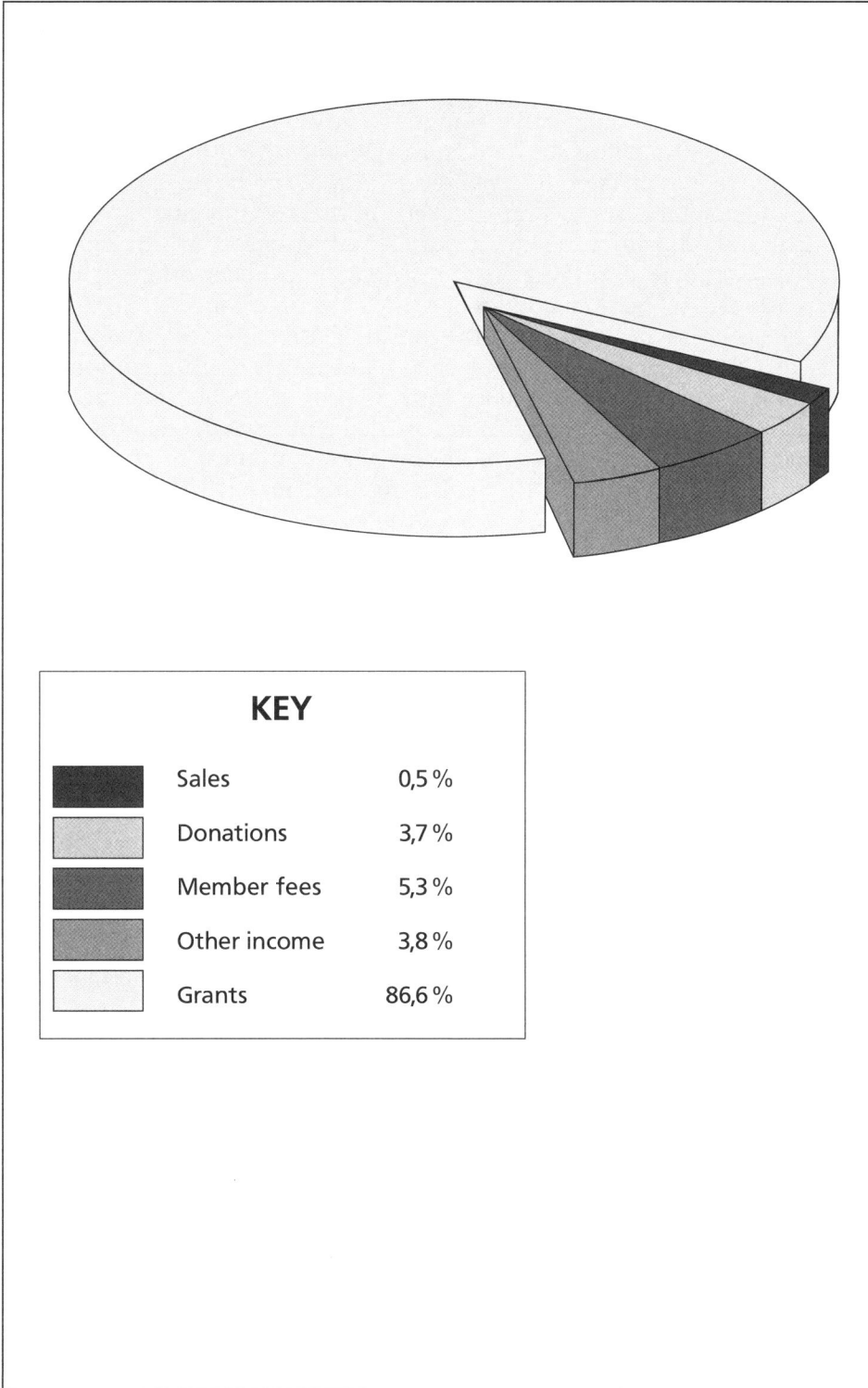

KEY		
■	Sales	0,5 %
▨	Donations	3,7 %
▨	Member fees	5,3 %
▨	Other income	3,8 %
□	Grants	86,6 %

The process of making the ANC financially self-sufficient began in earnest with the creation of a Business Unit within the Finance Department in September 1990. The task of the unit was to establish a merchandising section of the ANC, to protect and regulate the ANC's intellectual property, to establish an ANC travel agency, a printing company and garages, as well as computer and administrative training centres.[67] Movement Enterprise, coordinated by Pete Roussos, was subsequently established in November 1990 to operate as an ANC merchandising arm in the producing and selling of ANC memorabilia, such as caps, jackets, shirts and umbrellas.[68] While this initiative started with a boom, it was almost crippled by the spread of violence, as people displaying ANC insignia came under attack and retail outlets refused to carry goods with ANC logos or colours in their stores. Reacting to these developments the Business Unit opened its own retail outlet at ANC headquarters and reached its membership through a mailing list, a move which eventually bore fruit with up to 15 000 mailings being handled every month. Furthermore, cordial links were established with informal hawkers' networks such as the African Council of Hawkers and Information Business (ACHIB), which resulted in hawkers buying ANC goods in bulk and selling them at ANC rallies, meetings and conferences. A hawkers' scheme and jumble sale were introduced within ANC branches as alternative forms of fund-raising.[69] Some branches, such as the Johannesburg North-West branch, also used occasions such as the Nadine Gordimer Dinner in 1992 to raise funds.

By contrast, the attempt to set up a printing company was marred by controversy, much of which played itself out in the media. The controversy started with media revelations that the ANC had failed to account for R2,2 million donated by the Norwegian government to set up a printing shop.[70] According to these reports, the money was instead channelled by the ANC into the privately owned Thebe Investment Corporation (TIC).[71] The ANC maintained, however, that the funds were properly allocated for their intended purpose and that it had so informed the Norwegian government. While the TIC, generally perceived as an ANC business arm, reportedly intended to set up a printing shop[72] and appeared to be connected to rumours to establish an ANC daily newspaper and three magazines, the controversy surrounding it seemed to lie in the fact that it was registered with the Registrar of Companies Office in Pretoria as a private investment company. Further controversy flared up around the TIC's perceived role as a gatekeeper in handling business contracts between the ANC and foreign companies.[73] Criticism was not only levelled against practices seen as subverting sanctions at a time when the organisation was still calling for their maintenance, it was also directed against the nurturing of a culture of corruption, where access to corporate business was the private reserve of a few individuals who could make deals with the ANC elite. The implication was clear, particularly after reports of the TIC's involvement in a deal with the United States-based Digital Equipment Corporation, and in another deal with Macmillan Publishers Ltd to buy a small Johannesburg-based publishing house, Skotaville.[74] In a stinging criticism of the TIC's gate-keeping role in sanctioning business contracts in South Africa, Iden Wetherell, writing in the pages of the *Weekly Mail*, pointed to the anomalies of seeking to address past injustices to benefit the majority while creating conditions conducive to corruption and the enrichment of a few already mobile business elite.[75]

It was clear, though, that with the predictions of an ANC victory in the coming elections, a number of individuals, businessmen and companies would seek greener pastures under the umbrella of the ANC in various ways, including enticing its leaders into financial dealings. It was to be expected that the distinction between corrupt deals and deals that benefited the dispossessed would also become blurred. This was apparent in the business dealings entered into by the Head of the ANC's Department of Arts and Culture, Wally Serote, with Sun International and Elmo de Witt Films to establish an Arts Foundation and a National Film Trust of South Africa respectively. The first deal fell foul of ANC activists in Bophuthatswana who had been opposed to Sun International support for the Mangope government. The second came under attack from members of the Film and Allied Workers Union (FAWO) who opposed the granting of privileged status to one film company. But the alleged deal between some ANC leaders (Peter Mokaba, John Nkadimeng and Rocky Malebane Metsing) and the Miss South Africa sponsors to set aside R250 000 for the creation of a fund to train beauty contestants, appeared to be sensationalised news, conceived and blown out of proportion by the media. While this meeting did take place, its focus was to try to resolve mounting opposition by ANC supporters to the holding of the contest in Bophuthatswana.[76]

This, however, does not mean that there was no financial mismanagement within the ANC. The alleged squandering of funds of the Social Welfare Department by Winnie Mandela and Dali Mpofu[77] – and the lack of a visible inquiry into the allegation – created a precedent for others to use ANC property and funds without caring much about accountability. The result was a heavy price paid by the Treasury for property broken and unreported, cars recklessly driven, traffic fines accumulated and accidents left unreported, as well as for the incurring of high telephone bills. But much worse was that mismanagement created a fertile ground for conmen to use ANC official letterheads and business cards to extort millions of rands from private businesses. On 10 March 1993 Sakelo Llewellyn Ntile, an officer in the ANC Treasury Department, appeared in court on charges of fraud involving over R283 000. He had apparently made fictitious stationery purchases and deposited ANC cheque payments for the "goods" into his own business accounts.[78]

Not all the ANC's plans, such as the setting up of a travel agency and garages, had been adversely affected. However, despite the move towards financial self-reliance and the encouragement of regions and branches to similarly embark on their own fund-raising campaigns,[79] it was clear by 1993 that the ANC was still far from attaining these goals. Movement Enterprise was facing problems as interest in ANC products waned. Membership fees were also showing signs of falling off. It was against this background that the ANC continued to emphasise foreign funding to back its election campaign, hence the February 1993 international solidarity conference and Mandela's intensified fund-raising world tours.

The creation of ANC organisational structures inside South Africa and the management of its funds constituted one challenge, its political development was the other. The following chapter will analyse this political development, paying attention to relations with its youth, women's and other allied organisations, such as the UDF, COSATU, SACP and the civics. It will also focus on tensions, crises and democratic practice within the ANC.

ENDNOTES

1. It is important to note that this book only offers a synopsis of the ANC's history. For a comprehensive analysis of its history see Meli, F. *South Africa belongs to us: a history of the ANC.* Harare: Zimbabwe Publishing House, 1988; Holland, H. *The struggle: a history of the African National Congress.* London: Grafton, 1989; Karis, T. & Carter, G. (Eds). *From protest to challenge: a documentary history of African politics in South Africa, 1882–1964,* 4 volumes. Stanford: Hoover Institute, 1972; Lodge, T. *Black politics in South Africa since 1945.* Johannesburg: Ravan, 1983; Gerhart, G.M. *Black power in South Africa: the evolution of an ideology.* Berkeley: University of California Press, 1978; Walshe, P. *The rise of African nationalism in South Africa: the African National Congress, 1912–1952.* Berkeley: University of California Press, 1971; Tambo, A. *Preparing for power: Oliver Tambo speaks.* London: Heinemann, 1987; Motlhabi, M. *The theory and practice of black resistance to apartheid.* Braamfontein: Skotaville, 1984; Rantete, J. *The African National Congress: from revolutionary armed seizure to a negotiated transfer of power.* Honours dissertation, Faculty of Arts. Johannesburg: University of the Witwatersrand, 1990.
2. Report of the Office of the Treasurer-General, ANC National Congress. Durban, July 1991, 14–15.
3. The college was named after Solomon Mahlangu, an ANC cadre who was captured and executed in South Africa in 1979.
4. Report of the commission of inquiry into certain allegations of cruelty and human rights abuses against ANC prisoners and detainees by ANC members. 20 August 1993, 162.
5. Lodge, T. State of exile: the African National Congress of South Africa, 1976–86. In Frankel, P. Pines, N. & Swilling, M. (Eds), *State resistance and change in South Africa.* Johannesburg: Southern, 1988, 237.
6. See the Report of the Office of the Treasurer-General, op cit., 12 (statement of the Treasurer-General of the ANC), and 35 (report of the Transport Department).
7. Most of the ANC infrastructure in exile was either sold or donated to the host countries. The Dakawa and Mazimbu settlements were handed over to the Tanzanian government by Oliver Tambo on 9 July 1992. See ANC press statement on Mazimbu handover, 10 July 1992. According to Carl Niehaus, spokesperson for the ANC's Department of Information and Publicity, the ANC retained property in Uganda where MK members were maintained. Some diplomatic houses in foreign states were not disposed of.
8. Swilling, M. & Rantete, J. Organisation and strategies of the major resistance movements in the negotiation era. In Lee, R. & Schlemmer, L. (Eds), *Transition to democracy: policy perspectives.* Cape Town: Oxford University Press, 1991, 203–204.
9. This committee operated until March 1990 when it was disbanded after Mandela was released. See 'ANC's operation rebuild'. *Front File,* May 1990.
10. *Weekly Mail,* 16–22 February 1990. See also *The Star,* 14 February 1990.
11. Saki Macozoma, official of the ANC's Department of Information and Publicity. Interview.
12. The decision to establish the ANC inside the country was made by the NEC in its special meeting on 14–16 February 1990, convened to respond to the unbanning of the organisation by President De Klerk. See *Front File,* March 1990.
13. Saki Macozoma. Interview.
14. Rather than being caused by logistical problems, the initial idea of scattering offices seems to have been informed by the organisation's security consciousness and was reminiscent of the way offices were laid out in Lusaka, Zambia. See Lodge, op cit., 232–233. See also Uhlig, M. (Ed.). *Apartheid in crisis.* Harmondsworth: Penguin, 1986, 149.
15. 'ANC move almost complete'. *The Star,* 9 June 1991.
16. ANC press statement on the restructuring of the department of the organisation and the allocation of portfolios to members of the National Working Committee of the ANC, 2 August 1991.

17. See Appendix A for elected NEC members.

18. See Appendix A for members of the National Working Committee.

19. 'Building a mass-based legal ANC'. *SASPU National*, 1(2), 1990, 16.

20. 'Regions chart the way forward'. *Mayibuye*, December 1990, 21 & 23.

21. 'More ANC regions launched'. *New Nation*, 549, 7–13 December 1990.

22. 'Regional launches in congress strongholds'. *New Nation*, 541, 12–18 October 1990.

23. 'ANC grows amid the PWV violence'. *New Nation*, 536, 7–13 September 1990, 23.

24. Organisational report of the African National Congress Executive Committee. Presented by the Secretary-General CDE Alfred Nzo to the first legal National Conference of the African National Congress after 30 years of proscription, Durban, 2–6 July 1991, 13.

25. Barbara Hogan, Secretary-General of the ANC PWV region. Interview.

26. Joel Netshitenzhe (alias Peter Mayibuye), Editor of *Mayibuye*, NEC member and former Chairman of the ANC Northern Transvaal region. Interview.

27. By the time of the PWV Regional Consultative Conference in December 1990, the Katlehong branch had already enlisted 2500 members. This grew to 8000 in June 1991. See 'A super-branch success story'. *New Nation*, 624, 21–27 June 1991.

28. 'Brutal repression in Bophuthatswana'. *Mayibuye*, 1(2), September 1990, 22.

29. Chair Maselela, Secretary of the ANC Eastern Transvaal region. Interview.

30. Sam Louw, Secretary of the ANC Western Transvaal region. Interview. Repression by the Bophuthatswana police also occurred in the Northern Cape areas of the bantustan. See the interview with Manie Dipico, ANC Northern Cape Chairperson in *Mayibuye*, December 1992, 15–17.

31. 'Secret launch in Natal'. *Mayibuye*, 2(3), April 1991, 3.

32. See Chapter 4.

33. Ngoako Ramathlodi, Chairman of the ANC Northern Transvaal region. Interview.

34. Chair Maselela. Interview.

35. At the beginning of March 1991, the ANC had 57 cars inside the country with each department and regions being allocated either one or two. This was nevertheless incomparable with the fleet of cars the organisation owned outside the country, making a total of 269.

36. Raymond Suttner, Head of the ANC's Department of Political Education. Interview.

37. Vax Mayekiso, Deputy Secretary of the ANC Northern Orange Free State region. Interview.

38. Kaizer Sebothelo, Secretary of the ANC Southern Orange Free State region. Interview.

39. 'Moulding organs of struggle'. *Mayibuye*, 1(2), September 1990, 20.

40. It was this failure which prompted the Chairman of the PWV region, Tokyo Sexwale, to lambaste branch delegates at the regional conference in 1992, charging that "we have so narrowly politicised the character of the ANC since being unbanned that we have somewhat even further narrowed it down to a negotiations department of the struggle which concerns itself mainly, or only, with issues pertaining to the demand for an interim government, the constituent assembly and elections".

41. Pretty Javu, Administrator of the ANC Border-Kei region. Interview.

42. Joel Netshitenzhe. Interview.

43. 'ANC intensifies bid to recruit whites'. *The Star*, 18 June 1990.

44. See the establishment of the Pretoria Central branch on 18 October 1990 in 'ANC in die kol'. *Mayibuye*, 1(3), December 1993, 20.

45. 'ANC launches recruitment drive'. *Southern Africa Report*, 18 May 1990, 3–4.

46. 'Relaxing with oom Piet on the plaas'. *New Nation*, 624, 21–27 June 1991.

47. 'The ANC: never the same again'. *Mayibuye*, 2(3), April 1991, 16–17.

48. 'Build those branches'. *New Era*, 5(2), Winter, 1990, 16.

49. Gevisser, M. ANC enters political battlefield. *Weekly Mail*, 17–19 August 1990.

50. Harber, A. Can the ANC weave its strands into a thread? *Weekly Mail*, 7–13 December 1990.

51. Cargill, J. The same political home for hunter and the hunted. *Work In Progress*, 69, September 1990, 25.

52. The leadership's failure to resolve this challenge was also demonstrated by tensions around Ramodike, Lebowa's Chief Minister, who straddled the ANC and the NP. See 'Bantustan leaders cosy up to ANC'. *Work In Progress*, 80, 1992, 11.

53. Kaizer Sebothelo. Interview.

54. *City Press*, 4 November 1990.

55. *Vaal Vision*, 15 October 1993.

56. Joel Netshitenzhe. Interview.

57. Sam Louw. Interview.

58. There was, however, an exception to this trend as shown by the establishment of the Phola Park branch alongside the main Katlehong branch in the East Rand. This might have been caused by self-acknowledgement by the Katlehong branch, the biggest in the country, to effectively address squatter issues.

59. The London-based International Defence and Aid Fund contributed large amounts of money to the legal defence of apartheid victims in South Africa.

60. Swedish party political leaders, while feeling the need to review their financial backing of the ANC, were reluctant to cut financial support to the organisation during the transition period. See *Sowetan*, 21 September 1993.

61. See ANC press statement about reports emanating from Beijing that ANC President Comrade Nelson Mandela sent a letter to the government of the People's Republic of China regarding future diplomatic relations with Taiwan, 18 August 1993. This was a response to the confusion caused by the ANC in seeking support from countries which were historically enemies.

62. Report of the Office of the Treasurer-General, op cit., 3.

63. According to Jackie Selebi, NEC member by 1990 and convenor of the Organising Committee for the Return of Political Exiles, bringing about 20 000 ANC exiles home would cost R200 million. See 'Homecoming hassles'. *Enterprise*, March 1991, 20.

64. 'ANC fund appeal'. *Front File*, July 1990, 7. However, the approximately $5 million raised by Mandela in the United States was not readily available because of technical problems. In fact, American donors could not make tax-deductible donations unless they were directed at specific projects, meaning that the money would not come until the ANC provided details about how it intended using the money. See *Leadership South Africa*, 9(8), 1990, 22.

65. *The Star*, 11 January 1993.

66. In August 1993 a group of 27 MK members occupied the ANC Southern Natal offices and demanded that the ANC's leadership address their acute unemployment problem.

67. Report of the Office of the Treasurer-General, op cit., 16.

68. *Sunday Times*, 21 April 1991.

69. Letter sent to ANC branches by the PWV Regional Treasurer, Cassim Saloojee, entitled 'Launching of an ANC hawker scheme', 24 June 1992.

70. *City Press*, 7 February 1993; *Sunday Times*, 7 February 1993.

71. The corporation was directed by Vusi Khanyile and included Enos Mabuza and Tokyo Sexwale in its board of directors. Nelson Mandela and Walter Sisulu were members of the Batho-Batho Trust, which was a shareholder in the company.

72. By September 1993 the TIC reportedly revealed that it had made a deal with Macmillan and Skotaville to establish a printing company, Nolwazi Educational Publishers, which would print educational texts for the new South Africa. See *The Star*, 29 September 1993.

73. Joas Mogale, official of the Foundation for African Business and Consumer Services (FABCOS) official. Interview.

74. Relations between Macmillan Publishers and the ANC were cemented when the former donated 275 books worth R150 000 to the research library of the ANC on 26 October 1993.

75. *Weekly Mail and Guardian*, 17–23 September 1993.

76. ANC statement on the alleged ANC-Miss South Africa secret deal, 10 September 1993.

77. In the sensational love letter to Mpofu leaked to the press (*Sunday Star*, 6 September 1992) Mrs Mandela wrote that she was in trouble over the Simmonds Street account which reflected over R160 000 drawn, strengthening earlier press allegations (*City Press*, 24 May 1992) that she had squandered R400 000 of the Social Welfare Department with Mpofu. The ANC's investigation of this alleged financial mismanagement was never made public.

78. *Sowetan*, 11 March 1993.

79. However, some regions such as Northern Orange Free State had difficulty in raising funds because of right-wing-controlled businesses and junior managers who could not make such decisions without proper sanction from their headquarters, which were mostly based in the PWV area.

The ANC's political development

For most of its life in exile the ANC was esteemed and idolised by its supporters inside South Africa. To many it was the most effective and democratic organisation capable of replacing the white minority rule of the National Party (NP) government. However, the unbanning of the ANC revealed quite a different picture to the one often held by its supporters. As its leaders began returning home in 1990, not only was the organisation found to be fallible, but homogeneity was not as perfect as often assumed and internal democratic practice was not as publicly professed.

Media reports and statements by former detainees held in ANC camps depicted an ANC visibly divided between its leadership and the rank-and-file membership; between the military and security departments; and pervaded by personal rivalries. It portrayed an organisation highly secretive, authoritarian, and deeply influenced by the SACP. This bleak history posed an important challenge to the ANC's ability to engender a new sense of openness and democratic practice along with its organisational reconstruction. But a far more crucial challenge was the necessity to concretise relations with the heterogeneous organisations that had aligned themselves behind its political programme, and which by 1990 included the UDF, COSATU, SACP, the civic movement, as well as youth and women's organisations. Whatever form of interaction with these organisations and their internal political development was to evolve, would have an important bearing on the ANC's internal strength during the period of transition. This chapter will analyse the political dimensions of the ANC's re-emergence inside South Africa. It will pay particular attention to its relations with allied movements, tensions and crises within the ANC, as well as the question of internal democracy.

Relations with allied organisations

Internal relations with the ANC Youth League and the ANC Women's League

Despite being part of the ANC, the Youth and Women's Leagues operated as autonomous entities within the organisation. They had their own constitutions, offices and members. Their autonomy was, however, limited since they could not operate outside ANC policy parameters. Their role within the organisation is a story of mixed cordial relations, successes and tensions.

The African National Congress Youth League (ANCYL)

The ANCYL was formed in 1943 against the background of a growing class struggle in the factories. It was made up of young men led by Anton Lembede, Nelson Mandela, Walter Sisulu and Oliver Tambo. It formulated a militant programme of action, which was adopted by the ANC in 1949 and which came to inform the defiance campaign of the 1950s. However, the banning of political organisations in the early 1960s and their revival in exile were accompanied by the diminishing role of the league. The conditions of exile, which hampered links with people inside South Africa, complicated the rationale for a youth formation within the ANC. It was only in the 1970s that a Youth Section was formed to cater for the needs of thousands of youngsters who were fleeing South Africa after the 1976 uprising.

While the banning of political organisations resulted in a political lull inside the country, the continued legal existence of student organisations, such as the predominantly white National Union of South African Students (NUSAS), provided a sufficient loophole for the gradual resurgence of black student organisations. Dissatisfied with NUSAS's political programme, Steve Biko and Barney Pityane led a walkout at the NUSAS Congress at Rhodes University in 1969 and formed a Black Consciousness-orientated South African Student Organisation (SASO). This organisation was to be instrumental in the emergence of other political organisations, such as the Black People's Convention, South African Student Movement (SASM), National Youth Organisation (NAYO) and the formation of student representative councils in schools and universities. It would also be the driving force behind the wave of factory strikes that engulfed the country in 1973, as well as the outbreak of the Soweto uprising in 1976. While the prominence of this new political activity was predominantly aligned with Biko's Black Consciousness (BC) ideology[1] and succeeded in some degrees in eclipsing the ANC, the banning of BC organisations in October 1977 saw the resurgence and reanimation of the congress tradition, with the ANC being adored as the mother of the liberation struggle. The Azanian Student Organisation (AZASO), which was formed out of the ashes of the banned SASO, pledged its allegiance to the ANC, as did the Congress of South African Students (COSAS), formed in 1979, as well as various civic, women's and church organisations. The ultimate formation of the UDF in 1983 finally established a formidable internal mass support base aligned behind the ANC.

The role of the youth in the struggles of the mid-1980s was strengthened by the consolidation of their organisational structures, as well as the activities they embarked on. While student activities intensified between 1980 and 1985 through school boycotts, their support for rent boycotts, the dissolution of black community council structures and the declaration of successive states of emergency, which crippled effective organisation and mobilisation, saw the formation of the South African Youth Congress (SAYCO), led by Peter Mokaba on 28 March 1987. Taking place at the height of the state of emergency, the launch was a dramatic event. Deliberate misinformation was leaked directing the security police to Durban, while more than 200 delegates from youth congresses across the country met secretly in Cape Town. The Freedom Charter was adopted, as well as a militant programme of action which was reflected in the organisation's slogan, "freedom or death, victory is certain". Students also restructured their organisations in accordance with AZASO – adopting a new name in 1987, namely the South African National Student Congress (SANSCO) – to put themselves in line with the congress tradition. The period of emergencies in the mid-1980s ushered in new forms of political activity with militant student protest, particularly in tertiary institutions and universities. In the townships, the litany of slogans such as "liberation before education" saw COSAS intensifying its battle with the Department of Education and Training. Known as the "roaring young lions", the youth also intensified their militancy in township struggles. Their bravery was reflected in their creation and sustenance of street, area, zonal and block committees in the face of a concerted counter-revolutionary strategy employed by the security forces. But the aftermath of this intensified conflict with the security forces was a large element of disorientated youth in the wake of the mass detention, broken schooling and unemployment. While the mass pro-democracy demonstrations of 1989 were informed by this simmering militancy, they also underlined the extent to which the youth had come to embrace militant struggles as a dogma, to the exclusion of all other activities. This, together with the praises accorded to them by the ANC leadership,[2] was to create serious problems with the unbanning of organisations and the increasing predominance of negotiations and elitist middle-class politics in the struggle.

When the ANC was unbanned in February 1990, Mandelamania was to dissipate all the monumental achievements of the youth. Those who had aspired to be card-carrying members of the ANC found themselves sidelined, as the ANC restricted its membership to 18 years and upwards. Moreover, the increasing unemployment rate resulted in many young people wandering the township streets without jobs. Financial crisis and tighter admission criteria at universities and technikons also increased the pool of alienated wanderers. The result was either an increase in desperate attempts to leave the country to join MK in exile, despite the fact that its leaders had already returned, or to resort to gangsterism and criminality.[3]

Such was the state of affairs in 1990, when the leadership of SAYCO and the returned ANC Youth Section decided to relaunch the ANCYL. A Provisional National Youth Secretariat (PNYS) involving these two youth groups, SANSCO, NUSAS, COSAS, the Young Christian Students (YCS) and Students United for Christian Action (SUCA), was formed to prepare for the launch. This launch took place on Oliver Tambo's 73rd birthday, 27 October 1990.[4] Unlike SAYCO, which was a loose federal structure,[5] the ANCYL was to be a centrally coordinated organisation with regions formed in accordance with the ANC's 14 regions. It was to be an autonomous entity within the ANC. According to its constitution,

> ... the ANCYL shall be a voluntary youth association and mass organ of the ANC. The ANCYL will function as an autonomous body within the

overall structure of the ANC of which it shall be an autonomous part. It shall be based on the political and ideological objectives of the ANC. The ANCYL shall liaise closely with the ANC at all levels (national, regional, zonal and branch levels).[6]

ANCYL membership was open to all within the age group of 14 to 35. Membership of the ANC did not entitle a person to league membership. One had to make a conscious decision to join and be a card-carrying member of the ANCYL. A minimum number of 100 members was necessary for the launching of a new branch.[7]

After the ANCYL launch, Provisional Regional Youth Committees (PRYC) were established to organise the launching of regional and branch structures in preparation for the national conference earmarked for 6 April 1991. A membership target of half a million was set to encourage recruitment. However, by May 1991 a total of 460 000 members had signed up. Only 210 605 of this number were paid-up members.[8] Obviously problems that hounded the ANC's recruitment campaign also hounded the Youth League. These included the question of violence and the logistical problems of organisational capacity.

Another problem that dogged the ANCYL was galvanising its support into membership. Despite the success in mobilising the youth around ANC political programmes, and in drawing large support for campaigns around the National Youth Day, 16 June, transforming this into card-carrying membership proved to be difficult. This was to prompt a decision by the league's National Executive Committee to take its recruitment campaign directly to universities and technikons. According to Peter Mokaba, the ANCYL had to travel throughout the country, offering the youth organisational assistance, whether in schools, universities, technikons, factories, churches, businesses, sports or cultural arenas.[9]

But it appears that other factors were also accountable for the lacklustre recruitment campaign. While the league was well disposed to membership in existing student and other youth organisations, the decision to begin recruitment *de novo* among those not yet committed in any way, meant that a large body of potential support was ignored and consequently wasted. Relying on students and their contemporaries to make individual applications for membership, underestimated the wave of apathy and intimidation caused by violence, which was engulfing the country. The failure to use existing student organisations to its advantage also accounted for the increasingly low participation of whites, coloureds and Indians in the organisation – this despite their significant contribution to the student struggles of the 1980s. While a majority of SANSCO members were also Youth League members, they were not able to increase white participation in the league, even after their merger with NUSAS to form the South African Student Congress (SASCO) on 8 September 1991.[10]

The problems surrounding recruitment and contingent political developments resulted in the postponement of the national conference to 9 December 1991. Held in Kwandebele, the ANCYL national conference was the 17th since the formation of the league in 1943. Attended by 1600 delegates, the conference resolved to build a youth front to unite the youth from diverse political backgrounds, embark on a ''back to school and intensive learning'' campaign, and address gender issues such as the involvement of women in the Youth League, as well as the problem of poor participation among the whites, coloureds and Indians.[11] Notwithstanding the conference resolution on broadening the membership of the league, the basic situation continued unaltered. Lamenting over this, Lulamile Jojiyasi, Eastern Cape Regional Secretary for Political Education, stated that

> ... in our region, most branches were relatively weak and we had hoped that coming out of the conference with a clear programme of action and conference resolutions, our branches would implement them and grow from strength to strength. Exactly the opposite happened – ever since then our branches have been crumbling and collapsing like a house of cards. Some of our activists are no longer willing to continue serving in our branch executive committees. Very few branches are initiating activities and taking up campaigns on their own. Some branches have repeatedly failed to have their annual general meetings because members fail to turn up at meetings. Relatively speaking, our members are passive spectators of the whole current political process unfolding in the country today.[12]

The difficulty in consolidating the league's membership ran parallel to the league's failure to free itself from the shadow of the ANC's all-encompassing political programme, and to focus on and give prominence to its stated campaigns of fostering a culture of learning in schools and of raising issues of gender and health, for example, the need to increase public awareness of AIDS.

On the question of youth unity, however, the league achieved relative success. As a result of its initiative a National Steering Committee (NSC) was formed in February 1992 out of various youth formations, coordinated by the Institute for a Democratic Alternative in South Africa (IDASA), to prepare for a youth summit. This summit eventually took place on 28 August 1992 at the World Trade Centre, Kempton Park. Drawing its participants from diverse youth groups, the significance of the conference – though convened to discuss issues such as democracy, education, economic growth and peace and reconciliation – lay in underlining the crucial role of the ANCYL as a guide to youth aspirations. Ephraim Nkwe, ANCYL member on the conference steering committee, bluntly stated that ''participation was premised on the need to interact with the broadest possible range of youth formations. The purpose of this was to assert our influence and acceptance of our perspective on the ANC's political programme of transforming the country into a non-racial democratic order''.[13] It was envisaged that the youth unity initiative would be followed by the establishment of a national youth development forum in June 1992, which would implement a national youth development plan.[14]

Despite the relative success in initiating moves towards youth unity, achieving unity among diverse youth groups remained dogged by many serious problems. Without unity among the parent political bodies and with some still engaged in conflict, it was highly improbable that unity could be attained without the introduction of specific youth programmes not subject to political influence. In the circumstances, achieving unity even on non-political issues, such as a campaign against AIDS, proved difficult. During the youth conference discussions, for example, differences among participants almost produced a walkout by those dissatisfied with the process. Despite the ANCYL decision to broaden youth unity after the conference, the experience clearly demonstrated that, until national democracy was achieved in the country and apartheid indoctrination was overcome, youth unity would essentially remain an unattainable fantasy. After the conference, ANCYL Publicity Officer, Parks Mankatlana, lamented that the meeting had produced no sufficient basis for youth to act together.[15]

But youth unity was one among a handful of challenges that stared the youth of the country starkly in the face. Chief among these was the question of unemployment, which left many young people alienated and vulnerable to criminal behaviour, hence their association with appendages such as "the lost generation". The critical challenge that faced the league was how to promote the employment of the youth during the period of transition, when the ANC's position on sanctions still inhibited the inflow of foreign investment. While the idea of creating Self-defence Units (SDUs) in the townships provided a vehicle for youth involvement, this backfired, as the majority turned to criminality and held the townships hostage.[16] These structures may have been infiltrated by agents of the state to discredit them, but in any case the plan could not effectively succeed because of the lack of financial backing, hence the bullying tactics employed by some in collecting funds from the communities. Prompted by the criminal practices of the youth-manned SDUs, particularly in Sebokeng, Chris Hani proposed on the eve of his brutal assassination, the formation of peace corps.[17] According to Tokyo Sexwale, peace corps composed of the youth could become part of a reconstruction programme under a government of national unity.[18] They could be called the Chris Hani Brigade, be taught technical skills and used in repairing houses.

While the ANCYL did not create serious tensions within the ANC, the question of its autonomous existence and the explosive speeches of its president, Peter Mokaba, brewed tensions which sometimes soured relations with the parent body. The problem around the question of autonomy related largely to the different interpretations or usage of the term by both the league and the ANC. According to the ANCYL draft constitution, the league was to be organisationally autonomous. It would, however, base itself on the political programmes of the ANC and liaise with the ANC on all levels. The ANC's draft constitution stated that the league would function as an autonomous body within the structure of the ANC.[19]

Although the ANCYL finally altered its position in its adopted constitution to say that it would "function as an autonomous body within the overall structure of the ANC", as stated in the ANC constitution,[20] the different interpretations of this autonomy at the time when the two were busy with recruitment had serious implications. It had a negative impact on the campaign and soured relations between the league and ANC members. Most problematic was the competition for members between the two and their unwillingness to cooperate with each other. The ANC national conference in 1991 even passed a resolution setting up a special commission to investigate the inability to draw league members into the ANC.[21] In some cases, the strict adherence to autonomy by league members resulted in their lack of participation in ANC branch meetings in their areas. That league members, particularly those above the age of 18, were not automatically ANC members, clearly deprived the ANC of significant support, while exposing the league to the danger of being plagued by elements hostile to the ANC. As Andrew Masondo, the ANC's chief representative in Uganda, observed, the league's autonomy put it in the same position as the SACP, which allied and agreed with the ANC positions without being part of the ANC. This meant that, like the SACP, the league was outside the ANC and in effect had no valid claim to be an ANC organ.[22] While the debate on autonomy simply died, it was probably the explosive speeches of the league's President, Peter Mokaba, that involved the organisation in public controversy. Much of the controversy about Mokaba revolved around his chanting of the "kill the boer, kill the farmer" slogan. He was known to have chanted and popularised the slogan as early as the late 1980s. The furore around the chanting of the slogan in the 1990s was sparked by the noticeable increase in incidents of the killing of white farmers.

While Mokaba earned himself the presidency of the league as well as election onto the ANC National Executive Committee (NEC), because of his militancy and fiery speeches, like Mrs Mandela his public profile and political remarks always came under close media scrutiny. As early as 1990, Mokaba's militant rhetoric, though made in support of negotiations, was always interpreted by the media as representing the youth's opposition to negotiations. This was followed by damaging media revelations about his alleged role as a spy[23] and attempts to remove him from the presidency of the ANCYL on the grounds of his age. The media were inclined to pounce on his public pronouncements, even in instances where he made remarks similar to other ANC leaders about the need for self-defence, such as in Sebokeng, where he appeared with Tokyo Sexwale. While the ANC always made protective media statements about controversial remarks by its leaders, a less conciliatory stance was taken against Mokaba in 1993. This began in April after Mokaba's widely publicised chant of the "kill the boer, kill the farmer" slogan. An urgent meeting was subsequently called between the secretary-generals of the ANC and Youth League, after which a joint statement was issued, announcing that the chant did not represent ANC policy and would be reviewed.[24] Following Mokaba's agitation at a funeral of the Tembisa victims in August 1993 to demolish hostels, direct bullets at President De Klerk, remove the security forces from the townships and take the struggle into the white areas, another press statement was issued by the

ANC's Department of Information and Publicity. The statement denounced Mokaba's remarks and concluded by calling for "all South Africans to isolate and reject those who want to foster violence".[25]

Despite the fact that the ANC statement might have been directed at instigators of violence in general, it was abundantly clear that a concerted effort was being made to bring Mokaba in line with the organisation's stated positions. But it was difficult for the ANC to publicly subject him to discipline or isolate him from the organisation, as suggested by the conservative media. His popularity with the youth had already made him an independent leader whom neither the ANC nor the state could bring to book. Ironically, rather than diminishing because of these controversies, his political stature within the ANC continued to grow. This was further underlined by the NEC's acceptance of his suggestion to appoint Thabo Mbeki to the position of ANC chairman following the death of Oliver Tambo, a proposal which was earlier dismissed by Tokyo Sexwale and scorned by the media. For different reasons, the state also found it difficult to arrest Mokaba and make him answerable for his remarks, which allegedly contravened the provisions of the National Peace Accord (NPA). While there was abundant evidence of his remarks in the printed media and television, the police, rather than arresting him, chose instead to vent their anger on one journalist who happened to have covered Mokaba's "kill the boer" remarks at a Wits University meeting. The lack of decisive action by the authorities against Mokaba was not, however, a mark of their naivety. There were strong disincentives for them to take action against him. Prosecuting Mokaba would by implication have meant similar prosecutions of leaders such as the Afrikaner Weerstandbeweging's (AWB) Eugene Terreblanche, the Conservative Party's Ferdi Hartzenberg and the IFP's Mangosuthu Buthelezi, who had also allegedly contravened the NPA by their war talk and threats of civil war. Prosecuting these leaders was a decision for which the NP government was reluctant to pay the price.

The ANC Women's League

The struggle against the pass laws and the 20 000 strong march to Pretoria on 9 August 1956 represented a triumphant apogee in the women's struggle within the anti-apartheid democratic forces and the ANC in particular.[26] However, the banning of political organisations in the early 1960s and their resurgence in exile altered the tempo of the struggle, with more emphasis being placed on armed struggle and the mobilisation of the international community. While women's energies within the ANC were directed towards these new challenges, they were also able to take up issues and problems specific to women. These included the oppression of women through racial discrimination in society, the discrimination they suffered at their place of work, and their subordination to men in the home; men's indifference to issues such as rape and contraception, to which women were sensitive; and the lip-service attitude of the ANC to women's concerns, as shown by the paucity of practical steps taken to address them.[27] In 1981 Gertrude Shope became a member of the ANC's NEC and spearheaded the formation of the ANC's Women's Section. The success of this committee was reflected in the increasingly public stand taken by ANC leaders on women's issues. In their joint pledge to the women of South Africa and Namibia, ANC President, Oliver Tambo, and South West African People's Organisation's (SWAPO) President, Sam Nujoma, stated that their countries would not be free until women were liberated. Between 1981 and 1987 important ANC women's national conferences were held, with the ANC declaring 1984 the Year of Women of South Africa. Women's efforts were finally recognised by the United Nations, which declared 9 August the day of solidarity with the women of South Africa and Namibia. Inside South Africa, the re-emergence of the congress tradition also paved the way for the resurgence of women's organisations. From being committees of student organisations, women's organisations grew in strength, particularly in the Western Cape and Transvaal, and culminated in the formation of the UDF-aligned Federation of Transvaal Women (FEDTRAW), headed by prominent leaders such as Albertina Sisulu.

The ANC's 1985 Kabwe conference not only lauded these efforts but also made it the task of each and every woman and man to build and strengthen the women's organisation. In December 1989 an ANC in-house seminar on women, children and the family was held, in which the role of women in the struggle was discussed. The ANC's draft constitution which had been distributed for discussion, was amended during this seminar to incorporate women's concerns. However, despite attempts to reassert the rights and role of women in the struggle, the difficulty to liaise with women inside South Africa undermined effective maximisation of these efforts. In an attempt to bridge this serious fissure, the ANC's Women's Section convened a conference of South African women in Amsterdam in January 1990, under the name Malibongwe, which prioritised the need for the formation of a broad anti-apartheid women's organisation. This need, however, fell away due to the unbanning of the ANC in February 1990, which posed new organisational demands.

In April 1990 a workshop held in Lusaka between South African women and ANC exiles decided to launch the ANC Women's League (ANCWL) inside the country. Two preparatory teams, the ANC's Women's Section (comprising exiles) led by Gertrude Shope, and the ANC Women's League Task Force (comprising internal members) led by Albertina Sisulu, were formed to prepare the launch. Although the league was to operate as an autonomous and separate body to address what the ANC publication, *Mayibuye*, considered issues specific to women,[28] its organisational structure was to be the same as that of the ANC with 14 different regions. To league members, autonomy meant more than being an auxiliary organ of the ANC. It meant the right to take decisions and implement them without waiting for approval from the ANC. It also meant the right to elect its leading office-bearers and the right to raise and receive funds, as well as to open its own bank account.[29] League members were to be members of the ANC first and had to be over the age of 18.[30] Unlike the ANC, which required a hundred members to launch a branch, league branches could be launched by 20 women.[31]

The Women's League was formally launched in Durban in August 1990. Addressed by Gertrude Shope, Patrick Lekota, Harry Gwala and Govan Mbeki, the launch was interrupted by violence. The league's programme emphasised the need to establish a national commission on the emancipation of women. This had last been proposed at the 1987 women's conference, and supported in a special ANC NEC statement in May 1990.[32] The aim of the campaign was to sensitise, monitor, stimulate and report on the position of women. According to the NEC statement, "highest priority must be given to finding the means to facilitate women's participation in the struggle and within all political, administrative and military sectors of the ANC from the grass roots through to the NEC". The other issue in the league's campaign programme was the Women's Charter. It was felt that women's rights and concerns should be fully articulated and attached to the ANC's constitution.

While the launch of the league was an important step in creating a voice for women within the ANC, important issues raised during the launch were not fully pursued and no elections were held until the organisation's conference. However, for the first time since the ANC was unbanned, women took an organised role in ANC campaigns. Campaigns against violence were to dominate most of the league's activities before the conference. Immediately after the launch, in fact the very next day, the league's leadership embarked on a tour of all the war-torn Natal regions: Natal Midlands, Natal South and Northern Natal;[33] peace rallies were held in areas such as Entseleni and at the University of Zululand;[34] and the league organised a national march to police stations on August 25 to protest against the violence.

Intense work was also undertaken to establish branch structures and regions in preparation for the national conference. The PWV Regional Women's League was launched in January 1991, comprising a total of 38 branches.[35] However, the launch meeting was hurriedly convened, without sufficient consultation. Although attended by 400 delegates, issues were not thoroughly discussed, as the meeting started late. Elections were also not democratic, as voting was conducted by a show of hands. Most members of the Interim Committee were elected into the regional executive, with Winnie Mandela being elected chairperson. However, except for problems encountered in regions such as the PWV and Natal, much groundwork was done. By the time of its conference in April 1991, the ANCWL had enlisted 100 000 members with a total of 661 launched branches throughout the country.[36] The conference, attended by more than 1000 women, was held at the De Beers Stadium in Kimberley, home of the ANC's first Secretary-General, Sol Plaatjie, as well as of Ruth Mompati, one of only three women in the ANC NEC in 1990.[37] Important resolutions were taken, including the need for a Women's Charter campaign to articulate women's rights, the creation of a commission for the emancipation of women which would serve as a watchdog against the violation of women's rights within the ANC, and the decision to have at least 30 % of all elected ANC positions filled by women.[38]

It was the elections to the league's National Executive Committee, however, which drew most public attention. Already intense campaigning had taken place between Winnie Mandela, Albertina Sisulu and Gertrude Shope. Finally, the contest for the presidency of the league lay between Mrs Mandela and Mrs Shope, when Mrs Sisulu withdrew her candidacy. Despite the fact that Mrs Mandela was a popular candidate for the position, many factors combined to shift the balance in favour of Mrs Shope, who ultimately won the position by 422 votes to 196:

- Firstly, Mrs Mandela's appearance before a court on charges of kidnapping and assault and the negative media reports, as well as discontent with her appointment as Head of the ANC's Social Welfare Department, created reservations among the majority of women delegates. Days before the conference, a Western Cape women's branch was reported to have threatened a breakaway in the event of her election as president.[39]

- Secondly, Mrs Sisulu's last minute withdrawal and canvassing of her supporters to vote for Mrs Shope, tilted the scales against Mrs Mandela.

- Lastly, the democratic process followed in holding elections, and a secret ballot supervised by ten representatives from the ANC, COSATU and the SACP,[40] allowed members to exercise their democratic choice.

The failure of Mrs Mandela to win the league's presidency and the discontent felt by some members within the PWV Regional Executive, of which she was chairperson, set in motion a wave of bitter antagonism that was to culminate in some of the most divisive tensions within the ANC.

The increasing significance of the ANCWL was reflected in debates on gender and affirmative action issues throughout the movement. The league's proposal to the July 1991 national conference, read by the Secretary-General, Mr Alfred Nzo, included the amendment to the ANC's constitutional guidelines and the ANC's own draft constitution. The proposal further advocated taking a stand against child abuse and violence against women. Finally, the need to address the several obstacles hampering the growth of the league, such as poor recruitment of rural women and the poor showing of Indian, coloured and white women in the league, was also considered. Nzo recommended, among other things, that the organisation take a firm stand on its commitment to affirmative action, commit itself to signing various international agreements dealing with discrimination against women, and that women should be involved in debates on future economic policy.

Among these proposals, the question of affirmative action in favour of women and the NEC's decision that at least 17 % of all elected positions within the ANC be reserved for women, sparked a debate that lasted for two days. League members rejected the NEC's proposal and instead demanded a

30 % quota. A counter-argument to the 30 % quota proposal, which was supported by a majority of men, was that ANC leaders should not be elected on the basis of gender, but on the basis of their achievement and track record within the organisation.[41] League members contended, however, that this position ignored certain social and structural constraints within the society which inhibited women's participation. They argued that the quota would address the problem of the participation of women without any financial resources, and demonstrate the ANC's commitment to affirmative action. But contrary to their expectations, league members discovered during the debate the extent to which ANC men, including the leadership, had been paying lip-service to women's concerns. While many in the leadership had made public pronouncements on women's rights, not a single voice was heard from the front tables to support women's arguments from the floor. That there was no consensus at the end of the debate, when the matter came to the vote, signalled a critical defeat for one of the league's most important campaigns. After voting commenced on the 30 % quota demand, league members announced that their delegates would abstain. Left powerless, the chairperson of the session left the chair to consult with the leadership of the ANC and the ANCWL. While this was happening, league members started a song on the floor in support of the quota and, ultimately, even drew some men into their "toyi-toyi", who had earlier been opposed to the quota.

After a break of several hours during which a large women's caucus as well as other groups of delegates held discussions, the conference was reconvened. Nelson Mandela as Deputy President, appealed to the conference to adjourn and allow for a meeting between the NECs of the ANC, ANCWL and ANCYL to hammer out a compromise.[42] In a historic challenge to the leadership's autocratic decision making, Patrick Lekota and Andrew Maphetho stood up and opposed Mandela's proposal, arguing that the conference was the most authoritative decision-making body, and called for voting to continue. However, because of time constraints the conference was adjourned to the following day. When it reconvened the ANCWL President, Mrs Shope, read a statement apologising for the disruptions caused by the ANCWL 30 % quota demand and thus, by implication, put the issue to rest.

While the 30 % quota demand failed, the intensity of the debate it had sparked was of critical importance to the ANC's democratic practice. Not only did it put the league in the spotlight, but gender issues were now given more serious attention within the organisation.[43] Also crucial in the quota debate was the first public demonstration of how powerful leadership figures, such as Mandela, could be disciplined by the organisation's constitutional procedures. But the failure of the 30 % quota demand also served as a lesson to the Women's League. For the first time league members realised the extent of men's opposition to women's political role. They could no longer rely on men's nominal acceptance of their demands and concerns. Much work had to be done to combat men's insensitivity to women's issues and their stereotyped thinking, which continued to dominate the ANC even after the 30 % quota debate. The fact that the conference voted unanimously in favour of the constitutional proposal that MK commanders, most of whom were men, automatically be given seats on the NEC, pointed up the prevailing attitude. League members realised that for them to offer any meaningful challenge in the conference, they could not rely on men's support, but had to intensify work on the ground, combining mass female recruitment with sensitising men to women's issues, so that by the next conference they could muster more than the 17 % delegation which they had had at the July 1991 conference. Finally, league members also discovered that much work still had to be done to create an awareness of the issues involved in some women within the ANC who opposed the quota. While a mere 18 % (9 out of 56) of those elected to the NEC were women, the question of affirmative action on either gender or race within the ANC and South African society as a whole was firmly put on the agenda for debate.

The success of the league in cultivating debate within the ANC also gave impetus to the vigorous pursuit of its other campaign demands, such as instilling sensitivity to gender issues within the movement and intensifying the Women's Charter campaign. In accordance with the national conference's resolution in April 1992, the National Working Committee finally created the National Commission for the Emancipation of Women (NCEW) to advance gender issues within the ANC. Headed by Oliver Tambo with Frene Ginwala as his deputy,[44] the commission's terms of reference were

- to address the participation and representation of women in the structures of the ANC at all levels
- to ensure that women's experiences and perceptions inform ANC strategy and tactics, as well as its decisions
- to ensure that all departments, particularly the Human Resource Development Department, prioritised the development and training of women in all their programmes
- to promote and undertake research on gender issues.[45]

The NCEW would report to the National Working Committee of the ANC through its chairperson and operate as a department, with a secretariat consisting of a national coordinator, an administrative secretary and an organising secretary.

The Women's Charter campaign was conceived to update the existing Women's Charter drawn up by the Federation of South African Women (FEDSAW) during the 1950s.[46] This campaign was widened when the league convened a meeting of 40 organisations on 27 September 1991, which culminated in the formation of the Women's National Coalition (WNC). The coalition brought together women's organisations from the ANC, Democratic Party (DP), NP, IFP, Pan Africanist Congress (PAC), the Women's Bureau, Black Sash, Women's Legal Status, Young Women's Christian Association, Women of South Africa, as well as women from SACC, COSATU, the Disabled People of South Africa, Planned Parenthood Association, Bahai of South Africa, and university-based research groups. A

14-member interim committee was formed to broaden the coalition and clarify its objectives, terms of reference, process and structures and to prepare to officially launch the coalition. Launched in April 1992, the WNC's primary task was to produce a Women's Charter which would be incorporated into the new constitution of the country. Addressing the launch of the WNC, Frene Ginwala of the ANC stated that "women will have to make sure that the constitution goes beyond a ritualistic commitment to equality and actually lays the basis for effective gender equality".[47] On 25–26 April 1992, the WNC held its first national conference, where a steering committee headed by Frene Ginwala was elected.[48] At this conference the WNC decided to produce a charter of women's rights by the following year.[49] However, by the end of the year the campaign had not got off the ground.

Consequently, the executive committee of the WNC adopted an elaborate programme of action at its first meeting on 28 January 1993.[50] Divided into eight phases, the programme envisaged a public awareness strategy on women's issues, the collecting of information on gender issues, publishing reports and holding regional conferences which would culminate in a national conference. The campaign and the participatory research process were completed in December 1993 and regional conferences were presented with interim reports in January 1994. The WNC national conference was finally held in February 1994, where a draft working document of *The Women's Charter for Effective Equality* was adopted.

Apart from its campaign for the women's charter through the WNC, the league also took steps within the ANC to articulate women's rights. One such step was the vigorous discussion of ANC policy guidelines. Before the national policy conference, the league organised its own national workshop from 8–10 May 1992, where it perused the policy guidelines and made recommendations relevant to gender issues. Its efforts were reflected in the *ANC's policy guidelines,* which were finally adopted in May 1992. In the introduction, the guidelines stated:

> Gender discrimination has either excluded or subordinated the nature of women's participation in all socio-economic and political institutions. Combined with apartheid this has resulted in African women being the most exploited and poverty stricken of the South African population.[51]

The concern about women's equality also saw the league making persistent demands for women's inclusion in constitutional negotiations at the Convention for a Democratic South Africa (CODESA). Up to that time the few women who attended CODESA talks were only there in an advisory capacity without decision-making powers.[52] To spearhead the campaign for women's inclusion in negotiations, the league held a workshop from 11–12 January 1992, attended by representatives from all 14 regions. Opening the proceedings, the League's Deputy President, Albertina Sisulu, expressed concern about the small number of women involved in negotiations.[53] Arguing that the inclusion of women in negotiations was an integral part of its charter campaign, the league resolved to exert pressure on the ANC and CODESA Management Committee. The Management Committee was asked in particular to institute a Women's Advisory Committee which would evaluate all decisions of the working groups for their gender implications.[54] After concerted pressure, the CODESA Management Committee finally agreed to establish a Gender Advisory Committee (GAC), which started its work on 6 April 1992 until the breakdown of CODESA II in mid-May 1992. However, when negotiations resumed in the newly constituted Negotiating Council, which then included parties such as the PAC and the CP, women were excluded from the talks.[55] Through pressure on its ANC male delegates the league was able to force a discussion concerning the presence of female delegates in the Negotiation Council in mid-April 1993. The outcome of this discussion was to leave the female representatives to decide the issue. Given this power, the women finally resolved to expand the Negotiation Council with an extra female delegate in each party delegation, with full speaking rights. A chair for a woman in every delegation of ten, allocated to each party to the plenary, was also to be reserved.

In the end, though, while the league made significant strides in advancing the cause of women's rights within the ANC, this continued to be counterbalanced by serious weaknesses. In terms of its membership, the league failed to break the traditional barrier of its Africanism by recruiting women from other non-African communities. While this was a general problem within the ANC, the perceived cliquism and lack of open democratic practice, particularly with regard to tensions within the PWV region, served to scare away support from these communities. Indeed lack of unity within the league and allegations of "cabalistic" tendencies by a group of women who had been in exile, created a fertile ground for rumour mongering, which deepened tensions and deflected attention from important challenges facing the organisation. Petty politicking among women and the general hostility towards some white female academics, who were thought to be misrepresenting women's interests, also served to erode the basis for unity.[56] While the creation of the WNC was an important milestone, it ended up absorbing the cream of the league's able women and thus somewhat weakening the league. Some of the women in the WNC were already tied up in constitutional negotiations. Furthermore, as Jessie Duarte noted, there was no mechanism to make WNC members accountable to, and convey the needs of women at grass-roots level, since most of them came from professional backgrounds.[57] This was also complicated by the fact that the WNC did not interfere with activities of its member organisations. That the league's membership was heavily drawn from the urban communities clearly showed how far the organisation was from coming to terms with the concerns of the most underprivileged section of women in the rural areas.

The ANC and the United Democratic Front (UDF)

The major challenge to the ANC on its return to South Africa was how to cooperate with the UDF which had developed and intensified the struggle inside the country for most of the 1980s. The central questions were how to relate to it organisationally and how to accommodate its leadership, together with the leaders returning from prison, within the narrow and highly centralised ANC structures. While this was a difficult question to resolve, the UDF's stated political goals and the internal political developments in the country provided some of the elements necessary to come to a resolution of this problem. Formed in 1983 as a federal structure to harness hundreds of community, student, women, civic and worker organisations that were proliferating as a result of intense repression, the UDF publicly declared that it was not intended to replace the ANC. Its political programme focused on intensifying opposition to the tricameral parliament, the black local authorities and rent increases. To this end the UDF adopted strategies such as non-participation in governmental structures, boycotts and protests, the main objective being to weaken the apartheid system and pressure it into unbanning the ANC, so that the political future of the country could be jointly decided with the liberation movement.

That the UDF operated to further the political aims of the ANC was not only reflected in the profile former ANC leaders held in its political life. ANC decrees from Lusaka, such as making the country ungovernable, were often literally translated into practice by UDF activists. But some forms of political resistance and tactics, such as the abhorrent necklace killing of suspected police informants (which was not sanctioned by the leadership) and the creation of street, area and zonal committees, were the offspring of UDF politics.[58] The UDF objective of popularising the ANC and clearing the way for its central role in the resolution of the South African crisis was overtly mirrored in the mass demonstrations following the unbanning of the UDF in 1988, which called for the ANC's legalisation. Their objective was further reflected in the UDF-pioneered Conference for a Democratic Future held in Johannesburg, which rallied other political parties such as the Azanian People's Organisation (AZAPO) and the Pan Africanist Movement (an internal wing of the PAC) behind the ANC's negotiation proposals, outlined in the Harare Declaration. The declaration had proposed negotiations with the South African government, provided that the latter ended the state of emergency and unbanned all political organisations.

While these developments suggested that the ANC would politically have no serious problem in directly dealing with the UDF, there were fears that if the two organisations operated alongside each other, inevitable differences could lead to hostilities and divisions. But a much more serious question was how to absorb UDF leaders into the ANC. Because the UDF had taken up the political functions the ANC had performed before its banning, the unbanning of the latter in 1990 clearly implied that the UDF had to dissolve, as its purpose had been fulfilled. However, the UDF did not dissolve but continued to live in an uncomfortable relationship with the ANC until February 1991, leading to friction that resulted in a lack of decision on the role of the UDF. Marina Ottoway blames this state of indecision on the ANC.[59] She argues that the ANC deliberately ignored the UDF when it was unbanned, by not mentioning it in the provisional constitution adopted by the NEC in 1990.

She writes that, instead of availing themselves of the existing UDF set-up and particularly of its organisers, ANC leaders chose to rely on the return of exiles, arguing in late 1990 that the slow progress in building up the organisation lay in the government's preventing their speedy return. Ms Ottoway goes on to speculate that this attitude was informed by the fear of marginalising exiles, if the ANC was based on UDF structures, and further maintains that ANC leaders feared that the democratic and decentralised style of the UDF would not suit their own authoritarian leadership style.

But it would appear that, rather than being deliberate, the reasons for the ANC's ignoring of the UDF were much more complex. Given the long tradition of UDF leaders aligning themselves with the ANC, and with one of the objectives of the 1989 mass marches and demonstrations being to unban the organisation, most of them joined the ANC the moment it was unbanned. By then many UDF structures had already been badly affected by the state of emergency and, instead of resuscitating them, UDF leaders chose to spend their energy in preparing for the ANC's return. Most UDF leaders, including the returning Delmas treason trialists, were part of the Interim Leadership Group (ILG) and other ad hoc committees such as the Mandela Reception Committee, which prepared the way for the formal return of the ANC. During the course of 1990 most UDF activists had either joined the ANC or continued to be members of both. This was the case with activists such as Paul Mashatile, the UDF's Southern Transvaal Secretary, who also served as an organiser for the ANC Alexandra branch during that year.

Ottoway's speculation that the ANC feared to marginalise itself by building up an organisation along the lines of the UDF is not persuasive. If it really feared marginalisation and the democratic style of the UDF, the ANC would have prevented their active role in the ILG and would not have brought some UDF members into the extended NEC. By deciding to re-establish itself along party political lines with card-carrying mass membership, and by placing a new emphasis on intrademocracy, the ANC already anticipated that such diversification would jeopardise the positions of some of its leaders in exile. Despite the fact that a scramble for positions between ANC exiles and UDF leaders did ensue, the marginalisation of the UDF and the continuing deterioration in the relationship up to February 1991 was not the sole responsibility of the ANC, notwithstanding their attitude as described earlier by Ottoway. The question had much to do with the lack of decision within the UDF itself.

There was a lack of unanimity on the role of the UDF during the opening legal phase. Some argued that it should transform (or expand) itself into a broad anti-apartheid front, while others countered that it should in fact be dissolved. Popo Molefe, the UDF's General Secretary, maintained in an interview with the *New Nation* in December 1990 that the UDF had to be expanded into a broader front to provide a home for other "non-Charterist" formations.[60] Molefe, however, did not fully explain the political function of such a front, except for hinting that it would be non-partisan, a proposal that implied the potential creation of an anti-apartheid organisation which could end up competing with the ANC. But other leaders such as Steve

Tshwete felt its political function should be to support the ANC in negotiation.[61] In contrast to the proponents of an anti-apartheid front, other UDF leaders such as Paul Mashatile called for the dissolution of the UDF. Opposing Molefe's suggestions of a new front, Mashatile contended that the UDF had adopted the Freedom Charter and had hence aligned itself with a particular political position. It could not be non-partisan and thus had to be dissolved.[62] While the view for the dissolution of the UDF ultimately triumphed, the important issue that came to be the subject of heated debate was the ANC's relation to the civic movement, an important remnant of the UDF.[63] This issue was crucial because it stood midway between the ANC's attempts to strengthen its organisational structures on the one hand, and to promote the independence of civic associations and civic society in general on the other.

The ANC and the role of civics during the period of transition

Throughout the first two years of the 1990s, the ANC failed both on a theoretical and a practical level to achieve consensus on its relations with the civic movement. While it preached the concept of civic independence, the dictates of building a strong organisation capable of winning the first democratic elections often resulted in internal contradictions, manifested by tensions between ANC branches and local civic structures in the townships. Two clear positions on the approach to the civics developed within the movement, with one advocating the absorption of civics into ANC structures and the other calling for their autonomy.[64] The latter was further defined by civic leaders to mean the creation of strong civics which would function both as instruments of development and "watchdogs" of a future "ANC" government.[65]

However, the idea of civic autonomy raised difficulties, chief of which was the problem of dual membership of civics and the ANC. The idea also raised tensions between the ANC's interest in building a strong organisation and in promoting democracy. By allowing civics to be autonomous, the ANC sent out signals that were erroneously taken by some activists to mean that they could leave the strengthening of the organisation to others and concentrate solely on civic matters. The problem was further aggravated by the ANC's lack of clarity on whether autonomy should be maintained only during the period of transition or after the creation of a new democracy. The confusion caused by the call for civic autonomy was evident in Atteridgeville, where local civics competed with the ANC for members by issuing cheaper membership cards.[66] In other areas civics were created by activists excluded from ANC structures to establish political bases for themselves,[67] resulting in animosity and hostilities that often led to the weakening of the ANC branches. Furthermore, arguments by some activists within the civic movement that their structures would serve as watchdogs of a government, challenged the ANC's commitment to democratic practice and played into the hands of its rivals, who yearned to exploit whatever traces of division existed within the broad democratic formation.[68]

The potential of civics to challenge the ANC served as a basis for those who argued for the absorption of civics into the ANC. Criticising the proposal for civics to act as watchdogs, ANC analysts Nzimande and Skosana called for their incorporation into the ANC or, alternatively, their replacement with ANC branches.[69] The two argued that the idea of "watchdogs already assumes that the ANC would be a government and thus obscured the need to grapple with the process of reaching that stage". They maintained that such a position would discourage the need to build up a strong ANC in the light of forthcoming elections. Contending that local and political issues cannot be distinguished from each other to justify the autonomy of civics (which in fact would remain political as long as apartheid existed), the two analysts proposed that ANC branches should, rather than leaving it to civics, take up local issues to strengthen the ANC. They questioned the relevance of ANC branches if local issues such as electricity, rent and roads, were left to civics. By maintaining that the role previously played by civics could be played by ANC branches, the two effectively hinted at the disappearance of civics.

This position was bitterly criticised by activists within the civic movement. While maintaining their steadfast commitment to political issues, activists objected to the imposition of a particular line. Reacting sharply to Nzimande and Skosana's views, SANCO activist, Mzwanele Mayekiso, defended the independence of the civics, arguing that "civics must maintain their independence and ability to fight for the rights of constituents of many political perspectives, even if that is against a leading political party's short-term interests". Taking the argument further, Dennis Nkosi insisted that civics should empower the people instead of being forced into the ANC.[70]

In a bid to avoid the potential explosiveness of this debate some ANC leaders called for a symbiotic relationship between civics and ANC branches. But Raymond Suttner, while calling for their coexistence,[71] also strongly argued that ANC branches should organise and mobilise around the same issues civics were concerned with:

> While we recognise the independence of civic and other mass sectoral organisations they do not have the sole right to take up issues of daily concern to the people. Any national liberation movement is concerned with everything that affects the people. We must be there when there are shack demolitions, water and electricity cut-off[s], we must be with the people when they campaign. We must give leadership and direction in these campaigns.[72]

Though on a theoretical level these positions might be reconciled, in practice this debate produced serious tensions. ANC branches and civics continued to compete with each other, either for members or for the lead in local campaigns. These tensions were aggravated by the absence of any sort of liaison at national, regional and local levels between the ANC and civics. The reason for this would appear to lie in the ANC's perception of the civic movement. Unlike COSATU and the SACP which were treated as revolutionary allies, the civic movement was seen as another ally within the democratic formation, without being accorded any special position. Such an approach meant that no clear structural links were developed and communication links remained tenuous. While the formation of the South African National Civic Organisation (SANCO) was viewed by analysts and political observers as crucial in consolidating civic independence and facilitating the creation of a coordinated structural relation with the ANC, this did not happen. Instead, communication and friction continued to worsen. The difference of opinion between Nelson Mandela and Moses Mayekiso of SANCO on the question of bond payment boycott, raised by the civics in 1992, was a clear symptom of the poor relations between these two organisations.

The ANC and the Congress of South African Trade Unions (COSATU)

The forging of the Tripartite Alliance with COSATU and the SACP raises important questions about the alliance and its effectiveness. A close analysis of events in the early years of the 1990s not only shows an increasing marginalisation of working class interests, but also the severe strains to which the partners in the alliance were subjected to maintain their independence.

Despite ANC rhetoric about the role of the workers in shaping the content of, and leading the struggle towards a new political dispensation, in practice this was clearly not the case.[73] The cross-cutting leadership within the alliance served to bolster the fledgling structures of the ANC, while weakening COSATU by diversifying the energies of its leaders. This sparked intense debate, "the two hats debate", within the union federation on the acceptability of leaders occupying several positions within alliance organisations. While the debate was a healthy exercise, it nonetheless threatened to split COSATU as unions began to adopt opposing sides. Unions such as the South African Commercial, Catering and Allied Workers Union (SACCAWU), the Chemical Workers Industrial Union (CWIU) and the South African Clothing and Textile Workers Union (SACTWU) opposed the idea of leaders occupying leadership positions in other alliance organisations. Ebrahim Patel of SACTWU maintained that "we cannot adequately represent two, very different interests. Leadership has to be separated. It's more than a practical problem. It's a political problem and a question of who you represent. Merging the interests of all organisations is a fundamental mistake and one that has been committed elsewhere".[74] Proponents of this view feared in particular that trade union leadership would be absorbed into political parties, and hence pave the way for unions to become "sitting ducks" for bureaucratic control under a future political dispensation. They argued instead for union independence. SACCAWU, in particular, took a much tougher line, questioning the rationale of an alliance that excluded other liberation movements such as the PAC and AZAPO.[75]

Unions such as the National Union of Mineworkers (NUM) and the Food and Allied Workers Union (FAWU) and many leading figures of the Tripartite

Alliance supported the idea of leaders taking more than one position in the alliance.[76] Their starting point was that those who were against the "many hats" policy and who supported the complete autonomy of alliance partners, were indirectly supporting antidemocratic forces that were calling for the dissolution of the alliance and the transformation of the ANC into a "skinny" political party. To them, occupying several positions within the alliance was an important contribution towards strengthening the ANC and the advancement of the struggle towards democracy. According to Sydney Mufamadi, the practice was justified due to the scarcity of suitably trained organisational leaders.[77] Consequently, the fact that trade union leaders could take up positions in other alliance organisations was an important victory for the workers, as their grievances could be aired before a wider audience. In the words of COSATU's Vice-President and the President of FAWU, Chris Dlamini, dual leadership within the alliance "sharpens COSATU's political position and solidifies its objectives".[78]

Notwithstanding this debate, the overlapping of leaders across the alliance did not come anywhere near articulating workers' interests within the alliance and in the broader execution of the struggle.[79] Despite arguments about past histories of certain leaders who had efficiently worked with more than one portfolio, the siphoning off of union leaders into the SACP and the ANC clearly diminished the effectiveness of COSATU and its unions. That unionists such as Cyril Ramaphosa (of NUM), Kgalema Motlante and Sydney Mufamadi were elected into the ANC, and Moses Mayekiso and others had to serve all the alliance organisations, had a profoundly deleterious effect on the labour movement. Despite their professed intentions to continue to represent the interests of workers within the ANC, doing this within an organisation that professed to represent the whole country proved in practice virtually impossible. Instead, these leaders found themselves absorbed into the immense immediate challenges facing the ANC to the extent that sectoral working class politics became peripheral. But it would also appear that much of the blame for the increasing neglect of working class interests resided within COSATU and its unions. Unlike the 1980s, when the struggle by the federation was at its high point both on the labour and political fronts, the 1990s was a decade of major challenges. Having been replaced by the ANC at the political level, COSATU had to contend with increasingly bitter economic problems such as the government's privatisation and rationalisation policies, the closure of industries and retrenchment of its members, divisions and tensions within its unions, particularly in the Western Cape,[80] as well as endless negotiations with factory managements about job security. The movement towards centralised bargaining also impaired internal union democracy, resulting in union members no longer being able to participate effectively in their unions or in COSATU.[81] These factors had the combined effect of distracting COSATU's attention away from imprinting working class preoccupations on the alliance and its activities.

In spite of its weakness, COSATU played an important role in the formulation of economic and developmental policies within the alliance.[82] It also helped to inculcate the culture of democratic practice, mandate and consultation within the ANC (notwithstanding the latter's difficulty in implementing it), and was also central to the setting up of the National Peace Accord.[83] While COSATU did not ultimately participate in CODESA, it was nevertheless represented through its alliance partners, particularly the SACP. In fact, COSATU's leaders such as Chris Dlamini, Bernie Fanaroff, Peter Danjies and Sam Shilowa were part of the alliance delegation. Whether it succeeded in laying before CODESA the concerns of the workers could only be assessed in the contents of agreements reached there.

While the cohesion of the Tripartite Alliance remained intact despite internal problems and weaknesses, what was significant was the ANC's attitude to the independence of trade unions during the transitional period. The ANC took a somewhat imperious approach to the Tripartite Alliance in its failure to act in consultation with its partners. Moreover, in permitting the diversion of union resources and personnel to support its structures, the ANC weakened the alliance and undermined the effectiveness of COSATU. It also eroded the independence of the union-federation and alarmed the leaders about possible future relations. COSATU, however, did attempt to reassert its central role in the transition process. The decision to go on an anti-VAT strike in October 1991, the drafting of the workers' charter and the spearheading of mass action campaigns against "government intransigence" in negotiations, was part of the strategy. The same could be said of the march to the World Trade Centre in October 1993, over a clause in the draft interim constitution which empowered employers to lock out striking workers. A further indication was the decision taken by COSATU at its September 1993 conference to enter into a reconstruction and development accord with the ANC to advance workers' interests. However, the independence of COSATU under a future ANC government was still to be tested. Finally, the forging of the alliance advanced the ANC's interests over those of the other two parties. In spite of the significance of the alliance in coordinating the struggle for democracy, more often than not COSATU's strength was tapped to support what were political demands of the ANC. The decision by COSATU to help build ANC structures, the tolerance towards leaders occupying more than one position within the alliance, and the support given to the ANC's political demands such as an elected constituent assembly, the installation of an interim government and embarking on mass action to encourage progress in negotiations, projected COSATU as an "extension belt" of the ANC. While these actions were taken to represent what were claimed to be working class concerns, they raised questions about the independence of COSATU in a future political dispensation.

The ANC and the South African Communist Party

The prospect of legality posed serious challenges to the SACP. In exile the SACP's primary objective was to influence the ANC into adopting a radical liberation programme. The unbanning of previously banned organisations and the ANC's intention to become democratic and organise a broad-based mass membership posed a threat to the SACP's influence on the movement.

As a consequence a decision was taken to launch the SACP as a separate organisational entity with its own distinct leadership and offices. The launch took place on 29 July 1990 in Soweto, followed by a national congress in December 1991. Unlike the years before 1990 when the SACP successfully provided theoretical and strategic guidance to the ANC, the challenges of organisational reconstruction now proved daunting. The agreement within the Tripartite Alliance to strengthen the ANC's organisational revival tapped a considerable portion of the party's resources. Moreover, its high-ranking officials were also high-profile leaders in the ANC and COSATU. But a much more serious challenge facing the SACP was to establish the party against the background of disintegration of the communist regimes in Eastern Europe. Not only did the party have to explain the collapse of communism, it also had to justify continuing to pursue its goal. It had to explain the meaning of communism and how it would bring it about in South Africa.[84] This was a formidable challenge, more so because of the different conceptions of socialism and communism within the party itself. But these were not the only difficulties. The party also had to resolve an internal debate about whether to build a mass party or a vanguard party.[85]

Close relations with the ANC and the fact that party leadership also served in the ANC created public speculation about the party's possibly manipulative intentions.[86] This speculation became even more pronounced during elections to the ANC's NEC at the July 1991 national conference. The extent of the SACP influence over the ANC resides in the history of the two organisations. The relationship evolved from the decision by the Communist Party of South Africa, as early as the 1940s, to take part in the struggles of nationalist organisations with a view to transforming them into revolutionary forces. A suggestion was made that

> ... the party should pay particular attention to the embryonic national organisations among the natives, such as the African National Congress. The party, while retaining full independence, should seek to broaden and extend their activity. Our aim should be to transform the ANC into a fighting nationalist revolutionary organisation against the white bourgeoisie and the British imperialists.[87]

The criminalisation of communism in the 1950s and the banning of the ANC in 1960 opened a new era in the struggle against apartheid that saw the SACP forming an alliance with the ANC and playing an active role in its organisation. The growing influence of communist members within the ANC led to the latter's acceptance of the SACP's conceptualisation of the South African society as "colonialism of a special type", which needed to be confronted with anti-colonial strategies similar to those pursued by liberation movements elsewhere in Africa. The decision by the two organisations to transform the ANC's military wing, Umkhonto we Sizwe (MK), into a fully-fledged guerrilla movement saw the beginning of an armed struggle in which communist leaders played a pivotal role in supplying theoretical, strategic and tactical guidance.

Prior, in his analysis of the SACP's relationship with the ANC before their unbanning, contended that "the mutual involvement of the ANC and the SACP is, and has been extensive: that the SACP plays a prominent role in determining ANC ideology and policy objectives".[88] While his argument is persuasive about the two organisations, when they were still banned, to what extent does this still hold after the unbanning? What kind of positions did SACP members occupy within the ANC that gave them leverage to influence the organisation's policies? A microscopic analysis of the 1991 elected NEC of the ANC shows 20 out of 56 to be committed SACP members. These are Cheryl Carolus, Jeremy Cronin, Ebrahim Ismail Ebrahim, Harry Gwala, Chris Hani, Ronnie Kasrils, Ahmed Kathrada, Mac Maharaj, Gill Marcus, Raymond Mhlaba, Mohammed Valli Moosa, Elias Motsoaledi, Sydney Mufamadi, Joel Netshitenzhe, Billy Nair, John Nkadimeng, Siphiwe Nyanda, Reginald September, Joe Slovo and Raymond Suttner. Nine of them were in the 26-member National Working Committee, the most active decision-making body of the ANC. These were Chris Hani, Cheryl Carolus, Ebrahim Ismail Ebrahim, Ronnie Kasrils, Mohammed Valli Moosa, Sydney Mufamadi, Joel Netshitenzhe, John Nkadimeng and Joe Slovo.[89] While it is true that the SACP had significant representation within the ANC, was there any correlation between numerical strength and influence?

Despite historical influence over the ANC[90] and its constitution as an organised political caucus within the movement, the SACP's sectoral advancement of its interests and its inclination to control the ANC were undermined by differences within its ranks. The increasing disintegration of the SACP's ideological homogeneity during the early 1990s, caused by the crisis of communism in Eastern Europe, undermined notions of the party's consistent impact on the ANC's affairs. Since its unbanning, party leaders often took inconsistent and contradictory positions against one another. In characterising this as ideological confusion, Devan Pillay discerned three tendencies of thought within the SACP:

- One adhering to a Stalinist tradition of thought (Harry Gwala, Brian Bunting and Raymond Mhlaba)
- The second trying to recast "Marxism-Leninism" (Jeremy Cronin)
- The third leaning towards the New Left Marxism that espoused social democracy (as represented by the author, J. Steinberg)[91]

More than ever before, and even going beyond the limits of *glasnost*, SACP members publicly differed on a number of crucial issues. The conditions of legality had removed the basis for democratic centralism, Stalinist authoritarianism and secrecy, and created fertile soil for open debate and public criticism which increasingly revealed divergent opinions within the party. During the ANC's national conference in July 1991, Chris Hani and Mac Maharaj expressed different views on the question of negotiations. While Hani declared a commitment to continue with negotiations despite the killing of MK combatants by right-wing forces, Maharaj expressed reservations, stating that the liberation movement had made far too many concessions to the government and that it had failed to adequately mobilise its membership in support of its strategic goals.[92] Furthermore, while Hani held a moderate view on the demand for an interim government, moving as far as to state that "an interim government, is not an absolute non-negotiable",[93] statements and writings by Raymond Suttner suggested that he considered the matter of such importance that no deviations would be allowed. On the other hand, Harry Gwala's objection to a meeting between the ANC and IFP leadership differed from the stance taken by for instance Joe Slovo, who was involved in deliberations and meetings with the IFP.

This lack of unanimity within the party refutes claims of a conspiracy to control the ANC. Indeed, the party might have encouraged its members to join the ANC and it might have held "secret" meetings, but the fact that members differed in their views and in their interpretations was bound to weaken its determination to "manipulate" the liberation movement to its liking. Even if parallels could be drawn between the SACP and ANC, it would still be difficult to assert that a stand taken on a particular issue was that of the party and not of the ANC, primarily because of the problems of incorporation of the former into the latter. Moreover, policies and strategies of the two organisations were the same, except for the fact that the ANC's goal was national democracy while the SACP's goal included communism. Secondly, despite the fact that the SACP was an important factor within the ANC, its members often bound themselves to ANC policies, and even if they contributed in shaping those policies, no ANC policy or decision reflects communist inclinations.[94]

However, it was not only the extent of the SACP's influence within the ANC that provoked a fusillade of criticism by the government and other political parties. The continued relationship between the two in the context of what was described as the failure of communism in the eastern bloc impacted negatively on the ANC. ANC economic policies were criticised because of their supposed communist leanings. Serious attempts were also made to effectively sideline SACP members. Beginning with attempts to exclude Joe Slovo and Chris Hani from the ANC delegation to the negotiations, an anti-communist crusade was launched, culminating in the assassination of Hani by a right-wing Polish immigrant in April 1993.

While the ANC's alliance with the SACP discouraged support from the non-African communities on the one hand, the possibility of a negotiated deal with the government posed a serious dilemma for the SACP on the other. Having struggled with the ANC towards the creation of national democracy and having worked hard in providing theoretical justifications for the compromises made in the negotiation deal, the party was now faced with the problem of goal identity, particularly after the demise of communism in Eastern Europe. Moreover, it was clearly apparent even to party strategists that the attainment of a "bourgeois" democracy to which the ANC would be party, would not provide sufficient conditions for communism. Entering into a five-year long negotiated deal in which monopoly capital and free-market enterprise would be protected by the whim of a constitution, was no alternative to a vigorous proletarian democracy as espoused in Marxist texts. The success of a negotiated deal thus meant either that the party had to suspend its struggle or part ways with the ANC and lead a working class struggle against an ANC capitalist government. But opting for the latter required clarity about the nature of the communism to which it aspired, something which still needed agreement within its ranks.

In all, the ANC's relations with allied organisations demonstrate that the challenges of steering a broad spectrum of organisations in negotiations and the process of transition differed quite remarkably from coordinating the struggle against apartheid. Despite the fact that some degree of cohesion was maintained, the uncertainty of the transition process and the spiralling violence sometimes produced tensions, which in some instances led to public differences between the ANC and its allies.

Internal tensions, crises and democratic practice

Throughout the years of its struggle against apartheid, the ANC had set as its goal the creation of a democratic South Africa. Democratic principles were espoused and written into the organisation's historic document, the Freedom Charter, in 1955. But the extent to which the organisation committed itself to these principles became a subject for debate upon its return home. Historians of the ANC in exile provided a completely different picture – that of an organisation pervaded with tensions, crises and undemocratic practices.[95] The following sections will endeavour to give a clear outline and analysis of this bleak history.

Internal tensions, crises and the absence of democratic practice within the ANC during its period in exile occurred at a time when it was trying to flex its military muscles against the South African government. Having been banned inside the country and forced into exile, the organisation decided to mobilise the international community behind it and to strengthen the military capacity of its armed wing, MK. But launching an armed struggle against South Africa was impossible during the sixties, given the hostile regimes surrounding the country. It was only with the independence of Mozambique and Angola in 1974 that the ANC was able to secure overland transit into the country for armed incursions. The continuing war in Angola and the instability in Mozambique, however, posed problems for the organisation's armed struggle. In many respects the movement had to deflect attention from its armed struggle to assist host governments against their opponents.

The outbreak of the 1976 Soweto uprising and the flood of young recruits to the ANC put a further strain on the organisation. Tensions began to emerge between militant youth, yearning to fight at home after being trained, and the leadership, which was overly cautious about the execution of the armed struggle.[96] The discovery of a spy ring in March 1981 after the capture and confession of Piper (Kenneth Mahamba), and Pretoria's claims that of every ten recruits that joined the ANC five were infiltrators, aggravated tensions and laid the ground for human rights violations, internal divisions, personal rivalries and disregard for democracy. The ANC took the question of the spy ring seriously, particularly after its armed struggle had suffered serious setbacks under what were believed to be questionable circumstances.[97] These included

- the arrest in Botswana of senior MK leaders, including Joe Modise
- the seizure of the armed wing's 1982 programme of action
- the poisoning of cadres in the camps
- the destruction of food trucks and film projectors, resulting in boredom and dagga smoking in the camps
- the diversion of military equipment, which often landed in the hands of the South African security forces
- the sabotage of MK machinery in Natal
- the controversial decision by Thami Zulu to recklessly send through cadres who were killed by the security forces
- the inexplicable failure by some front commanders to intensify military activity
- the attack by South African agents on ANC facilities with remarkable precision
- the letter bomb aimed at Joe Slovo, but which ended up killing his wife, Ruth First, and wounding others like Pallo Jordan
- the vicious Lesotho and Matola (in Mozambique) raids
- the assassination of the ANC's chief representative in Zimbabwe, Mr Moabi Gqabi.
- the car bomb attack on Albie Sachs in Mozambique
- the capture of ANC operatives Grace Gele and Ismael Ebrahim in Swaziland in 1986 and the gunning down of their commanders, Cassius Make and Paul Dikeledi.

It was against this background that the ANC's Security Department, Mbokodo, was given additional powers to hunt, probe and prosecute suspects, measures which were carried out with excessive zeal at the Angolan camps where war was raging against the National Union for the Total Independence of Angola (UNITA) forces. The tightening of security and the resultant disregard of cadres' demands and grievances concerning unacceptable conditions in the camps were responsible for the simmering discontent within the army's rank and file, which culminated in mutinies of the Viana and Pango camps.

These mutinies were not the first within the ANC. In 1968 a group of MK soldiers defected from ANC camps in Tanzania and sought asylum in Kenya, alleging widespread dissatisfaction within the camps, ethnic favouritism and suppression of dissenting voices.[98] In 1978 MK cadres stationed at the Fazenda Camp (Villa Rosa) to the north of Quibaxe in northern Angola, grew restive and demanded to be allowed to go and fight in South Africa.[99]

The ANC responded by arresting its members, transferring some of its inmates to the other two camps, Pango and Quibaxe, and sending others to fight alongside Zimbabwe African People's Union (ZAPU) in Zimbabwe. The Fazenda camp was eventually closed in 1980, but with no attention having been paid to soldiers' demands and grievances. A prison camp (Camp 32), which later came to be known as Quadro (number four or "Buchenwald"), was hastily constructed to rehabilitate dissidents. Storerooms and backyard rooms were also used as detention centres in other facilities run by the ANC. Fazenda dissidents such as Ernest Khumalo, Solly Ngungunyana and Drake, who had decided to go to Luanda to submit their resignation to the ANC chief representative, Max Moabi, were taken in as the first inmates of Quadro. These measures did not succeed in stamping out discontent within MK. Tensions deepened as MK cadres in Lusaka also joined the chorus of criticism of the leadership's failure to deploy them inside South Africa.

Complaints were also levelled against what many perceived as corruption within the ANC leadership. Discontent was fuelled by the refusal of survivors of the Zimbabwean war to be sent back to Angola. Faced with this increasing restlessness, the ANC leadership, rather than conceding to the cadres' demand for a conference to review the organisation's conduct of the struggle, tightened security. Those who called for a conference and complained about the situation in the camps in Angola were branded as enemy agents and detained. The security department also grew autocratic and cruel. People were detained, interrogated, punished and sometimes executed. Divisions began to emerge between the security department and the rank-and-file members of MK. Favouritism and patronage set in, with security officials building up their stature by placing their protégés in positions within the security system. The security department was given unchecked powers to deal with what was labelled as an internal enemy to destabilise the movement. Some security personnel settled personal rivalries by accusing opponents of being enemy agents. Many of these were then detained indefinitely or subsequently released without clearance, thus making them victims of continued suspicion within the organisation. These developments fuelled vocal criticism of the security department and its head, Mzwai Piliso, as well as of the leadership's failure to attend to cadres' demands, and laid the ground for the 1984 mutiny.

In 1982 Oliver Tambo, as President of the ANC, asked cadres in all ANC camps to forward proposals to rectify the problems that were facing the movement. The Pango and Viana camps were harsh in their criticism of the leadership, but their proposal for the holding of a conference met with no response, as it was interpreted as casting doubt on the ANC leadership.[100] However, organisational changes were introduced in April 1983 when the Revolutionary Council was replaced by the Political Military Council, which was in turn divided into military headquarters, political headquarters and national security. Regional political military councils were also established in countries like Angola, Botswana, Lesotho, Mozambique, Swaziland, Tanzania, the United Kingdom, Zambia and Zimbabwe. These changes were not accompanied by a change in personnel; in fact, the announcement that Joe

Modise would continue as head of the army exacerbated the discontent among disaffected MK soldiers.

In December 1983 MK soldiers from the Quibaxe, Pango, Caxito and Luanda camps were deployed in areas of Cangadala and Malanje in eastern Angola at the request of the Popular Movement for the Liberation of Angola's (MPLA) People's Armed Forces for the Liberation of Angola (FAPLA) to ward off UNITA's threat to the region. Led by Chris Hani, this offensive was successful in driving UNITA out of the area. However, the decision to pursue UNITA to its bases across the Kwanza river after the departure of Hani and his replacement by a "Comrade Lennox" led to a serious defeat for MK. Soldiers were betrayed by FAPLA and fell into UNITA ambushes. As a result of this, MK members objected to fighting in Angola and demanded to fight in South Africa. On 16 December 1983 MK soldiers in Cangadala, as well as other camps such as Musafa, began shooting randomly into the air to draw the leadership's attention to their problems. The situation became tense as cadres began to interpret their deployment in eastern Angola as a means of deflecting attention from their call to be sent home and from the need for a conference. Groups of soldiers from Musafa and Cacuso moved to the ANC's transit camp in Viana, outside Luanda, where they were joined by soldiers from other camps. This was the mutiny of Mkathashingo against the ANC. Soldiers refused to hand over their arms when they arrived at Viana and instead disarmed the security personnel, some of whom fled to ANC facilities in Luanda. At this time the body of Solly Sibeko, who had been a vocal critic of the ANC, was found in a metal container, having died of bullet wounds. Rumours of his alleged elimination by the security department intensified the anger and animosity felt towards security personnel. A series of meetings were held in Viana by dissident soldiers, culminating in the election of a Committee of Ten comprising Zaba Maledza, the chairperson (whose real name was Ephraim Nkondo, brother of Curtis Nkondo, one of the leaders of the UDF inside South Africa); Bongani Motwa; Kate Mhlongo (Nomfanelo Ntlokwana); Jabu Mofolo; Sipho Mathebula (E. Mndebele); Grace Motaung; Moses Thema (Mbulelo Musi); Simon Botha (Sindile Velem); Khotso Morena (Mwezi Twala); and Sidwell Moroka (Omry Makgale). At this meeting it was resolved to call for an ANC conference to review the armed struggle and hold elections to the NEC. A resolution was also taken to suspend the security department and to investigate conditions in Quadro.

The ANC, with the help of FAPLA soldiers, reacted by invading the Viana Camp and arresting 13 dissident cadres, including members of the Committee of Ten. During this clampdown an MK combatant, Babsy Mlangeni (travelling name) was killed, as were two Radio Freedom staff members, Diliza Dumakude and Zanempi Sihlangu. Those arrested were sent to Luanda prison where they were subjected to intensive interrogation by the ANC security department; others were taken to Pango and Quibaxe camps where they were introduced to "reorientation". Soldiers were interrogated, with those found guilty or refusing to obey being secretly sent to Quadro prison. Torture by security personnel became commonplace.

A further mutiny broke out at the Pango Camp on 13 May 1984, when cadres killed two security guards and took control of the camp. The security department quickly mustered loyal soldiers and besieged the Pango Camp. After a running battle in which a number of dissident soldiers were killed, order was restored. Surviving mutineers were brought before a hastily created tribunal, headed by Sizakhele Sigxashe, and summarily executed. Those executed included James Nkabinde (Tambo's former bodyguard), Ronald Msomi, Bullet, Thembile Hobo, Mahero, Wandile Ondala and Stopper. Mutineers who had managed to escape during the invasion by the security department were recaptured and subjected to dehumanising forms of torture, such as being tied naked to trees and left there for weeks for all to see. Some were beaten, tortured and called derogatory names such as "Mozorewa" or "Mhlwembe". Others were placed in isolation for lengthy periods of time, denied medical care and subjected to cruel and inhuman conditions of confinement. Still others also went missing without being accounted for. The system of using code names or travelling names and that of shifting people from one camp or country to another, rendered efforts to trace them virtually useless.

During the course of this continuing internal discontent the ANC appointed as early as 13 February 1984 a commission of inquiry headed by James Stuart. Its terms of reference were to investigate the mutiny with a view to determining whether it was a conspiracy by enemy agents to subvert the organisation. The enquiry included an investigation into the role of the Committee of Ten. The report, entitled *Commission of inquiry into recent developments in the People's Republic of Angola* and dated 14 March 1984, and which was not publicly released until 1993, came to the following conclusions: that despite the fact that some agents exploited cadres' genuine grievances to fan disturbances, there was no evidence that enemy agents organised the disturbances from the beginning. The commission did not find the Committee of Ten to be an organised conspiracy to take over the leadership, nor was it instrumental in organising the disturbances in eastern Angola.[101] It found that the main reasons for the mutiny at Pango were that MK cadres were frustrated by the length of time they were kept in the camps without going to fight in South Africa; they wanted a national conference to debate policy and administrative issues; they felt that the older leaders should allow the younger generation a share in the decision-making process; and they wanted a review of the structures of the organisation, particularly the security department. Although the commission did not visit Quadro Prison, it commented on the brutality at the Pango Camp and found the food at Pango to be of extremely poor quality, while the inmates had been given no fresh meat, vegetables or fruit for months. There were virtually no recreational facilities and the level of cultural activities was low. The quality of tents, uniforms, boots and sports shoes was poor and there were no medicines.[102] Corruption and fear were pervasive. In the end the commission recommended that the NEC immediately appoint a committee to prepare for a national conference of the ANC. A drastic overhaul of the military should allow for two senior offices in the command structure, one for military operations inside South Africa and the other for military organisation outside South Africa. A committee should also be set up to handle cases of all those suspected of being enemy agents.

Reacting to these recommendations, the ANC called a consultative conference at Kabwe in Zambia, in June 1985. There it adopted a code of conduct and created three new offices – the Officer of Justice, the Tribunal and the Review Board. These initiatives did not, however, lead to democratic practice, nor did they stop human rights violations by the security department.[103] Ketelo et al. write that democratic practice was not even allowed at the conference. Delegates to the conference from Angola comprised mainly favourites of the security department. In some cases, at least, delegates were chosen by SACP units without consultation with the ANC rank and file. Ellis and Sechaba point out that there were also numerous officials, including security personnel, who attended ex officio, and who were granted voting rights, giving the leadership, the party and ANC bureaucracy effective control of the conference. The conference itself was dominated by party members. Jack Simons was the overall chairman, and politburo members John Nkadimeng and Dan Tloome chaired several sessions.[104] The issue of the Angolan disturbances was never tabled, because of its alleged divisiveness. Even candidates to the NEC were elected from a list ratified by Tambo. Thus, of the 30 elected NEC members, 22 had belonged to the previous executive.[105]

Despite some improvements as a result of the introduction of the code of conduct, the National People's Tribunal and the National Review Committee which acted as a court of appeal to cases handled by the tribunal, human rights violations persisted in the camps and in Quadro Prison. The Officer of Justice (under Dr Zola Skweyiya), whose office was supposed to play a role in checking the excesses of the security department, never worked in practice. Human rights abuses continued unchecked. The tribunal system was also not as effective as had been envisaged. Apart from the official tribunal, there were other military tribunals in ANC camps and facilities unknown in Lusaka, which continued to detain, interrogate and execute suspects.[106] In some cases people were detained to settle personal scores. Pallo Jordan, the ANC's Director of Research, was detained for six weeks because of his criticism of the security department;[107] Jacob Masondo was banished to a farm in Malanje, Angola, where he eventually died of diabetes; and others, such as Mzwakhe Ngwenya (alias Thami Zulu), were detained for long periods under suspicion, but no charges were brought against them.[108]

It was only in 1988 that effective democratic practice within the ANC appeared to gain ground, mainly in the ANC's Dakawa and Madzimbu settlements in Tanzania, where local bodies were elected and debate on a variety of issues was encouraged. Prisoners who were released in that year may also have contributed to this new development. However, even this innovation was to be met with resistance within the organisation. The Regional Political Committee in Tanzania was dissolved because of the election of former ANC dissidents into its higher positions, and was replaced by an interim Regional Political Committee comprising appointees. Having been prevented from holding positions within the ANC, ex-detainees decided to resign from the organisation and campaigned to put pressure on the ANC to allow investigations into human rights violations. They followed the example of similar attempts by SWAPO's former detainees in Namibia, who exposed cases of human rights abuses by the country's liberation movement.[109] But their campaign was to be difficult, though signs of its success began to emerge in early 1990. Ex-detainees gave interviews to the British media, appealed to Archbishop Desmond Tutu and Reverend Frank Chikane and eventually petitioned Nelson Mandela on 14 April 1990, requesting the appointment of a commission of inquiry into human rights abuses within the ANC.[110] Bandile Ketelo, Amos Maxongo, Zamxolo Tshona, Ronnie Massango and Luvo Mbengo jointly wrote a comprehensive article, published in *Searchlight South Africa* in July 1990, which vividly portrayed the ANC's hidden chapter of internal tensions and human rights violations. In the June 1992 issue of *Work In Progress*, Hein Marais publicised a discussion of the ANC's history in exile, when he summarised a book by Steven Ellis and Tshepo Sechaba, *Comrades against apartheid*[111] and the article by Bendilo Ketelo et al. in *Searchlight South Africa*.

The demand for a commission of inquiry into the ANC's past created tension within the organisation, with a majority of returned exiles resisting its appointment, as opposed to former internal leaders who wanted to clear the organisation of a blemish which could seriously damage its image and affect election results. Opposed to the appointment of the commission were reportedly Chris Hani, former Chief of Staff of MK and General Secretary of the SACP, Joe Nhlanhla, Head of the ANC's Department of Intelligence and Security, and Jacob Zuma, MK's head of counter-intelligence since 1987 and Deputy Secretary-General of the ANC.[112] Mandela, however, eventually appointed the Skweyiya Commission in September 1991.[113] Thembile Louis Skweyiya, who headed the commission, was the brother of Zola Skweyiya, a high-ranking member of the ANC's legal department and the Officer of Justice appointed during the 1980s to investigate and monitor ANC camps. But the Skweyiya Commission was deficient in several important respects: it was mainly comprised of ANC members and its impartiality was thus questionable; its terms of reference limited investigations to complaints by living persons, which meant that abuses committed to deceased persons were left out of consideration; the commission was not given powers to subpoena witnesses and thus had to rely on people's willingness to submit evidence. Moreover, fear of repercussions from ANC security personnel still employed at the organisation's headquarters prevented potential witnesses from coming forward.[114] The commission also had other problems to contend with, such as a weakened secretariat after its head, Dali Mpofu, had left to defend Mrs Mandela during her trial. In the end, though, the commission agreed with the findings of the Stuart Commission, recommending that they be published together with the inquiry into the death of Thami Zulu. It further recommended that the ANC appoint a neutral commission of inquiry into past abuses; and asked the organisation to apologise to people who had suffered under its control, as well as pay monetary compensation and medical costs to its victims and to assist those whose education had been disrupted.

Pressure on the ANC to appoint an impartial commission continued. The publication of the Skweyiya Commission's report and the ANC's NEC claim of collective responsibility was met with criticism from the media. In October 1992 the *Weekly Mail* published names of ANC members allegedly involved in human rights abuses.[115] In December 1992 Amnesty International published a report entitled *South Africa: torture, ill treatment and executions in ANC camps,* in which it criticised the shortcomings of ANC appointed commissions. According to this report, the failure to investigate the ANC's Security Department, which might disclose lines of responsibility, clearly precluded an investigation of senior leaders who held those positions. The report listed names of people alleged to have disappeared and recommended that ANC leaders guilty of human rights abuses should never be allowed to hold public office.[116] During the second half of 1992, the Douglas Commission, sponsored by the International Freedom Foundation, published its report after receiving submissions from a number of ex-ANC detainees. Unlike the previous ones, this report concluded that senior ANC leaders such as Oliver Tambo, Joe Slovo and Ronnie Kasrils were also responsible for human rights violations by virtue of their responsibilities.[117] It also recommended that the Goldstone Commission (appointed by the De Klerk government to investigate instances of violence) be extended to investigate human rights abuses within the ANC during its period in exile.

On 12 January 1993 Mandela appointed the Motsuenyane Commission, headed by Sam Motsuenyane, former President of the National African Chamber of Commerce. It included Advocate David Zamchiya, a respected jurist from Zimbabwe and Ms Margaret Burnham, a former judge from the United States of America. The terms of reference of the commission were to investigate the truth of allegations of torture; the manner in which the ANC's code of conduct had been breached; and whether persons had acted in any manner which brought the organisation into disrepute or in a way which justified disciplinary action.[118] The Motsuenyane Commission met from 13 May to 18 June 1993 at the FNB Stadium near Soweto. Twenty-seven affidavits were presented and 48 people made oral representation before the commission. Visits were also made to the ANC facilities of Mazimbu and Dakawa in Tanzania to determine whether people were still being held as detainees. Having heard about the disappearance of some 29 people, and about human rights violations by the complainants who appeared before it, the commission recommended that

- the ANC issue a public apology to the victims of abuses
- publicise its code of conduct and ensure that its members respect it
- review the flow of information between the NEC and the sectors under its control
- improve the NEC's capacity to supervise them and to bring to account the heads of those sectors responsible for abuses

- integrate into the ANC the victims of human rights violations
- create a claims settlement agency to compensate victims
- and publish a periodical about the whereabouts of missing persons.[119]

Despite the expectation of hearing the testimony of hundreds of complainants, only 19 appeared before the commission. Out of a total of 11 defendants who were alleged to have been involved in human rights violations, only six were found guilty by the commission. These were Floyd Huna, Dexter Mbona, Aaron Mokoena, Gabriel Mthembu, Golden Rahupe and Tim Williams. A number of people were found to be missing and could not be accounted for, because their whereabouts were unknown or their relatives did not come before the commission on their behalf. Despite public knowledge concerning certain senior officials, they did not come under scrutiny in the report, except for the recommendation to call to account before the NEC those heads of sectors involved in abuses. No mention of Mzwai Piliso, Sixashe, Joe Modise or Jacob Zuma was made for instance. Despite its limitations, the Motsuenyane Commission posed a critical challenge to the ANC leadership. The recommendation to make its members, some of whom held important positions within the organisation, account for their actions, carried with it the danger of creating internal divisions if followed up or of exposing the organisation to public criticism if disregarded. This was a critical dilemma, particularly at a time when elections were about to be held for a new transitional dispensation. It transpired that the organisation's NEC decided at its weekend meeting of 28–29 August 1993 to claim collective responsibility for human rights violations. While agreeing to make a public apology to the victims, it refused to take punitive action against the culprits and, instead, called for a truth commission to investigate all human rights violations, including those committed by apartheid agents.[120]

In sum, the ANC's history, as it is illustrated by Ketelo and Ellis and Sechaba, projects an organisation failing to exercise its democratic obligations, excessively flagrant on human rights violations, subject to manipulative communist influence and pervaded by personal rivalries. It would appear, however, that some of the criticism is overstated. Firstly, the human rights violations question is not presented within its wider context. To focus exclusively on the actual deeds fails to take into account the mitigating circumstances. That these things happened in the context of a war in which the apartheid security and defence forces went all out to decimate "ANC terrorists" wherever they were (including neighbouring independent states), is not equally emphasised. Secondly, the question of limited democracy within the ANC during the period of exile was not surprising. The necessity for a strong, central command, secrecy and a censured democracy is characteristic of all underground movements. The above notwithstanding, a framework for democratic practice did exist, as admitted by Ketelo et al.,[121] in the form of branches, zonal and regional structures, as well as conferences which despite limitations allowed some measure of membership participation. Critics of the ANC argue persuasively, however, that there was an authoritarian predisposition, which eventually bred human rights violations in ANC camps in Angola.

Homecoming and democratic practice

As much as the question of human rights violations continued to hound the ANC during the early 1990s, internal tensions and problems associated with democratic practice did not cease with its transition into a home-based legal organisation.

The ANC's return to South Africa took place against the background of diverse democratic discourses inside the country. These were

- the indigenous traditions of community consultation and communal life, as typified by the Kgotla gatherings
- the universal democratic demands made by the ANC, as enshrined in the Freedom Charter
- the political ideas of democratic representation, as practised by conventional political parties
- democratic concepts derived from the civil rights movement and the struggle against apartheid in general
- theoretical adherence to internal democratic practice within the ANC before it was banned and the limited democratic practices (convening of consultative conferences and creation of zonal and branch structures) during its period in exile
- the idea of direct democracy and people's power, as shown by the street committees of the mid-1980s
- industrial democracy within trade unions.[122]

While these were important tenets of a future democratic polity and indeed a democratic ANC, their synergy and efficacious use within the ANC were not always unproblematic. Despite the riches of universal democratic principles, as enshrined in the Freedom Charter and all the monumental endeavours to make proposals for a future democratic constitution, the serious limitations of democratic centralism which came to dominate the ANC in exile, the Mandela-centred leadership tradition of Robben Island prisoners, the autocratic populist behaviour of street committees inside the country, and the closed highly elitist democracy of MDM leaders during the emergency period, combined to significantly retard efficient democratic practice within the ANC. Despite the filtering through of union-orientated democratic practice such as accountability, mandate and consultation, these did not always succeed in checking leadership decision making.

The basis for internal democratic exercise only came to be consolidated with the creation of a hierarchy of regional and branch structures which connected with the national office, and the holding of conferences where major policy decisions were taken and elections to the organisation's executive committees were held. One such conference, to which ANC leaders attach the greatest praise for internal democratic practice, was the national conference held from 2–6 July 1991.

This conference, held at the University of Durban-Westville, Natal, was the 48th conference and the first legal one to be held inside the country following the organisation's consultative conference in December 1990. Other important conferences of the organisation had been held outside the country in Morogoro, Tanzania (1969) and in Lobatsi and Kabwe in Zambia (1985). The 1991 conference, entitled "Transfer of power to the people for a democratic future", was attended by 2000 delegates, 90 % of whom were directly elected by branches. The other 10 % were made up of the NEC, chief representatives of the ANC from 40 countries around the world, and delegates from branches of the ANC in exile. The latter structures were in Tanzania, Zambia, Uganda, the United Kingdom and the United States, and included delegates from the military camps of the organisation. Each branch had been allocated a certain number of delegates to the conference in direct proportion to the number of its registered members. Thus the smallest branch sent one delegate and the largest up to 24.

Mohammed Valli Moosa, a member of the National Preparatory Committee, who was subsequently elected onto the NEC, said before the conference that a great deal of work had been done in preparation for the historic event. He maintained that in order to ensure that the conference was democratic, "the process building up to the conference was as important as the conference itself".[123] Moosa mentioned that the issues that formed the agenda of the July national conference had all been discussed at branch and regional levels over the past six months. The delegates arrived, therefore, well prepared to put forward the position their branch wished to take on any particular issue. This process of involving the membership was repeated during nominations for NEC positions. According to Moosa, branches made individual nominations. These nominations were taken to regional conferences where regional lists of candidates were finally drafted. Exercising their democratic rights, regions were able to turn down an NEC suggestion to increase the number of NEC members to 126 and suggested 100 instead. Even the national conference itself had to follow certain democratic procedures. Organisational matters were first discussed in commissions where branch views could be directly articulated before being returned to the House during plenary session. Reflecting on his participation in the conference, an ANC branch delegate, Brahm Fleisch, wrote that "a strong culture of democratic participation was beginning to develop, of vigorous discussion, of decisions to be made by ordinary people, not carefully orchestrated behind closed doors".[124] Elections of NEC members were conducted through a secret ballot, with branches being allowed to vote for their candidates directly. Summing up his view of the conference, Moosa said: "I believe that this conference is a unique exercise in democracy. Not any political party can say it has held a conference as democratic as this one. The decisions that will be reached at the conference will reflect the views of our general membership – we haven't cut any corners".[125]

Similar feelings about the democratic process were expressed by Trevor Manuel after the ANC's national policy conference. According to him, the drafting of the ANC's economic policy, in particular, was a long process that began when the organisation was still in exile. The policy developed in stages. In 1988 the ANC's Constitutional Principles pronounced on economic policy. In 1990 the Department of Economic Policy released a discussion document which was formulated in Harare, Zimbabwe, to ANC branches when they were formed during the course of the year. After input from the branches, the document was reworked for the national conference in July 1991. Because of lack of time to discuss policy matters, the document was taken to branches and the public at large for input and comments. After workshops and feedback from the public, the final document was compiled and released to the ANC's policy conference in May 1992. Lauding the democratic process that preceded the adoption of ANC policies, Manuel said: "However imperfect the document may be, it is owned by thousands of people who drafted it and amended it".[126]

The democratic nature of the process leading to both the national and policy conferences was, however, not a microcosm of democratic practice within the broader liberation movement. Despite professed intentions by ANC leaders to implement this noble ideal, as reflected in the creation of regional and local structures, the realisation of this objective was blocked by problems and limitations. As early as the preparation for the consultative conference in December 1990, signs of these limitations were already evident. Although conference decisions were not to be mandatory, the late distribution of discussion documents to branches a mere two weeks before the start of the conference weakened considered input by members into the diverse political matters of the organisation.[127] But most crucially, the way certain decisions were taken by the leadership and the increasingly pivotal role of committees in decision making fundamentally weakened notions of democratic exercise.[128] While mandate and consultation were generally understood within the organisation as important foundations of internal democratic practice, these were constantly flouted by the leadership, as demonstrated by its lack of consultation with respect to the first meeting with the government in May 1990[129] and its unilateral suspension of the armed struggle without mandate and consultation with ANC members. The decision to call for an all-party conference in the January 1991 Anniversary Statement, without entertaining this idea at the December 1990 consultative conference, also showed the leadership's disregard of these fundamental principles of democracy. Mandela's overturning of an NEC decision to reshuffle departmental portfolios during his absence in August 1991, which resulted in his wife Winnie being placed under Cheryl Carolus in the Department of Social Welfare, also showed the serious limits of democracy within the liberation movement.

The tendency towards autocratic decision making by the leadership ac-counted to a great extent for the simmering dissatisfaction of various allied organisations. Not only did COSATU unions complain, with others hinting to break from the alliance, organisations such as SASCO and SANCO also began taking positions publicly opposed to those of the ANC. In its call for a two-day stay-away in August 1992, the ANC had urged students to continue with schooling. Opposing this decision, SASCO argued that it reserved the right to determine its own programme and urged students to stay away. In yet another dispute, bitter arguments in the media between SANCO's Moses Mayekiso and Nelson Mandela erupted after SANCO's decision to call for a bond boycott. Discontent did not however end here, but existed also in some ANC regions such as the war-ravaged Natal. Problems started here with the ANC's attempts to make peace with Buthelezi, a decision strongly opposed by at least two ANC regions, Natal Midlands and Northern Natal. The controversy began with the ANC's decision, following its meeting with an Inkatha delegation led respectively by Jacob Zuma and Frank Mdlalose in November 1992, to create a preparatory subcommittee made up of a representative from each of the three Natal regions.[130] Only Southern Natal participated, while the two other regions boycotted meetings of this committee and contended that the decision to meet Buthelezi had been imposed on them without their consultation. Although these internal differences were not allowed to surface in public, ANC Midlands leader, Harry Gwala, never hid his opposition to meeting Buthelezi. Even in the national conference in the commission on violence, Gwala strongly argued against conciliation with Inkatha, saying "while we talk peace they practise war".[131]

Problems relating to undemocratic practice were not limited to the leadership. Conduct at regional and branch levels also demonstrated the difficulty with which ANC activists sought to come to terms with democracy. In some cases campaigns were launched without consulting allied organisations, leading to complaints by some trade unions which charged the ANC with autocratic tendencies. Most often members would be informed of decisions without being democratically involved in the process.

Homecoming and continued internal tensions and crises

Like any other liberation movement or any other political party, differences over policy matters and purely personal squabbles have been part of the ANC's history. The integration of divergent political interests into the movement with a different understanding of the political struggle, had always been the main source of internal tensions and hostilities. Except for the breakaway of the PAC in 1959 over the question of whites and communist members within the ANC,[132] internal tensions that developed during the period of exile did not split the organisation, although they did lead to isolated factions, such as the African Nationalists or the Tennyson Makiwane faction[133] and the Marxist Workers' Tendency.[134] Throughout the early 1990s, differing traditions within the ANC battled each other in various subtle ways for strategic influence within the organisation. This struggle was manifested in the scramble for positions immediately after the unbanning of the movement. The decision to create the National Reception

Committee to welcome ex-prisoners and the subsequent formation of the Internal Leadership Core were strategic moves on the part of internal MDM leaders to avoid being sidelined in the event of the ANC's return. The NRC was also formed to prevent Winnie Mandela from using the release of her husband, Nelson Mandela, to promote her return to the political stage after her isolation following the killing of Stompie Moeketsi. Mrs Mandela did in the event use her husband and the support of some exile leaders to secure for herself senior positions within the ANC.

The ILC was formed in the main to create positions for ex-prisoners. But the creation of departments under the ILC and their assignment to ex-prisoners sparked tensions among exiles who had headed similar departments in Lusaka. The struggle for positions within the ANC also occurred on regional and branch level. In Northern Orange Free State the scramble assumed the form of personal vilification by regional leaders,[135] and the tension surrounding the ANC's PWV Women's League ended up being a struggle between former exiles and internal leaders. Media allegations against Mokaba's spy role also revealed a contrived strategy by a section of exile leaders to isolate the youth leader. But the leak of this information to the press allegedly by Jacob Zuma, Joe Slovo, Mac Maharaj and John Nkadimeng, either indicated an attempt to prevent unity among militant leftist leaders in the pending ANC national conference or indeed mirrored personal rivalries between Mokaba and leaders such as Zuma.[136] Mokaba and Zuma had reportedly clashed at an NEC meeting prior to the media revelation. The attempt to pre-empt a leftist militant faction appeared to be informed by continued tensions between those who favoured the continuation of negotiation after the ANC's withdrawal from constitutional talks and those who wanted it to abstain and instead opt for militant action. Mokaba and Zuma clearly held different views on this matter.

What was obvious in the various incidents of personal squabbles within the ANC was a systematic pattern of leaking sensitive information about certain individuals. According to Ivor Powell, one-time journalist with the *Weekly Mail*, some ANC leaders had approached the newspaper, asking its assistance in checking "corruption and undemocratic behaviour of certain ANC members". Despite the press quoting highly-placed sources within the ANC, the organisation was not able to address even a single case of a breach in confidentiality, something which clearly implied that such leaks probably came from leading office-bearers.

Potentially divisive internal tensions evolved, however, around the issue of the "cabal". The cabal question was a transfer into the ANC of an old division within the UDF during the 1980s. The issue became public after a lengthy letter written by Aubrey Mokoena of the then Release Mandela Committee to the ANC's NEC in June 1990. As defined in the letter, "cabal" referred to a clique or faction of comrades secretly pursuing their own agenda within the democratic movement or the ANC in particular.

[It is] a clique of activists who have been doing what is perceived as good work on the surface, but with a hidden agenda. The cabal adopts different types of strategies, *inter alia*, isolation, vilification, manipulation, infiltration and building its own leaders. It deploys its personnel in strategic organisational positions in such a manner that it is inexplicable how they got there.[137]

The cabal's political objective was to pursue a speedy negotiated settlement and to sideline and undermine militant politics (such as those of the youth in SAYCO and the MK), which could antagonise the state.[138] Grooming its personnel and placing them in strategic positions to influence ANC policy could be realised by taking control of the MDM. According to the cabal document, some of its people were already placed in influential positions. These included Cyril Ramaphosa (code-named CR), Azhar Cachalia (AC) and Murphy Morobe (MM). Others named by the centre-right International Freedom Foundation as belonging to the cabal were Mohammed Valli Moosa, who was acting UDF General Secretary; Elijah Barayi, who was COSATU President; Archie Gumede, UDF National Co-president; Fatima Meer, Natal Indian Congress member and researcher; Cassim Saloojee, Transvaal Indian Congress President; Eric Molobi, coordinator of the National Education Coordinating Committee; and Farid Essack, Western Cape UDF leader. Some of the names included in the list by the Inkatha Institute for South Africa were Billy Nair, Yunus Mohammed, Curnick Ndlovu and Pravin Gordan. Those who were felt to hamper the objectives of the cabal and had to be sidelined included Peter Mokaba (PM), Popo Molefe (PM) and Patrick Lekota.

Despite much publicity, the cabal controversy remained unresolved with insufficient evidence and conflicting leads. The ANC's failure to respond to the submissions by Aubrey Mokoena in 1990 might, however, have been influenced by the sensitive nature of the subject and the possible fear on the part of ANC leaders of its explosive potential if aired in public. Most significantly, that senior ANC members were allegedly involved made the issue difficult to follow through. While the ANC leadership was content to let the matter drop, the resurfacing of another "cabal" document in October 1992, contemplating more controversial measures such as sidelining Nelson Mandela as the leader of the ANC, squarely put the question of the cabal under the spotlight. The new document entitled *State of the nation: The road to victory, the path to power*, which was probably written before the March 1992 whites-only referendum, recommended the gradual replacement of Nelson Mandela by Cyril Ramaphosa through carefully contrived steps. While it re-emphasised the need for speedy negotiations, it propounded the idea of supporting De Klerk and allowing him "to score certain victories in the international arena".[139] It further reiterated the concern about MK, as well as the need to get rid of "this potential time bomb". Unlike the previous document, though, the new document expressed the cabal's opposition to exile leaders such as Josiah Jele, Mzwai Piliso, James Stuart and Alfred Nzo, who were seen to be consolidating their positions with the returning exiles. Furthermore, unlike the previously stated objective of a speedy negotiated settlement and the attainment of dual control with the incumbent regime, the document cited its ultimate aim as the transformation of South Africa into a true socialist state. It claimed success in having groomed certain leaders for senior positions, such as Mac Maharaj, Mohammed Valli Moosa, Popo Molefe, Cheryl Carolus, Allan Boesak and Dullah Omar.

What was confusing, though, was that some of the people the cabal claimed to have nurtured, such as Popo Molefe, were mentioned in the previous document as among those who had to be isolated. Others mentioned in the cabal documents were not even aware of their alleged allegiance. But more perplexing still, was the bringing together of communist members and those who advocated a compromise between liberalism and communism. It was an apparent contradiction that the cabal sought a speedy negotiated settlement and the creation of dual power at the cost of marginalising militant politics of the youth and MK cadres, and yet in the same breath sought to create a socialist South Africa. While it is true that there are different paths to socialism, including a liberal alternative, it is inconceivable how leaders such as Allan Boesak, who publicly disassociated himself from the South African Communist Party, could help the move towards socialism.

The confusing message in the second cabal document appeared to reinforce pervasive claims within the ANC that the document was probably the work of the state security department which sought to sow division within the organisation.[140] But how accurate were these claims? What about Winnie Mandela and Dali Mpofu's allegations concerning the existence of the cabal? Though not fictitious, it would appear that allegations about cabalism within the organisation lacked logical foundation and coherence. They seemed symptomatic of internal divisions and power struggles within the ANC. The allegation of cabalism by Mrs Mandela and Mpofu, and their associating Ramaphosa with the cabal, appeared to be a culmination of tensions that had built up since the Stompie Moeketsi controversy.

Since her return from banishment in Brandfort, Orange Free State, in the mid-1980s (she had been there since 16 May 1977), Mrs Mandela had not succeeded in building up cordial relations with the UDF leadership. This could be accounted for by her style of operation, which included attempts to project herself as a separate identity that directly articulated the ANC's voice in the country. Her ability to sway the emotions of the youth through fiery speeches and her cultivation of the spirit of militancy, effectively established her as the mother figure in the militant struggles that were being waged during the mid-1980s. While she emerged as a powerful force and spokeswoman for the interests of the oppressed amidst various oppressive measures against the democratic movement, this new, alternative platform turned into an empire that became too personalised. That she did not belong to any structure of the mass democratic formation clearly made it difficult for any attempts to advise, guide or even control her. Despite the acknowledgement of her increasing power, leaders within the UDF, COSATU, civics and the churches actually found it difficult to approach her. But it was after the assault at Mrs Mandela's house and the subsequent killing of a young veteran activist, Stompie Moeketsi, in December 1988, that pressure and protest against her mounted.

After concerted but fruitless efforts behind the scenes to persuade her to disband the Mandela United Team allegedly involved in the abuses, the MDM called a press conference in which it distanced itself from her and issued an embargo on her public appearance in mass meetings. Announcing the MDM's move in February 1989, Murphy Morobe, the UDF's General Secretary, stated:

> We have now reached the stage where we have no option but to speak publicly on what is a very sensitive and painful matter. In recent years Mrs Mandela's actions have led her into conflict with various sections of the oppressed people. In particular we are outraged by the reign of terror that the [Mandela United Team] has been associated with. Not only is Mrs Mandela associated with the team, in fact the team is her own creation. We are outraged at Mrs Mandela's complicity in the recent abductions and assault on Stompie. The MDM hereby distances itself from Mrs Mandela and her actions.[141]

The press briefing led to a rift between her and the leaders appearing in the press conference, such as Murphy Morobe, Elijah Barayi (COSATU President), Archie Gumede (Co-president of the UDF) and others, creating tensions that would be played out in the following years of power positioning. While Mrs Mandela was temporarily sidelined by the ban imposed on her, the release of Nelson Mandela saw her back onto the political stage. This was quickly countered, however, with the formation of the National Reception Committee, comprised largely of MDM leaders. The prominence of the NRC also saw surprising statements being made by Cyril Ramaphosa that Mandela would not automatically lead the ANC, but be an ordinary member. But Mandelamania and the return of exiled ANC leaders subsequently led to the downgrading of many prominent MDM leaders. Unlike before, Ramaphosa was no longer seen at the side of Mr Mandela. Except for those who opted for organising functions within the ANC, such as Patrick Lekota, or were employed by the movement, such as Vusi Khanyile (heading the Finance Department), the UDF leadership simply disappeared into oblivion. Murphy Morobe took a scholarship to Princeton University in the United States.

Meanwhile Mrs Mandela continued to consolidate her position in the ANC. She was appointed Head of the ANC's Social Welfare Department and was elected into the PWV Women's League. She was also elected onto the NEC of the ANC during the ANC's 48th national conference in July 1991. Her good fortune was, however, shortlived. The election of Cyril Ramaphosa to the Office of Secretary-General, replacing her ally Alfred Nzo, reduced her sphere of influence. This was followed by a series of damaging events which included her trial in the Moeketsi case and the ANC's distancing itself from her.[142] During Nelson Mandela's absence in 1991, ANC senior portfolios were reshuffled resulting in her removal from the Social Welfare post. Lodge describes this as party political manoeuvring by the SACP to place its members in strategic positions,[143] and to intentionally dethrone Mrs Mandela and place her Department of Social Welfare under Cheryl Carolus, a party member. While this move failed, because Mr Mandela ordered its reversal when he returned, Mrs Mandela was less than elated, as she had to contend with revelations about her alleged love affair with Mpofu and her poor relations with her husband.[144] Ultimately, her conviction in the Moeketsi case and the barrage of criticism in the press against her added weight to calls for her isolation from the ANC. That Mr Mandela was pressured into ostracising her was apparent when he publicly announced their separation on 13 April 1992, apparent not only from his emotional expression but also from the ironic declaration of separation and love in the same breath.[145] While no NEC member could apparently move for the sacking of Mrs Mandela following her conviction, revelations of the alleged embezzlement, together with Mpofu, of ANC funds, the new controversy surrounding the PWV Women's League which resulted in her suspension, as well as sensational media revelations of her angry love letter to Mpofu, were sufficient to lead to her resignation. Tendering her resignation, Mrs Mandela took a final parting shot at the "cabal", which she believed forced her out. She spoke of "enemies", some of whom were "inside our ranks", who "have rejoiced in reading about our problems" and who "for selfish political reasons have waged a vicious and malicious campaign against me, and through me the leadership of my husband and our organisation".[146]

It would appear on balance that Mrs Mandela's remarks about cabalism when she resigned her ANC positions, were made against the background of continued hostility towards former MDM leaders such as Ramaphosa. Mpofu's accusing Ramaphosa of cabalistic tendencies when he (Mpofu) was fired as Deputy Head of the Social Welfare Department, also seems to fall within this framework.[147] The close relationship between the question of "cabal" and the power struggle was further demonstrated by infighting in Natal, where a critical report by Robben Islanders on cabalism sought to undermine former UDF leaders.[148] The report's tabling at the regional conference and the urgent need expressed in it to create an ANC with an identity separate from the UDF, resulted in the exclusion of alleged cabal members such as Pravin Gordhan, Billy Nair, Farouk Meer, Curnick Ndlovu and Archie Gumede from the Executive Committee. Cabalism in Natal was, however, resolved when some of these members were elected onto the regional Executive Committee in subsequent years.[149] In short, while the cabal controversy did not breed factionalism, it nevertheless deepened tensions and mistrust within the ANC, much to the detriment of its unity.

This unity was further threatened by the crisis surrounding attempts to reinstate Mrs Mandela to her ANC positions. After her conviction to a six-year jail term pending appeal in the Moeketsi case and her subsequent separation from her husband, Mrs Mandela had resigned her position as Head of the ANC's Social Welfare Department. In her letter of resignation Mrs Mandela stated:

> False allegations have been made against me. I have always maintained my innocence and there is an appeal pending. My request that the

matter should be left in the hands of the courts has not only been ignored but appears to fuel the desire of those who wish to destroy me and to discredit the ANC. Their campaign of vilification has created a difficult situation for the ANC, my husband as its president, and myself. In view of all the considerations mentioned above, I have asked the ANC to relieve me of my duties as the appointed Head of the Department of Social Welfare as soon as a successor can take my place ... I have taken this step because I consider it to be in the best interest of the ANC whose cause and policies I will support until the end of my life.[150]

Her deputy, Dali Mpofu, also vacated the department, after being fired by the Office of the Secretary-General. On Thursday, 21 May 1992, five members of the PWV Women's League Executive Committee, including Nompumelelo Madlala, Maggie Nkomo and Maria Mojapelo, mobilised a group of women from ANC squatter camp branches of Carletonville, Phola Park, Sebokeng and Atteridgeville. Calling themselves the Social Welfare Support Committee, the group organised a march from the league's regional offices to the ANC's headquarters, demanding the reinstatement of Mrs Mandela and Mr Mpofu to the department.[151] They also charged certain congress leaders with victimising Mrs Mandela by leaking sensitive information on her private life to the press.[152]

While it was not clear why the women demanded Mrs Mandela's reinstatement, there was general unanimity that she was behind the demonstration. This was confirmed by a snap commission of inquiry appointed by the National Working Committee, and headed by Professor Dennis Davis of the Wits Law School and Durban lawyer Linda Zama. On the evening of the day of the demonstration, the deputy chairperson of the PWV Women's League convened an emergency meeting of the Regional Executive Committee (REC) to discuss the incident. On 22 May an interbranch meeting was called. Mrs Mandela, who was also present, left before the start of the meeting to consult her lawyers about media allegations. During discussions the meeting discovered that most participants in the demonstration were not fully aware of the purpose of their actions. Some had believed that they were demonstrating against the state. After it became apparent that demonstrators had used the league's resources to launch an anti-ANC demonstration, 11 of the 20-member REC threatened to resign.[153] But after intense debate a decision was finally taken to suspend the whole REC of the PWV Women's League and institute a commission of inquiry. This decision effectively removed Mrs Mandela from her leadership position. In its emergency meeting of 30 May 1992, the ANCWL endorsed the decision of the interbranch meeting and also suspended Mrs Mandela from its NEC because she was to be investigated. Nomvula Mokanyane was also suspended from the NEC because she was a member of the suspended REC. Taking an uncompromising position, the league argued that South Africa was writhing in pain from a past and present full of corruption and abuse of power and privilege, to the detriment of the interests of the majority. "Our ability to deal honestly and firmly with signs of similar situations in our ranks will go a long way in determining transformation of our society''.[154]

Formally instituting the Davis Commission of Inquiry, the National Working Committee of the ANC, however, ruled that the suspension of the REC of the PWV Women's League was unconstitutional. This decision was overturned by the ANC's NEC in its meeting of 8–10 June 1992, after the Commission of Inquiry, established by the National Working Committee, had found prima facie evidence to warrant disciplinary action against instigators of the demonstration.[155] Confirming the suspension, the NEC decided that the ANC at national level would assume responsibility for the day-to-day running of the regional office. On 10 September 1992, Mrs Mandela submitted her letter to the ANC, resigning from all her elected positions in the ANC's NEC, Women's League NEC and the PWV REC.[156] Her resignation followed media revelations of her vindictive love letter to alleged lover Dali Mpofu in the Sunday papers of 6 September 1992.

Acting on the decision taken at its previous meeting, the ANC NEC issued a press statement on 22 September 1992, announcing the names of a task force which would run the league's regional offices. These were Thandi Modise, Girlie Pikoli and Faith Mnguni from the ANC Women's League head office. They were to be assisted by Kediboni Mogotsi, Muntu Nxumalo, Thembi Moko, Kgomotso Rammego, Messie Sibiya, Lorna Motsoahae and Mrs Rivers. In May 1993 the Women's League decided to lift the suspension of the PWV REC. All were to resume their duties except five members, Mrs Mandela, Gwen Mahlangu, Marjorie Nkomo, Nompumelelo Madlala and Sally Peterson who, it was felt, had not repented their previous deeds. They were to be suspended for another year. According to Baleka Kgositsile, the league's Secretary-General, the five had continued to act in such a way as to bring the organisation into disrepute. Despite their suspension, she contended, the five continued to use the league's offices and facilities and incurred high phone bills, which ended up bringing the league's treasurer to court.[157]

While the idea behind the suspension of the PWV REC and Mrs Mandela was to correct the misdeeds of leaders and subject them to organisational discipline, the issue was handled in such a way that it failed to produce expected results. Despite the intervention of the ANC's NEC, differences of opinion within the organisation concerning Mrs Mandela always produced different approaches. This was clearly demonstrated by the NWC's decision not to recognise the suspension of the REC, a decision which was later reversed by the ANC's NEC. It was obvious that despite opposition by some ANC members to Mrs Mandela's political leadership, she still had the moral support of her husband, while a significant number of ANC members and powerful leaders such as Chris Hani, Harry Gwala and Peter Mokaba continued to pledge their support for her.[158] In fact, Hani had this to say of her during her trial:

> It would be an unbalanced judgement to Comrade Winnie to dismiss the considerable contribution she has made to our revolution, just because

she is accused of having had a hand in the killing of Stompie. Why should we recognise the cries of injustice coming from circles guilty of the most cruel injustice against our people? ... I am a good friend of Winnie. She is a leader. I admire her courage. I have seen her concern about the plight of the ordinary cadre. That side of Winnie is not known to many people. If I am too biased, it is because I have stayed with her and I have known streams of people coming to seek advice from her. It is very difficult for me even to conjure this image that she has been a cruel and ruthless woman.[159]

Though mandated to take disciplinary action against Mrs Mandela, the NWC could not find any practical way of effecting this, added to which was the perception that any disciplinary action against her would create divisions within the ANC and impact negatively on Mr Mandela.[160] Rather than being isolated into oblivion by this string of crises, Mrs Mandela continued to maintain her public profile by intensifying work in squatter communities. Her fiery speeches and public criticism of elitist politics by ANC leaders[161] won her sympathy and broadened her support in the ranks of ANC militants, who were already indignant at the leadership's handling of violence and negotiations. Her popularity was glaringly demonstrated by the tumultuous reception given her by ANC supporters at a rally in Richmond, Natal, where she shared the platform with Peter Mokaba and Harry Gwala.[162] Her election to chair SANCO's Southern Transvaal region, though constitutionally problematic,[163] firmly attested to her increasing political invincibility. This was to be further cemented by her successful appeal against the six-year jail term conviction, which removed an important stigma that had caused her temporary resignation from ANC-elected positions. The league's intention to make Mrs Mandela accountable for her alleged misdeeds never succeeded. In fact, Mrs Mandela was never brought before a disciplinary committee and continued to operate according to her own rules. She defied bad publicity and returned to the political limelight with her election as Deputy President of SANCO and President of the ANC Women's League in late 1993. Summing up the ANC's difficulty in reprimanding Mrs Mandela, Tokyo Sexwale said that

> ... anywhere in the world, Winnie would have been a written-off. But in South Africa, we are dealing with a different set of values where her errors were looked at in relation to what she stood for and still stands for. Winnie is a symbol – a symbol that has erred, sometimes seriously. Yet she has come to symbolise the hopes, the dreams and aspirations of ordinary people. How do you use a disciplinary code against such a symbol, who remains endeared to poor people all over – it is totally inadequate ... you would need a Herculean task to bring her down.[164]

In conclusion, the organisational and political development of the ANC in the early 1990s was important in many respects. Notwithstanding the problems and difficulties encountered, the development of an organisational structure with a centre, regions and branches provided a sufficient base from which ANC leaders could, with authority, enter into negotiations with other parties over the future of the country. It provided a framework for internal interaction which to a large measure allowed membership participation in decision making. This was mirrored by the many workshops and conferences that were convened on matters of policy and negotiation. On the other hand, its political development, though marked by tensions both within the ANC and between it and allied organisations, provided scope for negotiation and agreements over a broad political arena. The following chapter will focus on the development of policy within the ANC.

ENDNOTES

1. See Biko, S. *I write what I like*. London: Penguin, 1978. See also Nolutshungu, S. *Changing South Africa*. Cape Town: David Philip, 1983.
2. Addressing SAYCO's Easter weekend conference in 1990, Nelson Mandela said of the youth, ''Your contribution to the struggle, to our irreversible advance towards liberation, has been truly enormous. The sacrifices you have made and will still be called upon to make cannot but evoke our greatest admiration for your courage and determination.'' See *SASPU National*, 1(2), 1990, 9.
3. See Vogelman, L. Violence has corrupted the young lions. Quoted in *New Nation*, 12–18 June 1992.
4. 'A home for all the youth'. *Mayibuye*, December 1990, 41.
5. 'SAYCO eyes the ANC'. *Work In Progress*, 65, April 1990, 2.
6. ANC Youth League constitution and code of conduct, 12 December 1991, 3.
7. *New Nation*, 6–12 December 1991.
8. 'Youth League takes stock'. *Mayibuye*, May 1991, 27.
9. 'Reaching students'. Interview with Peter Mokaba. *Horizon*, 2(3), 1993, 15.
10. 'Students unite under SASCO'. *Mayibuye*, October 1991, 34.
11. 'Youth broadening horizons'. *Mayibuye*, March 1992, 17.
12. 'The youth in the last leap to victory'. *Horizon*, 2(3), 1992, 30.
13. 'Friends and foes meet'. *Horizon*, ibid., 19.
14. 'The challenge to build national youth unity'. *Mayibuye*, June 1992, 30.
15. 'National youth conference: only a beginning'. Interview with Parks Mankatlana, *Mayibuye*, October 1992, 20.
16. *Weekly Mail*, 5–11 June 1992.
17. Chris Hani's address to the East Rand Summit on Peace and Political Tolerance, 2 April, 1993.
18. 'Chris Hani's vision'. *Learn and Teach*, June 1993, 17.
19. 'A life of its own: the autonomy of the ANCYL'. *Mayibuye*, March 1991, 27. See also 'ANCYL speaks on the need for autonomy'. *The Spark*, 2(1), 1991, 37.
20. African National Congress constitution as adopted at the ANC National Conference, June 1991, 5, F4.
21. Report and resolutions from the Building the Organisation Commission, ANC National Conference, Durban, July 1991.
22. Masondo, A. The autonomy debate rages on. *Mayibuye*, June 1991, 45.
23. See 'Is this top ANC man a spy?' *Weekly Mail*, 24–29 May 1991. While the ANC released a statement defending Mokaba's innocence, a great deal of time was allowed to lapse before the announcement of a formal response, which created suspicions that cast doubt over Mokaba's integrity.
24. Joint press statement of the ANC Youth League and the ANC Secretary-General, Cyril Ramaphosa, 22 April 1993.
25. ANC press statement about the controversy regarding the remarks made by the President of the ANCYL, Mr Peter Mokaba, 13 August 1993.
26. For the history of women's struggles see Lodge, T. *Black politics in South Africa since 1945*. Johannesburg: Ravan, 1983, Chapter 6: Women's protest movements in the 1950s, 139–152. See also a brief but informative history of women's struggle in *New Nation*, 10–16 August 1990.

27. 'Frene Ginwala on feminism'. In interview with Frene Ginwala, *Work In Progress*, June 1992, 21.

28. 'What about the women?' *Mayibuye*, December 1990, 45.

29. *Political and structural relationship between the ANC Women's League and the ANC.* Undated internal ANCWL discussion paper, 2.

30. *Joining the ANC: an introductory handbook to the ANC.* Johannesburg, May 1990, 41.
See also 'Women: an auxiliary of the ANC'. *Mayibuye*, May 1991, 29.

31. 'The voice of women'. Interview with Gertrude Shope, *Mayibuye*, July/August 1990, 17.

32. Statement of the NEC of the ANC on the emancipation of women in South Africa, 2 May 1990.

33. See *Leadership South Africa*, 9(9), 1990, 36.

34. 'Launching the Women's League'. *Sechaba*, November 1990, 2.

35. 'PWV launch of the ANC Women's League'. *Mayibuye*, March 1991, 36.

36. Secretary-General's report to the ANC National Conference, July 1991, 20.

37. *The Star*, 25 April 1991.

38. This decision was a response to the ANC's NEC's constitutional proposal that 17 out of 105 NEC positions be reserved for women.

39. *Sunday Times*, 5 May 1991.

40. 'ANC women scrum down for key vote'. *Sunday Star*, 28 April 1991.

41. Ngoasheng, M. The ANC conference: Gearing to struggle for power. *South African Labour Bulletin*, 16(1), July/August 1991, 30.

42. Horn, P. ANC women's quota: the debate continues. *Work In Progress*, 77, September 1991, 37.

43. Daniels, G. Women chart the way forward. *Work In Progress*, 78, October/November 1991, 25.

44. Other members of the NCEW were Uriel Abrahamse, Kader Asmal, Jackie Cock, Baleka Kgositsile, Thenjiwe Mthintso, Bongiwe Njobe, Thutukile Radebe, Wally Serote, Bangumzi Sifingo and Arnold Stofile.

45. *Bulletin of the National Commission for the Emancipation of Women*, April 1990.

46. 'The women's charter campaign'. *Mayibuye*, May 1991, 31.

47. Meintjes, S. Dilemmas of difference: the Women's National Coalition. *Work In Progress*, April 1992, 17.

48. 'Women unite to map out their future'. *The Rock*, March 1992, 4.

49. 'Organising for a charter of women's rights'. *Mayibuye*, June 1992, 23.

50. 'Campaign for women's equality charter gains momentum'. *Mayibuye*, March 1993, 38.

51. *Ready to govern: ANC policy guidelines for a democratic South Africa.* Adopted at the National Conference, 28–31 May 1992, 2. See also 'Policy guidelines: a triumph for women'. *The Rock*, August 1992, 8.

52. 'League calls for more women in CODESA'. *The Rock*, March 1992, 3.

53. 'The women's charter campaign'. *Mayibuye*, February 1992, 32.

54. 'Women claiming the political terrain'. *Mayibuye*, April 1992, 22.

55. Manzini, M. Gender on the agenda: women in negotiations. *Mayibuye*, August 1993, 16.

56. Hassim, S. & Walker, C. Vive la différence: current debates on feminism. *Mayibuye*, August 1992, 32–33.

57. 'Vukan makhosikazi'. *Mayibuye*, May 1993, 13.

58. For a more detailed analysis of the UDF, see a draft manuscript by the author titled *The Vaal uprising: rent increases, community resistance and the struggle against apartheid*, 1995.

59. Ottoway, M. Liberation movements and transition to democracy: the case of the ANC. *Journal of Modern African Studies*, 29(1), 1991, 72.

60. 'The UDF: where to now?'. *New Nation*, 30 November – 6 December 1990.
It might also be true, as *Front File Bulletin* suggested, that the proposition not to dissolve the UDF was also influenced by the desire by some activists to retain the organisation's resources. See 'Mobilising the civics'. *Front File*, 5(3), March 1991.

61. 'ANC's programme of mass action to revitalise the movement and to seize the political initiative'. *South African Update*, 2(16), December 1990, 8.

62. *New Nation*, 30 November – 6 December 1990, op cit.

63. Rather than dissolving and joining the ANC, the Transvaal and Natal Indian Congresses, which were part of the UDF, opted instead to continue as separate entities.

64. For a full discussion of civics, see *Theoria*, 79, May 1992, Centre for Policy Studies, Special Issue. University of Natal Press.

65. Heymans, C. *Towards people's development? Civic associations and development in South Africa.* Paper presented to the Conference of the Development Society of South Africa, Grahamstown, 9–11 September 1992, 4.

66. Daniels, G. Beyond protest politics, *Work In Progress*, 76, July/August 1991, 13.

67. Lechesa Tsenoli, SANCO Deputy President (elected President in late 1993). Interview.

68. It was in view of this danger that CAST Vice-President Kgabisi Mosunkutu cautioned that ''we must do everything to guard against any attempt to translate autonomy into hostility towards the liberation movements''. See 'Civics line of march'. *New Nation*, 17–23 May 1991.

69. Nzimande, B. & Skosana, M. Civics are part of the democratic revolution. *Mayibuye*, June 1991, 38. See also Jeremy Seekings' criticisms of the viability of the watchdog function of civics in 'Civic organisations in South African townships'. *South African Review*, 6, Johannesburg: Ravan, 1992, 216–238.

70. Nkosi, D. Civics and the ANC. *Mayibuye*, 2(10), November 1991, 33.

71. Suttner, R. *The African National Congress and its relationship to civics*. Discussion paper no. 3, Department of Political Education, 1992, 2. See also 'The role of civics'. *Mayibuye*, December 1990, 31–32.

72. Suttner, R. *Where are we, where are we going from here and how do we get there? Current conditions and strategic priorities of the ANC*. Draft paper, November 1990, 6–7. See also Suttner, R. *One year of an unbanned ANC: the road ahead*. Draft, February 1991, 8.

73. Cyril Ramaphosa. Interview. See also Jay Naidoo's views in *Mayibuye*, 'Workers flex their muscle', September 1990, 25.

74. 'COSATU ponders over its alliance with the ANC and SACP: imperative or impediment?' *Work In Progress*, 75, June 1991, 39.

75. 'First signs of unease between unions and the ANC'. *Southern Africa Report*, 8(46), n.d., 8.

76. For FAWU's support for the ''many caps'' position, see its resolutions in 'NUMSA and FAWU congresses'. *Mayibuye*, August 1991. While NUMSA did not take a resolution on this matter, its Secretary-General, Moses Mayekiso, who himself held positions within the union movement, the civic associations and the SACP, supported the many hats position (see *New Nation*, 9 August 1990). The ANC publication, *Mayibuye*, also supported this position in the article entitled 'How many caps fit?' February 1991. While aware of its disadvantages, the SACP's Jeremy Cronin supported this position cautioning, however, that ''we should guard against the dangers of two hats but we should not stop people from joining and building political organisations like the ANC''. See his critique of Coperlyn and Zikalala on this subject in an article entitled 'Preparing ourselves for permanent opposition?' *South African Labour Bulletin*, 15(7), April 1991. See also 'Once more ... many caps'. *Umsebenzi*, 7(2), May 1991, 9.

77. 'The challenge facing COSATU'. Interview with Sydney Mufamadi, COSATU's Assistant General Secretary. *Mayibuye*, July 1991, 28.

78. See *Work In Progress*, 75, June 1991, op. cit., 37. See also 'A South African Communist speaks', Chris Dlamini interviewed by David Niddrie. *Work In Progress*, 68, August 1990, 4–6.

79. While it is difficult to separate working class interests from political ones in the South African situation, ''workers' interests'' is used here to mean those issues which are immediately specific to workers, such as the demand for a living wage or campaigning against retrenchment. The concern is whether these issues were given the same consideration within the alliance as were political demands.

80. See for example, Daniels, G. Fighting factionalism in the Western Cape. *Work In Progress*, 74, May 1991, 43–45. The federation had also to contend with the distressing revelation of spying by Maxwell Xulu, the President of its largest union member, NUMSA.

81. See 'COSATU: challenges of the 1990s'. *South African Labour Bulletin*, 16(1), July/August 1991, 62.

82. Pillay, D. & Webster, E. 'COSATU, the party and the future state'. *Work In Progress*, 76, July/August 1991, 33.

83. Jay Naidoo, interview by Glenda Daniels. *Work In Progress*, 77, September 1991, 20–21.

84. See Nzimande, B. & Skosana, M. Debating socialism. *The African Communist*, First Quarter, 1992, 37–51; Davies, R. 'Rethinking a socialist debate in South Africa'. *The African Communist*, Second Quarter, 1991, 37–46.

85. See the debate on vanguard party or mass party in *The African Communist*, Fourth Quarter, 1991, 7–22.

86. *The Citizen*, 13 July 1991.

87. Mackintosh, P. 'Is the Communist Party programme still valid?' *The African Communist*, 109, Second Quarter, 1987, 41.

88. Prior, A. South African exile politics: a case study of the ANC and the SACP. *Journal of Contemporary African Studies*, 3(1/2), October 1983/April 1984, 183. See also Francis, T.S. Communism, terrorism and the African National Congress. *Journal of Social, Political and Economic Studies*, 11(1), 1986, 55.

89. See the positions held by SACP members within the ANC in Appendix A.

90. Ellis, S. & Sechaba, T. *Comrades against apartheid: the ANC and the SACP in exile.* London: Indiana University Press, 1990, 198–206.

91. Pillay, D. Can the SACP change track? *Work In Progress,* 76, July/August 1991, 18 & 34. See also Cronin, J. Is the SACP travelling in the right direction? *Work In Progress,* 74, May 1991; Steinberg, J. Leninist fantasies and SACP illusions. *Work In Progress,* 74, May 1991; Kitson, D. Marxism-Leninism and absolute truth. *Work In Progress,* 77, September 1991. Here Kitson argues for proletarian democracy as opposed to the "bourgeois democracy" advanced by Steinberg.

92. *Business Day,* 5 July 1991. See also *The Citizen,* 5 July 1991.

93. *The Citizen,* 5 July 1991.

94. Joel Netshitenzhe. Interview.

95. Ketelo, B., Maxongo, A., Tshona, Z., Masango, R. & Mbengo, L. A miscarriage of democracy: the ANC security department in the 1984 mutiny in Umkhonto we Sizwe. *Searchlight South Africa,* 5, July 1990.

96. Thishang Makgabo, MK cadre and ANC representative at the National Housing Forum. Interview.

97. The ANC in exile was highly infiltrated by South African security agents. The uncovering of the spies Patrick Dlongwana (*Mayibuye,* September 1992, see also *Weekly Mail,* 14–20 August 1992), Craig Williamson (*Weekly Mail,* 28 June – 4 July 1991), Olivia Forsyth (*New Nation,* 23 February – 1 March 1989), Rodney "Khotso" Twala (*New Nation,* 6–28 June 1990) and a person called September, alias Glory Lephosa Sedibe (who coordinated the arrest of MK cadres infiltrating the country, such as Andrew Masondo and Jimmy Ngobeni – see *New Nation,* 22–28 June 1990) occurred after serious damage had been done to the organisation.

98. Lodge (1983), op cit., 300.

99. Ellis & Sechaba, op cit., 128–129.

100. Ketelo, op cit., 42.

101. Commission of inquiry into recent developments in the People's Republic of Angola. Stuart Commission, 14 March 1984, Lusaka, 24.

102. Ibid., 24.

103. Ketelo, op cit., 59.

104. Ellis & Sechaba, op cit., 148.

105. Lodge, T. The African National Congress in the 1990s. *South African Review,* 6, Johannesburg: Ravan, 1992, 46.

106. Reports of the commission of inquiry into certain allegations of cruelty and human rights abuse against ANC prisoners and detainees by ANC members. Motsuenyane Commission, 20 August 1993, 52.

107. Ellis & Sechaba, op cit., 120.

108. Report of the commission of inquiry set up in November 1989 by the National Working Committee of the National Executive Committee of the African National Congress to investigate the circumstances leading to the death of Mzwakhe Ngwenya (also known as Thami Zulu or TZ). Jobodwana Commission, n.d.

109. 'A report to the Namibian people'. *Free Azania,* 2 & 3, November 1989.

110. 'An open letter to Nelson Mandela from ex-ANC detainees'. *Searchlight South Africa,* 5, July 1990, 66–68.

111. Despite its incisive analysis of the ANC's history in exile, *Comrades against apartheid,* as Garth Strachan allegedly states in his review of the book, needs to be treated with circumspection. Stephen Ellis, who is the main author, had been the editor of *Africa Confidential,* which had for years allegedly concentrated its analysis on internal divisions within the ANC. Tshepo Sechaba is the pseudonym of Kenneth Mabandla who had committed serious breaches in the ANC, including misappropriation of funds. The major problem of the book lies in its unsourced and unsubstantiated accounts, particularly in the last three chapters. For a critique of the book see Strachan, G. 'Indecent obsession', *The African Communist,* Second Quarter, 1992, 47–49.

112. Trewhela, P. The ANC's prison camps: an audit of three years, 1990–1993, *Searchlight South Africa,* 10, April 1993, 13.

113. Report of the commission of inquiry into complaints by former ANC prisoners and detainees. Skweyiya Commission, Johannesburg, August 1992.

114. Ibid., 15.

115. 'The names the ANC tried to hide'. *Weekly Mail,* 21 October 1992.

116. 'South Africa: torture, ill-treatment and executions in ANC camps'. *Amnesty International Report,* London, December 1992, 26.

117. Report of the Douglas Commission, Durban, January 1993, 58–59.
    Intense debate ensued between Bob Douglas and Joe Slovo as a result of the publication of this
    report. See *The Star*, 27 January 1993.
118. Motsuenyane Commission, op cit., Appendix 1.
119. Ibid., 169–170.
120. African National Congress National Executive Committee's response to the Motsuenyane
    Commission's report, 29 August 1993. See also the media statement of the National Executive
    Committee of the African National Congress, 30 August 1993.
121. Ketelo et al., op cit., 53–65. Pallo Jordan also refers in a draft article to a tradition of internal
    democracy within the ANC in exile characterised by rigorous debate and discussion. See
    Jordan, P. *The politics of the democratic movement in South Africa*. Draft paper, Lusaka, May 1989.
122. Fitzgerald, P. Democracy and civil society in South Africa: a response to Daryl Glaser. *Review of
    African Political Economy*, 49, Winter, 1990, 105–107.
123. Press address by Mohammed Valli Moosa accompanied by Patrick Lekota and Carl Niehaus,
    June 1991.
124. Fleisch, B. Inside the ANC conference. *Searchlight South Africa*, 2(4), January 1992, 86.
125. Press address by Mohammed Valli Moosa, op cit.
126. Trevor Manuel's address to the Centre for Policy Studies on the ANC's social and economic
    policies, 21 July 1992.
127. 'Countdown to conference'. *Mayibuye*, March 1991, 19.
128. Michels contends that the more extended the bureaucratic apparatus of an organisation, the
    more central the role of committees in decision making and the more its rank-and-file
    members lose direct control of the organisation. See Michels, R. The bureaucratic tendency of
    political parties. In Merton, R., *Reader in bureaucracy*. New York: Free Press, 1952, 89–90.
129. 'The ANC on the road to negotiations'. *Searchlight South Africa*, 2(1), July 1990, 9.
130. *City Press*, 10 January 1993.
131. *Congress Militants*, a paper of the Marxist Workers' Tendency of the ANC, 8, October/November
    1991.
132. For a discussion of events leading to the split of the PAC from the ANC, see Gerhart, G. *Black
    power in South Africa: the evolution of an ideology*, Berkeley: University of California Press, 1978;
    Lodge (1983), op cit.; Pogrund, B. *How can a man die better: Sobukwe and apartheid*. London:
    Peter Halban, 1990; Farbian, J. *The split in the ANC, 1958. Searchlight South Africa*, 2(3), July
    1991, 60–64.
133. *Africa Confidential*, 20(5), 1.
134. For a discussion of the Marxist Workers' Tendency see Cronin, J. Marxist Workers' Tendency:
    trying to change the ANC from within. *The African Communist*, Second Quarter, 1991, 22–25.
135. Vax Mayekiso. Interview.
136. Powell, I. House cleaning. *New Era*, Spring, 1991, 25.
137. 'Conspiratorial cabal document'. Letter addressed to Walter Sisulu from the Release Mandela
    Committee, 6 June 1990.
138. 'State of the nation – negotiation: when and how?' An anonymous 'cabal' document which
    surfaced during July 1990, 4.
139. 'Row over cabal bid to sideline Mandela'. *Weekly Mail*, 9–15 October 1992.
140. ANC, SACP and COSATU joint media statement regarding the allegations in the *Sunday Star*, 22
    February 1993.
141. Quoted in Trewhela, P. The trial of Winnie Mandela. *Searchlight South Africa*, 2(3), July 1991,
    36.
142. Ibid., 33–47 and 3(1), August 1992, 32–46.
143. Lodge (1992), op cit., 59. See also *Weekly Mail*, 13–19 September 1991. However, in a press
    statement on 10 September 1991, the ANC denied that the reshuffling meant the replacement
    of Mrs Mandela by Ms Cheryl Carolus. It explained that the move was aimed at streamlining
    lines of accountability to the National Working Committee through one head rather than two,
    as was previously the case.
144. *Sunday Star*, 6 September 1992.
145. *City Press*, 19 April 1992.
    Norma Kitson, Deputy Convenor of the London Anti-Apartheid Group, states in a letter to the
    Weekly Mail (30 April – 7 May 1992) that Mandela confided to her in Harare that since his
    release from prison he has been led by the nose, implying that his ditching of Winnie was also
    upon an instruction.
146. *Weekly Mail*, 11–17 September 1992.
147. *Sowetan*, 14 May 1992. See also 'ANC cabal made sure I was sacked Mpofu'. *The Star*, 14 May
    1992.

148. 'Confusion and divisions in the ranks, the ANC and UDF'. *South African Update,* 2(16), December 1990, 7.
149. Mpho Scott, Deputy Secretary of the ANC Southern Natal region. Interview.
150. Statement by Nomzamo Winnie Mandela, 15 April 1992. Issued by the ANC's Department of Information and Publicity.
151. 'PWV women's region, half a league?' *Mayibuye,* July 1992, 30.
152. *The Citizen,* 16 June 1992.
153. 'League threatened by splits'. *Weekly Mail,* 5–11 June 1992.
154. 'ANC Women's League, PWV suspensions'. *The Rock,* August 1992, 6.
155. ANC press statement on the position of the PWV Women's League, 15 June 1992.
156. ANC press statement on Nomzamo Winnie Mandela's resignation, 10 September 1992.
157. 'The PWV Women's League saga'. *Mayibuye,* September 1993, 39.
158. During his overseas trip and immediately before Mrs Mandela's conviction, Chris Hani was reported to have publicly stated that a future ANC government would release her if she were jailed.
159. Quoted in 'Winnie Mandela trial: acid test for ANC'. *New Era,* Autumn, 1991, 30.
160. *Weekly Mail,* 24–30 April 1992.
161. *Sunday Star,* 10 January 1993.
162. *Weekly Mail,* 24–30 April 1992.
163. Lechesa Tsenoli, SANCO. Interview. Unlike other SANCO regions, Southern Transvaal had tendentiously interpreted the organisation's constitution to the effect of creating a chairperson's portfolio, apart from presidency, into which it voted Mrs Mandela. Despite her election, it was not clear what her functions were and she most often appeared on public platforms on an ANC ticket rather than that of SANCO.
164. *Sunday Nation,* 26 September 1993.

The ANC and policy development

In early 1994 the ANC released its policy document, the Reconstruction and Development Programme (RDP). The RDP was a product of two distinct processes which were nonetheless interlinked during the later phases of policy development: policies developed by the ANC and the Reconstruction Accord, engineered by COSATU to bind an ANC-led government of national unity in exchange for COSATU's election support.

Policy development and *Ready to govern*

A major part of the ANC's struggle against apartheid had been its constant attempt to provide an alternative vision. While the Freedom Charter is generally seen as the cornerstone of the ANC's vision of an alternative post-apartheid polity, the practice of propounding an alternative vision started years before the charter was adopted. On 16 December 1943 in Bloemfontein the ANC adopted a bill of rights called the *African Claims*, which espoused the national right to life, ownership of land, liberty and equality for Africans and coloureds.[1] This initiative was taken further with the adoption of the Freedom Charter at Kliptown in 1955.[2]

Since its adoption in the 1950s the Freedom Charter remained the main beacon in the struggle against apartheid until the mid-1980s. The controversy around some of its provisions, such as the nationalisation of the means of production and its alleged betrayal of the African ideals by declaring South Africa a land for both black and white, as well as the debate around its socialist inclinations, kept the charter alive throughout these years of intense repression. The emergence of the Black Consciousness Movement during the late 1960s and 1970s, asserting the fundamental role of blacks in the struggle, temporarily eclipsed the charter and its prospects for a non-racial, democratic South Africa. This nonetheless failed to confine it to oblivion and it re-emerged towards the end of the 1970s.

The Freedom Charter, in particular its economic provisions, was subjected to varying interpretations within the ANC. During the 1960s and 1970s, when the struggle against colonialism in Africa had reached its peak, ANC strategists interpreted the document in line with statist economic policies followed in most socialist states in Africa and East Asia. While the charter's provisions to transfer and restore the national wealth of the country to the people (the mineral wealth beneath the soil, the banks and monopoly industry) were interpreted by nationalists such as Mandela as implying the diversification of ownership of resources over all sections of the population, others read in these provisions the foundation for socialism. This latter interpretation came to enjoy broad acceptance during the period of armed struggle and was given further impetus by the socialist transformations that came with the independence of Mozambique and Angola. In line with this creed, the sections which related to the transfer of the ownership of resources and the central role of the state in the charter were seen to be in accord with the central features of socialism: central state planning and nationalisation. As a result a new perception of socialism from a South African perspective, based in part on events in the recent past, emerged and swiftly gained ground.

This analysis and the general predisposition towards socialism not only became ubiquitous in the orthodox literature of the struggle against apartheid; it also gained root within the different organisational formations which mushroomed during the 1980s. While the UDF finally adopted the Freedom Charter in the mid-1980s, it did not publicly commit itself to a socialist outcome, leaving this objective to be articulated by COSATU in the closing years of the decade. However, the growth of this popular view of socialism in South Africa during the mid-1980s ran parallel with a process that trammelled its hitherto unchallenged hegemony – exploratory negotiations between the liberation movement and forces that were until then regarded as part of the enemy camp. This challenge arose in 1985, when a group from the South African business community defied the Botha regime and consulted the ANC in Lusaka, Zambia, about the country's future. In response to this shift by the capitalist class, the ANC, while preparing itself for negotiations in 1987, also began moderating its position, particularly on matters that were of concern to this class.

The most visible product of these new relations was the ANC's moderate stance on nationalisation, which henceforth was presented not in its ugly face of confiscation of property without compensation, but as something which could be attained through state shareholding. But a much more important result of these interactions was the bold attempt by the ANC to develop and publicise its alternative policies on various matters. In 1988 the organisation released its *Constitutional guidelines* for general debate. It was in this document that the ANC's shift from "its utopian rhetoric of earlier years" was outlined.[3]

With its return to South Africa and faced with the varying challenges of building its organisational structures, contending with violence and negotiating with the government, the ANC's position on a number of issues tended to be very much ad hoc and in the main self-contradictory. This was particularly so on the question of nationalisation, with some ANC leaders stating that it was an ANC policy and others contending that it was not. It was in response to the need to develop a consistent policy that the ANC set up departments to coordinate policy proposals in their respective spheres. Tapping the resources and intellectual input of research institutes, universities, academics and contributions at branch level, the ANC policy departments produced draft papers which were distributed in preparation for discussion at the July 1991 national conference.[4] Because of time constraints, a decision was taken at the conference to set aside a separate date for such discussion.

The national policy conference which took place on 28–31 May 1992 in Johannesburg was preceded by an intense debate on policy proposals at all levels of the organisation. Branch meetings were called, culminating in regional policy conferences which set the scene for broader regional consensus. For instance, the PWV region convened a meeting of all its policy departments on 11 April 1992, where matters needing exploration were highlighted.[5] A decision to create a technical support group comprising ANC members and experts was taken, and the Regional Health Department was asked to prepare a draft discussion paper on policy making.[6] This groundwork laid the basis for the PWV regional policy consultative conference held on 9–10 May 1992, where policy resolutions were passed.[7] The ANC Women's League held its own national policy workshop on 8–10 May 1992 at the Down Town Inn Hotel in Johannesburg.[8]

Like the process leading to the adoption of the ANC economic policy, which is cited by Trevor Manuel in the previous chapter, the development of an ANC land policy broadly illustrates the breadth and intensity of the consultation and feedback proceedings. The skeleton of an ANC land policy had been shaped at the organisation's Land Commission Workshop held earlier on 14–21 October 1990. This workshop had convened to discuss issues such as nationalising the land, communal land, land claims, land acquisition, labour and gender issues, including macroeconomic matters. Tasks for the national secretariat and regional land commissions were set out to broaden the debate on land matters. These tasks included consultation and involvement of ANC regions and branches, CONTRALESA, COSATU, research institutions and other national organisations.[9] Out of this workshop and the consultation process, a draft discussion paper entitled *Discussing the land issue: A discussion document for ANC land commissions and branches*, had been produced early in 1991. Articulating the provisions contained in the Freedom Charter and operating within the parameters of the 1988 constitutional principles, the draft put forward principles and proposals which had been advocated by academics, institutions and research organisations associated with the MDM.[10] With comments and contributions from various sectors, the *Land manifesto for the ANC National Conference* was produced, ready for presentation at the organisation's national conference in July 1991. Discussion on this draft policy paper was deferred to a later policy conference. Before this policy conference was convened in May 1992, an intensive programme of consultation, debate and discussion of the land proposals was carried out. In February 1992 a simplified version entitled *Our land, a discussion guide for South Africans,* was published to guide discussions at branch level. This process having been completed, the draft land policy was ready for presentation and adoption at the national policy conference.[11]

After the May 1992 national policy conference, a composite policy document was released for broader public debate. Entitled *Ready to govern: The ANC policy guidelines for a democratic South Africa*, the document stated its vision as being

> ... to strive for the achievement of the right of all South Africans, as a whole, to political and economic self-determination in a united South Africa; to overcome the legacy of inequality and injustice created by colonialism and apartheid, in a swift, progressive and principled way; to develop a sustainable economy and state infrastructure that will progressively improve the quality of life of all South Africans; and to encourage the flourishing of the feeling that South Africa belongs to all who live in it, to promote a common loyalty to and pride in the country and to create a universal sense of freedom and security within its borders.[12]

The document outlined its policy on a democratic constitution for South Africa; a new system of local government; the economy; land; the environment; housing; health; social welfare; education, training and scientific development; education (broadly); the development of human resources; science and technology; the media; arts and culture; sport and recreation; peace and security; youth; and international relations. Other separate policy reports were released focusing on policing, regional policy, constitutional principles and a bill of rights. A policy report on farm workers was released in August 1993,[13] followed in October of the same year by *Foreign policy in a new democratic South Africa* and *Affirmative action and the new constitution*. An ANC regional policy document was also released proposing the creation of ten regions. Local government policy, which had been the subject of negotiation at the Local Government Negotiation Forum, was brought to fruition with the signing of the Local Government Transition Act at the World Trade Centre in Kempton Park in January 1994.[14] Signed by both Mandela and De Klerk, the Act provided for non-racial integrated local government councils as an interim measure towards fully-fledged democratic local government authorities. In January 1994 the *National health plan for South Africa* was also released, committing itself to transforming the entire health care delivery system and its institutions.[15]

Unlike any other political party in South Africa, the ANC was able to provide in its policy proposals a detailed, though not exhaustive, elaboration of its thinking. True to its liberation movement character of representing all sectors of society, its policy document touched every aspect of life. A cursory reading of the document revealed a clear bias towards the disadvantaged black communities, workers and women. The central themes were to build equality, empower the people and build democracy. There was strong advocacy for state centrality in economic and social planning and an accompanying desire to control the activities of the private sector, including banks and monopoly capital. Despite this tendency to interventionism, there was a significant departure from the socialist inclinations of the Freedom Charter.

Nationalisation of the mineral wealth was presented as an option rather than something that had to happen within a framework of command.

A comprehensive assessment of this policy document was made by the Urban Foundation's Development Strategy and Policy Unit and published in its journal, *Development and Democracy*.[16] Comprising commentaries and articles by leading South African intellectuals, the journal lauded the ANC's policy document as a pioneering example, while simultaneously subjecting it to critical appraisal. A general critique expressed in the commentaries was that *Ready to govern* was a "wish-list", promising everything to everyone, thus making the document too good to be true.[17] The policy document was criticised for its failure to target its audience and for a lack of prioritisation on issues it promised to deliver. In the view of critics, the document envisaged a welfare state where things would be dished out to people. It advocated an interventionist state which would regulate society without limit. The document spelt out aspirations or goals, rather than how economic growth would be attained to achieve these goals. It was contradictory in that it espoused socialist wishes which, ironically, would have to be met within a capitalist economy.[18] Moreover, the goals that needed to be achieved, such as education and health, were presented as a right in the policy document. This, according to Estian Calitz, implied that such goals were based on the rule of law, which in consequence were enforceable in courts of law. He doubted if such rights could be enforceable against the state's financial constraints.[19] The leaning towards state intervention and redistribution was seen by Henry Kenny as a precursor to an authoritarian outcome. According to Donald Ncube, the policy document lacked costing and did not mention where the source of funding would come from. It provided no incentives to foreign investors and deliberately called for less reliance on the World Bank and the International Monetary Fund.[20]

It would appear that some of the contradictions in the document were a product of the desire to appease different interest groups within the liberation movement. But they could also be a reflection of the various contributions made by these interest groups. Kaizer Nyatsumba identified some of these groups as the Women's League, youth, workers, COSATU, SANCO and MK.[21] As Tom Lodge noted, the influence of specialist technocrats and their specific role within the ANC's policy departments and outside were also instrumental in shaping the final policy product.[22] Significant commentaries and advice on policy making and drafting were made by Ann Bernstein and Charles Simkins. Attention to this advice is clearly revealed in the RDP document, as many of the deficiencies and omissions of *Ready to govern* are attentively addressed. In their commentaries Bernstein and Simkins called on ANC policy makers to give a lucid explanation of the problems facing the nation, putting facts in their context and outlining the political complexities of "current" South African society to enable clear choices to be made on what needed to be maintained, improved or restructured.[23] They contended that "policy formulation should be an exercise in the art of the possible – a weighing up of needs, resources, capacity, and priority rating in order to formulate a workable policy that accords with the organisation's values and its goals".[24] The ANC was also asked to clarify what it meant by "balanced development" and how this could be attained. Urban and rural policies needed to be fully developed, the dangers of affirmative action (promised to women and blacks) needed to be guarded against by stating attainable, defined targets. Furthermore, the contradiction of a strong state and a strong civil society needed clarification, as well as elaboration on the developmental role of the private sector. Finally, the style and arrangement of the policy document were also criticised.

While *Ready to govern* was neither a detailed prescription of policies ready for implementation nor an election manifesto, as Trevor Manuel explained,[25] it nevertheless was an important leap in policy development. A terrain was set for intense debate, with the various proposals in the document being thrashed out in newspapers and magazines. Although this debate came to be overshadowed by constitutional negotiations, mass action and violence during the later months of 1992 and in 1993, the proposals of the policy document came to find expression in a new policy development framework anchored to the RDP.

The Reconstruction and Development Programme

The birth of the RDP can be traced to the debate within COSATU on the need to review the alliance with the ANC. In fact, some activists were already calling for the formation of a workers' party distinct from the ANC and the SACP some time before this debate emerged within unions. Expressing this view, a radical socialist paper, *Qina Msebenzi*, stated in its May/June 1993 edition that "the ANC has crossed the class line, joining the camp of the bourgeoisie. It cannot be fire and water. Therefore workers must form their own workers' party to fight capitalism at economic and political levels".[26] Proponents of this idea, such as Ramadiro and Vally of Workers Organisation for Socialist Action (WOSA), saw the prospect of a government of national unity as a compromise that would betray workers' interests.[27] Following this line of argument, NUMSA and SACTWU formally resolved in their conferences in July 1993 to sever links with the ANC once an interim government was established. The call for an alternative organisation was grounded in the fear that constitutional negotiations would produce a compromise deal, which would not be sufficient to guarantee the gains and aspirations of the workers. SACTWU, in particular, resolved that its demands should be entrenched in the constitution, namely the right of workers to belong to trade unions, to organise, to bargain collectively and to strike without fear of dismissal.[28]

The call for a workers' party was, however, not unanimous within COSATU. Unions such as NUM opposed the call and resolved to remain closely linked with the ANC. This would be done by backing the ANC during the elections in exchange for the latter's attention to socio-economic demands of the workers. In a move that indicated the triumph of the anti-workers' party group, COSATU leaders were also beginning to talk about a reconstruction and development pact with the ANC. Writing in the *Sowetan*,

Jay Naidoo said: "We are proposing a programme for reconstruction and development aimed at addressing in a planned, coherent and systematic way the enormous social and economic problems we have inherited from years of apartheid misrule."[29] While these developments established the notion of a reconstruction pact, which in the eyes of unions would advance workers' interests, it was developments in constitutional negotiations that definitely set the path towards a reconstruction and development programme by bringing the ANC into the fold.

By mid-1992, after the collapse of the CODESA negotiations and the resultant mass action campaigns, the ANC's success in extracting compromises from the government in the *Record of understanding*, influenced the former to respond in kind by putting forward constitutional compromises. The "sunset clause" deal was propounded in *Strategic perspective*, agreeing to a government of national unity in which minority parties would be allowed participation irrespective of the outcome of the elections. During the debate of the "sunset clause" compromise, COSATU and SACP strategists such as Jeremy Cronin agreed to this compromise on the condition that the ANC bring into the government of national unity a definite socio-economic programme. To ensure that such a socio-economic programme would be adhered to, COSATU further demanded that its officials be included in the ANC election list. The acceptance by the Tripartite Alliance (ANC, SACP and COSATU) of this deal paved the way for the general acceptance of the ANC's strategic approach to negotiations. On the other hand, a strategic platform was secured by COSATU to develop a socio-economic programme which would be brought into the new government by the ANC.[30] From 10–12 September 1993 COSATU held a special conference to finally consider an accord with the ANC based on a reconstruction and development programme, and to elect officials who would go onto an ANC election list.[31] After these leaders were elected,[32] it was emphasised that they were mandated to enter into the new political dispensation with the sole purpose of realising the wishes of the workers. A fourth draft of the RDP was circulated at this conference as a working document for debate. The first, second and third drafts had actually been developed within COSATU before the fourth draft. It was agreed that the fourth draft would need to be gone into in detail by the Tripartite Alliance in consultation with other mass democratic organisations, including civics. The policy proposals outlined in the draft RDP broadened some of COSATU's earlier proposals. For example, economic proposals drew heavily on decisions reached at the COSATU economic conference held in April 1992, where a democratic mixed economy was advocated along with a selective nationalisation policy, an industrial policy and a public works programme.[33] These proposals did not differ in essence from ANC policy, except that COSATU saw these measures as a stepping stone towards socialism.

The fifth draft of the RDP was produced after intensive debate and consultation between the Tripartite Alliance and SANCO, the National Education Coordinating Committee (NECC) and other research organisations. In this broader consultation proposals produced by the ANC policy units and COSATU's proposals formed the backbone of what later became a coherent and more thorough draft of the RDP. Some proposals emanating from national sectoral negotiating forums, such as the National Housing Forum and the National Economic Forum, were refined and included in the document. The fifth draft was discussed at the conference of the MDM at the Chris Hani Memorial Centre, Nasrec, in Johannesburg in December 1993. In the 82nd ANC Anniversary Statement of January 1994, Nelson Mandela called for reconstruction and development, saying that "steps will have to be taken so that our country's resources are allocated and distributed in such a way that we can begin to end the racial disparities in terms of the distribution of wealth, income and opportunity".[34] The policy-making process gained further momentum in January 1994, when Nelson Mandela embarked on an election campaign which saw him addressing people's forums around the country. Critical questions addressed to Mandela by members of the public on how the ANC would be able to fulfil its commitments, influenced him to pressure convenors of the RDP to speed up the process. Contributions to and commentary on the fifth draft led to the production of the sixth draft, which was presented for discussion at an ANC RDP conference in Nasrec from 21–23 January 1994. This conference was attended by regional representatives and delegates from MDM organisations. The meeting resulted in the final touches being put to the printed version of the RDP.

During this consultation process a number of additions and changes were made to the RDP drafts. For example, the omnipresence of the state in every area of society was substantially scaled down. Attention was also given to democratising the state and civil society and giving the latter a more meaningful role in the developmental process. Published as an ANC official policy document in April 1994, the RDP was "an integrated, coherent socio-economic policy framework", which sought to mobilise all the people and the country's resources towards the final eradication of apartheid and the building of a democratic, non-racial, non-sexist future. The policy document was founded on six basic principles, namely the creation of an integrated and sustainable programme; a people-driven development process; promoting peace and security for all; embarking on nation building; linking reconstruction and development in a positive way; and democratising South Africa as a whole. The document put forward five major policy programmes: to meet basic needs, develop human resources, build the economy, democratise the state and society, and implement the RDP.

The RDP was a constellation of policy proposals that touched on almost all aspects of society. At the outset of each of the five major policy programmes the document began by providing a problem statement, which generally and specifically dealt with the problems inherited from the legacy of apartheid. For instance, in the problem statement for "meeting the basic needs", the document stated that "poverty is the single greatest burden of South Africa's people, and is the direct result of the apartheid system and the grossly skewed nature of business and industrial development which accompanied it".[35] As mentioned above, the detailing of a problem statement in each policy area indicated that the drafters of the RDP had paid attention to the advice given in the Urban Foundation's journal, *Development and Democracy*. A problem statement was followed by a "vision and objectives", which were then followed by a rigorous outline of policy proposals. It is important to note that one characteristic of the RDP was an inherent desire to restructure a phalanx of apartheid bureaucracy (with its attendant legislative, institutional and administrative complexities) both in the public and private sectors, including multiple and overlapping decision-making practices. Within this restructuring mode proposals were put forward to either rationalise, obliterate or create more effective institutions, which would enable the RDP to function. There was another striking characteristic, represented by innovative proposals to establish a workable and mutually beneficial relationship between state and society by providing a greater role for organisations of civil society and communities in general. This role accorded to civil society and the people was crisply captured by what the RDP called "people-driven development process". The document stated that

> ... the central objective of our RDP is to improve the quality of life of all South Africans, and in particular the poorest and most marginalised sections of our communities. This objective should be realised through a process of empowerment which gives the poor control over their lives and increases their ability to mobilise sufficient development resources, including from the democratic government where necessary. The RDP reflects a commitment to grass-roots, bottom-up development which is owned and driven by communities and their representative organisations.[36]

These proposals represented a radical departure from statist, top-down, secretive and unaccountable development practices. They provided a way in which most people would probably feel closer to determining their destiny at a local level. Through these proposals the question of governing and the realisation of development goals in South Africa was altered, at least in theory, from being the sole responsibility of elected officials to being the joint responsibility of both state officials and the communities. On "building the economy", the RDP stated that

> ... the fundamental principles of our economic policy are democracy, participation and development ... neither a commandist central planning system nor an unfettered free-market system can provide adequate solutions to the problems confronting us. Reconstruction and development will be achieved through the leading and enabling role of the state, a thriving private sector, and active involvement by all sectors of civil society which in combination will lead to sustainable growth.

The RDP further stressed that the goal for reconstruction and development was to create a strong, dynamic and balanced economy, which would "eliminate the poverty, low wages and extreme inequalities in wages and wealth generated by the apartheid system, meet basic needs, and thus ensure that every South African had a decent living standard and economic security". Nationalisation was seen as one of the options which could be considered on the basis of compelling evidence. Among other economic policies, a science and technology policy would be developed which would create an environment for innovation and international competitiveness.[37]

On "democratising the state and society", the RDP called for a democratic government and society, which would be realised through the enfranchisement of all people and their direct participation in the process of government. The RDP stated that

> ... democracy for ordinary citizens must not end with formal rights and periodic "one person one vote" elections. Without undermining the authority and responsibilities of elected representative bodies (the national assembly, provincial legislatures, local government), the democratic order we envisage must foster a wide range of institutions of participatory democracy in partnership with civil society on the basis of informed and empowered citizens (e.g. the various sectoral forums like the National Economic Forum) and facilitate direct democracy (people's forums, referenda where appropriate, and other consultation process).[38]

Implementing and financing the RDP was probably the most serious challenge and the policy document was quick to acknowledge this. The document cautioned that the uniqueness of the programme and the fact that it was the first time that it was being attempted in South Africa presented a major challenge.[39] For the RDP to be implemented, the document called for the establishment of RDP structures within national, provincial and local governments. These structures would monitor and coordinate the implementation of the programme by departments at the various tiers of government. A democratic government and parastatals would be required to establish priority-setting mechanisms to achieve measurable and attainable objectives within a definite time frame, including a plan and a budget. The implementation of the RDP would not be the sole responsibility of the government. The document stated that "the democratic government will reduce the burden of implementation which falls upon its shoulders through the appropriate allocation of powers and responsibilities to lower levels of government and through the active involvement of organisations of civil society".[40] A proposal was also made to establish a national system of monitoring with key indicators, which would measure the impact of the RDP on these indicators. It was also proposed that the RDP be legislated to give it legal effect. Furthermore, according to Jay Naidoo, the convenor of the RDP, this programme would be planned and implemented within the context of a five-year programme with certain quantifiable targets being set in the process. He stated that "we have harnessed not only the energies of thousands of activists at grass-roots level... but also the resources of experts and economists who are working in developing and verifying the quantification, the legislative and institutional programmes that will be necessary".[41]

Of relevance to the implementation of the RDP was the Commission on Development Finance, formed by SANCO at the instance of Jay Naidoo. Released on 11 April 1994 the Commission's report propagated a "people-driven" development process. It criticised the current flow of development finance in South Africa, which in the main benefited developers. It proposed the restructuring of development finance institutions such as the DBSA, IDT and the Kagiso Trust. While it proposed the merging of the latter two, the DBSA was seen as an anachronism which needed to be disbanded, because "it is an expensive luxury which South Africa cannot afford".[42] The report provided for the first time a detailed outline of how communities could be encouraged to participate in the development process. Notwithstanding the confusion of acronyms, the report spelt out the various roles of civil society organisations, such as community-based organisations (CBOs), community-based development organisations (CBDOs), non-government organisations (NGOs) and non-government development organisations (NGDOs). On the whole the report reinforced the RDP by exploring practical ways of implementing the flow of finance from the RDP offices to the people, and went a step further to suggest practical ways of mobilising civil society to participate in the RDP process.

With regard to financing reconstruction and development, the RDP argued that the success of the programme would lie not only in finance but also in labour, skills and coordinated effort. The greater portion of finance for the RDP would come from better use of existing resources. In this regard public expenditure of the national budget would be restructured and the revenue recovery capacity of the government improved. The existing tax structure would be reviewed with a view to creating a new, progressive, fair and transparent structure. New funds would be mobilised through the establishment of a Reconstruction Fund. Reconstruction levies might also be imposed on capital transfers, land and luxury goods. The proposal for a reconstruction levy was first made by Tito Mboweni, deputy head of the ANC Economic Planning Department, in June 1993 and repeated in September of the same year by ANC tax adviser, Dennis Davis. Making this proposal, Mboweni stated at the time that individuals and corporate groups would be expected to contribute a once-off proportion of the value of their fixed assets and income for reconstruction (5 % and 15 % were proposed respectively).[43] Earlier, in 1992, COSATU had proposed the introduction of a wealth tax which would be targeted at those in the higher echelons of the economy.[44] This proposal was abandoned after severe criticism by the business community and was not included in the RDP economic section.[45] Explaining the difference between a wealth tax and a reconstruction levy, Mboweni stated in *Mayibuye* in November 1993, that a reconstruction levy would be a once-off levy, whereas a wealth tax was a continuous part of the tax system. A reconstruction levy would be based on income and assets. Individuals whose income and assets were beyond a certain threshold would be expected to pay a specific percentage of their income and assets into a reconstruction development fund. The funds would be collected by the state and then transferred to the administrators of the RDP.[46] The RDP advocated a cautious approach to foreign lending, stating that such lending should not interfere with the integrity of domestic policy formulation. The private sector was also urged to undertake socially desirable investments.

Unlike previous reservations about ANC policies, the RDP was received with mixed feelings. Some of its provisions were lauded while others were criticised. That a mixed economy was finally endorsed as an ANC policy brought relief within the business sector, which had been sceptical of the ANC's economic policy. The fear of "nationalisation", which the ANC still maintained in the RDP as an option, had already declined partly because of some protection provided in the bill of rights of the interim constitution. The bill of rights upheld the right to property and outlawed expropriation of property without fair compensation. Joe Slovo had also cautioned that nationalisation could not be implemented mechanically, as it would tie up the budget and would result in the flight of capital and skilled labour.[47] *Finance Week Magazine* commended the RDP's shift from a punitive to a cooperative approach towards the private sector. According to the RDP, the private sector would be consulted in any future restructuring.[48] A spirit of cooperation and partnership developed between the ANC and the South African business community, strengthened by the ANC's newly moderate stance towards the private sector. This was further consolidated at a national conference called "Getting South Africa working: The ANC and business plan for the future", which was held in Sandton, Johannesburg, in March 1994.[49]

While commending certain RDP provisions, *Finance Week Magazine* also had criticism for some of its other provisions. It saw the document as a wish-list, stating that "until costing, a funding strategy and priorities are attached it cannot pass the test, set by the ANC itself, of being 'achievable' and 'sustainable'".[50] It claimed that the document "attempts to be all things to all people. It has a bit for those who believe in market-orientated economies and a bit for those who believe in centrally controlled socialist economies. In practice, it reflects the diversity of the ANC rather than a coherent economic policy".[51] A leading economist at the University of the Witwatersrand, Professor Charles Simkins, criticised the RDP for its overestimation of the capacity of the state and its underestimation of the capacity of the individual household and business.[52] The policy document was seen to contain too many sticks to beat the private sector with and provided few incentives for their involvement. It was not clear on its spending strategy, nor about its tax policy and how it would balance revenue and expenditure.[53] According to the *Financial Mail*, the RDP promised that many things would be free, such as free education, health care and nutrition for children, without equally elaborating on how it would be able to pay for these.[54] Certain institutions and practices, such as the private medical profession, also felt threatened by the RDP's proposal to restructure and centralise health care provision.[55] Proposals to change the directorship of the Reserve Bank came under fire: including COSATU representatives in the board of directors of the bank was seen as a dangerous proposal as this would erode the bank's independence, to which the ANC was committed, and probably stifle its efficiency.[56]

The major weakness of the RDP, as other analysts observed, was its lack of costing. The suggested budget of R35 billion was very conservative, as financial experts later claimed that the amount would in fact have to be doubled.[57] The policy document also did not say how these costs would be paid for and by whom. Achieving equity and extending socio-economic benefits to the disadvantaged section of the South African population became a key objective. By promising to deliver on almost everything, the RDP unjustly raised people's expectations. A careful reading of the document reveals ambivalence in some respects. It is neither a blueprint for socialism nor a free-market capitalist development plan. The document did not attack capitalism as an economic system, except to say that an unfettered free-market system cannot provide adequate solutions to the country's problems. At the same time it advocated the invigoration of the market economy in its full competitiveness. This, however, should happen within the context of the removal of restrictions imposed by apartheid, while simultaneously addressing its negative consequences.

In conclusion, then, the ANC's organisational reconstruction was important in providing a medium through which members could influence the organisation's direction on policy and negotiation. However, the interjection of violence impacted negatively on the process and in some respects influenced the ANC's strategic approach to negotiation. The following chapter will analyse the ANC's attempts to stop the violence.

ENDNOTES

1. Asmal, K. Three roads to freedom: human rights and the ANC. *Mayibuye*, December 1993, 21.
2. Suttner, R. & Cronin, J. *Thirty years of the Freedom Charter* . Johannesburg: Ravan, 1986, 262–266. See also Suttner, R. *The Freedom Charter: the people's charter in the nineteen-eighties.* The 26th T.B. Davie Memorial Lecture delivered at the University of Cape Town, September 1984; Polley, A. (Ed.), *The Freedom Charter and the future.* IDASA publication, Johannesburg: A.D. Donker, 1988; Hudson, P. Images of the future and strategies in the present: the Freedom Charter and the South Africa left. In Frankel, P., Pines, N. & Swilling, M. (Eds), *State resistance and change in South Africa.* Johannesburg: Southern.
3. Lodge, T. Context of the policy guidelines. *Development and Democracy,* Development Strategy and Policy Unit of the Urban Foundation, 3 December 1992, 4.
4. See, for instance, the release of a draft media policy by the ANC's Department of Information and Publicity on 23 November 1991.
5. Minutes of a meeting of all departments concerned with policy development. ANC PWV region Policy Department, 11 April 1992.
6. This draft was drawn up by Dawn Joseph and Anne Hilton, and is entitled *Inter-sectoral policy development – policy development in the PWV region,* 1992.
7. Resolutions of the Regional Policy Consultative Conference, PWV region, 9–10 May 1992.
8. See Resolutions of the ANC Women's League National Policy Workshop, 8–10 May 1992, Down Town Inn Hotel, Johannesburg.
9. ANC Land Commission Workshop. Discussion document, Broederstroom, 14–21 October 1990, 17. Also see Summary Report: ANC Land Commission Workshop. Comparative Studies Workshop on Agrarian Restructuring, 14–21 October 1990.
10. See Vaughan, N. Consensus and contention: a note on the current state of land debate. *Transformation,* 13, 1990, 96–103; Cloete, F. *Comparative lessons for land reform in South Africa.* Centre for Policy Studies Comparative Perspectives, April 1992; Qcabashe, K. *Land reform policy: the debate begins.* Centre for Policy Studies, 28 August 1990, unpublished research report. The government's *White Paper on land reform – a summary and background study* published in March 1991, added to the debate. See, for instance, 'ANC press statement on the government White Paper on land reform', 12 March 1991; Bekker, J.C. Land reform in African countries; and The changing face of South African land tenure, both in *SAIPA,* 26(1), 1991; Levin, R., Mkabela, S.

& Russon, R. The land: aspirations to strategy. *Mayibuye*, March 1993; Mkabela, S. Mawubuye – a social land movement. *Mayibuye*, April 1994; Randall, E. Back to the land. *Work In Progress*, 94, December 1993; Winkler, H. Direct action to restore land. *Work In Progress*, 81, April 1992; 'The graves of our ancestors are our title deeds'. *Work In Progress*, 82, June 1992.

11. The proposals made on land reform sparked a broader public debate which saw the Urban Foundation releasing a string of reports on land. See for instance, *A land claims court for South Africa? Exploring the issues*. Development Strategy and Policy Unit of the Urban Foundation, September 1993; *Rural land reform: the experience in Kenya, Zimbabwe and Namibia, 1950–1991*. Urban Foundation, September 1993; *Land ownership and conflicting claims: Germany 1937–1991*. Urban Foundation, September 1993; *Urban land invasion: the international experience*. Urban Foundation, March 1994. Other contributions included 'The land question', *SASH*, 34(3), January 1992.

12. *Ready to govern: ANC policy guidelines for a democratic South Africa*. Adopted at the National Policy Conference, 28–31 May 1992, 1.

13. *Policy on farm-workers*, August 1993, was a culmination of a process that started in mid-1992 when service organisations held a workshop in Stellenbosch to address the needs of farm-workers. The draft produced at this workshop was circulated to ANC departments, women and youth leagues, regions, branches, the SACP, COSATU, service organisations, the World Bank, and the South African Agricultural Union for discussion and debate. With submitted comments a redrafted document was presented to the ANC Policy Workshop on 8–9 June 1993, where the final draft was produced.

14. See Report on the ANC National Consultative Conference on Local Government, Johannesburg, October 1990, which forms the basis of the ANC's policy on local government.

15. *National Health Plan for South Africa*. African National Congress, January 1994.

16. *Development and Democracy*. Publication of the Development Strategy and Policy Unit of the Urban Foundation, 3 December 1992.

17. Ibid., 15. See comments by Henry Kenny and Masepula Sethole.

18. Ibid., 15. See comments by Herbert Vilakazi.

19. Ibid., 15.

20. Ibid., 30–31 and 34.

21. Ibid. See article by Nyatsumba, K. 'Making of the policy guidelines', 9–12.

22. Ibid. See article by Lodge, T. 'Context of the policy guidelines', 1–8.

23. Ibid. Also see article by Bernstein, A. & Simkins, C. 'Ready to govern? An essay on the ANC policy document', 50–51.

24. Ibid., 57.

25. Ibid. See Manuel, T. 'An ANC response to the two panel discussions', 43.

26. 'Fight for a workers' party'. *Qina Msebenzi*, paper of the Comrades for a Workers' Government, 7, May/June 1993.

27. Ramadiro, S. & Vally, S. Now is the time. *Work In Progress*, 94, December 1993, 29. See also Neville Alexander's argument for a workers' party in *Weekly Mail and Guardian*, 30 July – 5 August 1993. Alexander's call was a response to Jeremy Cronin's article in *Weekly Mail and Guardian*, 23–29 July 1993, where he cautioned proponents of the workers' party not to play into the hands of ANC opponents.

28. *City Press*, 25 July 1993.

29. *Sowetan*, 14 July 1993. See also Sam Shilowa's argument against a separate party in preference for workers' unity, in *Weekly Mail and Guardian*, 30 July – 5 August 1993.

30. Jeremy Cronin. Interview.

31. 'COSATU Congress, the path to reconstruction'. *Mayibuye*, October 1993, 8.

32. The following people were elected: For the national assembly – Jay Naidoo, Chris Dlamini, Moses Mayekiso, Alec Erwin, Kgabisi Mosunkutu, John Coperlyn, Nathie Nhleko, Marcel Golding, Don Gumede, Duma Nkosi, Phillip Dexter; for the regional list to the national assembly – Sipho Qcabashe, Salie Manie, D. Oliphant, T. Mufamadi, Leeuw, J. Mabudhafasi, E. Thabethe, S. Shabangu, G. Oliphant; nominees for the regional parliament – Thami Mohlomi, Dennis Neer and S. Mthethwa.

33. 'Workers grapple with the economy'. *Mayibuye*, May 1992, 31.

34. *Year of liberation for South Africans*. Statement of the National Executive Committee on the Occasion of the 82nd Anniversary of the ANC, June 1994, 8.

35. *Reconstruction and Development Programme*. African National Congress Policy Framework. Johannesburg: Umanyano, 1994, 14.

36. Ibid., 15.

37. A significant contribution to the ANC Science and Technology policy was made in *Towards a science and technology policy for a democratic South Africa*. Report to the ANC, COSATU and SANCO by a Mission sponsored by the International Development Research Centre, Canada, December 1992.

38. *RDP*, op cit., 120–121.

39. Ibid., 137.
40. Ibid., 140.
41. *Mayibuye*, February 1994, 26.
42. *Making people-driven development work.* Report of the Commission on Development Finance formed by SANCO, 11 April 1994, 78.
43. *South African Institute of Race Relations*, 1993/94, 430.
44. *South African Institute of Race Relations*, 1992/93, 568.
45. ANC tax adviser Professor Dennis Davis also opposed the tax. See *The Star,* 31 July 1993.
46. Mboweni, T. Reconstruction and development: where does the money come from? *Mayibuye*, November 1993, 32.
47. Slovo, J. Reconstruction demands sacrifices from all sides. *Business Day,* 27 January 1994.
48. *Finance Week,* 17–23 February 1994, 2–3. Organised black business (NAFCOC and FABCOS) appeared not to be the target of this future consultation. Despite the Mopani Understanding held at the Kruger National Park in November 1993, in which agreement was reached for cooperation between the ANC and black business, and despite the commitment of the RDP itself to bolster black business, there appeared to be few practical steps taken to deepen this relationship. Signs of frustration within black business were already evident when the RDP was released, with members dismissing the document as primarily concerned with appeasing the dominant white capital. See *City Press,* 20 February 1994.
49. *Finance Week,* 31 March – 6 April 1994, 25.
50. *Finance Week,* 20–26 January 1994. See also the criticism by Standard Bank Group Economist, Nico Czyplonka in *The Star,* 3 February 1994.
51. See comments by the Democratic Party's Ken Andrew on the RDP in *Financial Mail,* 21 January 1994, 29.
52. *Sunday Times,* 23 January 1994. See also the comments by Anglo American director, Bobby Godsell in *Sunday Times,* 13 March 1994; and comments by the International Monetary Fund economist in *Business Day,* 24 March 1994. There was also a string of comments on the RDP in leading South African newspapers between January and May 1994.
53. *Financial Mail,* 28 January 1994, 22.
54. Ibid., 77.
55. *Financial Mail,* 4 February 1994, 26–27.
56. *Finance Week,* 24 February – 2 March 1994, 11–12.
57. *Business Day,* 20 April 1994.

4 The ANC and the challenges posed by violence

Despite the relative advances made in developing an organisational structure, formulating policies and negotiating a political settlement, the ANC's major challenge lay in the spiralling wave of violence which threatened to emasculate its support base. As discussed in Chapter 1, violence had a tremendously negative impact on the building and operation of ANC branches. It also interrupted the negotiation process, as ANC leaders suspended talks in an attempt to force the government to stop the violence. Moreover, it influenced ANC strategic thinking as leaders opted for a speedy, compromised political settlement that would in the process seek to minimise its escalation.

In spite of the ANC's assertions about the fundamental causes of violence – which it pointed out, among other things, to be a result of the IFP's attempts to broaden its membership base,[1] third-force elements[2] and the government's strategy of destabilising liberation movements[3] – devising an effective panacea and countermeasures to stem the carnage proved to be daunting. Not only were suggested solutions always undermined by further outbursts of violence, but the state too was not always willing to exercise firm authority to this end.

Immediately after the upsurge of violence in Natal during July 1990, the ANC issued demands to police stations calling for the lifting of the state of emergency in Natal. It also called for the prosecution of warlords and the holding of a judicial inquiry. It demanded that security forces play an impartial and effective peace-keeping role and that freedom of association and political activity in the area be guaranteed. Ironically, rather than responding to these demands, the government amended the Natal Code of Zulu Law on 30 August 1990, authorising the carrying of traditional weapons, and introduced the Kwazulu Police Amendment Act, authorising cross-border operations.[4] On 11 September of that year Mandela led a delegation to a meeting with the government to expedite its response to ANC demands on violence. Detailing cases of police misconduct, acts of omission and brutality in places such as Imbali, Mpumalanga, Slangspruit, Edendale,

Vulindlela, Enseleni and Kwa-Mashu, a 50-page memorandum prepared by the organisation together with COSATU and the UDF, called for a two-pronged resolution to the conflict. This included a political approach envisaging talks with other parties such as the IFP and a proposal for joint supervision of the South African Police (SAP), which the organisation accused of not being impartial. A joint working group was also proposed to deal with a number of matters. These included setting up a common command structure for security forces, monitoring their conduct in handling complaints of misconduct, ensuring their rapid response to violence, and linking up ANC monitoring offices with the police in Pietermaritzburg, Durban and Empangeni.

The government's response was negative, as revealed by its lack of commitment to ANC proposals. While accepting the importance of the ANC's proposal for a joint supervision of the SAP, De Klerk, in a move that sought to boost Buthelezi's image, replied that such a move could only work if the IFP was also involved. The government, he contended, would play the role of a referee. Buthelezi also publicly stated that violence would not stop unless he met Nelson Mandela, giving the impression that both the government and IFP were pressuring the ANC to recognise the IFP as a powerful force to contend with, and one which had to be brought into the pre-talks initiatives.[5]

The ANC's response to calls for Mandela to meet Buthelezi would prove to be disastrous. Put under pressure by the Natal leadership, the ANC was compelled to block a meeting with Mandela and Buthelezi on the grounds that such a meeting would accord Buthelezi the recognition he did not deserve. It was further argued that meeting the IFP would mean that the organisation would in the future employ violence as an instrument to coerce the ANC to do things it would otherwise not do. The ANC weakened its position by putting off a meeting with the IFP, since in the long run the two organisations would have had to come to some understanding. By procrastinating, the ANC paradoxically gave the IFP more legitimacy.

On 29 January 1991 the ANC and the IFP, led by Mandela and Buthelezi, held a peace summit in which they agreed to develop practical steps to bring about an end to the violence between the two organisations in Natal and the Transvaal. Furthermore, they agreed to ensure that all persons, irrespective of political affiliations, would have access to public facilities and that they would cooperate in initiating and implementing non-partisan reconstruction programmes in areas devastated by violence. Finally, a code or codes of conduct would be developed for both organisations and all security forces.[6] But this meeting did not succeed in producing peace on the ground as expected. Hardly a week had passed before violence erupted in Natal. A youth was killed in Kwa-Makutha and a further 14 IFP supporters were killed in Sweetwaters a week later.[7] The spread of violence to other parts of the country and the alleged partisanship of the police in maintaining law and order led to vocal demands for arms and self-defence by besieged communities. The ANC responded to these demands by exploring mechanisms for self-protection. The ANC contended that

... terrorism and banditry are difficult to handle, even by states with resources and relatively huge armies such as Nicaragua, Angola and Mozambique ... [and that] our weakness is not the suspension of the armed struggle as such [which it did on 6 August 1990]. The right of self-defence has not been forfeited. What is at issue is our actual capacity to implement effective military self-defence against roaming bandits who strike indiscriminately.[8]

Evolving from this argument, the organisation proposed the creation of self-defence units (SDUs),[9] stating in a document entitled *For the sake of our lives* that "in the wake of the ugly violence unleashed against our people by security forces, vigilante groups and hit squads, it is imperative that our liberation movement takes responsibility for guiding and building people's self-defence units".[10]

While this proposal was welcomed by besieged townships and squatter settlements, it was not embraced by the government. The ANC in effect won the battle over the SDUs, as reflected in the National Peace Accord (NPA)[11] which acknowledged their legitimacy. Although SDUs were established in certain areas, they suffered from important weaknesses. The ANC was unable to arm the people sufficiently and most SDUs had to fend for themselves in defending townships. Furthermore, the proposal that MK would train these units[12] undermined their impartiality and led to resentment by other political organisations. In practice, only a few MK cadres participated in the setting up of these structures, which were mainly in the hands of undisciplined local activists. Indeed, despite the euphoria surrounding the SDUs, few were created. They were set up in places such as the Vaal and Phola Park. The reason for this was intensified police harassment and the logistical problems around their creation. Even where they were created, these units did not follow the command structure as outlined in the official document. Most crucially, rather than being an asset to the resolution of violence, the SDUs increasingly became an aggravating factor as activists held townships hostage.

As the SDU plan failed to make a difference, violence took a more ferocious turn with further flare-ups during moments of major political events. The sophisticated way in which attacks were conducted and the accompanying high levels of secrecy, the indiscriminate nature of the attacks which shifted to commuter trains, shebeens, funerals and other mass gathering places, ultimately sparked suspicions of a third force within ANC circles. These suspicions were further strengthened by what the organisation believed to be police complicity and omission in favour of IFP supporters. It was against this background that the ANC issued an ultimatum to the government on 3 April 1991, threatening to suspend further discussions regarding the all-party conference and all exchanges with the government on the future constitution of the country, if by 9 May 1991 it had not met the following demands:

• The banning of dangerous weapons in public places
• The dismissal of Ministers Adriaan Vlok and General Magnus Malan

- The visible public dismantling and disarming of all special counter-insurgency units such as the Askaris, Battalion 32, the CCB, Koevoet, the Z Squad, and the establishment of a multi-party commission to oversee this process
- The immediate suspension from duty of all police officers implicated in the massacre at Sebokeng on 22 March 1990 and the commencement of legal proceedings against them
- The immediate suspension from duty of all the police officers and constables responsible for the shootings in Daveyton, Benoni, on 24 March 1991, pending a commission of inquiry into that incident
- The satisfactory assurance that in future the SAP, the South African Defence Force (SADF) and other security organs would employ acceptable and civilised methods of crowd control
- A ban on the issue of live ammunition to the police on such occasions
- The phasing out of hostels and other labour compounds and their transformation into family units and single-occupancy flats
- The establishment of an independent commission of inquiry to receive, investigate and report on all complaints of misconduct by the police and other security services.

Besides seeking to stem the violence, the ANC's strategic objectives were to stop Buthelezi from exploiting the violence for political gains and to attempt to organise and recruit new members. The ANC also sought to recapture some of the political initiative from De Klerk and to correct the growing impression locally and abroad that Pretoria controlled the negotiation process. Further, it wanted to demonstrate its political muscle in the township in the run-up to its July 1991 conference. Given the efforts by the ANC to forge a united front with other anti-apartheid organisations and the preceding preliminary discussions with the PAC in Harare on this matter, the ultimatum won broader support from those organisations that wanted a tougher position in negotiations.[13]

While 9 May came and went without the ANC's demands being met, and mass protests nowhere in sight as the ANC threatened, the government nevertheless responded in important ways to the ultimatum. Both Ministers Vlok and Malan offered to resign if they were stumbling blocks to the process of negotiation. On 16 April 1991 Vlok announced a ban on the carrying of pangas, bush knives and axes in conflict situations, although he refused to include traditional weapons – shields, sticks, knobkerries and spears. On 18 April De Klerk announced plans for a two-day summit on violence, as well as the establishment of a standing commission of inquiry (which came to be known as the Goldstone Commission of Inquiry) to investigate, combat and identify the perpetrators of politically inspired violence and intimidation.[14]

While the ANC welcomed the idea of a standing commission, it nevertheless opposed the conference on violence because it was called unilaterally by the government, thereby giving the impression that the government was a mediator and not a participant. Countering these initiatives, the ANC sponsored and promoted peace initiatives taken by church and business leaders who set themselves to develop a code of conduct for the security forces and for political organisations, and to develop an enforcement mechanism to monitor the implementation of these codes. They also decided to develop a programme of reconstruction. This position was endorsed by the ANC's national conference in Durban in July 1991.[15] But these efforts remained in suspense as violence resurfaced. The press provided documentary evidence about the involvement of certain agents within the state's security system in the spiralling wave of violence. Visual material provided by the state's television network on police inactivity or "collusion" with armed bands also existed. Yet the government responded with denials and absolution. At the same time the government argued that "we do not have enough police to act against the violence" and that "police were afraid to tackle these huge violent bands". In some cases misleading statements were made about the prosecution of perpetrators of violence.[16]

It was only late in the day and after many lives had been lost that concrete evidence about the state's role in violence and destabilisation was divulged.[17] On 19 July 1991 the *Weekly Mail* published police documents detailing how R250 000 was paid into an IFP bank account by the police for rallies held in November 1989 and March 1990. These revelations, which came to be known as the Inkathagate scandal, led to further revelations and an admission, for the first time, by the government of its collusion with the IFP and other organisations opposed to the ANC. It was revealed that about R5 million was paid to the IFP's United Workers Union of South Africa (UWUSA) and over R100 million was given to parties opposed to SWAPO in Namibia in the run-up to the 1990 elections. In addition, organisations such as the Federal Independent Democratic Alliance (FIDA) of Mr Gogotya, the Eagles Youth Group and the National Student Federation also received money from the state's secret funds. The amount of money channelled into secret funds to fund secret projects suspected of inciting violence was enormous. For the year 1991/92, about R80 million was allocated for secret projects. The following six secret accounts with huge sums of money were created for this purpose:

- The Account for Special Services, created under Act 56 of 1978 and administered by the Department of Foreign Affairs
- The Foreign Affairs Special Account, created under Act 38 of 1967 and administered by the Department of Foreign Affairs
- The Security Service Special Account, created under Act 81 of 1969, also administered by the Department of Foreign Affairs
- The Information Service of South Africa Special Account, created under Act 108 of 1979, administered by the Department of Foreign Affairs
- The South African Police Special Account, created under Act 74 of 1985
- The Special Defence Account, created under Act 6 of 1974 and administered by the Department of Defence[18]

The revelations of the Inkathagate scandal embarrassed the government and tarnished the image of the IFP, sparking condemnation by other political parties. The demand by the ANC to oust Malan and Vlok was acceded to when De Klerk removed the two ministers and relegated them to junior ministerial positions. Malan vacated his defence post to become Minister of Water Affairs in the House of Assembly, while Vlok parted with his law and order post to become Minister of Correctional Services and the Budget. De Klerk's image as an honest politician had been dented and attempts to absolve himself failed to redress the damage. Foreign countries in the process of reconsidering sanctions suspended their intended rewards for De Klerk's bold reform initiatives.

In contrast to public outcry, the ANC's response to the Inkathagate scandal was cautious. While it called for a consumer boycott in the PWV region, the organisation restrained itself from taking full advantage of this momentum to deepen the crisis. Although calls for the resignation of De Klerk came from within its ranks, the ANC used the Inkathagate scandal to rally support behind its demand for an interim government. For the first time, a majority of the parties rallied together with the ANC in their call for an interim government to supervise the transition to democracy. Still reeling from the damage of the scandal and operating from a position of isolation, the government also began talking about the need for transitional arrangements.

While the Inkathagate scandal put a halt to the spread of violence, this was short-lived as factional fighting, train killings and attacks on civilians soon resumed. About 583 incidents of violence with 128 deaths were reported in July 1991, the month in which the revelations were made.[19]

Apart from strengthening the ANC's demand for an interim government, the scandal was equally important in rallying internal parties behind the search for peace. This was reflected in the high level of interest shown in the peace initiative already taken by church and business leaders, which paved the way to the signing of the NPA on 14 September 1991 in Johannesburg.[20] While the NPA was a product of multi-party negotiations, its provisions were still subject to existing laws, rules, procedures and budgetary constraints of the country.[21] They did not replace existing bilateral agreements between the ANC and the government, such as the Pretoria Minute. Nor was the question of MK dealt with in the accord, because it formed the subject of the Working Group under the Pretoria Minute.[22]

In an attempt to implement the provisions of the accord, the ANC in its turn created the Operations Committee which coordinated the work of the Tripartite Alliance. Further subcommittees of the operations committee were created: a complaints office to coordinate complaints from the alliance against other parties in terms of the accord, and an organising committee of ANC/COSATU/SACP organisers to play a role in setting up Local Dispute Resolution Committees (LDRCs), Regional Dispute Resolution Committees (RDRC) and Joint Working Committees. The Joint Working Committees, when established, were to take over the following functions of the operations committees:[23]

- Giving political leadership
- Exposing the perpetrators of violence
- Pursuing legal methods of dealing with the violence
- Ensuring disciplined self-defence
- Coordinating reconstruction and development
- Ensuring that head offices of the alliance partners consulted the regions

Notwithstanding the ANC's resolve to implement the provisions of the NPA, the latter made little impact on the ground. Violence continued as if nothing had happened. Despite the fact that an RDRC was established in Natal/Kwazulu under the chairmanship of Roman Catholic Archbishop Denis Hurley, assisted by Mr M.C. Pretorius, and despite the fact that this structure endeavoured to establish LDRCs in areas such as Umlazi (7 January 1992), there appeared to be no end in sight to the killing in the region.[24] As Mpho Scott commented, the NPA was a good document, but it was not able to halt the killing spree.[25] Except for the relative successes of the Mpumalanga peace initiatives, violent attacks continued in conflict areas such as Bruntville, Richmond, Empangeni, Ozwathini-Maphumulo, Port Shepstone, Bulwer and Wembezi near Estcourt. During September 1992 a total of 65 people were killed in Natal alone.[26] In the PWV region, another area ravaged by violence, LDRCs were established in areas such as Alexandra (where other efforts were made, such as the creation of the Alexandra Peace Forum) and Soweto (headed by Charles Nupen). Problems existed in the setting up of these structures, notably the continued friction between local ANC and IFP leaders. Even where these committees were established, many local leaders were also involved in CODESA committees. This deprived the LDRCs of the attention they deserved. The campaign to publicise the work of the NPA did not reach the intended audience and few people knew where to find their offices or the people involved in its structures to whom they could report cases of violence.

The ANC's PWV REC also established the Violence Monitoring Committee.[27] The committee, which preceded the signing of the NPA, had no meaningful powers to impact upon the spiralling wave of violence. It was simply a monitoring mechanism which provided advice to affected communities on the formation of SDUs, visited areas before and after the eruption of violence, visited the next of kin of victims and attended or addressed funerals of victims, as well as contacting the police concerning the threat or outbreak of violence.[28]

By the end of 1992 it was evident that the signing of the NPA had had no effect on the of violence in the country. Violence continued unabated in the surrounding townships and shack settlements, and train killing became more vicious. The Goldstone Commission of Inquiry was formed to look into the Thokoza massacre, the Bruntville violence, train massacres (in particular, the Nancefield train attacks), taxi wars and the President Steyn Mine killings on 3 November 1991, and to find ways to prevent public violence and intimidation. This, however, did not stop the violence. Most frustrating was the fact that even when the ANC made a public outcry and forwarded voluminous evidence of alleged agent provocateurs, the government and its security apparatus responded with denials and criticism instead of acting on the information provided. While the provisions of the NPA were hailed as a breakthrough because of their potential to eliminate violence, those who held the resources to make it work would be the decisive catalyst. The government was reluctant to blow life into the accord by providing necessary funds, and its security forces were not keen to operate by the established rules. Reg Mason, former Chairperson of the Border/Ciskei RDRC, cited the lack of funds as one of his reasons for resigning. Dr Antonie Gildenhuys, Chairperson of the National Peace Secretariat, was also worried by the government's lack of interest in the accord, saying that he found it

> ... a matter of great concern that political consensus at CODESA on a range of issues can be reached; a referendum mobilising thousands of people and costing millions can be put together in the space of a few weeks – and yet so little is done to ensure the success of the Accord, which can deliver long-lasting peace, growth and prosperity for all South Africans.[29]

The ANC's dilemma with regard to the accord's provisions for policing was that while it (the ANC) accused the police of allegedly taking part in the fanning of violence, it was forced to rely on them. Despite the proposed police boards and the code of conduct for the police, it was the police who in the final analysis had the power to make the difference in the maintenance of peace.[30] Furthermore, the accord's failure to reach agreement on the question of cultural weapons and the government's refusal to treat them as dangerous weapons, meant that IFP followers were given the sanction to display these weapons in public and to continue with acts of provocation. That a person could carry a spear or a handgun onto a commuter train with the police refusing to act because the accord and the law did not see this as a possible incitement to violence, created a mockery of the entire peace process. The belated ban on cultural weapons also did not stimulate the security forces to disarm IFP followers.

Despite the ANC's identification of hostels as the primary source of violence, its lack of material resources and the power to effect its decisions meant that it was unable to impact upon the ongoing violence. Protests to the government on the issue, as well as bilateral agreements, simply went unheeded while mass demonstrations and marches to notorious hostels such as the Kwa-Madalas in Boipatong and Alexandra were thwarted by a heavy police presence. It was only in the case of the train killings that initiatives by the ANC and other democratic organisations actually produced positive results. Already in the first three months of 1992, a total of 126 people had been killed in the trains. This exceeded the total of 97 deaths recorded in 1990 and 1991.[31] The rise of the death toll to 260 in May of that year prompted an unprecedented mass boycott of commuter trains on the Reef. Organised by the ANC, SACP, COSATU, PAC, National Council of Trade Unions (NACTU), the Civic Association of Southern Transvaal (CAST) and the Institute of Contextual Theology, the boycott lasted for a week and cost Spoornet an estimated R78 000.[32] The boycott, which was preceded by and carried along with activities including a sit-in and picket at Spoornet offices and prayer services, was significant in pressuring Spoornet and the SAP into an accord to provide security to train commuters. The Train Peace Accord, which was signed on 14 May 1992, obliged the SAP to deploy more police in the Witwatersrand and Soweto regions. Spoornet was obliged to prohibit dangerous weapons on trains, to educate the public against carrying danger-ous weapons, to erect a permanent screening system at all railway stations, to erect fences around stations and to consider installing television cameras on trains and the employment of guards. The demand for the compensation of victims of train violence was, however, rejected by Spoornet.

While the scale of train killings declined during the week of the boycott, a few days after the signing of the accord the police failed to arrest or at least curb IFP followers who boarded a train from Germiston (heading for Kempton Park and CODESA II) with an assortment of weapons. Notwith-standing this, the boycott and the accord on train killings contributed to a significant reduction of violence at least for the following months. But there was nothing to demonstrate that it, like other previous agreements, could not be subverted by the lack of commitment of those who had the power and resources to make it work. What was specifically significant was that Spoornet incurred losses as a result of the boycott and this propelled it to exert pressure on the government to help stop the carnage on the trains. Spoornet also took strong measures to implement the provisions of the accord because its business was at stake. But the success of the train accord did not enjoy publicity as it came to be subsumed by renewed ferocious violence which surfaced in townships such as Alexandra, where agent provocateurs and statements by some IFP leaders, such as Musa Muyeni, about unfounded impending attacks left such areas in a state of agitation. The cycle of killings which followed funeral after funeral in Alexandra, the abduction and murder of activists in the Vaal, the mysterious hit-squad shootings and the revenge killings between township residents, hostel dwell-ers and squatters in Soweto and the East Rand, as well as the army onslaught on the settlement of Phola Park in 1992, showed that violence was out of control.

At its policy conference on 28–31 May 1992 the ANC decided to embark on a mass action campaign against violence. The aim of the campaign was to expose the government's alleged complicity in the violence by focusing public attention on police and army death squads, covert and third-force operations, the killings on the trains and in taxis, as well as the revelation of the involvement of top government officials in these operations. The sig-nificance of this campaign reinforced and gave further impetus to the revelations made by newspapers such as the *Weekly Mail, New Nation* and *Vrye Weekblad* and affidavits before the courts and the Goldstone Commis-sion, as well as secret dossiers in the possession of General Bantu Holomisa of the Transkei. While the exposure campaign was crucial in putting the state under focus, it had no substantial effect in abating the violence.

It was only after coming to the conclusion that it could not devise any viable strategies against the violence (with its PWV region threatening to withdraw from the NPA) that the ANC made a firm call for the involvement of the international peace-keeping forces in the South African conflict. While this demand was raised by Mandela after the Alexandra violence, it was only after the horrific mass slaughter of innocent women and children in Boipatong on 17 June 1992 that the organisation took a firm stand on this issue.

The Boipatong massacre sparked a war of words between the ANC and the government, with the ANC charging President De Klerk with being personally involved in the violence. In its view, De Klerk's involvement in violence was corroborated by a series of events. The killings in Boipatong occurred immediately after he warned during his overseas visit that he had contingency plans to deal with the ANC's plans of mass action. He also threatened to reimpose a state of emergency. Soon after, Law and Order Minister Hernus Kriel, spokesman Captain Craig Kotze, Mangosuthu Buthelezi and Themba Khoza also warned of the possibility of violence. On 14 June "cultural weapons" and guns which had been confiscated from IFP members by the police in the full glare of publicity were secretly returned to the organisation the following day. This raised fears of possible attacks. On 16 June, the day of commemoration of the 1976 Soweto uprising, De Klerk visited Buthelezi and addressed the Kwazulu legislative assembly. The following day, innocent people were killed in Boipatong by what survivors alleged was a mission by IFP members from the nearby KwaMadala hostel accompanied by white policemen. A week later, ANC intelligence and the Goldstone Commission discovered a secret Koevoet base in Witbank whose members were reported to have also taken part in the Boipatong killings.[33]

In its July 1992 issue of *Mayibuye*, the ANC disclosed the government's two-pronged strategy called "Operation Springbok" and "Operation Thunderstorm", which it claimed sought to secure white power through methods of both negotiation and violence. To add salt to the wound, the Goldstone Commission submitted, at the start of an investigation into the Boipatong massacre, that the government had failed to respond to almost all the recommendations the commission had made so far on the question of violence. These recommendations included the banning of the public display of weapons, the fencing and upgrading of hostels and the continuous presence of the police, the withdrawal of Battalion 32 from the townships, and the granting of protection to witnesses appearing before the commission.[34]

It was against this background and the conclusion that the government was involved in the violence, with the IFP being "used as an extension of the system", that the ANC decided to withdraw from CODESA negotiations in mid-1992. A detailed memorandum was sent to the government demanding the immediate resolution of violence-related matters before negotiations could resume. This included

• an end to the campaign of terror

107

- the termination of all covert operations
- the disarming, disbanding and the confinement to barracks of all special forces made up of foreign nationals
- the suspension and prosecution of all officers and security force personnel involved in the violence
- an end to repression in some self-governing and "independent" states.

The ANC also insisted that the government implement agreements which were made the previous year on curbing violence. These included

- an immediate implementation of the programme to phase out hostels and convert them into family units[35]
- the installation of fences around these establishments
- the guarding of these buildings by the security forces on a permanent basis and monitored by multilateral peace structures
- the expulsion of those who occupied the hostels illegally
- regular searches of hostels with the participation of multilateral peace structures
- the banning of the carrying of all dangerous weapons in public on all occasions, including cultural weapons.

Further demands were made that the government agree to the establishment of an international commission of inquiry into the Boipatong massacre and all acts of violence, as well as international monitoring of violence, the release of all political prisoners and the repeal of all repressive legislation, including those laws which were hastily passed into law during the last days of the 1992 parliamentary session.

Besides its memorandum to the government, the ANC also made strenuous efforts to bring international involvement into the South African crisis. Its efforts, taken with the PAC, saw the convocation of the Organisation of African Unity (OAU) and the United Nations' (UN) Security Council on 15–16 July 1992, culminating in the passing of Resolution 765, which obliged the South African government to end the violence and create conditions for the resumption of negotiations. The UN emergency meeting on the South African question also resolved to send a special representative of the General Secretary (Cyrus Vance was appointed) to study the situation and help the parties in their efforts to end the violence and resume negotiations. While the UN intervention was important, it fell short of meeting the ANC's expectations. Despite unanimous criticism of the government during the UN debate, the final resolution was so drastically modified, particularly at the instance of Britain, that it was more favourable to the government than to the ANC. While it did not directly demand an international monitoring force, the ANC had hoped that international outrage against the Boipatong massacre would *ipso facto* result in a meaningful role for the UN in South Africa. By placing the ball in the court of South African parties and arguing that only they could resolve the crisis, the UN clearly supported the government's view that the crisis was parochial and could only be resolved by talks between the ANC and the IFP. The lukewarm approach by the UN to the South African crisis clearly meant that the ANC had no viable alternative except mass action to pressurise the government to address violence-related matters.

Although the government addressed some of the ANC's demands when it announced the disbandment of Battalions 31, 32 and Koevoet, a ban on dangerous weapons and the upgrading of hostels, it was clear that the decision was prompted by the need to provide Foreign Minister Pik Botha with ammunition to counter and dilute ANC criticism during the UN debate. These measures contained nothing new. Soldiers serving in the regiments that were to be disbanded were to be redeployed in other SADF structures, raising fears about the difficulty of monitoring and controlling them. It was not the first time dangerous weapons had been banned, and in the past this had not led to any action by the police against those wielding them. The fact that such a ban was restricted to "unrest areas" seemed to sanction their legal use in other, non-unrest areas. The decision to upgrade hostels was also not new. Since 1991, the government had failed to implement this decision, arguing that it could only start to upgrade hostels with the consent of the ANC, the IFP and hostel residents.

Notwithstanding efforts to internationalise the South African crisis, the killings continued. According to the Human Rights Commission report, *Three years of destabilisation*, a total of 9325 people were killed between July 1990 and June 1993. Even when negotiations resumed in 1993, and despite the fact that the media took a deliberate step to remove violence-related news from the headlines, the carnage continued unhampered. In the East Rand townships of Katlehong, Thokoza and Vosloorus, ANC and IFP members clashed, setting in motion a cycle of violence which was to continue into 1994. According to the Human Rights Commission, a total of 1318 people were killed in these townships in the first ten months of 1993.[36] Violence assumed a pattern of ANC versus IFP, or community versus IFP hostel residents. People were abducted, maimed and killed, while others got caught in what was becoming crime-related violence. The shooting and wounding of Radio Metro DJ, Trevor Tshabalala, bore testimony to this new development.

The controversial role of the Internal Stability Unit of the SAP in maintaining law and order in the townships and indeed the infighting within the SDUs also worsened the carnage. Except for the East Rand townships and some parts of Natal, violence in other townships subsided considerably towards the end of 1992 and the beginning of 1993. In the Vaal townships, where it had continued since the Boipatong massacre, violence came to an end after the death in detention of the "Vaal monster", Victor Khethisi Kheswa, who was alleged to have masterminded almost all the massacres in the area. The revelation that he was a member of the IFP and the World Apartheid Movement suggested for the first time a clear pattern that certain organised forces were behind the carnage wrecking the townships. At the same time a new pattern of eliminating ANC leaders emerged with the assassination of the ANC leader and SACP Secretary-General, Chris Hani, in April 1993. Plans to assassinate, among others, Joe Slovo, Tokyo Sexwale, Peter Mokaba, Winnie Mandela and Matthews Phosa were also revealed. While their assassinations were not carried out, a number of MK members and security personnel of ANC leaders were killed. Starting with the killing of Walter Sisulu's bodyguard, the bodyguards of Winnie Mandela, Jacob Zuma and Obed Bapela were also either killed or attacked.

It was in view of this ceaseless wave of violence that a peace campaign initiative was taken in September 1993. Beginning with the observation of a moment of silence at noon on 2 September, the campaign was a success in that for the first time people poured into the streets to pledge their support for peace. But while this was given public profile, it nevertheless did not succeed in stopping the killings on the ground, which were becoming even more ugly with the Azanian People's Liberation Army's (APLA) attacks on white civilians and right-wing violence against blacks.

Rather than being a product of societal change, as Huntington suggests in his *Political order in changing societies*,[37] violence in South Africa seemed to be orchestrated to effect a particular outcome. But its uncontrollable escalation highlighted an important gap in the ANC's approach to the transition process. Entering negotiations without a mutually binding ceasefire stripped and exposed the organisation to the sort of challenges the violence had created. It also implicitly allowed the state and reactionary forces to continue in their war against the ANC and to undermine the negotiation process. Their alleged complicity in violence vindicated what O'Donnell and Schmitter concluded in their study of transitions to democracy, that forces previously involved in repression have the propensity to either block or undermine the transition process.[38] Moreover, the lack of trust between the main negotiating partners worked, as Larry Diamond observed,[39] to the detriment of successful negotiations.

In conclusion, the ANC's organisational reconstruction in South Africa was an enormous task. An organisational structure with regions and branches had to be built to allow smooth administration and participation of members in the decision-making process. Relations with allied organisations such as the UDF, COSATU and the SACP had to be developed to enable cooperation on various matters. Policies on a range of issues also had to be developed to give direction to the organisation's vision of a future democratic South Africa. Undertaking these tasks was not easy and under conditions of heightened violence, proved very daunting. However, like organisational reconstruction, the other challenge the ANC had to deal with was entering into negotiations with other parties over the future of the country. The following section will provide a critical analysis of the ANC and negotiations.

ENDNOTES

1. This position was strengthened by the findings of the International Commission of Jurists which blamed Inkatha for the violence. See *Sowetan*, 30 March 1992.

2. Mapheto, A. The violence: a view from the ground. *Work In Progress*, 69, September 1990, 5–8. Mapheto was the regional organiser of the ANC's PWV region during 1990–1991.

3. 'Dealing with terrorism'. *Mayibuye*, December 1990.

4. 'Keeping a watchful eye on the peace-keepers'. *Work In Progress*, 69, September 1990, 17.

5. Tjonneland, E.N. *Negotiating apartheid away? Constitution-making, transition politics and conditions for democracy in South Africa.* International Peace Research Institute, Oslo, 1990, 29.

6. 'The ANC/IFP Agreement'. *Mayibuye*, March 1991, 21.

7. Bhagowat, C. After the Peace Accord: conflict continues in Kwa-Makhutha. *Work In Progress*, 73, 1991, 8.

8. Ibid., 26–27.

9. The call was announced by Nelson Mandela in his address to the Soweto mass funeral (drawing 50 000 people) for the victims of violence. See 'MK defence units for the Reef'. *New Nation*, 21–27 September 1990.

10. *For the sake of our lives: guidelines for the creation of self-defence units*, 2.

11. Point 7 entitled 'Self-protection units' of Chapter 3 (General Provisions for Security Forces) of the National Peace Accord stated that "the law accords all individuals the right to protect themselves and their property and to establish voluntary or self-protection units in any neighbourhood to prevent crime and to protect any invasion of the lawful rights of such communities".

12. 'The case for self defence units'. Ronnie Kasrils, interviewed by Devan Pillay. *Work In Progress* 77, September 1991, 19.

13. 'ANC shock therapy'. *Front File*, Southern Africa Brief, 5(4), April 1991, 2.

14. 'ANC ultimatum to the government'. *South African Barometer*, 5(8), 26 April 1991, 121.

15. See "Resolution on violence" in the Report of the ANC National Conference, July 1991, issued by the Department of Information and Publicity, 1991, 28.

16. 'Peace and the police'. Interview with General Johan van der Merwe, the SAP's Commissioner of Police. *Mayibuye*, October 1991, 12.

17. This does not mean that there was no concrete evidence before. It means that this latter evidence was such that the government could no longer absolve itself through denials.

18. *South African Barometer*, 5(16), 16 August 1991.

19. *South African Barometer*, 5(16), 16 August 1991, 244.

20. Signatories to the accord included the following organisations: the ANC, SACP, COSATU, IFP, UWUSA, Kwazulu Government, National Party, South African Government, QwaQwa Government, Dikwankwetla Party (QwaQwa), Lebowa Government, United People's Front (Lebowa), Kwandebele Government, Intando Yesizwe Party (Kwandebele), Kangwane Government, Inyandza National Progressive Party (Kangwane), Gazankulu Government, Ximoko Progressive Party (Gazankulu), Solidarity Party, National Forum, Labour Party of South Africa, Democratic Party and Contralesa.

21. The National Peace Convention, 14 September 1991, 4.

22. Papers of the ANC National Workshop on the National Peace Accord, held at the Johannesburger Hotel, 19 and 20 October 1991, 1.

23. Ibid., 3.

24. *Sowetan*, 20 March 1992.

25. Mpho Scott. Interview.

26. 'Between freedom and barbarism'. *Work In Progress*, 78, November 1991, 9.

27. The committee was initially comprised of Cyril Jantjies, Winnie Mandela, Bavumile Vilakazi and Tokyo Sexwale.

28. Report of the Violence Monitoring Committee. ANC PWV Regional Conference, 5–6 October 1991.

29. 'Peace accord: is it working?' *Mayibuye*, May 1992, 18.

30. Shearing, C.D. Policing transformation. *Work In Progress*, 72, 1991, 22.

31. *Sowetan*, 24 April 1992.

32. 'Six days that shook Spoornet'. *Monitor*, 1(3), 1–8 May 1992, 2.

33. *Business Day*, 26 June 1992.

34. *Sunday Times*, 5 July 1992. See also *The Star*, 7 July 1992.

35. Hostels accounted for much of the violence in the Reef townships. Of the 135 hostels in Transvaal, there were at least 30 hostels on the Reef (eight in Soweto, three in Johannesburg, three in the Vaal townships, one in Krugersdorp, two in Alexandra, three in Tembisa, one in Daveyton, one in Benoni, one in Brakpan, three in Thokoza, one in Katlehong, two in Vosloorus and one in Kwa-Thema). See 'Hostels to continue as central focus of political conflict',

Business Day, 26 June 1992; also 'Blame it on the hostels flash-points for too long', *Weekly Mail,* 26 June – 2 July 1992.

36. *Business Day,* 6 January 1994.

37. Huntington, S. *Political order in changing societies.* New Haven: Yale University Press, 1968, 357.

38. O'Donnell, G. & Schmitter, P. *Transition from authoritarian rule: tentative conclusions about uncertain democracies.* Baltimore/London: John Hopkins University Press, 1986, 28–29.

39. Diamond, L. 'Beyond authoritarianism and totalitarianism: strategies for democratisation'. *The Washington Quarterly,* Winter, 1989, 144.

Section B

The African National Congress and the negotiated trajectory to power in the 1990s

This section will analyse factors behind the ANC's decision to negotiate and the organisation's approach to negotiations. It will also analyse the movement towards the conclusion of a negotiated settlement, the election campaign and the installation of the Government of National Unity.

Factors behind the ANC's decision to negotiate

5

The road to negotiations cannot be seen in isolation from the overall struggle against apartheid. In fact, the history of the ANC is one of a decades-old struggle against white colonial domination and oppression since the arrival of white settlers in 1652. The ANC's decision to negotiate with the South African government should therefore be understood against the background of the various forms of colonial domination, the ANC's resistance and the consequent deepening of the conflict between the parties. Without delving too much into this history, this chapter will analyse the factors behind the ANC's decision to negotiate. It will focus on the armed struggle, its successes and limitations. It will also analyse the impact of Nelson Mandela's personal initiative in negotiations, pressures on the ANC to negotiate, as well as the dynamics of internal mass struggles, including the political and diplomatic achievements of the organisation.

The armed struggle – from propaganda warfare to people's war

The ANC was formed in 1912 against the background and in continuation of the memorable wars fought by African chiefs in defence of the land against colonial conquest.[1] Wars such as those led by the valiant Sekhukhuni, Moshoeshoe, Dingaan, Makhado, Ngungunyane and Magigwane served as an inspiration in the overall struggle against white domination. However, the defeat of the Bambata rebellion in 1906 marked the end of the first phase of struggle and set the stage for the handing over of the administration of the country to the local whites in 1910. Notwithstanding the defeat and the formation of the Union of South Africa, the war did not come to an end. Instead it transformed itself into a protracted struggle as national consciousness gained ground and primary organisations of the people developed. The formation of the ANC in 1912 crystallised this nascent consciousness into a formidable national ideology and brought to an end tribal sectionalism and strife. The convenor of the inaugural conference for the formation of the ANC, Pixly Ka Isaka Seme, said in his historic message:

... The aberration of the Xhosa-Fingo feud, the animosity that existed between the Zulus and the Tsongas, between Basutos and every other native must be buried and forgotten, it has shed among us sufficient blood. We are one people. These divisions, these jealousies, are the cause of all our woes and of all our backwardness and ignorance today.[2]

Although the presence of the chiefs within the ANC reflected the continuity of the struggle for power and the return of the land (an issue which was to be central in the struggle following the passing of the Land Act in 1912), the predominance of people from middle-class social backgrounds (priests, teachers, etc.) consequently diluted the militancy of the organisation and propelled it into moderation. Writing petitions and sending deputations to the authorities were to assume centrality in the overall conduct of the struggle until the 1940s.

For 37 years, that is until 1949, the ANC adhered strictly to constitutional struggles in the belief that African grievances could be settled through peaceful discussion.[3] However, these constitutional methods of struggle were rendered obsolete as the state hastened to construct an apartheid regime using in the process multipronged strategies, including coercion, to batter black political demands. Utter intransigence and brute force became the mark of its response to black aspirations. In the end, the apartheid framework and the approach adopted by the state left no room for black political activity except in precipitating their organisations towards a militant disposition. By developing mass workers and township struggles, culminating in the 1946 miners' strike, and establishing the militant nationalist (ANC) Youth League in 1943, the ANC manifested its inclination towards a new mode of political action. When members of the Youth League won seats in the ANC National Executive Committee and Walter Sisulu, a worker, was elected as the secretary-general, the class composition of leadership of the organisation altered, with workers assuming a more dominant role.[4]

A programme of action drafted by the Youth League was adopted by the ANC in 1949, jettisoning old forms of struggle in favour of the militant ones. Mass defiance of apartheid laws, stay-at-homes, boycotts, demonstrations, picketing and marches that were to dominate the 1950s became the main characteristics of a new resistance strategy based on the Gandhian principle of non-violence. The fruits of these struggles were marked by the formation of the Congress of the People (comprised of the ANC, the Congress of Democrats, the South African Indian Congress and the South African Coloured People's Organisation), culminating in the historic drafting of the Freedom Charter in Kliptown on 25 and 26 June 1955.[5]

Formation of Umkhonto we Sizwe

Despite the peaceful campaign against apartheid in the 1950s, the state responded with vicious repression. It arrested, detained and prosecuted thousands of political activists, drowning their spirit of resistance with the 1960 Sharpeville massacre.

By banning the ANC and the Pan African Congress under the Suppression of Communism Act, it also frustrated their non-violence strategies. The chapter of peaceful resistance was therefore closed and a new chapter of frustration and indignation was opened, bringing a new array into the politics of resistance – the armed struggle. Umkhonto we Sizwe (MK), the military wing of the ANC, was formed as an independent organisation by a group of ANC and SACP leaders in December 1961 to take the organisation onto a new path of struggle.[6] Speaking from underground through the ANC's Radio Freedom, Walter Sisulu said: "In the face of violence, men struggling for freedom have had to meet violence with violence. How can it be otherwise in South Africa? Change must come. Change for the better, but not without sacrifice. My sacrifice, your sacrifice".[7]

The resort to the armed struggle was later to be defended by the ANC leader, Nelson Mandela, at the Rivonia trial where he said that "the hard facts were that 50 years of non-violence had brought the African people nothing but more and more repressive legislation, and fewer and fewer rights ... it was only when all channels of peaceful protest had been barred to us, that the decision was made to embark on violent forms of political struggle and to form Umkhonto we Sizwe".[8]

The clarion call of the MK manifesto declared that "the time comes in the life of any nation when there remain only two choices: submit or fight. That time has now come to South Africa. We shall not submit and we have no choice but to hit back by all means within our power in defence of our people, our future and our freedom".[9]

The primary objective of the armed struggle in its sabotage form was aimed at scaring the white public in the hope that they would change their minds and persuade the government to change its attitude towards blacks. But the state responded with brute force and uprooted the underground MK command cell in Rivonia, Johannesburg. Even those who escaped the clampdown in Rivonia and persisted with acts of sabotage were later arrested and prosecuted in the Fischer trial some time after the Rivonia trial.[10] The internal underground network of MK was therefore destroyed and the remaining members of the ANC were demobilised. Only a few ANC leaders, who were sent abroad, and some MK trainees in Ethiopia and Tanzania were able to revive the two organisations, but now in exile.

The decimation of MK's underground network, the Rivonia trial and the revival of the ANC and its military wing in exile saw the emergence of a different conception of the purpose of the armed struggle. Although there was a general realisation that the armed struggle on its own would not accomplish the strategic objective of the organisation, namely the transference of power, there was a parallel, if not dominant, belief that the armed struggle was the most crucial means towards this end. The ANC was henceforth referred to as a liberation movement and MK was elevated from a sabotage organisation to a fully-fledged insurgent guerrilla movement.[11] *Operation Mayibuye*, an MK planning document which was found by the police in Rivonia, stated that

... the white state has thrown overboard every pretence of rule by democratic process. Armed to the teeth it has presented the people with only one choice and that is its overthrow by force and violence. It can now truly be said that very little, if any methods exist for the smashing of white supremacy other than by means of mass revolutionary action, the main content of which is armed resistance leading to victory by military means.[12]

Joe Matthews argued that the decision to adopt the armed struggle for the overthrow of the regime involved a complete change of strategy, tactics, propaganda, organisational machinery and so on, which meant abandoning previous forms of struggle.[13] Oliver Tambo, on the 25th anniversary of the formation of MK on 16 December 1986, recalled that when they had formed the military wing they had known that they were

... striking out along a new road for the liberation of the people; that once we took that road there would be no going back; a road that was going to necessitate total dedication, self-sacrifice and a determination that knew no surrender; a road along which the commitments not to submit but to fight would have to be transformed into the uncompromising warrior pledge – victory or death![14]

But what motivated the new thinking on the armed struggle? Why did the struggle against white domination have to be advanced from merely influencing the white electorate to one that sought to seize power violently and transform South Africa into a unitary, non-racial and democratic society? The period within which the ANC adopted a militarist strategy was very important in moulding the organisation's perception of the political struggle in South Africa. The spread of the spirit of nationalism all over the African continent was awakening the oppressed and exploited black masses to break the shackles of imperialism and colonialism. The visits paid by the ANC leadership to African countries, in particular Nelson Mandela's visit to Algeria, significantly influenced their thinking on the struggle. While this milieu of Africa's yearning for Uhuru moulded a new conception within the ANC about the objective of the political struggle in South Africa, the actual strategy and prescription of the path the struggle had to pursue were shaped by the ANC's association with the SACP.

The SACP played a crucial role in theorising the nature of the political struggle in South Africa and in evolving the concept of "national democratic struggle" later to be adopted by the ANC. The concept cannot be fully comprehended without an introspection into the theory of Colonialism of a Special Type (CST), dexterously coined by the party's leading theoretician, Michael Harmel. This theory was a product of long debates within the democratic movement around issues such as the Native Republic, the Atlantic Charter and the African Claims.[15] Although an in-depth investigation into the genealogy of the theory will not be made, a sketchy outline will be attempted in order to provide an insight into the correlation between the CST theory and the national democratic revolution.

When Harmel theorised the South African society and the political struggle of the oppressed masses, most of his work was drawn from Lenin's theorisation of imperialism and colonialism. Lenin identified the conditions under which capitalist exploitation produces a loss of political autonomy for certain countries and peoples. According to him, the loss of political autonomy occurs when finance capital, in order to maintain satisfactory profit levels in an advanced capitalist economy which has become "overripe", exports capital to countries in which there is an available supply of cheap labour and raw materials. These countries are deprived of their political autonomy, that is, they are colonised in order to guarantee the supply of these commodities. Finance capital now benefits from the exploitation of two proletariats (its own and that in the colony) and as a consequence reaps what Lenin refers to as "super-profits".[16]

Applying Lenin's theory in the formulation of the CST thesis, Harmel contended that the social formation in South Africa exhibited most of the features of the relationship between a colonial power and its colony, but the relationship occurred within a single social formation, hence the term "special colonial".[17] While South Africa is a semi-independent state, black South Africa is its colony. The colonial relations are maintained by the colonists by the same mechanisms of cultural domination, political oppression and economic exploitation which, at the international level, produce the development of the advanced capitalist state through the imperialist underdevelopment of the colonial satellites. This is the central feature that characterises South Africa as a unique society.[18]

The significance of Harmel's conceptualisation of South Africa as CST was that it helped in the choice of appropriate strategies. According to Harmel, the unique colonialism of South Africa necessitated an amended theory of struggle. Reacting against the claim by some Marxists in South Africa that class struggle should be the primary mode of challenging colonial oppression and exploitation, he contended that the struggle in South Africa was between two blocs, black versus white. He argued that the pervasion of national consciousness across the class divide within the black nation belied the claims of class consciousness and class struggle, and opted instead for the national democratic struggle as the most appropriate form of struggle consistent with the South African reality. Although the CST theory did not specify the precise forms of struggle in advancing the notion of the national democratic struggle, the armed struggle was perceived as consonant with the general premise. Colin Bundy put it lucidly that "a theory which specified the South African social formation as a variant of colonialism naturally directed the search for models to anti-colonial struggle".[19] Logically, therefore, the launch of guerrilla warfare by MK was set within the context of other previous and current guerrilla warfare, particularly in Angola, Mozambique, Algeria, Guinea-Bissau, Sierra Leone, Cuba and China.

The CST theory and the national democratic revolution were formally adopted by the SACP in a document entitled *The road to South African freedom*

119

in 1962. The cooperation and overlapping of members of the SACP and the ANC ultimately led to the adoption of the CST thesis by the ANC, with Joe Slovo playing an important role in this regard.[20] The document *Strategy and tactics of the South African revolution* officially adopted by the ANC in 1969, setting out the four strategies of the organisation, was drafted by Slovo as a shortened version of the party's programme.[21] The Morogoro conference held in 1969 finally concretised the ANC's option of military strategies to overthrow the state. In the above document guerrilla warfare was declared to be the special, and indeed in the case of South Africa the only, form in which armed liberation struggle could be launched. Learning from the lessons of the Luthuli Brigade, the conference warned that guerrilla warfare was not to be conducted in a vacuum and stressed the primacy of the political struggle.[22]

Slovo was to make the same point at a later stage when objecting to Debray's approach. He contended that Debray in *Revolution in the revolution* tended to proceed from the proposition that the most important form of propaganda is military action to a conclusion that in most of Latin America the creation of militarily skilled guerrilla foci is sufficient to bring about favourable conditions for an eventual military victory by the people. Slovo berated Debray for underrating the vital connection between the guerrilla struggle (which in the early stages must of necessity be of a limited magnitude) and other forms of militant mass activity. He criticised Debray for treating the foci as the main revolutionary nuclei which should assume overall political and military leadership and which had to cut themselves off from the local population. Contrary to Debray's thesis, Slovo contended that there were many indications, including the increasing devotion of resources to mass illegal propaganda throughout South Africa, that the ANC's approach on this important question was different.[23]

The Morogoro conference paid serious attention to the unfavourable conditions under which guerrilla warfare was to be executed inside South Africa. As early as the formation of MK, its military planning document, *Operation Mayibuye*, cautioned that "we have no illusions about the difficulties which face us in launching and successfully prosecuting guerrilla operations leading to military victory. Nor do we assume that such a struggle will be over swiftly".[24] The document highlighted the following problems:

- They were faced with a powerful armed modern state with tremendous industrial resources which could at least in the initial period count on the support of three million whites.
- The people were unarmed and lacked personnel who were trained in all aspects of military operations.
- The absence of friendly borders and long-scale impregnable natural bases from which to operate were both disadvantages.

Notwithstanding the above, however, the ANC argued at the Morogoro conference that there were more favourable than unfavourable conditions for guerrilla warfare. Guerrilla warfare, it was argued, almost by definition presents a situation in which there is a vast imbalance of material and military resources between the opposite sides. It is designed to cope with the situation in which the enemy is infinitely superior in relation to every conventional factor of warfare. It is par excellence the weapon of the materially weak against the materially strong. The survival of the people's army is assured by the skilful exercise of tactics. Surprise, mobility and tactical retreat should make it difficult for the enemy to bring into play its superior firepower in any decisive battles. No individual battle is fought in circumstances favourable to the enemy. Superior forces can thus be harassed, weakened and, in the end, destroyed.[25] The struggle by the masses and their gallant preparedness to engage the regime in violent confrontation were seen as proof of the ripened consciousness among the oppressed to fight. Arguing against the precondition of a physical environment propitious for successful guerrilla warfare, Slovo contended that

> ... guerrilla warfare can, and has been, waged in every conceivable type of terrain, in deserts, in swamps, in farm fields, in built up areas, in plains, in the bush and in countries without friendly borders. The question is one of adjusting survival tactics to the sort of terrain in which operations have to be carried out.[26]

A precise blueprint for future military activity was not provided in *Strategy and tactics*. It was only elaborated in the early 1980s in MK's publication, *Dawn*. Writing on this military strategy, Hough outlined that it was envisaged that the sequence of revolutionary warfare in South Africa would evolve in stages, starting with guerrilla warfare, which would involve "hit-and-run" tactics coupled with armed propaganda. It was hoped that this would lead to the reduction of enemy personnel and material through sabotage. Guerrilla warfare would be followed by the "stage of equilibrium" in which it would evolve into mobile warfare where bigger guerrilla units armed with advanced weapons would be formed. This would allow lightning attacks to be launched against the enemy. The last stage was the "stage of offensive", which would see offensive attacks. At this stage, it was expected that South Africa would be internationally isolated, the economy exhausted and the security forces demoralised. This would enable the establishment of liberated zones in the rural areas and the encirclement of the cities.[27]

Although it is not clear whether the ANC did intend to go this far, a number of guerrilla warfare models such as the Maoist, Guevara-Debray, Marighella and the mass insurrection models were available as possible options.[28] Nevertheless, despite all military plans and the availability of these types of models in its military arsenal, the execution of the guerrilla programme in the early 1970s started on a pessimistic note. Firstly, complications and hurdles emerged in the ANC's attempts to infiltrate MK cadres back into South Africa. Secondly, the movement's arch ally, ZAPU, collapsed owing to an internal feud, thus complicating the ANC's mission. Thirdly, the final ANC expedition into Rhodesia (which followed the foiled Wankie Campaign) ended prematurely with the ambush of Flag Boshielo and two others while they were crossing the Zambezi River from Zambia.

With the failure of armed infiltration by MK soldiers into South Africa, the ANC had to resort to other options. Lodge writes that between 1970 and 1975 the known attempts by the ANC at infiltration took the form of efforts to enter South Africa at official border points using forged identification documents.[29] In the course of the 1970s ANC members were, however, able to enter the country using other routes. The independence of Mozambique and Angola in 1975 opened opportunities for the ANC to infiltrate and establish bases inside the country. In addition, the cordial relationship forged with the Soviet Union, strengthened by the ANC's association with the SACP, ensured continued support in terms of funds, equipment, training, as well as diplomatic accommodation. The outbreak of the workers' strikes in 1973 and the Soweto uprising in 1976 saw a number of South African youths crossing the borders to join the movement in exile. The influx of the Soweto activists (heroically named the June 16 detachment within the MK hierarchy) enabled the ANC to establish itself inside the country on a hitherto unprecedented scale. Recounting the significance of the June 16 detachment, Oliver Tambo said that

> ... in the decade since the Soweto Uprising Umkhonto we Sizwe has become entrenched inside our country. Combat operations have dramatically increased in number, in daring, audacity and sophistication. Our combatants, by our operations, have wrenched away the mask of invincibility that the enemy sought to wear. Inspiration and hope and the certainty of victory today surge through the veins of the masses of our people.[30]

MK's presence inside the country coincided with, and in some instances was instrumental in the development of people's organisations. Armed incursions and the arrest and prosecution of MK combatants helped build the army's image in the minds of the people. This was critical in reinforcing people's struggles against the state, either in the form of resistance to rent increases, undemocratic local authorities or the anti-apartheid struggle in general. It was the intensification of these struggles inside the country that was to bring about a change of thinking within the ANC. Talk about concepts such as "people's war" and the advocacy of "arming the people" became increasingly salient. Although MK succeeded in making itself felt within the country through escalating attacks on specific targets, it did not adhere to the prescriptions enunciated at the Morogoro conference. Much more effort was focused on military attacks than on building the political underground, except in isolated cases such as the Transkei. Lodge contends, however, that such sabotage attacks functioned to promote the conditions under which political organisation could take place.[31]

"Mayihlome" – the ANC towards people's war

The concept of a people's war, which emerged from the ANC's consultative conference at Kabwe in 1985, signalled the departure of the liberation movement from guerrilla warfare to mass insurrection involving the strug-gling masses on the ground. The concept had developed in the period preceding the conference, influenced by the heroic struggles waged by the masses inside the country. Already reservations were being expressed about protracted guerrilla warfare as the only form of the armed struggle. These reservations were further deepened with the study tour by a high-level delegation of the ANC leadership to Vietnam in 1978. The Vietnamese experience confirmed the belief that the armed struggle had to be based on, and grow out of mass political support, eventually involving all the people. All military activities had to be guided and determined by the need to generate political mobilisation, organisation and resistance.[32] Adopting this approach, the ANC decided to focus its attention on building an under-ground political network to mobilise and organise the masses. From then onwards, MK cadres infiltrating into the country were directed to execute this task instead of concentrating solely on sabotage.

The concept of a people's war involving the people on the ground received encouraging support in the debate among members of the libera-tion movement. But before a formal position could be taken the Vaal uprising erupted in September 1984, setting the stage for continued mass violent action against the state throughout many parts of the country. When the ANC finally assembled at Kabwe, Zambia for its second consultative conference on 16 June 1985, its decision on a people's war was to be highly influenced by these developments. In opening the Kabwe conference and arguing the case for MK to establish mass revolutionary bases among the masses, Oliver Tambo said that

> ... as a result of the strength and tenacity of the people's offensive many
> areas in our country are emerging, perhaps in a rudimentary way, as
> such mass revolutionary bases. The people are engaged in active struggle
> as a conscious revolutionary force and accept the ANC as their vanguard
> movement. They are organised in mass democratic organisations. They
> have destroyed the enemy's local organs of government and have
> mounted an armed offensive against the racist regime, using whatever
> weapons are available to them. What is missing is a strong underground
> ANC presence as well as a large contingent of units of Umkhonto we
> Sizwe.[33]

The Kabwe conference took a decision to direct the revolutionary struggle towards mass insurrection. The armed struggle was not discarded, but would form a component of the broad revolutionary strategy. Strikes to jeopardise the economy were emphasised, as well as the creation of an anti-apartheid alliance and alternative local authorities. According to the people's war plan, small bands of armed youth equipped with home-made weaponry were to be formed to lead township struggles. Such bands would have to attend weekend lectures offered by MK cadres. Explaining the organisation of the revolutionary army (MK) and how it would be located inside the country to facilitate the arming of the people, Ronnie Kasrils, a senior MK member, explained that the organised advanced detachment was the nucleus of the revolutionary army. In his opinion, the trained, full-time MK combatants were central to it, but they must themselves have different specialisations and be grouped into combat units of various types:

- Guerrilla units of the countryside whose size and mode of operation would depend on the terrain. Their aim was to link up with villagers and farm labourers.

- Underground urban combat groups based in factories and other work-places, including residential areas. They might be combat groups, sabotage units and elimination squads or part-time combatants who worked by day and operated by night.

- Self-defence units, which had already begun to emerge out of necessity as the popular democratic organisations had been forced to defend themselves, their leaders, their homes, offices and meetings from the "enemy". Self-defence units could be organised by legal or underground organisations and could form the basis of a people's self-defence militia. Trained MK cadres had to merge into these people's self-defence units and lead them.[34]

The implementation of the people's war strategy was comprised of three elements: to "render South Africa ungovernable", the erection of liberated zones, and the arming of the masses. Calling on the people to render South Africa ungovernable, Oliver Tambo in his famous address said:

> ... We must begin to use our accumulated strength to destroy the organs of government of the apartheid regime. We have to undermine and weaken its control over us, exactly by frustrating its attempts to control us ... render the enemy's instruments of authority unworkable ... [and] creating conditions in which the country becomes increasingly ungovernable.[35]

The call to render South Africa ungovernable and to establish organs of people's power and liberated zones coincided with, and in some cases underlined the internal mass struggles that had been taking place at the time since the Vaal uprising. Since 1984, violent unrest had been spreading to other townships in the country. Towns and townships such as Saulsville, Phomolong, Oberholzer, Tžaneen, Ikageng, Thabong, Odendaalsrus, Clocolan, Virginia, Vryburg, Bothaville, Beaufort West, Paarl, Parys, Galeshewe, Mangaung, Somerset East, Fort Beaufort, Newtown and Cradock[36] were also joined by familiar names such as Sharpeville, Soweto, Alexandra, Langa, Sebokeng and Duduza. Mass protest marches, stay-aways, consumer boycotts, strikes, coupled with gruesome killings by "necklacing", firebombs, hand grenades and limpet mines, all aimed at strategic targets associated with the state, became the main characteristics of the apogee of the militant struggles against the state. Organs of people's power were established in townships such as Cradock, New Brighton, Lamontville, Alexandra, Mamelodi and Soweto. Village committees were also created in Sekhukhuneland and Kwandebele together with shop-steward committees on the East Rand. Writing on people's democracy, Murphy Morobe, the Assistant Publicity Secretary of the UDF, said that

> ... the rudimentary organs of people's power that have begun to emerge in South Africa (street committees, defence committees, shop-steward structures, student representative councils, parent/teacher/student associations) represent in many ways the beginning of the kind of democracy that we are striving for.[37]

While organs of people's power were established, the creation of liberation zones in the true sense of the word failed to materialise, although "no-go areas" were created in some parts of the country. But despite the absence of liberated zones, the prospect of a people's war increased in momentum with the masses being called to arm themselves against the state. According to the ANC directive, the interpretation and implementation of the war pledge "every patriot a combatant" was to be realised by the people's resort to arms and their direct or indirect participation in the armed struggle.[38] Encouraging people to take the initiative in arming themselves, the ANC through its Radio Freedom broadcast asked:

> ... Where are the weapons to destroy this regime? They cannot be found anywhere else countrymen. They can only be found in our country itself. The weapons are there in front of you. They are in the hands of the policemen themselves. Some of these policemen are coming back to sleep within our midst in the townships. We know where they live. Let us break into their houses and take those guns that the apartheid regime gave them to kill us and turn those guns against them. Let us break into their barracks and take those guns and machine guns ... We should attack the police stations and army barracks and capture those weapons.[39]

In its call in 1986 to the people to advance "from ungovernability to people's power", the ANC urged for the intensification of the struggle saying "let us together, under the leadership and umbrella of the ANC, render apartheid South Africa even more ungovernable. Let every township and every community become a stronger organised fortress of our revolution".[40] Either as a result of this call or as a spontaneous reaction to brutal repression, a number of military activities in the form of sabotage, bombs, hand grenades, land mines, etcetera were carried out in the course of the 1980s. Increasing from four in 1976 to 895 by October 1988,[41] the attacks conducted by MK not only kept the government forces in a state of agitation, but also demystified the notion of the invincibility of the apartheid state. When the SADF launched an attack on alleged ANC bases in Maputo, Mozambique in 1978 killing 13 people, MK responded with a bomb blast at the Koeberg nuclear power plant in December 1982. When the SADF launched another attack on an ANC outpost in Maseru, Lesotho, killing 42 people, MK responded with a car bomb attack in Pretoria in May 1983. These developments, including political trials involving MK cadres, served to give the ANC's military wing a clout of heroism. Although this popular heroism was out of proportion with what was happening in reality, it had the desired effect of mobilising a majority of the people, in particular the youth, behind the movement's programme. Important also was MK's involvement in the clandestine formation of organisations inside South Africa. It was for this reason that the political objective of the armed struggle was by far the most effective.

However, although the revolutionary struggle gained momentum and nascent forms of alternative democracy developed, the setbacks suffered by the ANC and the limitations of its revolutionary strategy increasingly jeopardised the prospect of an immediate or at least foreseeable defeat of the apartheid state. South Africa's conclusion of treaties with neighbouring states, starting with the Nkomati Accord with Mozambique in 1984 and proceeding to peace pacts with Swaziland, Lesotho and Angola, led to the removal of MK cadres from these countries, complicating communication between inside and outside MK structures. For example, the conclusion of an accord between South Africa, Angola and Cuba leading to the implementation of Resolution 435 for the independence of Namibia, compelled the ANC to withdraw its armed forces from Angola to Tanzania, Ethiopia, Ghana and Uganda.[42] Incursions by the state into the neighbouring states also saw it attempt to destroy the ANC's regional structures in those areas.[43] Hit-squad activities, sanctioned by the government to eliminate anti-apartheid opponents and in particular ANC members, also dealt the armed struggle severe blows. Captured MK cadres were forced against their will to betray their comrades and to participate in their murder (the Nofomela case). The uprooting of other internal cells such as the predominantly white Broederstroom cell and the discovery and confiscation of large quantities of ammunition, some highly sophisticated, increasingly exposed – even to the public eye – the serious limitations of the armed struggle.

By the beginning of 1987, a total of 507 trained MK combatants had been neutralised in South Africa, 379 of them having been arrested and 128 killed. More than 3000 hand grenades, 150 limpet mines, 31 RPG-7 rocket launchers and 378 AK-47 rifles were discovered and confiscated by the SAP over the same period.[44] These developments had serious implications for the conduct of the revolutionary struggle. Although mass political struggles were not emasculated and continued to resurge through strikes, boycotts, defiance and marches, the absence (or weakness) of the underground network of trained cadres to guide in the execution of the revolution meant that these struggles could not mature into the formidable force required for the making of a revolution. In addition, the declaration of the national state of emergency in 1985, to be repeated in subsequent years, seriously reversed the gains achieved through mass struggles. Mass arrests, detentions and, to some extent, the maiming and killing of activists demobilised the people, while the banning of political organisations in 1988 left a vacuum in terms of directing the struggle into a concerted action against the state.

Using South American counter-revolutionary strategies, particularly the strategic theory of Lieutenant-Colonel John J. McQueen, the state also ventured into the political terrain often dominated by the opposition forces to win the hearts of the dominated communities.[45] The State Management System and the "win the hearts and minds" of the people strategy, coupled with a sophisticated network of security spies, dented the effective organisation and mobilisation of the people. Thus by 1987 the prospect of the revolutionary struggle was so undermined that it was apparently too weak to shake, let alone destroy, the military might of the apartheid state. In assessing its achievement and in a prelude to the ultimate acknowledgement of these limitations, the ANC, in a document circulated to national command centres in October 1986, soberly said that

> ... we are observing this year as the year of Umkhonto we Sizwe. At the beginning of the year, in the January 8th statement, we set out the task that we had to achieve in the area of armed struggle. Nine months on, it is clear that, despite all our efforts, we have not come anywhere near the achievement of the objectives we set ourselves. It seems obvious that with a few exceptions we have as yet not succeeded to build up the required links between professional Umkhonto units and the mass combat groups that exist in many parts of our country.[46]

The document also mentioned serious reversals suffered by the organisation in Mozambique, Swaziland, Lesotho and Botswana. "This cannot be but a matter of serious concern because it means that the enemy has gained ground at our expense. We have been forced to withdraw many people, dismantle machinery and rethink our plans and programmes." Internal organisational shortcomings, particularly within the UDF, COSATU and the religious community, were perceived to have hindered the ANC from exploiting the revolutionary preparedness in certain communities such as Duduza, Kwandebele and Lebowa. On a sober note, Ronnie Kasrils observed that

> ... the past three years have shown us how relatively underdeveloped the subjective factor is. We have had endless discussions and meetings about how it should be done. Differences of approach exist between military and political organs of the movement. We appear to agree in meetings but differ in practice. Confusion exists among rank-and-file cadres going home as to what structures to create, and between externally trained cadres and those activists who have never left home.[47]

Similar observations about the limitations of the revolutionary strategy were also expressed in an issue of *Mayibuye* under the title 'People's war and insurrection: the subjective factor'.[48]

In conclusion, it was against these setbacks and limitations of the revolutionary armed struggle and the strategy of people's war that the question of negotiation began to receive more attention and support within the liberation movement by 1987. The political and diplomatic achievements, the pressures exerted on the organisation by different forces and Mandela's personal initiatives on negotiations ultimately pressured it to consider negotiation as the most affordable strategic option to materialise its vision of the transfer of power. The revolutionary struggle was officially pronounced a failure by the organisation in Lusaka on 18 January 1990. At the opening of the meeting between the NEC and the eight visiting leaders from South Africa led by Walter Sisulu, Acting President Alfred Nzo said that "looking at our situation realistically, we must admit that we do not have the capacity within our country, in fact, to intensify the armed struggle in any meaningful way".[49] Nzo's statement on the limitations of the armed struggle was important for two reasons. Firstly, it publicly put to rest the clamour by ANC militants that the prospect of overthrowing the state by force of arms was imminent. Secondly, while the statement was made within the context where the momentum for negotiating with the government had already gained ground, it provided an official rationale for the ANC leadership to pursue negotiations seriously.

The Mandela factor – setting the stage for negotiations

While the prospects for negotiations arose out of the intensified struggle inside South Africa, the pressure upon the ANC to negotiate and out of the government's reluctant overtures to negotiate, it is probably Nelson Mandela's initiatives in prison that built the foundation for serious negotiations. After serving 19 years of his life sentence on Robben Island, Mandela, together with his long-time comrades, was transferred to Pollsmoor Prison in 1982. Pollsmoor had a much more relaxed atmosphere than the harsh conditions of Robben Island. Prisoners were allowed some degree of liberty. Mandela used this new-found liberty to do things that were close to his heart such as reading, developing a garden and, most importantly, giving thought to ways of resolving the political crisis in South Africa. Although he was convinced that negotiations were the only way to resolve the political crisis, it was very difficult for him to enter into such a discussion with his prison colleagues. In fact, the political conditions at the time made any discussion of talking with the regime highly treasonable.

It was initiatives by the government that were to avail Mandela of a secure opportunity to pursue negotiations seriously. During the ten years that preceded 1984, the government had already made six conditional offers to release him in an attempt to sideline him. At one stage, Minister Kruger had offered to release him to the Transkei.[50] Overtures to Mandela by the government can well be explained by the deepening conflict that had developed at the beginning of the 1980s, caused to some extent by MK's violent attacks, as well as internal mass mobilisation led by the UDF. This deepening conflict and in particular the loss of white civilian lives had propelled the government towards seeking an alternative solution to the political crisis. The promulgation of the 1983 constitution, which created a tricameral parliament accommodating Indians and coloureds into the corridors of power, was an attempt at creating a new political dispensation. But this failed to stem the tide of resistance. The adoption of the Black Local Authorities Act and the relegation of black political participation to local level added fuel to an already volatile situation and conditioned more organised forms of resistance. The UDF and a number of grass-roots organisations were formed that were, in the following years, to trouble the government. More resources were thus invested in the military machine to contain resistance, but the brute force used to quell resistance served only to annoy the international community.

Its frustration in handling resistance to its rule prompted the NP government to begin exploring other alternatives. The renascence of charterist organisations rallying their support behind the ANC and Mandela in particular precipitated the government, at least initially, towards seeking to ostracise Mandela from the democratic movement. It was in pursuit of this strategy that Mandela was moved from Robben Island to Pollsmoor Prison. After his operation for an enlarged prostate gland at the Volks Hospital in Cape Town in 1985, Mandela was separated from his prison mates. He was offered a solitary apartment in another cell on a different floor of the prison. The government used this opportunity to have exploratory talks with Mandela, but with the purpose of seeking a compromise on his position. Apart from the semi-luxury of his prison conditions and the relaxed attitude of prison officials towards him, Mandela was allowed more visits in prison. His wife, Winnie, and family lawyer, Ismail Ayob, were allowed regular visits. In 1984 he was allowed a visit by Lord Nicholas Bethel, a member of the British House of Lords and the European Parliament. This was followed by a visit by Samuel Dash, a professor of law at Georgetown University and a former counsel to the United States Senate Watergate Committee. These were fact-finding missions by Western states about Mandela's perspective on the political situation. That Mandela was a man of violence was of great concern to Western governments. This was clearly reflected by two American editors of the *Washington Times* who visited Mandela simply to find out whether he was a terrorist and a communist.

It was this well-orchestrated distortion of facts by the South African government – that Mandela was committed to violence – which underlined President P.W. Botha's request to Mandela to renounce violence as a precondition to his release during a debate in parliament on 31 January 1985. Mandela was more than disturbed by this distortion of facts. In his first public statement read by his daughter, Zinzi, at a rally in Soweto's Jabulani Stadium, Mandela said:

> ... I am surprised at the condition that the government wants to impose on me. I am not a violent man ... It was only then, when all other forms of resistance were no longer open to us, that we turned to armed struggle. Let Botha show that he is different to Malan, Strijdom and Verwoerd. Let him renounce violence.[51]

In spite of the government's insistence that negotiations could be possible only if the ANC renounced violence, Mandela focused his mind on a peaceful resolution of the political crisis. His separation from his prison mates allowed him room to concentrate his attention on this subject. Reflecting on this initiative, Mandela wrote in his autobiography:

> I was not happy to be separated from my colleagues, and I had been pondering for a long while: begin discussions with the government. I had concluded that the time had come when the struggle could best be pushed forward through negotiations. If we did not start a dialogue soon, both sides would soon be plunged into a dark night of oppression, violence and war.[52]

Talking with the government was Mandela's personal initiative which he undertook, at least at the beginning, with absolute confidentiality. Reflecting on this, Mandela wrote that

> ... a decision to talk to the government was of such importance that it should only have been made in Lusaka. But I felt that the process needed to begin, and I had neither the time nor the means to communicate fully with Oliver Tambo. Someone from our side needed to take the first step, and my new isolation gave me both the freedom to do so and the assurance, at least for a while, of the confidentiality of my efforts.[53]

In a move to implement his decision to begin talks with the government, Mandela wrote several letters to Minister Kobie Coetzee. However, all his efforts were to no avail as the minister failed to respond. In 1986 Mandela was allowed a visit by the Eminent Person's Group (EPG) sent by the British Commonwealth meeting held in Nassau in October 1985. The purpose of the visit was a fact-finding mission on the issues of violence, negotiations and international sanctions. It was here that Mandela first made known his support for negotiations. His views on negotiations were passed on to the ANC in Lusaka and to the government in Pretoria. It was these initiatives by Mandela that were to influence the ANC's move towards strengthening its negotiation approach in 1987.

Internal mass struggles including political and diplomatic achievements of the organisation

Despite the limitations of the armed struggle and the remoteness of mass insurrection in destroying the state, the ANC continued during the 1980s to make enormous advances in political and diplomatic terms. The historical legacy of its leadership of the liberation struggle enabled it to remain the main source of inspiration during the mass upheavals of the mid-1980s. The fact that emergent organisations during this period refused to challenge its vanguard role in the struggle also strengthened this general notion. In fact, the UDF declared when it was formed that it did not intend to be a substitute for the liberation movement. The re-emergence of campaigns around the Freedom Charter and the employment of strategies and tactics used by the movement in the 1950s not only eulogised the ANC's politics, but also symbolically placed it at the forefront of the struggle. This contributed to its re-emergence as a dominant force across the South African political landscape.

The significance of internal mass struggles not only undermined white minority rule, it also provided a platform for a united mass resistance against apartheid. The repression that followed and all the anti-resistance strategies that were adopted led to more calls for sanctions and to South Africa being declared a pariah among all the nations of the world. As a result of the deepening of the crisis and the government's inability to resolve it, an array of white support began to align behind the ANC. During the period August 1983 to early 1989, a significant number of white organisations and high-profile personalities consulted the ANC in London and Lusaka. This demonstrated in essence the popularity of the organisation, as well as its indispensability in the resolution of the South African political conflict. Starting with Professor H. van der Merwe of the University of Cape Town and Anglo American Corporation Chairman Gavin Relly, in August and September 1985 respectively, the number of visits surged to well above 70, possibly more if one were to include other unpublicised meetings.[54] Of chief importance were the Dakar conference in Senegal between the ANC and the Afrikaner intellectuals, the Harare meeting between the movement and South African lawyers, and the Five Freedom Forum/ANC Meeting in Lusaka.[55]

While the visits and contacts started as an exploratory mission on the part of whites, they ultimately became a strategic initiative on the part of the ANC to draw the white population into the struggle.[56] Added to the above political milestones, the ANC also scored a diplomatic coup against the state at an international level. Besides the gains it made through its sanctions campaign against the state, it also won the support of many international states. Even those states which opposed some of its strategies supported instead the objective of its struggle to end apartheid in the country. While the Soviet Union, the German Democratic Republic and Sweden had been the ANC's major donors,[57] from 1983 onwards China, previously the donor of the PAC, began to extend support to the ANC, arguing that it treated all organisations struggling for national liberation in Southern Africa alike, without discrimination.[58] The ANC also strengthened its diplomatic initiatives in Britain, the United States and other Western countries. Besides its host states, Zambia, Tanzania and Ethiopia, it won further support from many African states and was given observer status both at the UN and the OAU. The International Conference against Apartheid held in Arusha, Tanzania in December 1987, bringing together not only ANC members and representatives, but also representatives of foreign governments, agencies, support organisations, the democratic movement from within the country and members of the English and Afrikaans language press corps, reflected in essence the apex of the political legitimacy that the liberation movement had achieved.[59] In the words of the ANC, many countries and governments were beginning to treat it virtually as a government-in-waiting.[60] Adding to these gains, the ANC President, Oliver Tambo, went on a diplomatic offensive during 1987 to increase the organisation's credibility among the international community. At the end of January 1987, he met the US Secretary of State, Mr George Schultz. At the end of March, he visited Australia and proceeded to New Zealand and Japan in April, ending in Canada in August.[61]

However, although the political and diplomatic achievements of the ANC contributed to bolstering its stature, they also significantly impinged on its approach to the struggle. The intensification of the struggle inside the country assuaged by tactical negotiations between representatives of democratic organisations and the state's local government structures demonstrated to the ANC the fruits of negotiation in the process of the struggle. While the idea of entering into political negotiations with the state was still remote in its thinking, the ANC did not show its indifference to local-level negotiations that sought to resolve the rent crises. This lukewarm acceptance of local-level negotiations was later transformed into a force within the movement as more pro-negotiations arguments were advanced. As transpired during the local-level negotiations, activists within the democratic movement began arguing that negotiating was another dimension that advanced rather than underscored the struggle. It was in the end this sort of argument that was to be critical in acclimatising comrades to the concept of negotiations.

The growing support received from the white population inside the country and from moderate foreign governments also resulted in a change of thinking within the ANC concerning certain tactics in the conduct of the struggle. The outcry in 1987 against the decision to hit soft targets resulting in civilian loss of life successfully coerced the ANC into remorse and abhorrence of the system of necklace killing by activists in the townships. Most significantly, these criticisms and suggestions to the ANC to consider the question of negotiation added more weight to the already swelling pressure on the movement.

Pressure exerted on the organisation by the Soviet Union and the front-line states

Besides the above dynamics, the ANC found itself under further pressure from the Soviet Union and the front-line states on the question of negotiating with the South African government.

The Soviet Union

By 1987 feelings about the concerns of South African whites had reached unprecedented proportions among political strategists in the Soviet Union. These concerns also infiltrated into the analytical search for solutions for the South African political crisis. Expressing these concerns, a leading member of the Moscow-Africa Institute, Dr Gleb Starushenko, argued that anti-racist forces should not put forward the argument for a broad nationalisation of capitalist property as indispensable, and should give the bourgeoisie relevant guarantees. He encouraged the ANC to work out comprehensive guarantees for the white population which could be implemented after the elimination of the apartheid regime. Such guarantees would suit the liberals and the pragmatists from the white community, while at the same time neutralising the diehards. The examples of Kenya and Zimbabwe, where the white minority felt absolutely safe after a postcolonial settlement, were said to attest to the practicability of such a solution.

However, Starushenko also mentioned that the above precedents need not be regarded as rigid models. He contended that "for instance, the parliament may consist of two chambers: one formed on the basis of proportional representation and the other possessing the right of veto on the basis of equal representation of four communities".[62] He also contended that South Africa might not yet be ready for an entirely non-racial system and that it would be unnecessary for the liberation movement to impose solutions for which the people were not yet ready; hence his options for a tactical guarantee.

Starushenko further warned against an underestimation of the ethnic question (differences) which in his opinion might last for years and might be difficult to abolish.[63] His views on ethnicity were partly influenced by contemporary Soviet politics in which demands for national and regional autonomy were surging as the key issues of the day. Despite the fact that Starushenko's views were not Soviet policy, his speech was not contradicted by the Central Committee of the Communist Party of the Soviet Union or the Foreign Ministry who were present at the conference at which he delivered his paper. Starushenko's views were, in fact, in tandem with the whole Soviet foreign policy. Conflict resolution through negotiations and other peaceful bargaining had become the central key in Soviet foreign policy.

Already Soviet policy towards Africa was laden with growing disillusionment about the possibility of effectively expanding and implementing the Marxist-Leninist model. The failure of this model in the area of economic development, particularly agriculture, was one of the most important factors in the difficulties which they were facing. The catastrophic developments in Mozambique and Ethiopia and the serious difficulties in Angola had an effect on its military and economic policies towards the continent. Under Gorbachev, cost-benefit calculations were already playing a greater role in the formulation of Soviet policies.[64] It was also in line with this approach that the Soviet Union sought to reduce international tensions and the danger of nuclear war through dialogue. Its new approach was to promote political solutions to global and regional conflicts, as well as exploring and promoting a political solution for South Africa.[65] Friedman and Narsoo argued that the key reason for this policy, particularly the search for stability, was that the Soviet Union urgently needed to devote its resources to developing its own economy. It did not want to become involved in expensive foreign commitments which would sap these resources. If reasonable and peaceful foreign arrangements with the West could be achieved, the Soviet Union would then be able to proceed with the task of modernising its economy.[66]

Starushenko's views on a peaceful resolution of the South African conflict were later officially embraced by the government of the Soviet Union, as clearly articulated by the Soviet Senior Foreign Ministry official, A.A. Makarov. The Soviet analytical approach characterised the South African crisis as having been generated mostly by contradictions between the development of South African productive forces in the age of revolution in science and technology and the apartheid-based institutionalised system of monopolistic state control and regulations governing national manpower. It argued that South Africa's intensive economic development was made directly contingent on freedom from racial discrimination and on political rights. This approach saw the balance of forces around these contradictions as relatively stable: "Organisationally, politically and militarily, the anti-racist resistance movement is not yet ready to topple the regime and capture power, while the regime is no longer capable of curbing the growth of resistance".[67]

Although a direct revolutionary overthrow of the state was understood to be remote and despite the new approach that sought a negotiated settlement, the Kremlin did not stop supporting the armed struggle of the liberation movement. Against speculations that the Soviet Union would foist its thinking on the liberation movement, Oliver Tambo was promised more support for the armed struggle when he visited the country in early 1989. Unlike Angola and Mozambique, the material assistance given to the ANC did not cause a drain on the Soviet economy and this explains the unconditionality of the support given to the movement.[68] However, even if it had wished for a negotiated settlement for South Africa, the Soviet Union was not in a position to force the ANC to adopt its stance. It was in the final analysis the prerogative of the ANC to formulate, change or adapt its policies. But while this is true, and in view of the changing conditions that favoured negotiations and a negotiated settlement, it was highly probable that the ANC would not be indifferent to the propositions advanced by its ally. In fact, a significant amount of pressure had been exerted on it by the Soviet Union to negotiate with the state.

The front-line states

In addition to the pressure exerted by the Soviet Union, the ANC experienced further pressure from the front-line states. By 1987, a sense of weariness had developed among these states in sustaining the war with the South African government. Already the economies of Mozambique and Angola had been crippled owing to blunders in policy implementation. The aggressive and offensive posture adopted by the South African-propped insurgent groups, RENAMO (the Mozambican National Resistance Movement) and UNITA, in these countries inflicted more wounds onto these ailing economies, resulting in mass demobilisation, misery and starvation of the majority of the local population. Mozambique came out clearly supporting negotiations while Angola, in its desperate search for an end to the war in order to secure Western economic aid, told the ANC through its President Dos Santos that there might not be time to wait for the democratic forces to build up their strength before negotiations. The Zambian President, Kenneth Kaunda, the United States, particularly the Secretary of State for Africa, Herman Cohen, and Britain individually placed further enormous pressure on the ANC to consider the question of negotiations.

Internal debates within the ANC on the questions of theory, strategy and tactics for attaining power through negotiations

The intensified struggle against apartheid inside and outside of South Africa, Mandela's personal talks with the government and pressure on the ANC to negotiate initiated one of the most intense debates within the movement on the question of revolutionary strategies and negotiations. This debate was to be critical in the ANC's movement towards this new political discourse.

During the height of liberation politics and the mass defiance campaign of the 1980s, the idea of negotiating with the apartheid regime was believed to be antithetical to the revolutionary objectives and paths to power. Towards the end of the 1980s, however, the theme of negotiations assumed prominence as civics and unions successfully bargained with local governments and company managements. ANC strategists, too, began pondering the possibility of a negotiated settlement with the South African regime. While negotiations were part of the ANC's political strategy before its banning in 1960, it was, however, differently understood. Prior to 1960, the political objective of negotiating was to secure an essentially accommodative political settlement that would extend political rights to the excluded black majority. But in the period following the banning of the ANC, negotiations were conceptualised simply as one of several possibilities for the actual transfer of power to the people. Revolutionary armed seizure was seen as the central way to power.

While the idea of negotiations was abandoned in the 1960s and 1970s because of existing repressive conditions and a confident belief in revolutionary theory, its emergence inside South Africa in the mid-1980s presented serious challenges to the ANC and the SACP's orthodox revolutionary approach. As the ANC's theoretical and strategic think-tank, the SACP had hitherto excluded negotiations and assumed the armed struggle and mass insurrection as the decisive political strategies for attaining political power. Its political programme, *The road to South African freedom*, adopted in 1962, characterised South Africa as a CST, thus justifying intensified anti-colonial strategies to overthrow the incumbent regime. It identified the following four pillars of the struggle: the armed struggle, the mobilisation of the international community, the underground political network, and mass struggles. Negotiations did not feature in this vision. This programme was endorsed by the party's eighth congress programme, *The path to power*, as late as 1989.

135

The litany of revolutionary theory constrained the SACP's strategic conception of a politically negotiated settlement in South Africa. While Slovo had talked about the possibility of an eventual negotiated settlement in the 1960s, the subject was not given any thoughtful analysis. Even when the prospect of negotiations presented itself during the mid-1980s and despite the ANC's 1987 statement on negotiation and its Harare declaration in 1989, the SACP had still not embraced negotiations as an important vehicle to power. There was a visible absence of a theory and strategy of negotiation which could explain the South African conjuncture with the same rigour as the CST theory. This bred confusion and resulted in the emergence of differing strategic perspectives on negotiation within the party and the ANC. These differences were reflected in a thoughtful internal debate towards the end of the 1980s. This debate grew from changed circumstances inside South Africa and was also underlined by classical revolutionary approaches of Marxism and Leninism. To understand the debate, we need to review, briefly, these revolutionary texts.

Revolutionary politics had as late as the 1980s made talking with the regime an anathema, and the general belief within the liberation movement was that negotiating was defeatist and tantamount to capitulation and that embracing reforms was an apologetic acceptance of weakness. However, this belief had little foundation in the classical revolutionary texts on which the SACP and the ANC had hitherto based the struggle. Despite their opposition to reformism and the preaching of the bourgeois democracy school,[69] the leading theorists of revolution, Marx and Lenin, had not been opposed to tactical flexibility and the use of non-revolutionary methods, including negotiation, to achieve political objectives. Lenin wrote in this regard that "we might have to go in zigzags, sometimes retracing our steps, sometimes going up the course once selected and trying various others".[70] He elaborated that

> ... Marxism does not tie the movement to any particular combat method. It recognises the possibility that struggle may assume the most variegated forms. For that matter, Marxism does not "invent" those forms of struggle. It merely organises the tactics of strife and renders them suitable for general use ... [Marxism] will never reject any particular combat method, let alone reject it forever. Marxism does not limit itself to those types of struggle, which at a given moment, are both practical and traditional. It holds that due to changes in social conditions, new forms of battle will arise inevitably.[71]

Commenting on the necessity of reforms and negotiation to advance the course of revolutionary struggle, Ralph Miliband much later maintained that in classical Marxism, reforms in bourgeois democratic regimes were never incompatible with revolutionary aims.[72] In fact, Stalin had written that

> ... with revolutionary tactics under the existing bourgeois regime, reforms inevitably serve as instruments that disintegrate the regime, instruments that strengthen the revolution ... the revolutionary will

accept a reform in order to use it as a means wherewith to link legal work with illegal work, in order to use it as a screen behind which his illegal activities for the revolutionary preparation of the masses for the overthrow of the bourgeois may be intensified.[73]

He also argued that "every little helps, that under certain conditions reforms, in general, and compromises and agreements, in particular, are necessary and useful".[74]

The ANC's disposition towards negotiation was informed by the changing dynamics of international politics which propounded peaceful negotiated settlements, as well as by the fledgling negotiations led by civics and unions inside the country, including Nelson Mandela's personal initiatives on negotiations in prison.[75] However, the crucial question of strategy and tactics in negotiation evolved within the broader framework of revolutionary theory. Already in the mid-1980s, ANC, SACP and MDM strategists, as well as academics aligned to them, were advancing postulations that called for tactical flexibility.[76] Brenda Stalker, an ANC activist, crisply captured this emerging thinking. Writing in the ANC's journal, *Sechaba*, in 1988, she argued that "a conscious policy of choosing the most peaceful path, as long, of course, as it is not connected with lack of principle, offers the revolutionary and democratic forces the most favourable basis for further progress".[77] This position was strengthened by further arguments within the ANC that

> ... a principle of "no compromise" is neither useful nor realistic to serious movement. Circumstances arise which force revolutionary movements to compromise to avoid being weakened or defeated ... Compromises made to maintain an organisation's mass base, because of the greater strength of the enemy on a particular terrain, or because it becomes impossible to continue a particular form of struggle indefinitely are necessary.[78]

The ANC's internal allies in the MDM also argued in 1989 that

> ... we cannot always choose to negotiate from a position of strength or in a situation where we expect to achieve important advances, or make maximum gains. A national movement may be forced to negotiate in some situations, in order to achieve a more limited goal, for example, a breathing space or a tactical retreat before resuming the struggle on a more intense basis. It may hope, on the other hand, that meeting at the negotiating table necessitates a greater degree of recognition of its legitimacy and may possibly lead to more space within which to operate, especially legalisation in the case of banned organisations.[79]

Finally, the SACP journal, *The African Communist*, stated in 1990, after quoting Lenin, that

... to enter into discussions with the government does not in itself constitute compromise, but compromise of one sort or another may eventually be forced upon us by circumstances. The test will be whether that compromise can open the way to the ultimate achievement of our objectives and whether the alternative to compromise would constitute a setback for the revolutionary cause. These matters must not be decided by rhetoric but by careful analysis of the objective situation which prevails at the decisive moment.[80]

While broader consensus was achieved within the ANC, SACP and MDM about the importance of negotiating, the question of negotiating to achieve limited victories or to strengthen a revolutionary seizure of power gave rise to intense debate. This internal debate produced two schools of thought: the negotiation versus the revolutionary school. The negotiation school contended that the ANC had always been disposed to negotiations, and that the resort to the armed struggle and other forms of struggle was prompted by the desire to force the state to negotiate. In this view, negotiation and other revolutionary strategies were not contradictory but compatible and mutually reinforcing. They were compatible in the sense that, should the opportunity for negotiation present itself, it must be given priority. This would imply suspending forms of struggle seen to be inimical to it. It was contended that "armed struggle cannot be counterposed with dialogue, negotiation and justifiable compromises, as if they were mutually exclusive categories".[81] The negotiation school also maintained that to advance the course of the struggle, the liberation movement should embrace the principle of compromise and partial victories. In the words of Mashinini,

> ... since we are confronted with conditions under which absolute victory is impossible, conditions in which both sides must necessarily make compromises on certain positions, we can conclude that the outcome of any negotiation that can be successfully conducted must end up in partial victories for warring parties. Both sides would have failed to defeat each other absolutely and would have to be content with partial victories.[82]

In contrast, the revolutionary school believed the ANC was a liberation movement destined to seize and transfer power from the minority to the majority. While also adhering to the idea of the compatibility of negotiation and revolutionary strategies, the revolutionary school understood this to mean that negotiations should accompany revolution. This perspective saw negotiations as another terrain of struggle which should be violently contested. It saw it simply as another strategy which should complement existing revolutionary strategies.[83] The armed struggle and the commitment to a people's war remained the central focus of the movement's strategic objective of seizing power. It meant intensifying the struggle so that when negotiations took place, they did so under the terms of the ANC, which were aimed at the transfer of power – neither power-sharing nor partial victories were contemplated.[84] Arguing against Mashinini and in particular against the notion of compromises and partial victories, Zumana maintained that

> ... history would never forgive our liberation movement if it adopted such a defeatist position when our enemy is in such crisis, and is holding power only by strained threads ... History is on our side. If this is so, is revolution impossible in our case? If it is not, why then settle for partial victories? All revolutions are about state power, and ours is no exception.[85]

Thando Zuma, criticising Brenda Stalker's hinting at compromise through negotiations, strongly argued that "the seizure of power by the people is, after all, the central point of departure of the struggle, and as such cannot be reduced to the level of 'concern' by this or that comrade. Does the strategy of 'talks' mean that we are abandoning the perspective of insurrection and people's war? Not at all".[86]

These two schools of thought sometimes overlapped. However, this did not fundamentally efface the existence of these differences represented symbolically within the organisation by the late Moses Mabhida, who espoused the violent, armed seizure of power (the revolutionary school) and Oliver Tambo, who contended that the ANC's main objective lay not "in a military victory but to force Pretoria to the negotiating table" (the negotiation school).[87] It was ultimately the views of the negotiation school that triumphed, as reflected by the ANC's attempts to prioritise negotiations over other forms of struggle. This, together with the momentum which had already built up in the late 1980s, provided the platform for negotiations to be pursued vigorously.

ENDNOTES

1. Wilton Mkwayi. Interview. 1989.
2. Seme, quoted in Bernstein, H. 'The ANC – seventy years on'. *South,* March 1982, 28.
3. Mandela, N. Speech delivered at the Rivonia Trial. A booklet of *Learn and Teach.* Published at the 70th birthday of Mandela on 18 July 1988, 3.
4. Meli, F. South Africa and the rise of African nationalism. In Van Diepen, M. (Ed.), *The national question in South Africa.* London, 1988, 70.
5. Marcus, G. *The Freedom Charter: a blueprint for a democratic South Africa.* Occasional paper. University of the Witwatersrand: Centre of Applied Legal Studies, 9 June 1985, 15.
6. Slovo, J. *The unfinished autobiography.* Johannesburg: Raven, 1955, 146–148.
7. Walter Sisulu and Ahmed Kathrada, interviewed by Jo-Ann Collinge. *Work In Progress,* 63, November/December 1989, 12.
8. Nelson Mandela, quoted in Meer, F. *Higher than hope: a biography of Nelson Mandela on his 70th birthday.* Braamfontein: Skotaville, 1988, 177–179.
9. *Umkhonto we Sizwe: born of the people.* Statement of the National Executive Committee of the African National Congress, delivered by President Oliver Tambo on Heroes Day, 16 December 1986, 7 & 9.
10. Wilton Mkwayi. Interview.
11. Prior, A. South African exile politics: a case study of the ANC and the SACP. *Journal of Contemporary African Studies,* 3(1/2), October 1983 – April 1984, 189.
12. Document 73 "Operation Mayibuye", document found by the police in Rivonia, 11 July 1963. See Karis, T. & Carter, I. *From protest to challenge.* 111, 760–761.

13. Matthews, J. False theories and pessimism. In De Bragança, A. & Wallerstein, I. (Eds), *Africa liberation reader – document of the national liberation movements*, 3, 141.

14. *Umkhonto we Sizwe: born of the people*, op cit., 2.

15. See Lodge, T. *Black politics in South Africa since 1945.* Johannesburg: Ravan, 1983, 9.

16. Hudson, P. The Freedom Charter and the theory of national democratic revolution. *Transformation*, 1, 1986, 25–26.

17. Anonymous. 'Colonialism of a special type'. *Africa Perspective*, 23, 1983, 76. See also Wolpe, H. (Ed.), 'The Oxaal'. *Beyond the Sociology of Development*, 1975.

18. Lambert, R. *Political unionism in South Africa: the South African Congress of Trade Unions, 1955–1965.* Thesis, Faculty of Arts, University of the Witwatersrand, 1988, 62. See also Lambert, R. *Trade unions and national liberation in South Africa: past perspective and current strategies.* Paper read at the Centre for Southern African Studies Conference, 1986, 3.

19. Bundy, C. Around which corner? Revolutionary theory and contemporary South Africa. *Transformation*, 8, 1989, 5.

20. Callinicos (1988) op cit., 68.

21. 'South Africa: inside the Communist Party'. *Africa Confidential*, 29(17), August 1988, 3. See also the similarity of language between the ANC's *Strategy and Tactics* and Slovo's article 'Objective and subjective conditions' in De Bragança & Wallerstein (Eds), op cit.

22. Bundy, op cit., 6.

23. Slovo, op cit., 135.

24. *Operation Mayibuye*, op cit., 161.

25. 'ANC strategy and tactics'. In Turok, B. (Ed.), *Revolutionary thoughts in the 20th century*. London: Zed, 1980, 151. See also a reprint in La Guma, J. (Ed.), *Apartheid*. Berlin: Seven Seas, 1972.

26. Slovo, op cit., 139.

27. Hough, M. Revolutionary warfare in the Republic of South Africa. *ISSUP Strategic Review*, University of Pretoria: Institute of Strategic Studies, 1986, 10.

28. Ibid., 6–9. For more information about the Debray model, see his book *Revolution in revolution*, 1987.

29. Lodge, op cit., 302.

30. *Umkhonto we Sizwe: born of the people*, op cit., 5.

31. Lodge, T. The African National Congress after Nkomati. *South African Institute of Race Relations – Topical Opinion*, 16 September 1985.

32. Bundy, op cit., 7.

33. Opening statement of Comrade Oliver Tambo at the Second ANC National Consultative Conference, 16–23 June 1985, 5.

34. Kasrils, R. The revolutionary army. *Sechaba*, September 1988, 5.

35. Tambo quoted in 'The Communist Party' in *International Viewpoint*, 30 September 1985, 4. This is a reproduction of an article written by Mzansi entitled 'United front to end apartheid, the road to mass action in South Africa'. *The African Communist*, 97, Second Quarter, 1984.

36. Murray, M. *South Africa – time of agony, time of destiny: the upsurge of popular protest.* 1987, 272.

37. Morobe, M. Towards people's democracy. *South Africa International*, 18(1), 1987, 34.

38. Kev (pseudonym). A contribution to the discussion on people's war. *The African Communist*, 115, Fourth Quarter, 1988, 121.

39. Callinicos (1988), op cit., 4.

40. *From ungovernability to people's power.* Statement of the National Executive Committee of the ANC, 1986.

41. 'Resurgence of the ANC, 1976–1988'. *Indicator South Africa, Issue Focus*, 1989, 86.

42. *Sowetan*, 27 January 1989.

43. The Regional Political-Military Councils (RPMCs) were established by the Political Military Council (PMC) formed in 1983 to replace the old Revolutionary Council. The purpose of the RPMCs was to establish area PMCs in the townships to construct one chain of command from Lusaka to the street committees. See *Africa Confidential*, 29(16), August 1988. Lesotho, Swaziland, Botswana, Zimbabwe, Mozambique, Angola and Malawi were, in one way or the other, destabilised by South Africa. See Asmal, K., Asmal, L. & Roberts, R. *Reconciliation through truth.* Cape Town: David Philip, 1996, 168–175.

44. Adam, H. Exile and resistance: the ANC, the SACP and the PAC. In Berger, P. & Godsell, B. (Eds), *A future South Africa: visions, strategies and realities.* Cape Town: Human & Rousseau/ Tafelberg, 1988, 98–99.

45. Sarakinsky, I. *State strategy and the extra-parliamentary opposition in South Africa, 1983–1988.* Paper presented at the Political Studies Seminar, University of the Witwatersrand on 12 April 1989, 3– 4. On counter-revolutionary strategies see Swilling, M. & Phillips, M. *The power and limits of the*

emergency state. Paper presented at the African Studies Institute, University of the Witwatersrand on 14 August 1989. See also the same authors, State power in the 1980s: from total strategy to counter-revolutionary warfare. In Cock, J. & Nathan, L. (Eds), *War and society: the militarisation of South Africa,* 1989.

46. *1987: What is to be done?* Document distributed by the Politico-Military Council to Regional Command Centres, October 1986. See also Lodge, T. The ANC after the Kabwe Conference. *South African Review,* 4, 1989, 10; and Callinicos, op cit., 133.

47. Kasrils, op cit., 4.

48. 'People's war and insurrection: the subjective factor'. *Mayibuye,* 2, 1989, 16.

49. *The Star,* 19 January 1990.

50. Gregory, J. *Goodbye bafana: Nelson Mandela, my prisoner, my friend.* London: Headline Books, 1995, 227.

51. Mandela, N. *Long walk to freedom.* Randburg: Macdonald Purnell, 1994, 510–511.

52. Ibid., 513.

53. Ibid., 514.

54. See the list of organisations and persons who had visited the ANC, in a paper prepared for the Five Freedoms Forum, May 1989.

55. *City Press,* 9 July 1989.

56. Zuma, T. 'The surest way to people's power: a response to Brenda Stalker'. *Sechaba,* February 1988, 13. See an outline of the ANC's strategy towards the visiting whites.

57. Lodge, T. State of exile: the African National Congress of South Africa, 1976–86. In Frankel, P., Pines, N. & Swilling, M. (Eds), *State resistance and change in South Africa.* Johannesburg: Southern, 1988, 237.

58. Costea, P. *Eastern Europe's relations with the insurgencies of Southern Africa (ANC and SWAPO).* Paper presented at the Bi-annual Conference of Political Science Association of South Africa, Port Alfred, 9–11 October.

59. Phillips, I. After Kabwe and the emergency, lessons of the 1980s. *Indicator South Africa Issue Focus,* 1989, 99.

60. *1987: what is to be done,* op cit., 12.

61. South African Institute of Race Relations Survey, 1987/88, 704–705.

62. Starushenko, G. *Problems of the struggle against racism, apartheid and colonialism in South Africa.* Paper presented to the second Soviet-Africa Conference for Peace, Cooperation and Social Progress. Moscow: USSR Academy of Science, the African Institute, 1988. See also *Black politics in South Africa and the outlook of meaningful negotiations.* Report of the International Conference held at the Foundation of Science and Politics (Stiftung für Wissenschaft und Politik), Ebenhausen, 10–12 December 1986, 9.

63. Friedman, S. & Narsoo, M. *A new mood in Moscow: Soviet attitudes to South Africa.* South African Institute of Race Relations, 1988, 10.

64. Ebenhausen Conference Report, op cit., 41.

65. 'Negotiations, fighting with new weapons'. *New Era,* 4(2), August 1989, 8.

66. Friedman & Narsoo, op cit., 6. See the same argument by Swilling, M. 'The politics of negotiations'. *Work In Progress,* 50/51, October/November 1987, 22.

67. Phillips, M. Negotiations: it takes two to tango. *Work In Progress,* 60, August/September 1989, 15.

68. Costea, op cit., 26.

69. See Lenin, V. 'After the seizure of power (1917–1918)'. *Selected Works,* Vol. VII. The Marx-Engels-Lenin Institute, 1937, 152–160. See in particular, the postscript 'The proletarian revolution and the renegade Kautsky'. See also Reglar, S. & Young, G. Modern communist theory: Lenin and Mao Zedung. In Wintrop, N., *Liberal democratic theory and its critics.* 1983, 262–266.

70. Lenin, V. Quoted in Stalin, J. *Leninism.* Moscow: Cooperative Publishing Society of Foreign Workers in the USSR, Moscow, 1934, 84–85.

71. Lenin, V. Partisan warfare. In Sarkesian, S.C. *Revolutionary guerrilla warfare.* Chicago: President Publishing, 1975, 187.

72. Miliband, R. *Marxism and politics.* London: Oxford University Press, 1977, 160.

73. Stalin, op cit., 85.

74. Ibid., 84.

75. Rantete, J. & Giliomee, H. Transition to democracy through transaction? Bilateral negotiations between the ANC and the NP in South Africa. *African Affairs,* 91, 1992, 527.

76. Cronin, J. National democratic struggle and the question of transformation. *Transformation,* 2, 1986, 74. See also Sisa Majola on the flexibility of revolutionary movements in 'The two stages of our revolution'. *The African Communist,* 110, Third Quarter, 1987, 45.

77. Stalker, B. The crisis in our country: a realistic political solution. *Sechaba*, May 1988, 26.

78. 'The politics of talking power'. *New Era Magazine*, 4(2), August 1989, 10.

79. *Negotiation as a terrain and method of struggle.* Discussion paper for the Conference for a Democratic Future, issued by the Mass Democratic Movement, December 1989, 8.

80. 'Editorial notes'. *The African Communist*, Third Quarter, 1990, 11.

81. Callinicos, A. *Between apartheid and capitalism.* London: Bookmarks, 1992, 30.

82. Mashinini, A. People's war and negotiations: are they fire and water? *Sechaba*, August 1988, 27.

83. 'The politics of talking power'. *New Era Magazine*, 4(2), August 1989, 10.

84. Meli, F. South Africa and the rise of African nationalism. In Van Diepen, M. (Ed.), *The national question in South Africa.* London, 1988, 76.

85. Zumana, N. Revolution or negotiations? *Sechaba*, 23(4), April 1989, 27.

86. Zuma, op cit., 10.

87. Lodge (1988), op cit., 249–251.

The ANC – taking the initiative in negotiations

6

Actions by the government also played a role in hurrying the ANC towards the negotiating table. Having been pushed by mass struggles and the military defeat in Angola to the point where it had to negotiate with the black leadership, the government under P.W. Botha sought to create a negotiating forum, the "Great Indaba", aimed at bringing together black representatives, particularly those who had been "elected" into the government-created structures. Responding reluctantly to the programme of negotiations introduced in 1986 by the Eminent Persons' Group (EPG), the government hinted at the creation of a national forum which would negotiate a new constitution for the country. However, organisations such as the ANC were to be excluded from this forum on the basis of "their preference for violence".

The ANC's 1987 Negotiation Statement and the 1989 Harare Declaration

Against the background of the above scenario, the ANC increasingly felt a sense of urgency in taking the initiative positively and constructively in the question of negotiations. The objective here was not only to pre-empt the state's treacherous plans, but also to take the struggle in general to a different plateau. It was clear that the organisation could not afford to lose mass support from both the West and the East by staying out of negotiations while the whole world was shouting for a peaceful settlement to the South African conflict. It also could not afford to let the sanctions pressure on Pretoria be lifted because of its unwillingness to negotiate, or to isolate the democratic forces from the mass of the people and create divisions among them.

Although the revolution had not ripened as the organisation had anticipated, it could not afford to remain "obsessed" with its military strategies in the face of practical reality. In the final analysis, therefore, the same pragmatism that forced FRELIMO to tone down its Marxist-Leninist scientific socialism in Mozambique and the Soviet Union to decentralise the monopoly of socialism in Europe, awakened the ANC to the realities of South African politics. More organisational energy was therefore concentrated on attempts to set the negotiation wheels in motion. Despite the ANC's indifference towards negotiations in the 1960s and 1970s, the talk of negotiating did not originate from Mandela's discussions with the government behind bars. Rather, there had been speculations on this issue for some time before Mandela's contact with government officials. Opening the Kabwe conference in 1985, President Oliver Tambo made an observation regarding the growing speculation about negotiations between the ANC and the state, but expressed the NEC's conviction that the state was not interested in a just solution to the South African question. More significantly, he contended that "the NEC is of the view that we cannot be seen to be rejecting a negotiated settlement in principle. In any case no revolutionary movement can be against negotiations in principle".[1]

While this signalled the ANC's willingness to negotiate, a precondition was set for the release of political prisoners in order to test, in a certain sense, the state's seriousness about negotiations. The conference sealed the position by passing a resolution stating that "we cannot even consider the issue of a negotiated settlement of the South African question while our leaders are in prison". In March 1986 the EPG formed subsequent to the Commonwealth meeting in Nassau was sent on a mission to Southern Africa to persuade parties to the South African conflict to seek a peaceful settlement through negotiations. A "possible negotiating concept" was presented to the South African government, envisaging the ANC "entering negotiations and suspending violence" in exchange for the withdrawal of the SADF from the townships, the release of Mandela and other political prisoners, and the unbanning of the ANC and the PAC.[2]

Although the ANC's response was encouraging, it nevertheless expressed scepticism about the necessity of negotiations under conditions which it perceived to be unfavourable. It mistrusted the state's seriousness on the urgency of dismantling apartheid and urged that "immense pressure would be required before the South African government would be ready to negotiate seriously".[3] It further argued that "nothing had changed and nothing would change and that if that proved to be the case, then the conditions for negotiation did not exist". The ANC's scepticism about the regime's commitment to negotiation was confirmed by the latter's frustration of the peace initiative through its military aggression on alleged ANC bases in Zimbabwe, Botswana and Zambia. The aggressions led the EPG to issue the following statement:

> From these and other recent developments, we draw the conclusion that while the government claims to be ready to negotiate, it is in truth not yet prepared to negotiate fundamental change, nor to countenance the creation of genuine democratic structures, nor to face the prospect of the end of white domination and white power in the foreseeable future. Its programme of reform does not end apartheid, but it seeks to give it a less

inhuman face. Its quest is power-sharing, but without surrendering overall white control.[4]

With the failure of the EPG mission to promote a negotiated settlement in South Africa, the concept of negotiation disappeared from the headlines only to resurface in 1987. Responding to pressure exerted on it to negotiate and the government's continued insistence on the concept of the "Great Indaba" to resolve South Africa's political conflict, on 9 October 1987, the ANC issued its first official statement committing itself to negotiation:

> Once more, we would like to reaffirm that the ANC and the masses of our people as a whole are ready and willing to enter into genuine negotiations provided they are aimed at the transformation of our country into a united and non-racial democracy. This, and only this, should be the objective of any negotiating process.[5]

The statement further outlined the organisation's rejection of the demand by the state to abandon or suspend its armed struggle and instead called for the intensification of the struggle on all fronts. However, conspicuous in the statement was the organisation's scepticism about the regime's seriousness regarding negotiations:

> We are convinced that the Botha regime has neither the desire nor the intention to engage in any meaningful negotiations. On the contrary, everything this regime does is directed at the destruction of the national liberation movement, the suppression of the democratic movement and the entrenchment and perpetuation of the apartheid system of white minority domination.

Calling on the state to demonstrate its seriousness and to create a climate conducive to negotiations, the ANC put forward the following preconditions:

- The unconditional release of all political prisoners, detainees, all captured freedom fighters and prisoners of war, as well as the cessation of all political trials
- The lifting of the state of emergency
- The withdrawal of the army and the police from the townships and their confinement to the barracks
- The repeal of all repressive legislation and all laws empowering the regime to limit freedom of assembly, speech, the press and so on. Among these would be the Riotous Assemblies Act, the Native Administration Act, the General Laws Amendment Act, the Unlawful Organisations Act, the Internal Security Act and similar acts and regulations.

The ANC negotiation statement did not, however, call specifically for the unbanning of banned organisations. Swilling and Van Zyl Slabbert wrote that presumably the unbanning of political organisations was subsumed in the last point which called for the repeal of repressive legislation. The call for the unbanning of political organisations was made explicit by the UDF later in 1989 when it broadly outlined its preconditions for negotiations.[6] Also expressing its scepticism about the government's seriousness, the UDF outlined its preconditions for negotiations as follows:

- The release of political prisoners (convicts and awaiting trial) and detainees, and the unconditional return of all exiles. Obviously the leaders could not take part in the negotiation process from behind prison bars or outside the country.

- The unbanning of the ANC and all banned organisations; the outlawed liberation movement had to be free to fully consult with the people and the entire democratic movement in order to obtain a mandate to enter negotiations.

- The police and the SADF had to be withdrawn from the townships and villages and confined to their barracks. This was necessary to create a climate of free and open discussion, so that apartheid forces would be unable to intimidate and harass people and to prevent them from meeting about any proposed negotiations. Apartheid vigilantes and death squads had to be dismantled.

- For the same reason, all laws restricting free assembly, press freedom, and free speech had to be repealed. All repressive laws such as the detention laws would also have to be repealed, as would all laws restricting freedom of movement.

- Bantustan authorities, including the so-called "independent bantustans", had to be stripped of their powers equivalent to those listed above, so that people in those areas would have the same freedom to organise in their areas.

- The state of emergency had to be lifted throughout the country.

The cessation of political trials as mentioned in the ANC statement, was not mentioned in the UDF precondition but appeared in the preconditions outlined by COSATU in its congress resolutions of July 1989. Here COSATU called for "the end of all political trials and executions". The ANC's 1987 negotiation statement, as supported by statements by its allies, firmly demonstrated the organisation's seriousness about entering into negotiations with the government. Statements on preconditions were coupled with reservations and opposition to secret negotiations, with the organisation calling for a definite time-frame for negotiations. Its negotiation statement stated that

> ... the conflict in our country is between the forces of national
> liberation and democracy on the one hand and those of racism and
> reaction on the other. Any negotiations would have to be conducted by
> these two forces as represented by their various organisational
> formations.[7]

The response of the National Party government to the question of negotiations was again negative. In November 1987, State President P.W. Botha ruled out negotiations with the ANC as a far-fetched idea and argued that organisations such as the ANC entered negotiations only to force others into capitulation.[8] Despite the state's refusal to negotiate with the ANC, the latter continued to emphasise its commitment to negotiations. Addressing the Arusha conference in December 1987, the ANC President, Oliver Tambo, reiterated the organisation's willingness to negotiate, emphasising that it had never been opposed to negotiations. The purpose of the existence of the organisation, it was contended, was to protect the lives of the people and to create conditions whereby everyone, without regard to race or colour, can develop as a free and complete human being. There could have been no deliberate resort to the path of war in the quest for liberation if an alternative, non-violent path were available to the ANC. He also emphasised that the ANC was not interested in talking merely for the sake of dialogue. Any discussions were to be seriously meant to end immediately the tyrannical and murderous system of apartheid. He added that

> ... there could be no solution to the South African question until our country is transformed into a united, democratic and non-racial entity, until the people themselves exercise power through a system of one person one vote in a unitary state. Without acceptance of this perspective there can be no negotiations precisely because without this political result South Africa can know no peace.[9]

While the government was still dragging its feet on the question of negotiations, the ANC embarked on another offensive that sought to strengthen its negotiating position. After a long period of discussion, the organisation passed the constitutional guidelines for discussion.[10] The constitutional guidelines were in fact a product of the struggles that were being waged during the mid-1980s. The climax of the mass resistance inside the country and the resurgence of the ANC as the dominant force across the political landscape had increasingly tilted the balance of support in favour of the liberation movement and aligned world support behind its struggle to eliminate apartheid in South Africa. Many international states and organisational entities were beginning to look at the ANC as a potential alternative to the apartheid state, hence the pressures on it to elaborate its conception and vision of an alternative post-apartheid policy. For several years since 1955, the ANC's guiding document had been the Freedom Charter. Although the charter provided a glimpse of the configuration of a future order, it did not elaborate on the details. It only provided a broad outline which was so ambiguous as to have different meanings to different people. By the mid-1980s the ANC felt that a detailed outline of its vision of a future South Africa was needed. As the Freedom Charter had formed the basis of its thinking on questions of the struggle, such a vision had to conform with the fundamental principles it endorsed.

The guidelines were drafted by the ANC's Constitutional Committee, set up in January 1986.[11] They merely expanded on the fundamental principles enshrined in the Freedom Charter and were not by themselves an end product, a constitution, but an auxiliary tool that would guide in the drafting of a new constitution. They were devised to invoke debate and full contribution by the masses with a view to ultimately carving a formidable constitutional option. According to Zola Skweyiya, the constitutional guidelines were

> ... an ideological instrument, a morale booster and a clarification of our objectives in our present struggle against apartheid. At this time when the signs are clear that the apartheid regime has been shaken to its foundations, its allies frightened and confused, and its overseas supporters on the defensive, the guidelines are meant to strengthen the confidence of the liberation forces, deepen the conviction of all those who have lost their faith in the viability of the apartheid system. They are meant to increase the pressure on the apartheid regime on all fronts and make our force irresistible. They are a response to the demands of the stage the struggle had reached.[12]

The constitutional guidelines contained 25 clauses covering areas such as the state, franchise, national identity, a bill of rights, affirmative action, economy, land, workers, women, the family, and the international dimension.[13] They gave content to the ANC's vision of a united, non-racial and democratic South Africa. They committed it, among other things, to a unitary state, one person one vote, a bill of rights, a multi-party system, mixed economy, land reform, extensive rights for workers and women, and the protection of the family and other private formations in civil society.[14] Adding momentum to its negotiating position, the ANC embarked on a massive campaign to sell its formula to the international community of states. After much consultation with various segments of the MDM, all sectors of the liberation movement and other international parties, the ANC, headed by Alfred Nzo, submitted its negotiating position to the OAU conference held in Harare on 22 August 1989. There was no problem on the part of African states in adopting the ANC's negotiating position. Only the PAC, which had an observer status in the OAU, objected, arguing that conditions were not yet ripe for negotiations in South Africa and that it would continue with the armed struggle. The declaration of the OAU Ad Hoc Committee on Southern Africa on the question of South Africa was worded as follows:

> We believe that a conjuncture of circumstances exists which, if there is a demonstrable readiness on the part of the Pretoria regime to engage in negotiations genuinely and seriously, could create the possibility to end apartheid through negotiations. Such an eventuality would be an expression of the long-standing preference of the majority of the people of South Africa to arrive at a political settlement. We would therefore encourage the people of South Africa, as part of their overall struggle, to

get together to negotiate an end to the apartheid system and agree on all the measures that are necessary to transform their country into a non-racial democracy. We support the position held by the majority of the people of South Africa that these objectives, and not the amendment or reform of the apartheid system, should be the aims of the negotiations.[15]

The Harare Declaration agreed with the major principles of the ANC and further reiterated the organisation's preconditions before meaningful negotiations could start. The declaration stated that "together with the rest of the world, we believe that it is essential, before any negotiations can take place, that the necessary climate for negotiations be created. The apartheid regime has the urgent responsibility to respond positively to this universally acclaimed demand and thus create this climate". It called on Pretoria to

- release all political prisoners and detainees unconditionally and refrain from imposing any restrictions on them
- lift all bans and restrictions on all proscribed and restricted organisations and persons
- remove all troops from the townships
- end the state of emergency and repeal all legislation such as and including the Internal Security Act, designed to circumscribe political activity
- cease all political trials and political executions.

Although the Harare Declaration called for the "removal of all troops from the townships", it did qualify where the troops should go after their removal. The previous formulations had suggested that they should go back to the barracks. Similarly, "the return of exiles", which had featured in other formulations on creating a climate for negotiations, was not mentioned in the ANC/OAU proposal. An ANC official said that "logically, we do not think the return of exiles can be a precondition. It is a matter which is related to the cessation of hostilities. If you put it as a precondition, and the regime accepts it before a cease-fire is negotiated, what guarantee is there for the safety of our cadres?".[16] The formulation of preconditions before negotiations was viewed by some commentators as a reflection of the ANC's reluctance to negotiate. It was assumed that by setting conditions which it knew the government could not meet, the ANC ensured that negotiations would not be possible.

Looking at these assumptions from the angle of the balance of forces obtainable at the time, it would have been foolhardy for the ANC to be enticed into negotiations in an environment inimical to it. Arguing this case, the UDF mentioned that "it is true that both itself and the ANC have set conditions for negotiations. This does not indicate a lack of commitment to negotiation. On the contrary it is a recognition that for parties to negotiate they must be truly representative of their constituencies".[17] This meant that all barriers to free political activity had to be removed before negotiations could start.

Friedman meticulously outlined the reasons why preconditions had to be met by Pretoria before negotiations could start. He wrote that the most obvious point was that the black leadership could not arrive at the negotiation table unless it was no longer in jail or exile. Leaders also did not negotiate as individuals, but as representatives of organised movements. If leaders were to negotiate on behalf of their constituents, they needed to know what settlement terms would be acceptable to their supporters. Labour relations negotiations had shown long ago that bargains which were not endorsed by those they affect were not worth the paper they are written on. Both parties to a negotiation needed to canvass support freely for their position. In the end, Friedman argued that steps such as the release of prisoners, unbanning, repealing security laws and creating opportunities for free tests of black political allegiances were not unreasonable preconditions set by people who did not want to negotiate. They were measures which had to be taken if bargaining was to work.[18] These were the initiatives that had to be taken by the government. As Cyril Ramaphosa emphasised, "we cannot talk to De Klerk about unbanning the ANC until he does it. We cannot talk to him about releasing political prisoners until he does it. He has to fulfil certain conditions before there can be any negotiation".[19]

The question of negotiations stagnated into a stalemate during the Botha era with the state insisting on its precondition requiring the ANC to abandon "violence" before negotiations could start. But the ANC countered that it had resorted to violence in response to state violence and that it could not abandon violence before the state did so.

P.W. Botha's political dilemma and the crisis of stalemate

Although the ANC and the state tried to demonstrate that they were willing to negotiate during the period from 1987 to early 1989 (the Botha period), their practical actions demonstrated that they were not yet ready for real negotiations. Neither party wanted to compromise and most of their actions were aimed at trying to discredit each other on the political terrain. There was nothing to entice them into negotiations. Attempts by the two parties to avoid each other were grounded in their deeply rooted mistrust and fear of each other's needs and aspirations. Thus the fusillade of accusations and counter-accusations on the question of sincere commitment to negotiations served well to prevent their actual contact and did no harm to either's position. While on the one hand the state declared itself open to negotiations with the black communities and tried to create structures such as the National Statutory Council and the National Forum to facilitate the talks, it was not on the other hand committed to opening such talks to the broad spectrum of the black population. It conceived of such talks taking place within the parameters it defined and only about the agenda it introduced. It was not prepared to lift the state of emergency, release political prisoners or unban political organisations. It kept the ANC out of the talks by demanding that it renounce the armed struggle before it could be allowed to be party to the talks. On the other hand, the ANC's statements on negotiation continued to be contradicted by belligerent words about intensifying the armed struggle. The liberation movement insisted on the fulfilment of its preconditions before any meaningful negotiations could commence between it and the state. It insisted on the intensification of the struggle on all fronts. Its joint statement, released after meeting the UDF and COSATU on 6 June 1989 in Lusaka, stated that

> ... it is necessary for us to effectively review our position on negotiations. Our perspective on doing so is to find the appropriate response that fends off this initiative in a manner that does not create confusion or division in our ranks; does not result in the demobilisation of the masses; does not result in any lessening of pressure from the international arena and results in us maintaining the initiative against the regime.

Despite its commitment to negotiations, the ANC also called for the intensification of the armed struggle and mass political actions, declaring 1989 as the "year of mass action for people power".[20] In its discussion paper of 16 June 1989 on negotiations, it stated that

> ... discussion of the whole question of negotiations in no way affects and should not affect the overall strategic orientation of our movement and the tasks that arise from that orientation. Our strategic task is the destruction of the apartheid regime and the transfer of power to the people. This we seek to achieve through mass political action, armed struggle, the international isolation of the apartheid system and by ensuring that the ANC plays its proper role as the revolutionary vanguard of our struggling people.[21]

The emphasis on escalating the armed struggle and the all-round political mass offensive was not only induced by the ANC's scepticism about the state's seriousness, but also by its analysis of the state, which it perceived as vulnerable and divided. In its call to the people of South Africa to press home the attack, the ANC said that

> ... our struggle stands on the brink of a very crucial moment. Through bold mass action, we have driven the racist bully into a corner. Through militant mass defiance and skilful organisation, we are rendering martial law unworkable. Through heroic armed actions, we have made the regime more insecure, more unsteady on its feet. Our duty now, the duty of all patriots, is to press home the attack! The apartheid ruling clique is confused, divided and more vulnerable than ever before. Faced with a people determined to achieve their birthright now rather than later, the racists no longer understand one another and are fighting among themselves.[22]

In a pamphlet issued by the ANC underground structure from "Pretoria's Church Street" and distributed at the December 1989 Conference for a

Democratic Future in Johannesburg, the liberation movement urged the masses to participate in a people's war and provided a broad guideline on participation. It contended that the armed struggle was not only for trained combatants, but for everyone, and explained that people participate in the armed struggle when they set up barricades and fight the police and soldiers; when they supply MK combatants with food, shelter and information, and when they form combat groups and self-defence units. It urged for the building and strengthening of underground networks; the drawing in of active militants; the making of home-made weapons and the seizing of weapons from the enemy; the skilful observation of targets; the gathering of information about the enemy; the spreading of the politics of the movement; and the fusion of mass and armed actions to weaken the enemy. The call for a mass offensive was repeated on 8 January 1990, the 78th anniversary of the ANC, when the organisation declared 1990 to be the "year of people's action for a democratic South Africa".[23]

Although the insistence on intensifying the revolutionary struggle could be interpreted as indicating a lack of commitment on the part of the ANC to negotiate, it was nevertheless reflective of the genuine, practical problems confronting the organisation. Being a banned organisation operating from exile, the ANC did not have much leverage vis-à-vis the state in terms of spearheading the negotiation process, nor did it have any feasible means of mobilising popular support behind its negotiating position. In addition, it could not, for the sake of negotiations, start suspending its military activities while the state still wielded its mechanisms of repression. Nevertheless, the ANC used the calls for an armed struggle during this period only as a means of keeping the government in a state of agitation and reassuring the masses of its unwavering commitment to defending their cause. It had in effect already imposed a de facto suspension of armed activity. The reduction of armed activities in 1989 and the emphasis by the released Rivonia leaders on the need for discipline (i.e. avoidance of violence) in the struggle were contributing towards the normalisation of hostilities with the state. While it earnestly sought to take initiatives in negotiations, it also had to adopt a threatening posture towards the state to harass it into serious dialogue. But its refusal to renounce violence and the state's arrogance to meet its demands ultimately created an impasse.

This stalemate around preconditions – where each party demanded that the other renounce violence – increasingly became the main characteristic of the stillborn negotiation prospect during the Botha era. Despite public statements, the reality was that the actions of the government and the ANC did not suggest that a mutually hurting stalemate was fundamental to their respective consideration of negotiations. Arguably, both parties had sustained injuries in the conflict, but still felt that they could manage the worsening problem. On top of this, the parties differed in their understanding of the purpose of negotiations. Commenting on this unqualified commitment to negotiations, Zartman wrote that "the majority expects to negotiate the surrender of the minority .. [while] the government, contrarily, believes it is in charge of the country and conceives of negotiations as a grant by central authority, necessarily involving unequals".[24]

The parties did not feel the urgency to negotiate quickly; there were no deadlines to compel them to work swiftly towards negotiations, as was the case with Resolution 435 in Namibia. According to Zartman "the government believes it can handle things in the short run whereas the majority believes in the wave of history in the long run. All these aspects open up some prospects of negotiation but do not yet constitute a ripe moment".[25] Schlemmer contended that there was no stalemate in South Africa to warrant objective negotiations.[26] He pointed out that parties first had to agree on what was to be negotiated, for example, the transfer of power. He argued that the parties were still divided on the subject of negotiations. While the ANC wanted the transfer of power, the state wanted power-sharing based on race groups. The absence of a stalemate therefore, Schlemmer concluded, led parties to negotiate in bad faith, with each party trying to discredit the other.

Negotiations therefore became to both parties another terrain of the struggle on which they sought to tackle each other with new instruments. For the state, negotiating was a strategic initiative that sought to demobilise mass resistance and to foster divisions within the black community and the liberation movement. The ANC, on the other hand, did not see negotiations as the penultimate step towards the ultimate resolution of the conflict. It saw negotiations as another terrain of the struggle from which to launch a mass political offensive against the crumbling regime.

The De Klerk era: the normalisation of hostilities and the building of a peaceful climate conducive to negotiations

While the possibility of negotiations remained trapped in the quagmire of preconditions during the Botha era, the drastic developments in 1989 and the ascendance of F.W. de Klerk as the State President saw an emergence out of the quagmire and the creation of conditions conducive to dialogue between the main political adversaries. The creation of a climate conducive to negotiations in 1989 would have been inconceivable had it not been for the stroke suffered by P.W. Botha on 18 January. Botha's stroke and his subsequent resignation on 2 February opened the way for the election of De Klerk as the State President.

Even during the period when De Klerk served as Acting State President, there was evidence of a new spirit of optimism across the South African political spectrum. For the first time a new vision of a future South Africa was advocated, envisaging a complete break with the past. Calls for genuine negotiations with the authentic leaders of the black community were made, with De Klerk taking practical steps to demonstrate his government's seriousness about negotiations. Still serving as Acting State President, De Klerk crossed the border to talk to President Chissano of Mozambique on bilateral cooperation, went to see President Mobuto of Zaire about the Angolan peace talks, and visited Zambia to introduce himself to President Kaunda. Bell wrote that De Klerk's visits were a practical demonstration to the electorate of the value of negotiations. They could see on television that black leaders obviously found De Klerk an acceptable man to deal with.[27] The warm reception he received from African leaders, as well as Britain's Margaret Thatcher when he visited her in June, was underlined by South Africa's impressive contribution to the negotiations that led to the withdrawal of the Cuban forces in Angola and the implementation of UN Resolution 435 for the independence of Namibia. However, the leaders that De Klerk met similarly used the opportunity to pressure him into resolving the conflict in South Africa through negotiations.

Unlike during the Botha era, where such outside pressures and calls for negotiations were condemned as unwarranted meddling in South Africa's domestic affairs, the call for negotiations during the De Klerk era received warm acceptance and was translated into the NP election propaganda for the general elections to be held on 6 September 1989. The party's election manifesto, the *Five-year action plan*, emphasised the intention of the Nationalists to break with the past and move towards true democracy. The NP victory with 93 seats, together with the impressive return of the Democratic Party (DP) with 33 seats and the marginalisation of the Conservative Party (CP) with 39 seats, was interpreted as a 70 per cent mandate for reform and negotiations.[28] Within a few weeks after his election as South Africa's second executive State President, De Klerk took practical steps to implement his promises:

- He allowed peaceful marches to take place, resulting in the biggest ever protest marches being staged all over the country on 14 October 1989.[29]
- He released Walter Sisulu and other Rivonia political prisoners (except Nelson Mandela) on 15 October 1989.
- He allowed mass welcome rallies to be held in Soweto.

Other informal attempts were made to allow the creation of a peaceful climate towards negotiations. Police powers for handling political demonstrations were greatly circumscribed and mass detentions of political activists curtailed. Reacting to the barrage of criticism by the CP on the handling of demonstrations and rallies, the NP responded in a voice that a few months previously would have been most unfamiliar among its ranks. Speaking at Voortrekkerhoogte, De Klerk appealed to those who felt threatened by events in recent weeks not to allow fear to override the need for initiative towards peaceful solutions.[30] In another unfamiliar expression, particularly from the ranks of the South African security establishment, Minister of Law and Order, Adriaan Vlok, contended that opportunities must be created in South Africa where people can express their political views in an orderly fashion. "Peaceful protest provided a political outlet for certain political feelings. It was an opportunity for protesters to present their grievances so that the government could give its attention to them".[31]

The appointment of Gerrit Viljoen as the Minister of Constitutional Development and Planning in the De Klerk government also saw an increasing urge on the part of the state to speed up negotiations. The normalisation of hostilities and the creation of a climate conducive to negotiations received utmost priority, with the state initiating preliminary talks with a broad spectrum of the black communities. Unlike during the Botha period, the prioritisation of political accommodation over constitutional mechanisms received more favour under De Klerk. Intransigence on certain apartheid principles such as group rights was toned down, with new emphasis being placed on such issues forming the subject of negotiation.[32]

Between September 1989 when De Klerk assumed the leadership of the country, and January 1990, significant reforms were introduced to help "remove the layer of suspicion" from among the different population groups and to create a climate conducive to negotiations. In addition to releasing political prisoners and allowing peaceful protests, De Klerk opened all beaches to all South African citizens and scrapped the Separate Amenities Act. With a strong fist, he opened the apartheid Boksburg central business district to all races and announced the first free settlement areas. He reduced the national service period and ended bureaucratic control of the National Management System.[33] In January 1990 he relieved the police force of its role in political affairs,[34] promised to lift the state of emergency and to release Nelson Mandela in the not too distant future. Although the ANC remained banned during this period, the release of the Rivonia leaders and their unrestricted operation as ANC leaders effected a de facto unbanning of the organisation. There was also back-stepping on certain previous positions. The display of the ANC and the SACP's flags or the promotion of their image – something that had led to mass prosecutions in the past – was now said "to have never been prohibited". Of greater significance in the attempts to speed up negotiations, the old insistence on the ANC to renounce violence was toned down into something to the effect that "the ANC had to show its commitment to peace" before it could be allowed to enter into negotiations.

In summary, the drastic liberalisation steps taken by De Klerk, the reforms he introduced and the diplomatic initiatives he took to sell his initiatives abroad had by the beginning of 1990 enhanced the image of his government quite considerably. Unlike the Botha regime, De Klerk's initiatives drew much sympathy from many international states. He successfully warded off the imposition of more sanctions and scored a coup against the ANC when he successfully negotiated the rescheduling of foreign debts and even ventured to win support from the Eastern bloc, particularly Hungary. While the above initiatives were significant in maximising the political image of the government and in building a climate conducive to negotiations, they nevertheless were underpinned by blurred ulterior motives. While the liberalisation project and the reforms introduced were aimed at the creation of a peaceful climate, they also sought to demobilise and defeat the opposition forces. Despite the fact that the release of Sisulu and other Rivonia leaders was a product of the struggle waged by the masses and the international lobby, the timing of their release on 14 October 1989 before the commencement of the Commonwealth Heads of State Summit meeting, served on the part of the government as a means of giving Thatcher a tangible defence to block the imposition of further sanctions against South Africa.

The permission for these leaders to operate legally as ANC members inside the country showed an earnest attempt by the state to drive a wedge between them and the external ANC in Lusaka. In fact, negotiating with these leaders instead of the external mission would not be as problematic to the state in the long run. Other attempts were also made to sidestep the ANC. In calling for the participation of all groups and organisations in the negotiation process and proposing the election of black representatives, the state contended that the ANC was not the single representative of black opinion. This message was conveyed by Viljoen at the Transvaal National Party Congress where he said that "it is a fundamental misunderstanding that there are only two real opposing parties, namely the government and the most extreme of the militant radical organisations".[35] The ANC was said not to be the only pebble on the beach and De Klerk vowed that his government would not allow its "elected homeland and municipal leaders" to be sidelined out of the negotiation process. "There is no single party or grouping that can lay claim that it alone speaks on behalf of black South Africans."

The decision to allow protest demonstrations also saw attempts by the state to shift the responsibility of consequent violence into the hands of the ANC and its MDM ally. While the introduction of reforms and the creation of a peaceful climate were welcomed by almost the whole of humanity, the fact that the state was responsible for these initiatives allowed it the freedom of timing the implementation or the spacing of such reforms over a long period of time during which it could weaken the opposition forces. In fact, the vein of negotiating in bad faith, though covert, ran through the body of the liberalisation initiatives introduced by the state thus far. However, despite the blemish of these covert attempts to demobilise the opposition forces, the initiatives taken by the state had by 1989 and early 1990 shaken the ANC out of balance, hence its desperate urge to take the initiatives away from its opponent. Fundamental changes that were taking place all over the world in 1989 also served as a continuum within which the ANC had to consolidate its position on a negotiated trajectory to national liberation. Communist Party governments in Eastern Europe (Poland, Hungary, Czechoslovakia) were either crumbling or introducing fundamental reforms in the face of popular protest and pressure.[36] Enthused by *perestroika* and *glasnost*, but instinctively driven by fundamental grievances, national movements in different republics of the Soviet Union were demanding independence. The fall of the Berlin Wall, which had divided Germany in two, symbolically opened the way for the unification of the West and the East and undermined the decades-old threat of global war between the superpowers. Finally, the defeat of despotic rule and the shunning of foreign-propped insurrectionary groups in Latin America (Nicaragua, El Salvador, Chile, Panama, Colombia) and the search for political solutions to regional conflicts in Africa (Angola, Mozambique, Ethiopia-Eritrea) and the Middle East (Palestine) broadly provided a context for the unfolding of the struggle in South Africa.

Acknowledging De Klerk's positive signals to a peaceful solution of the political crisis, the ANC began rethinking its hard insistence on preconditions. The question was asked: "Do all our previous preconditions need to be met before there can be negotiation, in other words, must all apartheid laws be scrapped before the democratic forces negotiate with the forces of apartheid?"[37] A distinction was made between negotiations and a negotiated settlement. "Negotiations" as a term was defined as "meetings between conflicting parties at which they try to find a mutually acceptable resolution to their conflict, or some aspect of their conflict". A "negotiated settlement" was defined as a "binding agreement reached through talks which create a new order". It was asked whether all the preconditions needed to be met before there could be any negotiations, or whether this applied only once a negotiated settlement, that is a situation of transfer of power to the majority, had been arrived at.

> What we need to consider is whether we do not need to be more precise and examine whether it is not perhaps a case of some preconditions needing to be met immediately to ensure participation by authentic leaders, acting with a mandate from organisations etcetera, in an atmosphere where consultation is facilitated. Can we not see some other preconditions as ones over which we negotiate, that is, the overall goal being the abolition of apartheid and its replacement by a democratic people's South Africa. Can we not meet in the interim subject to a climate being created where leaders can conduct proper consultation etcetera, to negotiate for the achievement of the ultimate goals, or to create a climate that is more favourable for its achievement?[38]

It was argued that while this suggests a shift "in the way we tackle preconditions, it does not mean that we abandon our demand for the total abolition of apartheid laws. It means that we recognise that we may be in a better position to achieve our fundamental preconditions if we negotiate in a climate conducive to such negotiations".[39] Underlying the ANC's rethinking on preconditions was the urge to take the initiative away from the government. In its 1989 discussion papers on the issue of negotiation, the ANC contended that

> ... as a revolutionary movement, it is however our task and responsibility that we should at all times keep the initiative in our hands, particularly with regard to strategic questions. The issue facing us is how to keep the initiative in our hands on this strategic matter of negotiations. What positions should we elaborate to ensure that it is our opponent who is forced to respond to us and not the other way round? Clearly, as a revolutionary movement, we cannot afford to trail behind the regime and allow ourselves to fall into a defensive posture with the regime maintaining the offensive.[40]

The organisation decided to rally for mass support both inside the country and abroad behind its Harare Declaration on negotiations and to deepen mass discussions around its constitutional guidelines. Significantly, the Harare Declaration was adopted by the Non-aligned States and was endorsed by the MDM during the Conference for a Democratic Future held at Wits University on 9 December 1989. It was finally adopted by the UN's General Assembly on 14 December 1989. In intensifying mass political action the ANC decided to exploit the space provided by De Klerk's liberalisation process, resulting in the mass defiance campaigns, the "unbanning" of restricted organisations and the mass protests against the Labour Relations Act. Despite the ANC's attempts to take the initiative in negotiations, the drastic reforms and the ebullient commitment shown by the state to speed up negotiations had by the end of 1989 not only left the organisation in a state of shock, but also faced with a swelling list of challenges. It had to contend with several serious problems. Beside the threats confronting its arch-allies in the East, particularly the Soviet Union and East Germany, the liberation movement had to contend with the following problems at home:

- The question of unity between itself, the MDM and the PAC on the question of negotiations
- The search for a solution to the Natal violence
- The underdevelopment or failure of MK activities in raising and supporting the revolutionary momentum
- The drastic steps taken by De Klerk in meeting its preconditions – something that had left the ANC uncertain of his and its next moves
- Finally, and most significantly, the Mandela question.

The emergence of Mandela from the shadows of legend into a real politician, though operating behind the scene, left the ANC trailing behind his initiatives. While Mandela maintained his loyalty to the ANC and saw himself as only attempting "to bring the country's two major political bodies to the negotiating table", his initiatives had a significant impact on the ANC. Even if it might have been indifferent to his initiatives, the organisation could not afford to be seen to be against him.

The release of Nelson Mandela from prison

In a historic speech at the opening of parliament on 2 February 1990, De Klerk declared the unbanning of all political organisations, including the ANC, and announced the release of Nelson Mandela from prison. This watershed speech opened a new chapter in the history of South Africa. It provided the first real basis for a negotiated end to apartheid rule. Despite initial attempts by the government to release Mandela unceremoniously, the ANC leader was finally released on 11 February 1990. A number of welcome rallies were organised around the country to welcome him from prison, starting with the Grand Parade rally in Cape Town. For the following weeks and months Mandela became the main celebrity both at home and abroad with crowds of people gathering at every place he visited.

The significance of Mandela's release lay not only in clearing one of the most important obstacles to negotiations, but also in allowing the ANC to sort out its leadership problem following Oliver Tambo's debilitating stroke. The election of Mandela as Deputy President and his effective take-over from Oliver Tambo of the leadership of the organisation allowed more room for consensus on negotiations. These developments were important for they brought to an end the time-consuming consultation process between the triumvirate centres of power (exile, prison and internal leadership) that had developed within the mass democratic organisation at the end of the 1980s.

ENDNOTES

1. Communiqué of the Second National Conference of the ANC. Presented by President Oliver Tambo at a press conference, Lusaka, Zambia, 25 June 1985.
2. Callinicos (1988), op cit., 135–136.
3. *Mission to South Africa: the Commonwealth Report*, 1986, 86.
4. Ibid., 132.
5. ANC statement on negotiation, 9 October 1987.
6. 'The United Democratic Front statement on negotiations', *Phambili*, 1, April 1988.
7. ANC statement on negotiation, op cit.
8. South African Institute of Race Relations (SAIRR) *Annual Report*, 1987/88, 702.
9. *The spear of the nation (Umkhonto we Sizwe): armed struggle, strategy and tactics of the ANC*. Address by President O.R. Tambo, Arusha, December 1987, 18. See also "People of the world united against apartheid for a democratic South Africa", ANC Arusha Conference, Tanzania, 1–4 December 1987, 21–22.
10. Anonymous. *The constitutional guidelines of the ANC: a Giddensian perspective*, 1988, 6.
11. Skweyiya, Z. *The ANC constitutional guidelines: a vital contribution to the struggle against apartheid*. Paper presented at the Harare Conference of Lawyers, 31 January – 4 February 1989, 3.
12. Ibid., No. 6. Workers.
13. Anonymous, op cit., 7.
14. Swilling, M. & Van Zyl Slabbert, F. *Waiting for a negotiated settlement: South Africans in a changing world*. Centre for Policy Studies "Negotiation Package", University of the Witwatersrand, 1989, 6.
15. Declaration of the OAU Ad Hoc Committee on Southern Africa on the question of South Africa. Harare, Zimbabwe, 21 August 1989. This document is popularly known as the "Harare Declaration".
16. Cargill, J. Scoring points off Pretoria. *Work In Progress*, 61, September/October 1989, 17.
17. 'The United Democratic Front today'. *United Democratic Front Publication*, September 1987, 7.
18. Friedman, S. Enter the playing fields of negotiations. *Weekly Mail*, 5(26), July 1989.
19. Ramaphosa, C. Interview in *Leadership Magazine*, 18(9), November 1989, 23–24. 'Negotiations as a terrain of and method of struggle', op cit., 12.
20. Cloete, F. *Prospects for a democratic process of political change in South Africa*. Paper presented at the Conference on Perspectives on the Contemporary South African State. Centre for Policy Studies, University of the Witwatersrand, 27–28 February 1989.
21. ANC discussion paper on the issue of negotiations, 16 June 1989.
22. *ANC call to the people of South Africa: press home the attack!* ANC statement, 22 August 1989.
23. *The Star*, 8 January 1990.
24. Zartman, W. Negotiations in South Africa. *The Washington Quarterly*, 11(4), Autumn, 1988, 143.
25. Ibid., 143.
26. Schlemmer, L. *Negotiations in South Africa: a balance sheet of opportunities and constraints*. Centre for Policy Studies "Negotiations Package", University of the Witwatersrand, 1989, 4.
27. *The Star*, 21 December 1989.
28. *Sunday Star* and *Sunday Times*, 12 October 1989.
29. *Sunday Star*, 3 November 1989.

30. *The Citizen*, 30 October 1989.
31. Bell, P. Feeling the way. *Leadership Magazine,* 8(9), November 1989, 18.
32. *Sunday Star*, 17 December 1989.
33. *The Star*, 29 January 1990.
34. *The Star*, 23 October 1989.
35. 'A year of turmoil and change'. *New Era Magazine,* 4(4), December 1989, 20–21.
36. 'Negotiations as a terrain of and method of struggle', op cit., 12.
37. Ibid., 113.
38. 'Negotiation as a weapon, view of the MDM'. *New Nation*, 4(40), October 1989.
39. *Business Day*, 20 July 1989.
40. Harare Declaration, op cit.

The ANC and substantive negotiations

Preliminary negotiations and the removal of obstacles to substantive negotiations

In spite of subscribing to the concept of combining its negotiation with other liberation strategies, the ANC concentrated its efforts on building a strong foundation for negotiations. The objective of this move was to harness and take control of the negotiation process, to set the agenda and to determine the parameters within which it would evolve. Unlike the government which was still locked in dismantling apartheid, the ANC had recourse to the provisions of the Harare Declaration in its attempts to steer the direction of the negotiation process.[1] According to these provisions, preliminary negotiations had to be entered into with the government to discuss the removal of obstacles to negotiations. This would pave the way for negotiations on an interim government, and elections to a constituent assembly that would draft the new constitution.

Taking the first step towards official talks with the government, the ANC NEC in its meeting held in Lusaka in February, decided to send a delegation to South Africa to explore preliminary talks with the South African government. Intensive preparatory work was initiated that culminated in the Groote Schuur meeting on 4, 5 and 6 May 1990. This historic meeting ended with an agreement to establish a working group which would define the parameters for ANC-government negotiations. The working group had to define political offences and discuss time scales in this regard. Furthermore, it had to advise on norms and mechanisms for dealing with the release of political prisoners and the granting of immunity in respect of political offences to those inside and outside South Africa. According to the Groote Schuur Minute, an "offence" applied to any person who had left the country without a valid travel document and to acts committed by organisations which were previously prohibited. Temporary immunity from prosecution for political offences committed before the date of the meeting, would be granted to NEC members to enable them entry into the country. The government undertook to review the existing security legislation and to work towards lifting the state of emergency. A further aspect of the agreement was that channels of communication between the government and the ANC would be established in order to curb violence.

The Groote Schuur agreement was an important breakthrough for the ANC in that it was able, for the first time, to force the government to clear obstacles in the way of constitutional negotiations. At the same time, nevertheless, it marked the beginning of a string of countless problems that were to create major headaches for the organisation throughout the period of transition. The commitment, in principle, by the government to part ways with apartheid and to implement decisions reached at Groote Schuur, compelled the ANC to adopt a stance of believing in these signals of goodwill. However, within three months it became clear that the government did not always act in good faith. It failed to implement the Groote Schuur agreements. The question of indemnity which could have been successfully handled in a month was effectively paralysed by administrative bureaucracy. Moreover, an unprecedented wave of violence washed over Natal and spread into the townships on the Rand in mid-1990.

While the ANC insisted on the continuation of the armed struggle to back up its negotiation strategy, and despite a developing understanding of the insincerity of the government, it called for a second bilateral meeting in Pretoria on 6 August 1990. At this meeting the NEC unilaterally agreed to suspend the armed struggle to advance the course of negotiations. This action was taken to induce a positive response from the government, particularly the clearing of remaining obstacles to negotiations. On the government's side, specific dates were given for the release of political prisoners and the indemnification process. The government gave the assurance that it would fulfil its obligation with regard to security legislation and the state of emergency. The major thrust of the Pretoria Minute, however, lay in the ANC's suspension of the armed struggle. According to the Minute

> ... in the interest of moving as speedily as possible towards a negotiated peaceful political settlement and in the context of the agreements reached, the ANC announced that it was now suspending all armed actions with immediate effect. As a result of this, no further armed actions and related activities by the ANC and its military wing, Umkhonto we Sizwe, will take place.[2]

A working group was set up to resolve all outstanding questions arising out of this decision and to report on 15 September 1990. Raymond Suttner justified this compromise on the armed struggle saying that

> ... the leadership saw the armed struggle as a blockade in the way of continuing the peace process. Even though it was felt that the government's objections to armed struggle were unreasonable, it was regarded as necessary to make this compromise in order to realise our broader strategic objectives. We made a tactical retreat in order to be in a better position for a strategic advance.[3]

The unilateral suspension of the armed struggle, against the background of escalating conflict in which the IFP and right-wing organisations were consolidating their military capabilities and the state still maintained the apparatus of repression, raised serious questions within the ANC about the implications and timing of this decision. While the leadership of the ANC saw their decision as a tactical shift to maintain the moral high ground on the question of negotiations, it nevertheless raised two major problems. It not only violated the precepts of the Harare Declaration that envisaged the conclusion of a truce only after the removal of obstacles, but was taken without consultation with branch members and regional leadership, much to the discontent of the rank and file. In the context of escalating violence in the East Rand townships and in parts of Natal/KwaZulu in particular, the rank and file increasingly felt the need for a defensive strategy involving arms. Moreover, the provision in paragraph 3 of the Minute to "set up a working group to resolve outstanding matters relating to the suspension of the armed struggle" raised legitimate fears about another compromise on mass action. In fact the government had, contrary to its decision to allow mass demonstrations and protest in 1989, exerted enormous pressure on the ANC to reconsider this form of action in the light of the opening political phase. Finally, the manner in which the decision was taken vindicated growing criticism that the organisation was gradually degenerating into elitist politics and ignoring the views of its membership.

While the suspension of the armed struggle formalised what was already a de facto move by the organisation to reduce confrontational politics, it nevertheless had little bearing on the other parties involved in the ongoing violence. Instead, violence continued unabated, leading to increasing dis-illusionment among both ANC supporters and the members of victimised communities. Contrary to expectations that 1990 would see the removal of obstacles and the paving of the way for constitutional talks by 1991, the question of violence significantly disrupted the organisation's efforts to rebuild its structures and its zeal in setting the terrain for negotiations. Violence and the inability of the state to stem it, the lack of a clear programme of action that linked negotiations to other forms of political action, the increasing prominence of deals behind closed doors and the poor state of organisational development, became crucial issues that formed the subject of the ANC's consultative conference in December 1990. High on the agenda of ANC leaders was the clearing of hurdles and replacing negotia-tions on the agenda.

The consultative conference held at Crown Mines, Johannesburg, on 16 December 1990, provided a medium for self-criticism and proper planning in the organisation. Although its decisions were not binding, they nevertheless provided guidance on what it conceived as the most effective way forward to achieving its goals of liberation. The adoption of the theme "1991, the year of mass action for the transfer of power", reflected an attempt by the organisation to bring mass struggle into the theatre of negotiations to bolster the leadership and to avoid major compromises. Besides resolutions on sanctions, violence, the underground and MK, on the question of negotia-tions the conference resolved to mandate the leadership to continue ex-ploratory talks with the government, but under strict conditions.[4] The conference emphasised that future deliberations with the government should be undertaken without any secrecy. It resolved that

- the NEC regularly consult with ANC membership in all regions on all major issues

- appropriate mechanisms be set up for such consultations and communication with the membership by the end of February 1991

- the NEC involve its revolutionary allies in the negotiation

- a comprehensive negotiating team composed of chief negotiators, working groups and researchers be created, including a fair representation of women

- the NEC serve notice on the government unless all obstacles had been removed on or before 30 April 1991, after which the ANC would consider the suspension of the whole negotiation process.

A programme of action was drawn up, centred upon the conference theme. This provided for the launching of a mass action campaign which would culminate on Solomon Mahlangu Day (6 April), for the release of prisoners, the return of exiles, the cessation of political trials and detention. It further provided for demonstrations around the opening of parliament to highlight the demand for an interim government and a constituent assembly, as well as the demand for the abolition of the tricameral parliament and the bantustan system. This was to be followed by a mass door-to-door signature campaign to popularise the objectives of an interim government and a constituent assembly, and to mobilise the people in this regard. The programme of action also provided for a patriotic front conference to mobilise all anti-apartheid forces against the government. While the programme started with massive marches during the opening of parliament, the ANC was unable to force the government to speed the release of prisoners and the return of exiles. In fact, the Groote Schuur and the Pretoria Minutes had reduced the organisation to a spectator by entrusting the government with the power to deal unilaterally with the question of obstacles. Not only could the latter manipulate this matter in its favour, it also had the power to introduce major reforms to its benefit.

Early in 1991 the ANC, faced with the danger of prolonging the transitional process by waiting for the complete removal of obstacles, opted to speed up negotiations. It hoped this tactic would also resolve these obstacles. The concern to speed up the process was reflected in the organisation's Anniversary Statement of 8 January 1991, which called for the holding of an all-party conference to discuss the creation of an interim government and a constituent assembly. The idea of an all-party conference had not been discussed at the December conference, and raised further fears of continued elitism and the apparent evasion of the conference's resolutions. A resolution had been passed at the conference, binding leaders to consult broadly before making important decisions. At the same time, ANC members had also resolved to give the leadership sufficient scope to act. The all-party conference was to address issues related to a constituent assembly, such as criteria for the selection of parties, mechanisms of representation and the size of a delegation, a convenor, chair and dates, an agenda, methods of decision making and deadlock resolution. It was suggested that after completing its work within a definite time the all-party conference would dissolve, unless it obtained a specific, popular mandate to continue as a constitution-making body, an interim government or both.[5]

The demand for transitional mechanisms: interim government and a constituent assembly[6]

Unlike the idea of an interim government, the views about a democratically elected body to draft a new constitution for the country had deep historical roots within the ANC. Although different in name, the concept of a forum for the drafting of a constitution within the ANC dated back to Nelson Mandela's call for a national convention in the early 1960s. Mandela believed that a national convention could be the turning point in the country's history. In a letter addressed to Sir de Villiers Graaff, leader of the United Party, he had written:

> The country is becoming an armed camp, the government is preparing for civil war; none of us can draw any satisfaction from this developing crisis. We for our part have put forward, in the name of the African people, a majority of South Africans, serious proposals for a way out of this crisis. We have called on the government to convene an elected national convention of representatives of all races without delay, and to charge that convention with drawing up a new constitution for this country which would be acceptable to all race groups.[7]

Notwithstanding creative and peaceful intentions around the question of a national convention, the idea was dealt a fatal blow by the arrest, prosecution and imprisonment of ANC leaders. Until the 1970s, this idea remained submerged within a culture of revolution.

When Mangosuthu Buthelezi, the Chief Minister of KwaZulu, resurrected the concept of a national convention in 1971, the ANC quickly responded in support of such a forum, with certain conditions. It stated that the convention should have sovereignty and have the authority to change South African society in all its aspects, and that it should be attended by representatives of all national groups in proportions that reflected the composition of the South African population.[8] Although the national convention was seen by the ANC as a vehicle to introduce change in South Africa, it was later abandoned and the organisation began talking of a mechanism for the transfer of power to the people, hence the idea of a constituent assembly. When proposals for a national convention – resurfaced in 1985, Nelson Mandela was reported to have declared on 18 August of that year that "the time is past for a national convention all there is to talk about now is the mechanics of handing over power to the people of South Africa".[9] The first comment within the ANC on the idea of a constituent assembly was made by Mzala in 1985. Mzala suggested that a people's democratic republic in South Africa could be established through a constituent assembly elected, not on the grounds of the 1971 proposal, but on the basis of equal universal franchise. He argued that the assembly would have to be sovereign to have the necessary power to formulate a new constitution.[10] The call for a democratically elected constituent assembly was put forward as an ANC position during a meeting with COSATU and the UDF on 6 June 1989. In a joint statement, the organisations proposed the holding of negotiations for the establishment of a constituent assembly which would be empowered to draw up a constitution. The statement also called for the suspension of parliament and the establishment of an interim government that would facilitate the process during the period of transition.[11]

At the COSATU congress held in July 1989, the trade union federation resolved that "only a sovereign body mandated by the people as a whole can have the authority to develop a new constitution and decide on the method of implementation".[12] Although the idea of a constituent assembly was not specifically mentioned in the 1989 Harare Declaration, articles 21.2–3 and 21.5 gave effect to this idea and to that of an interim government. The declaration stated that after the suspension of hostilities between the warring parties

> ... negotiations should then proceed to establish the basis for the adoption of a new constitution by agreeing on, among others, the principles enunciated above [see statement of principles in the OAU Harare Declaration]. Having agreed on these principles, the parties should then negotiate the necessary mechanism for drawing up the new constitution. The parties should agree to the formation of an interim government to supervise the process of drawing up and adopting a new constitution, governing and administering the country, as well as effecting the transition to a democratic order, including the holding of elections.

In 1989 the ANC emphasised that a constituent assembly should consist of democratically elected representatives of all the people of South Africa and should not be based on groups or minorities, as the government demanded.[13] During this period a transitional government, which would prevent the NP from being both a player and a referee, would be elected to take charge of the governing of the country and to facilitate the transition to a new political order. In its words,

> ... the early installation of an interim government, as a body with real power in fact and in law, and in control of all instruments of state power, is critical to the process of the transition to the new order. Quite clearly this process of transition away from apartheid cannot be supervised by an apartheid institution, which is precisely what the present government is.[14]

Without according them an automatic role, the organisation also called for the involvement of international forces to supervise the transition.[15] The Harare Declaration had clearly stated that "the parties shall define and agree on the role to be played by the international community in ensuring a successful transition to a democratic order".[16] The organisation also proposed the involvement of specialists in the drafting of the constitution, but cautioned that "these specialists would be accountable to the Assembly. The constitution which results must derive primarily from the majority of South Africans. It is very important for the process of specialisation to be democratised".[17]

On 3 May 1990 Mandela called for national elections for a constituent assembly to draw up a new constitution.[18] In the "Programme of mass action to destroy apartheid and transfer power to the people" in December 1990, the ANC gave priority to the demand for a constituent assembly and an interim government. This was reiterated at the national consultative conference in December 1990 and in the anniversary statement of 8 January 1991, leading to its final endorsement at the ANC's national congress in July 1991. The ultimate acceptance of these transitional mechanisms within the ANC was of greater significance to the fulfilment of its strategic objectives. By establishing an interim government, the ANC hoped that this would help in the fair management of the transition by scaling down acts of violence and destabilisation, controlling the security forces and supervising elections for a constituent assembly.[19] It also argued that an interim government would enable it to maximise its power vis-à-vis the nationalist government. An interim government would limit the power of the NP to determine the course of the transition and would ensure the creation of a new democracy.[20] As regards the constituent assembly, the ANC believed that if delegates to this body were elected, this would result in a legitimate constitution. It also believed that through an elected constituent assembly it would be able to win a majority of votes and hence draft a new constitution, and possibly form a new government.[21]

While the ANC's transitional mechanisms were influenced by the heightened violence and the inclination of the government to favour an undemocratic way of drafting the constitution, the extent to which it stood to fulfil its strategic objectives was highly questionable. Although the demand for an interim government in South Africa was prompted by the need to create an impartial structure that would manage the process fairly, African countries in which interim governments had been created provided evidence of difficulties and problems which disadvantaged liberation movements. As for the maintenance of peace and the prevention of intimidation, the interim governments in Africa's decolonisation process had proven to be weak and, in most cases, incapable. In Zimbabwe, the transitional government of Lord Soames which was agreed to at Lancaster House, had no effective control over the security apparatus of the Ian Smith government and the Rhodesian security forces continued their operations against guerrillas.[22] The South African forces, too, had been reluctant to leave and continued with acts of terrorism against communities.[23] Sithole and Muzorewa auxiliaries, paramilitary armies, also contributed to the wave of intimidation. In spite of the evidence of widespread "dirty tricks", the interim government could do little with the limited human and material resources at its disposal. Furthermore, the monitoring force made up of British, Australian, Fijian, Kenyan and New Zealand soldiers made no significant effort to control the Rhodesian security forces.

The transitions in Namibia and Angola were also not without enormous constraints. In Angola, the transitional government of Brigadier General Silva Cardoso, assisted by a presidential council with rotating chair shared by the National Liberation Front of Angola (FNLA), MPLA and UNITA collapsed within days of its formation because of its failure to maintain stability among the contending liberation movements.[24] The limitations demonstrated by these experiences provided a lesson for South Africa and it was highly unlikely that an interim government in this country would be any different. The "war of position" by the major parties which was being translated into violence, the existence of paramilitary forces and increasing disillusionment of the populace served to block sustained peace efforts. While the ANC favoured an interim government of which it would be part, it was, at least during the 1990–1992 period, not clear at what level it would seek participation. The issue of integrating MK cadres with the SADF was undecided, as was the establishment of joint structures of control.

The proposal for the involvement of international forces in monitoring South Africa's transition was not easy to contemplate. In those international cases where UN peacekeeping forces were deployed during transitions to independence, the only observable achievements related to supervising and monitoring the elections. Where the maintenance of stability and the prevention of intimidation were concerned, they had little success. This was due to the deficiency of both human and material resources, as well as a low moral commitment by foreign soldiers to sacrifice themselves for a war with no bearing on their lives. Peacekeeping forces deployed in the Congo and Lebanon, for instance, failed dismally to restore stability. While South Africa, like Zimbabwe and Namibia before it, sought to resolve the problem of white minority rule over the black majority, there were significant differences in the conceptualisation of the transitions. Although all three countries went through bitter conflicts before arriving at negotiations, Zimbabwe and Namibia were seen by the incumbent parties and the international community as going through a process of decolonisation, which provided legitimacy and a central role for the involvement of international forces. While this had negative consequences in the sense of foreign interference in determining the parameters within which new African polities were to emerge, these parties nevertheless made an invaluable contribution to mediating and providing some form of interim government. In the case of Zimbabwe, outsiders provided an impartial system of monitoring. The principle of majority rule was agreed upon as the point of departure, accompanied by mechanisms to allay the fears of whites.

In contrast to the above, there were differences of opinion in South Africa as to whether or not the country was going through a process of decolonisation. The government and a number of South African scholars viewed the transition as a democratisation process similar to that in Latin America and in some totalitarian regimes around the world.[25] For its part, the ANC saw the transition as little or no different from other cases of decolonisation, hence its insistence on the formation of an interim government and the holding of national elections for a constituent assembly that would ultimately facilitate the transfer of power to an elected government. While it was the ANC's position that international forces be given a role in the transition,[26] the government, despite its changing attitude on the matter during CODESA, argued to preclude them on the basis that the transition was an internal matter that would be settled by internal parties. Although the debate on the involvement of international forces no longer concerned whether they should be invited or not, the important question was: on what basis would they succeed in maintaining stability during South Africa's transition?

The other ANC objective behind the demand for an interim government was to maximise power against contending parties. However, the extent to which it would be able to achieve this depended on a number of factors. The first related to the composition and the type of interim government it was seeking. In the second instance, the sorts of tasks it would be entrusted with and whether the ANC would compromise its organisational strength for the success of such a government were also at issue. A careful analysis of the ANC's proposals for an interim government reveal serious shortcomings and difficulties that significantly narrowed the scope within which it could maximise its power. Towards the end of 1991 proposals for three optional forms of interim government were circulated within the organisation for discussion:

- The first was an interim government vested with sovereignty. This implied the transfer of legislative and executive powers from the existing parliament and cabinet. This transfer would have to be sanctioned by an interim constitution passed by the existing parliament after the repeal or amendment of the existing constitution. This would, *inter alia*, provide for the dissolution of the existing structures, define the composition and tasks of the interim government, as well as pronounce on various aspects such as the administration of the country during the interim period, the role of the existing state departments, provincial and local government administrations, and the procedure in decision making.

- The second option that was considered was an interim governing council. This body would leave the existing legislative and executive structures intact, but would have the power to veto bills passed by parliament and decisions taken by the cabinet. It would also be empowered to amend and make new laws by proclamation.

- A third option was an independent council, composed either of representatives of political parties or of people of acknowledged integrity. This structure would only deal with certain functions that would be taken away from the present government, such as the holding of free and fair elections and the creation of a conducive climate for the elections. It would be given the power to assume control over the security forces, to regulate and control access to the public media, to place a moratorium on "controversial" projects, and to require the government to take or refrain from taking particular actions.[27]

All three options had their own limitations. The establishment of a sovereign interim government sanctioned through an interim constitution that would depend on the approval of the existing parliament, accorded the apartheid structures the recognition and legitimacy that the organisation had resisted over the years. If a governing council model comprising a coalition of different political parties was introduced, bitter conflict would arise as to who should head the state. Problems of duality could also arise if the governing council made laws alongside the existing parliament without a clear demarcation of authority. It would, for instance, be difficult for an interim governing council, detached from the structures of governance, to adequately control the security forces. The historical record of the NP government also made it naive to believe that it would enjoy harmonious relations with a contending governing structure. Finally, it was possible that the governing council could end up making or repealing laws that might never be implemented by the existing government. This could also apply to an independent council which might not have the means to tame the security apparatus.

The ANC was vague about the composition of an interim government and about how parties would be drawn into the structure. While it said that it should be composed by the NP and itself, another option put forward was to involve all political parties, whatever their size. It was argued that in order to guarantee impartiality, none of these organisations should be treated as though they were major or minor.[28] While it would be easy to identify the major parties that would participate in the interim government, the question of minor parties was bound to create problems. If the country ended up with, say, a thousand political parties, how would this be handled? Of most significance, on which procedural basis would such a government be constituted? Would it be elected or simply be composed of appointees? If elected, would this not duplicate elections to a constituent assembly? If appointed, who would be assigned this task, and on what basis would the interim government be sovereign and enjoy popular legitimacy? If the interim government used consensus decision making, as mooted by the ANC, the possibility existed that certain parties might withhold consent, thereby halting its functioning. It could be argued that consensus only works if there has been an agreement among parties. The problem was, however, that parties were manoeuvring for position. For its part, the ANC faced the problem of what it would do if it did not like the decisions reached through consensus or if consensus was never reached on certain issues. Would it undercut a stalemate by demanding that "sufficient consensus" (i.e. minimum agreement) between the major players be taken as the standard barometer to enable progress? What if a majority of other parties objected to certain decisions reached through "sufficient consensus" or if they rejected this formula altogether?

The different options of an interim government that the ANC was considering in the early 1990s had limitations that had the potential to undermine its objective of maximising power. Moreover, whatever form of interim government the organisation ultimately opted for, maximising power against other parties had the potential to contradict efforts at creating a broadly accepted government that would be able in all fairness to supervise the transition. The tasks assigned to an interim government also had the potential of narrowing the scope of the organisation's ability to maximise its power. While the organisation maintained that the primary tasks of an interim government should be to create a climate conducive to fair elections and to maintain stability, there were other governmental tasks that were unclarified. Would an interim government attend to the basic needs of the population? Would it embark on fundamental socio-economic restructuring? There was a lively debate within the ANC on these questions.

Of significance in this regard was the debate involving Raymond Suttner, Head of the ANC's Department of Political Education, an analyst, Maria van Driel, Thabo Mbeki, Head of the ANC's Department of Foreign Affairs and contributions by the organisation's journal *Mayibuye*. All agreed that an interim government should supervise the transition and maintain peace. Differences, however, existed as to whether it should undertake other governmental tasks which would effect fundamental transformation. Raymond Suttner argued that an interim government should not take responsibility for tackling pressing issues such as housing and unemployment. Similarly, the September 1990 edition of *Mayibuye*, in its summary of a workshop on an interim government, argued that

> ... an interim government is not the forum – nor the transitional period the time – for emphasis to be put on resolving the housing question, unemployment and other structural problems of apartheid. Conditions can be created for this in the transitional period, but the basic mandate and tasks of the interim government should not be submerged in this.[29]

However, eight months later, *Mayibuye* contended that "life will not stop simply because society is in a state of transition". In an about-face, it propounded the idea that an interim government would have to manage all these matters during a period of transition. "This will require the involvement of all the parties concerned, in the running of ministries, departments and public corporations."[30] Expressing the same perspective but in a different tone, Thabo Mbeki[31] argued that those issues that demanded structural change would have to be tackled during the transitional period, and that an interim government could not shy away from them. "When the masses would demand from you to attend to their problems because you are involved in the government, you would not fold your hands and say you have no powers."[32]

Approaching the issue differently, Maria van Driel proposed that the transition be divided into two phases, so that two interim governments operated in succession.[33] The first, she suggested, would be established before the election of a constituent assembly. During this phase the task of this government would be to create a climate for free and fair elections. This phase would end with elections of a constituent assembly. The second interim government, which would replace the previous one, would be created after the first sitting of the constituent assembly. This government would have legitimate powers to address the immediate problems of the population, including restructuring the economy, since it would be accountable to an elected constituent assembly. The essence of her argument, which came closer to that of Suttner, was that an interim government should attend to transformative tasks after elections for a constituent assembly, and not before. However, her proposals did not consider that a government established by a democratically elected constituent assembly might not be an interim government but a sovereign democratic government. Furthermore, her proposal for two interim governments carried the danger of prolonging a process that was planned to move quickly.[34] It was clear, out of this debate, that one of the major challenges facing the ANC was that participating in an interim government to maintain peace, to supervise elections and to effect socio-economic restructuring, would demand responsibility from the movement without granting it real power to run the government.

The strategic objectives behind the demand for an elected constituent assembly were also not without problems, despite the fact that this appeared to be the most comfortable procedure through which a legitimate constitution could be drawn up. The argument that a constituent assembly would ensure democracy because delegates would be democratically elected was questionable, given existing conditions of violence and destabilisation. Fair elections could not be held under such conditions. Furthermore, the enthusiasm for the view that an elected constituent assembly would ensure democracy overestimated the extent to which elected delegates could represent the original will of the people in the drafting of the constitution. The Namibian experience demonstrated that elections were not the equivalent of democratic practice. While national elections legitimised delegates to the Namibian constituent assembly, once elected, these delegates operated much like an all-party conference, often behind closed doors and without much contact with their electorate.[35]

The ANC also did not make it clear whether elections of representatives to the constituent assembly meant that the party with a majority of votes would automatically form the new government or whether further elections would be held for this purpose. It was not clear whether it saw elections as essential for a democratic constitution or a democratic government, or both. It appeared prima facie that, drawing from the Namibian experience, the organisation saw elections for a constituent assembly as crucial in deciding what party would form the new government. The insistence on elections for a constituent assembly, while valid, appeared set to exclude minority parties that would not be able to muster the necessary votes, and to allow the majority party the uncontested freedom to write the constitution. Such a move could incite resentment from other organisations which would feel sidelined and alienated. It was not unthinkable in such a scenario that parties might disassociate themselves from the constitution and even undermine it.

Notwithstanding the latent problems within its proposals for an interim government and a constituent assembly, the ANC maintained the moral high ground over the question of transitional mechanisms towards a democratic South Africa. Its proposal for the holding of an all-party conference to discuss the details of these matters, was translated into practice with the convening of the Convention for a Democratic South Africa (CODESA) in December 1991.

The Convention for a Democratic South Africa (CODESA) and the beginning of substantive negotiations

While the ANC insisted, in terms of the prescriptions of its Harare Declaration, that the government remove obstacles to negotiations, the unending spiral of violence in 1991 prompted it to call for the speedy commencement of constitutional negotiations. Having developed some understanding about the nature of the transition it wanted, and with its call in January 1991 for the convention of an all-party conference, the ANC began arguing that the removal of the remaining obstacles could only be accomplished by entering into constitutional negotiations. However, the continued escalation of violence marked by clashes between supporters of the ANC and the IFP, and mass shootings in the Vaal and East Rand townships, deflected attention away from embarking on talks for most of 1991. In April 1991 the organisation sent an ultimatum to the government, threatening to break off preliminary negotiations if by 9 May it had not attended to its demand to ban the public display of dangerous weapons and had not taken measures against Ministers of Law and Order and Defence, including security officials implicated in perpetrating violence. The tensions and hostilities that ensued between the two parties over the issue of violence paved the way for a vigorous search for violence-controlling mechanisms. This led to preparations by church and business leaders for the signing of the National Peace Accord in September. The momentum for negotiation grew at the ANC's national conference held in Durban on 5 and 6 July 1991. While the ANC leadership came under scathing attack for the compromises they had already made to the government on the armed struggle, they were nevertheless given a mandate to pursue negotiations.

The revelation of the Inkathagate scandal two weeks later, on 19 July, pointed to massive government financial support for Inkatha and strengthened the ANC's call for the installation of an interim government. For the first time, and deviating from its earlier resistance to the idea, the government agreed to the creation of some sort of transitional arrangement which

173

would govern during the period of transition. The coming together of various parties in September to sign the National Peace Accord also added momentum to the cordial relations and understanding developing among them. This made it easier to sign the Declaration of Intent for the Convention of a Democratic South Africa on 20 and 21 December at the World Trade Centre, Kempton Park. That convention was also made possible by the ANC's success in rallying behind its demand for transitional mechanisms a variety of anti-apartheid organisations into a Patriotic Front in October. The withdrawal of the PAC from the preparatory meeting of CODESA on 29 November, the glaring absence of the CP and the insistence by Buthelezi on a separate delegation for the IFP, the KwaZulu government and the King at the talks, created a set of problems that were to hound CODESA in the months to come.

CODESA was a historic gathering in South Africa since the constitutional convention of 1909, which led to the formation of a united republic out of the British colonies of Natal and the Cape and the Boer republics of Transvaal and the Orange Free State. CODESA, comprising 19 parties, became the negotiating forum until 1992. It was divided into five working groups, each dealing with specific issues: the creation of a climate for free political activity, constitutional principles, transitional arrangements, the future of the TBVC states, and time-frames and implementation. The most significant were Working Groups 1 and 4. Working Group 1 (the creation of a climate for free political activity) had three subcommittees dealing with the completion of the reconciliation process, the continuation of the security and socio-economic process, and the creation of a climate and opportunity for political organising. Working Group 4 (the future of the TBVC states) had four subcommittees focusing on testing the will of the people, citizenship, administrative, financial and practical implications, as well as political, constitutional and legal implications. A management committee, comprising a secretariat with chairpersons of the negotiation forum (Mac Maharaj and Fanie van der Merwe) and an administration section under the ANC's Murphy Morobe, oversaw the process. The spread of ANC representatives in the working groups was as follows:

- Working Group 1: Joe Modise, Jacob Zuma, Penuel Maduna and an adviser, Professor Kadar Asmal

- Working Group 2: Cyril Ramaphosa, Mohammed Valli Moosa, Frene Ginwala and an adviser, Mr Arthur Chaskalson

- Working Group 3: Thabo Mbeki, Joe Nhlanhla, Joel Netshitenzhe and an adviser, Mr Dullah Omar

- Working Group 4: Alfred Nzo, Matthews Phosa, Barbara Masekela and Pius Langa

- Working Group 5: Pallo Jordan, Zola Skweyiya, Lucille Meyer and Mr George Bizos

During the course of negotiations significant understanding, accompanied by strategic shifts, began to emerge in the forum as parties compromised with and accommodated each other. Although the ANC attempted to foster a decolonisation approach in the resolution of South Africa's political crisis, it made important compromises. Its insistence on the installation of an interim government and a constituent assembly were negotiable. The adoption of a pragmatic approach and the willingness to relent on certain matters pertaining to an interim government, were evidenced in its discussion document entitled *Reflections on interim government*. This document clearly cautioned against the cost of taking full responsibility for an interim government.[36] It outlined possible problems and difficulties likely to emerge from the ANC's participation. It stated that an interim government composed of unelected representatives would be difficult to run since each party would seek to assert its policies. Decision making would also be complicated. If the ANC became party to such a government, it would inherit an apartheid machinery which it would not be able to transform within the timescale of the transitional period.

> The ANC would become part of a structure vested with complete responsibility for running the country. At the same time such an interim government would be a power structure which would be unable to address in any meaningful way the ongoing socio-economic crisis, to effectively transform the apartheid power institutions and the racial imbalances which it will inherit at every level. In such circumstances we run the grave risk of discrediting ourselves in the eyes of our constituency.[37]

The paper pointed out that participation in an interim government with other parties would mean continuous compromises in order to achieve unity. It also questioned the practicability of demanding the dissolution of the existing parliament, the abandonment of the constitution and the submission of the entire state structure to an interim government. It contended that if the interim government were given total responsibility for the administration of state apparatuses, the effective participation by the ANC and its allies would absorb a massive proportion of talent and resources. "There is a grave risk that these will be stretched to the point where we undermine effective attention to one of the principal and talent-absorbing tasks facing us, i.e. to build our organisation on the ground in preparation for an election victory."[38] In a move aimed at avoiding these possible difficulties, the ANC, in a working paper entitled *Interim government: towards a viable option*, opted for a safer and less costly path. Carefully selecting the positive aspects of the different options of an interim government discussed above, the paper suggested important pragmatic compromises. It proposed that an interim government be composed of an interim governing council made up of senior representatives of the major parties. It should have commissions to deal with defined strategic areas, and should assume responsibility for managing those areas where practical actions and negotiations had led to sufficient agreement for implementation structures to be set up.

The significance of this new position lay in its ability to encapsulate positive aspects raised in the debate around the options, composition and tasks of an interim government. However, it also proposed important compromises, chiefly the jettisoning of the call for a sovereign interim government. This was reflected in the proposal for an interim government with limited functions. Arguably, no government, even with a short life span, could claim sovereignty if it left certain functions of government to other bodies. Even if control measures were devised to subordinate structures of the previous government under the new interim government, such a government would not, in effect, be sovereign. The interim governing council, which was the supreme body within the hierarchy of the proposed interim government, would, besides supervising the work of the joint interim government structures, act retroactively in vetoing bills and approving the repeal or amendment of legislation passed by the existing parliament. If the existing government still had the power to decide on governmental matters and sent its decision to the interim government for approval only, it would be a spurious suggestion that the latter had complete sovereignty since, although it had the mouth to pronounce judgement, it did not have the hands to act.

ANC strategists also used the concept of "tactical flexibility" to the extent of compromising what had hitherto been the starting point of the organisation's struggle against apartheid. While the demand for an interim government was premised on the illegitimacy of the regime,[39] it was also argued that this illegitimacy should not determine the ANC's choice of options for an interim government.[40] For the ANC, negotiating with the government and participating with it in joint structures such as the National Peace Accord was a tactical manoeuvre that was not meant to confer legitimacy on the regime. Notwithstanding this postulation, an ANC suggestion for a role for the apartheid parliament, the constitution and some parts of government indicated an inclination to compromise. This inclination was reflected by the argument that the ANC did not have the power to force the regime to dissolve the tricameral parliament and abandon the constitution.[41] This kind of thinking, which was informed by the sweeping mood of sobriety creeping into the ANC leadership, was far removed from the orthodox viewpoint that saw mass struggle, and not reliance on the invincibility of the regime, as the tool of change.

Compromise on the notion of the illegitimacy of the regime was already reflected in suggestions within the organisation that the decisions of CODESA would have to be passed by the existing parliament to give them legal force. Mandela also stated that parliament was the highest legal authority in the country. "Decisions of CODESA cannot be invested with legal authority without getting that legal authority from this parliament."[42] The passing of the decisions of CODESA by parliament would also apply to decisions of the interim government. The fear that these decisions would lack legal force if not legislated through parliament testified not only to an erroneous self-judgement of incapacity, but also to an increasing tendency to abdicate other forms of struggle to constitutionalism and negotiations. Without a special relationship with the NP, it was unrealistic to expect the decisions of CODESA to be passed smoothly by the existing parliament.

Strategic shifts were also made on the question of a constituent assembly. Until January 1991 popular support for a constituent assembly and statements by ANC leaders suggested that the issue was non-negotiable.[43] However, the proposal for an all-party conference that was made in the Anniversary Statement of 8 January 1991, clearly revealed an inclination to renege on the question of elections for a constituent assembly. The proposal that a popularly mandated all-party conference would continue to function either as a constituent assembly or an interim government or both, showed that ANC strategists were not entirely opposed to an unelected constitutional forum. For them, a constitution drafted by such a conference, or CODESA as the conference came to be known, would suffice if mandated by a national non-racial referendum.[44] It was not unthinkable, therefore, that CODESA could be transformed into a constituent body in its advanced stage of development.

Given the urgency with which the ANC sought to strike a deal in negotiations, the leadership tried on a number of occasions to water down the tone of the demand, arguing that the constituent assembly should not be a non-negotiable precondition. The mandate given to Nelson Mandela at the ANC's National Congress in July 1991 to convene an all-party conference, and Mandela's call to seize the moment, indicated that successful compromises could be made on the matter. In an interview with *The Star* after the conference in July, Mandela indicated that the ANC would be willing to make compromises (which were not specified) if the government displayed the will to fulfil its obligations. Although the ANC would have difficulty in compromising a constituent assembly because of the overwhelming support for the idea shown at the Patriotic Front conference in October 1991, it could entertain shifts on certain matters, including elections in favour of representatives of all parties.

A discussion paper entitled *Notes on a constituent assembly*, which dealt with such details of a constituent assembly as the procedure for its convention, composition, powers, functioning, decision making and implementation,[45] also frankly asked if there could be room for flexibility on these matters without compromising principles of importance. Contrary to the Harare Declaration that the next step after the installation of an interim government should be elections for a constituent assembly, it was suggested that parties should first agree on the principles of the constitution which would be recorded in legislation. Thereafter, parliament would pass legislation which would sanction the holding of elections for a constituent assembly. The constitutional principles would also provide for the holding of a referendum either to confirm those principles or to confirm a new constitution. It was also suggested that, to avoid the holding of a multiplicity of elections which would be costly, time-consuming and could lead to conflict, a constituent assembly be converted into a national assembly (parliament). The rationale behind the new thinking was that such a trajectory, if properly pursued, would ease discussions in a constituent assembly because prior consensus would have been achieved on constitutional principles. It was further contended that, without departing from the Harare Declaration, this move would go some way towards winning the support of the government if it knew, in advance, the legally binding constitutional framework within which the constituent assembly would work. It was also suggested that for the sake of unhindered progress, constitutional deliberations should take place behind closed doors so that parties could find scope for flexibility.

The discussion in CODESA of constitutional principles which would bind an elected constituent assembly was not a compromise, since the Harare Declaration had stated that they should be discussed after the removal of obstacles. Despite its opposition to the idea, the PAC also understood in its participation in the Patriotic Front inaugural meeting in October 1991, that discussing the "modalities of a constituent assembly with the regime", entailed constitutional principles.[46] The problem around constitutional principles, however, which the PAC adamantly opposed and which the ANC was inclined to go along with, was the limits and depth of discussion to be entertained. Notwithstanding earlier anticipation that negotiating constitutional principles entailed producing a broadly generalised statement of principles, the pressure by the government and the IFP to be given security about the future form of state ultimately led to addressing the issue in detail. While the ANC justified its acceptance of this state of affairs by arguing that it would smooth debate on the constituent assembly or what was increasingly called a constitution-making body, it was clear that elected delegates would become hostages to fundamental principles devised by unelected multi-party negotiators.

While the demand for elections for a constituent assembly signalled the ANC's intention to exclude minority parties from drafting the constitution, this position was later abandoned, with the emphasis being placed on their inclusion to achieve a legitimate and broadly accepted constitution. A discussion paper on the constituent assembly outlined that smaller parties would be represented, provided they obtained a minimum of 3 % of the votes to be able to occupy three seats in a 100-vote chamber or twelve seats in a 400-seat chamber.[47] The discussion paper further outlined that another way in which smaller parties could be assured some say in the decision making, was if the voting procedure moved away from a simple majority.[48] It proposed that, in the interests of having a constitution to which most people would be reconciled, the ANC should allow a decision-making process by a two-thirds majority or some such proportion. It contended that

> ... where you operate by a simple majority and an organisation has 51 % of seats, there is little incentive to seek compromise that is likely to ensure that all organisations feel that they have played a part in making the constitution. A two-thirds majority requirement may ensure that the new constitution is not simply an ANC constitution but a South African one.[49]

Accommodating other parties in decision making through this requirement was, however, not enough for parties such as the NP and the IFP. The NP, in particular, required 75 % for the ratification of the constitution, which far exceeded the minimum requirement accepted in most democracies. The ANC's decision to offer a 70 % majority requirement to entice the NP into a deal would have amounted to a serious compromise, had this been accepted by the NP before the breakdown of CODESA talks.

In sum, proposals at CODESA induced a significant shift from the ANC's earlier positions. The ANC compromised on the rejection of the legitimacy of the South African parliament. Insistence that all matters pertaining to the constitution be deliberated within an elected forum was dropped. The call for all deliberations to be open to public scrutiny and the earlier insistence that the party that won the majority of the votes should have an uncontested discretion to write the constitution, were discarded. Notwithstanding this, the ANC's strategic shifts and certain compromises were crucial in allowing the negotiation process to move forward. Despite the major hurdles that impeded the process, the fact that agreement was finally reached in CODESA to install an interim government and to hold elections for a constituent assembly, as demanded by the organisation, gave it the moral high ground in determining the course of transition.

Shifts and compromises did not, however, come from the ANC alone. The NP government too, shifted from a paradigm of sole control of the transitional process towards accommodation. The NP embraced options that had previously been regarded as unacceptable or impracticable. In November 1990 the NP had publicly rejected the ANC's proposals for an interim government and a constituent assembly. Dr Viljoen had said that

> ... the government has made it quite clear all along that it is not in favour of either a constituent assembly nor an interim government. We are a sovereign independent country. We are not like colonies becoming independent ... and there is no question of handing over power to an interim government.[50]

Objections were also raised against the involvement of the international community in the South African transitional process, with arguments being made that local parties have the capacity to resolve their differences. It was also strongly contended that the NP government should continue to govern during the transitional period and that its security forces should maintain law and order. However, the vicissitudes of the transitional process, its indeterminacy and its vulnerability to influence also saw the NP shifting positions and compromising to accommodate opposite viewpoints and proposals. Revelations of its funding of Inkatha compelled it to embrace the ANC's proposal for an interim government. Negotiations at CODESA also influenced it to accept the notion of an elected constituent assembly which would draft the final constitution. The uncontrollable flames of violence highlighted the need for an independent violence monitoring commission (the Goldstone Commission) and an increasing role for the international community. Furthermore, the earlier insistence on entrenching group rights in the constitution also faded as NP negotiators began talking about the protection of minority rights, which were also eventually abandoned in favour of the ANC's concept of individual rights and one person, one vote.[51]

In spite of the shifts and compromises in CODESA negotiations, these did not mirror nor were they mirrored by what was happening outside the negotiating forum. The lack of publicity of what was happening in the closed sessions of CODESA, coupled with the general antipathy brewed by right-wing organisations and the PAC towards the forum, heightened emotions and created anxiety among those who believed that their rights were being eroded at the forum. The flight of white support away from the NP into the right-wing organisations and the radicalisation and growth of the AWB posed a serious threat to the transitional process. Clearly aware of this trend which had gathered momentum in 1991, De Klerk, during his opening speech of parliament on 24 January, sought to allay fears of the whites. Written mostly in Afrikaans, his speech sought to reassure whites that they would not be left behind in future constitutional changes. While agreeing to the need for a transitional government as demanded by the ANC, De Klerk told parliament that "the institutions of any transitional government will have to take place constitutionally and be based on power-sharing". He assured parliament that his constitutional proposals would be passed by the existing parliament, after having been put to a whites-only referendum.[52]

Flowing from these earlier promises, and particularly after suffering defeat in the Potchefstroom by-elections at the hands of the CP, a decision was taken to call a referendum on 17 March 1992 to test the white electorate's support for negotiations. To bolster confidence in its course of direction, a range of the party's basic constitutional principles were published. These included the maintenance of standards, the effective protection of ownership of private property against any arbitrary action by any future government, a free-market economy in a multi-party democracy, and the prevention of domination and the abuse of power by any particular group. A bill of rights and an independent judiciary were included. State employees were offered job and pension security. The NP also promised impartial security forces, the maximum devolution of power, strong regional government and a separation of power, limiting the power of a state president. A two-chamber parliament, elections on the basis of proportional representation, and the maintenance of language and cultural rights, as well as community-orientated education for those who wanted it, were put on its manifesto.[53]

While the results of the referendum were a resounding "yes", which logically implied speedy movement towards the conclusion of a negotiated deal, the NP interpreted the results to mean that it was then unassailable and could dictate the terms of transition. This thinking was to be demonstrated by a number of positions taken by government ministers. Government negotiators began slowing down negotiations. They also began to arrive at meetings late. In addition, a young junior minister, Tertius Delport, was made head of the government negotiating team, coming into talks without a full mandate.[54] Most disturbing to other parties was the tabling of a string of new constitutional proposals, including one calling for a troika presidency council which deviated from earlier positions, and which were rejected by a majority of CODESA delegates. Outside the forum the government took a tougher stance. It called upon the ANC to terminate the armed struggle and to disband MK, despite the fact that some understanding on these points had been reached in the Pretoria and D.F. Malan agreements. It also called upon political parties to end calls for sanctions and the isolation of South Africa, and insisted that black leaders themselves solve the issue of violence.

In spite of broader consensus in CODESA around a number of issues, stalling by the government continued into May. To a considerable extent, this accounted for the lack of consensus in Working Group 2 (constitutional principles). Even when last-minute attempts were made on the eve and in the morning of the first day of the two plenary sessions of CODESA II on 15 and 16 May to break the logjam, there was no indication of a serious will on the part of government. According to delegates, what the government wanted in Working Group 2 was an agreement that the new constitution would be ratified by a 75 % majority. As a result of the lack of sufficient consensus (a decision-making procedure which in practice came to mean agreement between the ANC and the government), negotiations began to teeter on the brink of collapse. Political party leaders indicated in their speeches that the CODESA process was being threatened. It was, however, the SACP's Secretary-General, Chris Hani, who captured the mood of the delegates and a majority of followers outside the corridors of the World Trade Centre. Elucidating the suffering and expectations of millions of South Africans and the failures of the government to end violence, the corruption scandals revealed by the Pickard Commission and Inkathagate, Hani conveyed to the government that the time had come for its "exit-gate". He clearly stated to the delegates that the future of the country would not be dictated by the government but by the force of the "masses" in the streets – a reflection of what the ANC had already decided in expectation of CODESA's failure. Clearly aware of the explosive potential of the anger of delegates, Mandela and De Klerk intervened and sought to repair the damage during the following day. The failure of CODESA had, however, already been registered on television and in the minds of millions of South Africans and the international community.

Except for the deadlock in Working Group 2, CODESA had made significant agreements in other working groups. Working Group 1 (the creation of a climate for free political activity) agreed upon the speeding up of the release of political prisoners and the return of exiles and their families. In addition, there was agreement that

- the interim government could impose emergency regulations and detention without trial on the advice of the multi-party executive council

- discriminatory laws should be repealed

- the use of military means to pursue political objectives would end

181

- the political neutrality of and fair access to state-controlled media, including the SABC and television, as well as those in the TBVC states, would be established

- an independent body to control the media would be established, which would focus on finance, licensing, conditions and standards

- the National Peace Accord would be implemented – CODESA committed itself to a peaceful settlement

- the security forces would be placed under the control of an interim government and mechanisms be established to ensure the accountability of the security forces

- the funding of political organisations and parties to six years after the general election should cease

- a spirit of tolerance would be fostered among political parties and an intensive educational campaign would be embarked on in respect of political tolerance.

In Working Group 2, consensus had been reached on a transitional interim constitution, providing for a constitution-making body operating within the framework of that constitution. This body would have two chambers, one of which would comprise regional representatives. The deadlock in this working group that led to the collapse of CODESA, revolved around the percentage needed to take decisions on a final constitution. The government and the IFP insisted on 75 % while the ANC and its allies argued for a two-thirds majority.

In Working Group 3 (transitional arrangements), it was agreed that the transition to democracy was to be in two phases: one being the preparation for the holding of elections and the second being the period after the holding of elections to adopt a new democratic constitution. It was agreed that during the first phase a multi-party transitional executive council (TEC) would be put in place to prepare for the elections. The TEC would be appointed by the State President on the recommendation of CODESA. It would have executive powers and would include at least one representative from CODESA participants. Alongside it, independent media and electoral commissions would be established. TEC decisions would be taken by consensus, failing which by an 80 % majority. Five subcouncils would be established directly under the TEC to ensure a climate of free political activity and the levelling of the political playing field. These subcouncils comprised regional and local government, law and order, finance, safety and security, defence and foreign affairs.[55]

In Working Group 4 (the future of the TBVC states), agreement was reached on the reincorporation of the TBVC states. These states would participate in the transitional arrangement, bearing in mind that the decisions of these structures would affect them. Moreover, citizens of these states would take part in national and regional elections. South African citizenship would be restored to them after the elections and no more land transfers would be made to these states.

The task of Working Group 5 (time-frames and implementation) was to monitor progress in the other four working groups and to establish time-frames within which CODESA decisions would be implemented. It achieved little, however, because of the lack of tasks emanating from the other working groups. It was therefore decided to convene the working group only when agreement had been reached in those working groups.[56] It seems that at the time of the CODESA breakdown the government would have been at an advantage, had the deal been struck. It would have obtained a high percentage (70 % which the ANC had offered) for the ratification of the constitution, and the clause on detention without trial would have been passed without much opposition.

With the failure of CODESA, the management committee was mandated to carry forward the work of the working groups which had been disbanded. Its task was to resolve all outstanding issues of the working groups, to examine all agreements to explore ways of their speedy implementation, and to establish technical committees or subcommittees to assist it when necessary. Finally, it was to convene a CODESA plenary session to adopt these agreements, and was empowered to constitute a mechanism to draft all legislation required as a result of these agreements.

The fall of CODESA and resultant mass mobilisation

The collapse of CODESA negotiations resulted in a wave of militancy within the ranks of the ANC, with calls for more militant mass action. Hani's threat to resolve the deadlock in negotiations in the streets gained wide support within ANC structures, with a decision being taken by the Tripartite Alliance to embark on a national programme of rolling mass action. A series of mass action activities were outlined, beginning with rallies and marches on 16 June, the holding of a people's parliament in Kliptown, Soweto, on 27 June, organising a number of public demonstrations and rallies to police stations under the banner of peace and democracy, occupying government buildings, and embarking on an indefinite strike aimed at forcing the government to speed up the negotiation process. The ANC's resort to mass action, which began in earnest on 16 June, soured relations with the government. However, Mandela defended it as a middle course between armed struggle and negotiations.[57]

On 17 June, immediately after launching its mass action programme and after a concerted negative media campaign, 23 innocent women and children were killed in their sleep in Boipatong in the Vaal Triangle. It was alleged that Inkatha members from the nearby Kwa-Madala hostel were responsible. The ANC claimed that the killings were part of the government's strategy, as they occurred after De Klerk had warned of a counter-strategy to mass action. De Klerk's visit to Ulundi on 16 June also gave weight to ANC claims. These events led to the ANC's withdrawal from negotiations. Addressing ANC supporters in the Evaton Stadium after visiting Boipatong, Mandela said: "I can no longer explain to our people why we continue to talk to a government which is murdering our people ... we are now convinced that his [De Klerk's] method of bringing about a solution to this country is war". Emphasising this at a later meeting, Mandela stated that "the negotiation process is completely in tatters ... the gulf between the oppressed and the oppressor has become unbreachable". On 22 June the ANC NEC formally announced its withdrawal from negotiations with the government. The ANC presented the government with 14 demands which called for the ending of violence as a prerequisite for the resumption of negotiations. The ultimatum to the government gave birth to a new form of negotiation, as the parties exchanged bitterly worded memoranda containing accusations and counter-accusations.

The Boipatong massacre sparked widespread anger. It also rekindled cooperation between the ANC and the PAC as the two embarked on joint mass action programmes. These programmes had different strategic objectives. While the ANC, at least its leadership, saw mass action as a means of forcing the government into meaningful negotiations and the resumption of CODESA, the PAC sought to use mass action to "bury CODESA". The irony of its militant rhetoric, however, was its simultaneous exploration of talks with the government. What was most significant in the aftermath of Boipatong, was the momentum given to the mass action programme by the labour movement.

At the beginning of the year, COSATU had unveiled its mass action programme which was to be implemented on an unprecedented scale. This programme had been abandoned on the advice of the ANC because of "improper timing". With the government having "shown to be uncaring about black lives", the increasing retrenchment of workers and unilateral restructuring by the government, this programme was invoked with much vigour. Members from a variety of unions, ranging from the South African Railways and Harbour Workers Union (SARHWU), and NUMSA to SACTWU, began swarming onto the streets and factory premises. Marches under the banner of the campaign against corruption and murder proliferated in cities and towns. On 26 June thousands gathered at Kliptown to listen to the speeches of veterans who had been part of the gathering that drafted the Freedom Charter on that spot in 1955.

While mass action activities mushroomed countrywide, the post-Boipatong tensions did not simply end in a showdown in the streets. In July the ANC and the PAC succeeded in putting their case about the government's lack of commitment to democracy to the OAU, which passed the issue to the UN Security Council. On 15 June 1992 the struggle for democracy in South Africa was placed under the international spotlight when South African parties appeared before a packed UN Security Council to explain their respective cases about developments in South Africa. While the intention of the ANC and the PAC in putting the case to the UN was to pledge for more international involvement, the response given by the UN seemed to throw the ball back into the court of the South African parties. While it held the South African government responsible for terminating violence, the UN insisted that only South African parties had the capacity to resolve their differences. It offered to send Mr Cyrus Vance to assist the parties to resume negotiations. In the light of this UN response, which fell short of meeting the ANC's expectations and coupled with the belief within the ANC that the government was not serious about curbing violence, particularly as it only announced steps to stop violence on the eve of the UN debate to arm Foreign Minister Pik Botha with ammunition against ANC allegations of inaction, the liberation movement decided to intensify its mass action programme.

A successful two-day stay-away was called on 3 and 4 August, with more than 90 % of the population staying away from work and schools country-wide. Marches, demonstrations and strikes by unions culminated in an unprecedented "march to Pretoria with Mandela" on 5 August. In September the rolling mass action campaign was taken to the bantustans in demand of free political activity. Targeted at Ciskei, Bophuthatswana and KwaZulu, the programme backfired when a 100 000 strong march to Bisho on 7 September was fired upon by Ciskeian soldiers. Although thousands of people rallied behind ANC campaigns, and in spite of the perceived legitimacy of launching such mass action programmes, the ANC became nervous of further risking the lives of its supporters in bloody confrontations. As a result other planned marches in KwaZulu and Bophuthatswana were cancelled. Immediately following the aftermath of Bisho, Mandela indicated the need to return to multi-party negotiations. De Klerk was also becoming nervous and urged the ANC back to negotiations. It would appear that the potential risk of militant mass action undermining negotiations influenced the ANC leadership to be more cautious in defence of what Mandela regarded as the only alternative to the resolution of the South African political crisis. It was this concern for safeguarding negotiations which saw the leadership's systematic marginalisation of other forms of struggle such as mass action activities, the armed struggle and the sanctions campaign.

Putting a tap on mass mobilisation: whither the armed struggle and the sanctions campaign?

Much as the ANC would have liked to continue with mass action and the armed struggle to back its negotiation efforts, the theoretical assumptions about the compatibility of liberation strategies and negotiations proved to be virtually impossible to translate into practice. The Bisho massacre clearly demonstrated the danger and difficulty of simultaneously sustaining negotiations with militant mass action activities. The quest for an intensified armed revolution, backed by mass action, had already proved to be costly and difficult to realise in the short term,[58] and it was clear that the organisation was reluctant to indulge in such an experiment at the expense of negotiation. Most crucial was the potential danger of antagonising the state and jeopardising the prospects of a peaceful settlement. It was against this background that the ANC opted for a speedily negotiated settlement in which its negotiation strategy would assume primacy vis-à-vis other forms of struggle. While the latter were not abandoned in theory but seen as complementary to the negotiation strategy, in practice they came to be marginalised.

Military options during negotiations: whither the armed struggle?

In spite of the prospect of negotiations with the South African government towards the end of the 1980s, the ANC and its alliance partner, the SACP, had continued to insist on the intensification of the armed struggle. Almost at the same time as the announcement of its negotiation position in 1987, the ANC embarked on a strategy later to be known as "Operation Vula" (meaning "operation opening") to strengthen its underground network in the country. While the operation was an important response to the weakness of the past, as Mac Maharaj and Siphiwe Nyanda pointed out in *New Nation* and *Mayibuye* respectively,[59] its strategic significance was twofold: to create a defence network against attacks on communities and to lay the foundation for a revolutionary armed insurrection. ANC strategists firmly believed that if the underground structure was consolidated and supported by a strong contingent of MK cadres with a military arsenal based in the country, a decisive mass insurrection involving the people could be launched.

Operation Vula was headed by President Oliver Tambo. The command and operational structures comprised the President's Committee, including Mac Maharaj, Siphiwe Nyanda, Joe Slovo, Ronnie Kasrils, Ivan Pillay and Archie Abrahams. Under it was the Vula Head Committee consisting of Mac Maharaj, Siphiwe Nyanda, Chris Hani and Janet Love, who were to command twelve regional committees. Only one committee, the Durban Political Committee headed by Pravin Gordhan and Billy Nair, was formed by the time the project was uncovered by the police.[60] There were 70 people involved in the project, but the police arrested only eight for prosecution. These were Mac Maharaj, Siphiwe Nyanda, Raymond Lala, Catherine Mvelase, Sussanna Tshabalala, Dipak Patel, Pravin Gordhan and Amnesh Munnessar Sankar.

The project was launched in earnest in July 1988, when Mac Maharaj and Siphiwe Nyanda were sent into the country by President Oliver Tambo to spearhead its implementation. According to Nyanda, "the initial task of the project was to bring into the country as much military hardware as possible so as to launch any assaults from within the country".[61] For almost two years before its discovery in July 1990, the operation established structures, made widespread contacts and smuggled into the country large quantities of arms and sophisticated military hardware. The capture of its top leadership, along with critical operational computer documentation detailing the Vula project, effectively neutralised what was to have been a five-year plan to set up a people's revolutionary army, including underground MK support structures in South Africa.[62] The discovery of Operation Vula embarrassed the ANC at a time when it was enjoying the limelight in spearheading the negotiation process. In fact, Mandela had not known about Vula until it was uncovered by the police.[63] Operation Vula fuelled the debate on the compatibility of negotiation and revolutionary armed struggle within the movement, and the role of MK was spotlighted during the unfolding process of transition.

While the ANC and the SACP tried to defend the Vula project, the way in which this controversy was handled by the ANC leadership clearly demonstrated a tendency to forsake and even disown the mission. Operation Vula operatives were detained, interrogated and even assaulted in ways reminiscent of the era preceding the unbanning of the ANC. While the ANC protested against the arrests and called for the release of Vula detainees, it did not put all its energy behind securing their release. There are two ways of understanding the ANC's actions: they signalled either a distancing from armed struggle by the leadership, or the beginning of new tensions with the SACP whose leadership manned the operation. The temporary resignation of Mac Maharaj from the ANC immediately after his release testified to the tense relations created by the Operation Vula controversy.

The destruction of the foundations of the underground network intercepted what could have been a vital connection between MK operations and ANC grass-roots membership. It broke the foundation upon which the revolutionary dimension of mass insurrection was to be based. This resulted in a radical subversion of MK's revolutionary role. Though unbanned, MK was unable to return and develop township links, nor could it impose its structures upon ANC branches without proper coordination. To uphold the revolutionary banner of mass insurrection, MK needed access to the people through organised underground networks. With this connection broken, coupled with the lack of interest by the leadership to repair the damage, the revolutionary agenda of the liberation movement appeared to be disappearing.

Within a month after the Vula operatives were discovered, the ANC leadership decided at the Pretoria Summit on 6 August 1990 to suspend the armed struggle. The decision was taken without consultation with ANC members and even MK cadres, fuelling further dissatisfaction. MK cadres inside and outside the country were the most disgruntled. Furthermore, the precise meaning of "suspension of armed struggle and related activities" in the Minute created misunderstanding between the organisation and the government, which resulted in bitter arguments. Although a working group was set up under Paragraph 3 of the Minute to analyse this phrase, the government was vehement in insisting that the ANC stop all other forms of struggle except negotiation. Mandela, however, countered that the suspension did not include mass action and added that it did not mean any change to the status quo of MK, except that it would stop engaging in armed combat. Winnie Mandela contradicted him when she hinted that the suspension did not entail an end to violence and that the armed wing should continue to fight. The government, on its part, understood the suspension to include an end to mass action, as well as the dismantling of MK and the handing over of arms caches. This misunderstanding dominated and complicated the task of the working group. Originally set to report on 15 September 1990, it was only able to do so early in 1991.

In another move that further weakened the ANC's resolve on armed struggle, Mandela and De Klerk headed delegations to a meeting at D.F. Malan Airport, Cape Town, on 15 February 1991, where the ANC agreed to abandon military training in South Africa, to end the infiltration of men and material and to halt the creation of underground structures, in exchange for the return of exiles to the country.[64] However, it was agreed that membership of MK did not constitute a violation of any of the provisions of paragraph 3 of the Pretoria Minute, and that the population at large had a right to express its views through peaceful demonstrations. The security forces were to be directed to take cognisance of the suspension of armed action and related activities, and the parties would remain in close liaison with one another to ensure prompt and efficient reporting, investigation and redressing of all allegations of unlawful activities or activities by the security forces.[65] A liaison committee comprising members of both parties was to be created to monitor the implementation of the agreement. Like the compromise made at the Pretoria Summit, the D.F. Malan undertakings, though they secured a space for the ANC on the question of mass mobilisation, were one-sided. The fact that the government conceded to the demand for the return of exiles and accepted that mass action was a legal peaceful activity, did not amount to a compromise of any substance. While the government's decision to allow mass demonstrations in 1989 acknowledged the legality of this mode of political action, the unbanning of organisations also implied that exiled members of these organisations would be allowed back into the country. It was clear that, rather than fulfilling its obligation, the government was using every available opportunity to extract compromises from the ANC.

While the ANC secured space for mass action at both the Pretoria and the D.F. Malan meetings, this did not end the bickering with the government. Instead, in the months following these agreements, the government continued to put pressure on the ANC to terminate mass action and to dismantle MK. The dividends of what the ANC thought was its contribution to the negotiation process, ultimately turned out to be a defence against an onslaught on its image and cohesion as a liberation movement.

The Pretoria Summit and the arrest of Operation Vula operatives raised fresh questions about the role of MK in the new phase of negotiations. Its role as an army tasked with spearheading the revolutionary programme of the liberation movement was in question. There appeared to be two answers to this question within the ANC. The one tended to see the continuation of MK's revolutionary programme through its involvement in self-defence units (SDUs) in the townships. The other sought to redefine its role by propounding the idea of transforming it into a regular national army that would lead to its integration with the SADF and other bantustan and political party armies.

While the role of MK hung in the balance during the period of transition, earlier thinking by its leaders pointed to an inclination to see it confined to barracks. In an interview with *Mayibuye*, Chris Hani hinted that if an interim government were to be put in place, he would expect MK and the SADF to be confined to barracks to prevent them from interfering in the political process.[66] He did, however, see a role for MK in policing and argued that the South African Police (SAP) had been biased and brutal in their maintenance of law and order and, as such, could not be entrusted with the task of supervision during the transition. In later statements, however, more emphasis was laid on the integration of MK with the SADF and other bantustan armies to form a national people's army. Joe Modise, the commander of MK, pointed out in December 1991 that they were in the process of changing the army from a guerrilla army into a regular army.[67] Acting against the pressure to disband the military wing, the ANC's national conference in July resolved to maintain and develop MK until the adoption of a democratic constitution and the creation of a new defence force into which MK cadres could be integrated.[68] By the time MK's conference was held in September 1991, MK leaders were already talking of a training programme in the airforce, navy and ground forces in countries such as India, Uganda, Libya, Cuba, Nigeria, France and Britain.

While the transitional period and the process of negotiations forced a reorientation of the role of MK, its leaders persisted in seeking an alternative route through which the organisation's revolutionary programme could be advanced. Although the idea of establishing SDUs was prompted by the carnage of violence sweeping the townships, it had, in addition, much to do with promoting the organisation's revolutionary agenda. Drawn up by a committee mostly comprising SACP members,[69] the SDU plan sought to repair the damage caused to the underground network through the revelations of Operation Vula. Its objective was to build a people's militia through SDUs which would not only defend the townships, but would also respond to an armed insurrection against the state using an assortment of home-made weaponry, backed by trained MK cadres. The guidelines for the creation of SDUs entitled *For the sake of our lives*, clearly stated that

> ... self-defence structures need, by definition, to be paramilitary. They differ from all the other forms of organisation referred to, including street committees. They must be tightly structured to repulse aggression and ensure law and order; they need a specific command and control system; their members must be trained and have a high degree of discipline.[70]

To many ANC members the idea of SDUs appeared to be limited to security. To SACP and MK leaders, SDUs were linked to a broader revolutionary strategy. As early as 1988 Ronnie Kasrils had explained in *Sechaba* that SDUs, together with guerrilla units from the countryside and underground urban combat groups, formed part of the revolutionary army (MK) that would be located in the country to facilitate the arming of the people and directing the course of insurrection.[71] The SACP's meeting that was held in Tongaat from 19–20 May 1990, clearly put SDUs within an insurrectionary perspective. SDUs backed by trained MK cadres were to combine with the masses, culminating in mass insurrection.[72]

In spite of its intentions, the SDU programme could not get off the ground in the way it had been projected. MK cadres did not appear to take active steps to implement this initiative. Only a few SDUs were created, some without the input of MK.[73] The lack of enthusiasm by MK cadres appeared to be rooted in the simmering problems within their military structures. Although the organisation had been unbanned, MK cadres continued to be the targets of harassment by the security forces. Some were arrested, detained, tortured and killed, whereas others simply disappeared. Describing this type of harassment, Mbulelo Mdledle, a returned exile, noted that cadres were harassed for crimes allegedly committed before they left South Africa, while others were subjected to routine checks by the police which involved rude knocks in the dead of night.[74] In many cases returning cadres found no peace of mind, as they became victims of Askaris (their former comrades turned agents of the security police). Moreover, MK cadres felt that they had been spurned by the leadership's turn to negotiations. A majority of those outside the country felt completely abandoned after the leadership's return to the country. The suspension of the armed struggle, without their consultation, appeared to them to be a prelude to their ultimate marginalisation.[75] Although Mandela visited MK camps in April 1990 where cadres' complaints were discussed, the lack of clarity on their indemnity and return to the country left them with an uncertain future.

It was primarily because of these dissatisfactions that MK cadres were able to influence the conference in July 1991 to pass resolutions committing the ANC to accept full responsibility for cadres arrested or detained by the police and security organs in the course of the execution of their duties in defence of the people. The conference also resolved that the ANC establish MK structures at all levels throughout the country, including the establishment of offices and the provision of resources for such activities. The ANC would encourage MK cadres to join and to channel their political concerns through these structures. Finally and of most significance, the conference resolved that the NEC take full responsibility for the transferring of funds to regions for the maintenance, development and general welfare of all MK cadres, both inside and outside the country. Proper and appropriate binding mechanisms were to be established to ensure this. Strengthening this resolution, the MK conference held in Thohoyandou, Venda, from 9–10 August 1991, called for the establishment of a social welfare department within MK to look into the specific needs of the entire membership of MK, inside and outside the country.[76]

Notwithstanding the ultimate success of MK in making its voice heard within the ANC, the failure of its cadres to actively participate in creating SDUs, coupled with its internal problems,[77] set back attempts to create a revolutionary role for MK. The Chris Hani report on SDUs in the Vaal, which revealed their corruption and role in the violence, also damaged the image of these structures as crucial components of the revolutionary struggle. That some MK members were allegedly involved in the dirty work of

SDUs diluted MK's revolutionary mission. Unable to find a revolutionary role in SDUs, MK became, for most of the early 1990s, an army that hung in the balance waiting for orders from its leadership locked in negotiations.

Farewell to mass mobilisation and militancy?

In every statement during its re-emergence in the country, the ANC maintained that negotiations did not replace mass struggle. Rather, it was one method and terrain of struggle which had to be complemented by other forms of struggle, including mass action. According to Suttner, "just as we try to mobilise the masses in organised formations on a number of different fronts of struggle, our task in the process of negotiations is to involve the people, to ensure that their influence is felt at the table and that their power is decisive".[78] The ANC's chief military strategists, Ronnie Kasrils and Mandla Khuzwayo, also urged the coordination of negotiations with mass action to prevent the ANC being tied to a negotiating process defined and controlled by the regime.[79]

Notwithstanding these statements, no effective programme was devised to connect these two dimensions of struggle, at least for most of 1990. Instead of involving the people or even consulting them on major political decisions such as the suspension of the armed struggle, the ANC, in practice, became elitist. Even when mass action campaigns were called, they appeared as an afterthought to deal with the problems faced in negotiations. While the ANC purportedly had valid strategic reasons for its employment of mass action campaigns, these were not clearly spelled out. The result was confusion, disillusionment and a widening gap between the leadership and the grass-roots members.

The lack of a clear programme integrating mass action and the negotiation strategy, and the resultant marginalisation of grass roots came under review at the consultative conference in December 1990. In a move to revitalise the role of its members in the conduct of the struggle, the conference urged the termination of secret negotiation deals and the implementation of internal democracy that would ensure broader consultation. It adopted a programme of action that would not only put mass action back on the agenda, but that would also develop a dynamic recruitment plan which would build active and democratic regions and branches. These would ensure mass participation in campaigns, make negotiations a terrain of mass struggle and broaden consultation with the mass formations. The "Peace and Democracy Now Campaign" of 6 December 1990 which was part of the programme of action, urged, among other things, the capturing of the moral high ground, support for the gains of negotiations with mass struggle and connecting the mass base to negotiations. Its campaigns included marches against Bophuthatswana's independence, the demand for the return of exiles and prisoners, as well as focusing on local issues such as housing and electricity. The mass demonstrations and stay-aways that took place throughout the country during the opening of parliament in 1991 found uneven support: in some areas like Port Elizabeth, Border and the Eastern Cape it was large, but attracted smaller crowds in Durban, Johannesburg and Cape Town. Marches in areas such as Bophuthatswana and some Northern Transvaal towns were not permitted by the local authorities.

The Million Signature Campaign to pressure the government to yield to the demand for an interim government and a constituent assembly, revealed signs of failure immediately after it was launched on 11 March 1991. Only about 28 700 people attended the launch of the campaign across five different areas in the Pretoria-Witwatersrand-Vaal Triangle region. Apart from the factor of violence, there appeared to be little enthusiasm at leadership, regional or branch levels to embark on door-to-door work. It was only at mass meetings such as those at Wits University and the Johannesburg City Hall which were addressed by Mandela, that this campaign featured prominently. The PWV region which was given a target of 300 000 signatures collected only a total of 55 347 from its 41 branches. Only four of the branches met their targets: Soshanguve (11 595), Mabopane (5895), Johannesburg North West (2700) and Sebokeng (3375). Fifty-nine of its branches failed to submit forms.[80]

Marches which were organised on 6 April 1991 by the ANC's National Campaigns Committee and the Human Rights Commission to demand the release of prisoners ranged between success and complete failure. About 20 000 people marched in Kroonstad, about 30 000 in the Vaal, 20 000 on the East Rand in the PWV, and a low turnout of 3000 in Soweto. No activities took place in the Eastern Cape, Border, Natal and Northern Transvaal.[81] A consumer boycott which was planned for the weekend of 8–13 April, as well as a stay-away on 2 May to add weight to this campaign, had to be called off due to inadequate organisation. Most surprising, was the silence by the leadership immediately after the government's failure to meet the deadlines of 30 April and 9 May. Despite widespread indignation at the government's failure to contain violence, the leadership approached the matter with caution for fear of fuelling confrontation that could bedevil the negotiation process. The result of this inaction, however, was increasing vocal criticism at grass-roots level. Calls to support the day of fasting on 22 May, in solidarity with political prisoners, failed to arouse mass participation. Although marches on 15 June around the theme of "Peace, freedom and jobs" succeeded in drawing large numbers in smaller towns such as Welkom (50 000) and Virginia (50 000), less than 5000 supported the marches in the big cities such as Johannesburg, Pretoria and Cape Town. While the campaign for open schools gained momentum with the government indirectly coercing these schools to open their doors to other population groups, the campaigns for land and local government, as well as the campaign against AIDS, did not proceed as expected.

Compared to the euphoria that followed Mandela's release, the number of people attending rallies, demonstrations and other campaigns organised around the programme of action, dwindled. In spite of urging by some ANC leaders to use the opportunity of opened political space,[82] mass enthusiasm failed to reach the level shown in earlier marches, such as those in 1989 when De Klerk first introduced his reforms. The reassurance by the national conference of July 1991 to place the masses at the centre of the struggle[83] made no difference to subsequent mass campaigns, apart from the massive two-day stay-away organised by COSATU on the question of value added tax (VAT) in 1991. The national day of protest which focused on the release of Operation Vula operatives, was a failure.

It would appear from a superficial analysis of the poor support in mass action campaigns between mid-1990 and early 1992 in particular, that the intimidatory element of violence was the key factor responsible. A closer analysis reveals that other factors played their part. There was incontrovertible evidence that the public was increasingly losing interest in ANC campaigns.[84] A sense of complacency, bemoaned by General Secretary Alfred Nzo during the national conference in July, pervaded a majority of the rank and file. There seemed to be a belief in general that the ANC was a government in waiting and that it was negotiating itself into power. Negotiations also dampened mass enthusiasm, since almost every problem appeared to be able to be resolved through dialogue by the leadership.

The failure of campaigns did not, however, lie only in the intimidatory factor of violence or in mass apathy. The way in which campaigns were organised also had a significant bearing on their level of success. This was the case with the decision by the Tripartite Alliance to call for a national consumer boycott. The call was met with indifference in ANC regional structures. While most Transvaal regions responded through localised boycotts around local towns, the PWV consumer boycott found little support. There were several reasons for the failure of the boycott:

- There was little preparation: no consultation occurred with branches or with the regional leaders.

- The ANC regional representatives in the Tripartite Alliance were severely criticised by the branches for having proceeded without properly consulting with branch structures.

- The consumer boycott proved to be highly controversial and impracticable. Calling for a boycott of white shops was not only racist, but also ignored the fact that the ANC had branches in these areas which would have difficulty in effecting the boycott.

- Even the demands around the boycott, which ranged from local grievances to political issues such as the release of political prisoners, were unrealistic.

In general terms, the inefficient operation and often moribund ANC branch structures made the coordination of campaigns from national, regional and local levels difficult. Lack of communication about intended campaigns was a consequence. Quite often, branch executive members discussed campaigns and took decisions on the basis of their own analyses, without the input of members of the branches or that of allied organisations such as unions and civics. The traditional use of mass meetings to discuss campaigns was submerged in a growing tendency to communicate with members through pamphlets. The changed attitude of the ANC to boycotts and stay-aways also had an impact on the performance of these campaigns. While in the past, activists took campaigns seriously by actively mobilising the people through different techniques such as door-to-door mobilising and even an element of "intimidation", the new approach discouraged coercion and promoted voluntarism which allowed people the scope to ignore calls for action.

Mass action, however, made an impressive return to the political stage in mid-1992, following the collapse of CODESA negotiations in May. Commemoration Day rallies on 16 June were rapidly followed by countrywide protest, spearheaded by the ANC after the Boipatong massacre on 17 June. Trade unions, teachers and students poured into the streets to support ANC demands. The ANC also led marches to police stations in cities and towns, demanding an end to corruption and a vote for democracy. On 3 and 4 August 1992 a successful two-day stay-away was organised across the country, followed by an unprecedented mass march "with Mandela" to Pretoria on 5 August. Mass action mushroomed during this period. Marches of thousands of ANC supporters were organised in the homelands of Ciskei, KwaZulu and Bophuthatswana to demand free political activity. The massacre of protest marchers in a hundred thousand strong crowd led by Ronnie Kasrils, marching to Bisho in the Ciskei in September 1992, cut short the resurgence of mass action. This incident demonstrated the potential danger of jeopardising negotiations and disposed the ANC leadership to a more cautious approach. Henceforth, mass action was treated as a tap to be turned on and off at times congenial to the movement. This, however, had an unintended effect of disempowering supporters.[85]

The erosion of the sanctions campaign

Until 1990 the ANC and the Anti-Apartheid Movement abroad had been able to win world support for their struggle against apartheid. Numerous resolutions condemning the South African government were passed by the UN and other international organisations. Some states and agencies pledged their support for the cause of the anti-apartheid struggle through financial assistance for development programmes and the upliftment of the social conditions of the disadvantaged communities. Other states even supplied military equipment to the organisation to bolster its military struggle. The extent to which the ANC enjoyed international support was demonstrated by Nelson Mandela's successful world tour in 1990. He was warmly received in all the world cities he visited. Thousands of people poured into the streets and crammed the halls and stadiums wherever he went. In New York, for example, a million people witnessed his procession through the city. In the previous 30 years the ANC had, through the establishment of 40 missions and the building of contacts with a broad variety of governmental, political, anti-apartheid, religious, social, cultural and sporting organisations around the world, succeeded in building a diplomatic weapon that turned South Africa into a pariah among the nations of the world. From the establishment of one mission in Tanzania, the organisation had over 30 years established

20 missions in Africa, eight in Europe, four in the Nordic countries, four in America and five in Asia and Australia. In the words of Nzo,

> ... over these three decades we established ourselves as an influential force in the United Nations and its Allied agencies, the Non-Aligned Movement, the OAU and the Commonwealth. We built ties with religious forces in many countries and have maintained an admirable relationship with the World Council of Churches and the World Alliance of Reformed Churches. We succeeded in building a world-wide anti-apartheid movement based in the smallest towns to the major cities of the world.[86]

While the balance of support at an international level weighed in favour of the ANC, the beginning of the liberalisation process and De Klerk's swift removal of apartheid legislation that formed the basis for international sanctions altered the situation. International solidarity was eroded and left the ANC in a defensive position. For the first time in the history of the NP government, De Klerk became its only leader to sway international opinion in his favour.[87] Not only was he warmly welcomed in the states he visited, he also commanded respect and built cordial relations with states which were once staunch opponents of apartheid. Even before world bodies decided on the question of sanctions, De Klerk had already made important inroads on sanctions, apart from the sanctions-busting operations by certain companies.[88] His visits to the Ivory Coast, Senegal, the Netherlands, Luxembourg and many other foreign states, led to the resumption or creation of consular and diplomatic relations, as well as the consolidation of trade relations.[89] Even East European states such as the Soviet Union were eager to build ties with South Africa. While the international arena was dominated by the ANC and the anti-apartheid movement with regard to the internal political crisis in South Africa, the 1990s saw it being transformed into a theatre of struggle in which the anti-apartheid forces were on the defensive. The ANC was aware of the difficulty of sustaining its dominant moral position at an international level. However, it failed to devise a coherent approach to manage the demise of the sanctions campaign. This failure arose from internal divisions on the subject. A proposal by Oliver Tambo to the consultative conference in December 1990 that the ANC take a sober look at this question, particularly in view of the disintegration of sanctions, was completely ignored. Instead a resolution was passed calling for the maintenance of existing sanctions. While this resolution opened the door for the promotion of sport, the reasoning behind it was unconvincing. It insisted that "we should oppose the lifting of financial sanctions especially by the IMF, on the grounds that the country is still governed by a white minority regime".[90] Opposition to the lifting of the arms and oil embargo was made on similar grounds.

The ANC's insistence on maintaining sanctions misinterpreted the changing world politics and put the organisation in a defensive and contradictory posture. A majority of international agencies and states – some of which were staunch opponents of apartheid – were anxious to exploit the loophole created by the reform process to begin trade relations with South Africa. European Economic Community (EEC) states were eager to reconsider sanctions by December 1990. These developments made it difficult for the ANC to convince the world of its judgement of the South African situation. Despite the alleged involvement of the government in township violence, the ANC had little evidence to convince a world keen to reward De Klerk for his reform initiatives. Even the anti-apartheid movement abroad seemed to have lost its ability to put pressure on foreign governments to comply with the ANC's prescriptions on the question of sanctions. While the ANC suffered setbacks on sanctions, it nevertheless made important gains on the readmission of South African sport into the international sporting community. Almost all the sports bodies in South Africa had to obtain ANC clearance to be readmitted. Steve Tshwete, Head of the ANC's Organising Department, played a pivotal and constructive role in promoting the image of the ANC as an indispensable broker on the sports question. Cultural contacts and diplomatic visits could also not happen without the blessing of the organisation.

The difficulty in defending the sanctions position in a changing world order became an important issue. The ANC adopted a more sober approach during its national conference in July 1991. During his presentation of the Secretary-General's report, Nzo emphasised that

> ... we succeeded in the imposition of sanctions by a wide range of governments and international organisations. We therefore must be able to work out a clear strategy for managing and controlling their lifting. At this conference we must once and for all determine a clear policy on this issue taking into cognisance the reality around us.[91]

A resolution argued that ways and means should be found to arrest the erosion of sanctions because of its strategic value as a weapon of the struggle. Consequently, a decision was taken that specific groups of sanctions should be used to achieve specific strategic objectives. These included the removal by the government of obstacles to negotiations, the implementation of effective measures to end violence, the installation of an interim government, the adoption of a new constitution and elections for a non-racial parliament and a representative government. Although the ANC's position on sanctions was flexible, foreign states and agencies were hardly influenced by its resolutions. They made their own decisions in lifting sanctions or resuming diplomatic ties with the South African government.

In conclusion, the subjective or objective marginalisation of the armed struggle, mass action and sanctions during the period of transition left negotiation as the dominant form of political activity pursued by the ANC. Mass action campaigns continued to be invoked at times to bolster negotiations, but they were seen as nothing more than that.

Back to negotiations and the Record of Understanding

The mass action campaign and Mandela's triumphant march to Pretoria demonstrated the power of the ANC's mass support base. However, the killing at Bisho also sensitised the ANC to the danger of undermining negotiations. While the ANC opted for mass action following the collapse of CODESA, it did not terminate further contact with the government. In fact, during the mass action campaign bilateral meetings between the ANC Secretary-General, Cyril Ramaphosa, and the new Minister of Constitutional Development, Roelf Meyer, laid the foundation for the resumption of negotiations.

These meetings sought to find a mechanism to resolve deadlocks, which would be used in the event of disagreement in future negotiations. Indeed, CODESA had collapsed in May 1992 primarily because there was no effective deadlock-breaking mechanism. The ANC, however, apart from resolving this issue, also wanted government commitment towards the speedy creation of an interim government and elections for a constituent assembly. On 1 September 1992 the organisation's NEC held a meeting at which it resolved to resume constitutional negotiations. The Transition to Democracy Bill was released proposing amendments to the South African constitution that would facilitate the establishment of an interim government and a constituent assembly. The bill proposed a four-chamber national assembly, elected by proportional representation, to serve as an interim legislature and a constitution-making body. It defined South Africa by its 1910 boundaries and sidestepped the homeland system and key issues of regionalism by retaining, for the interim, the provincial system as the only form of regional government. The president would be elected by a simple majority of the national assembly. The cabinet would have a multi-party, two-thirds majority. All parties with 5 % or more of the membership of the assembly would be entitled to nominate cabinet ministers. The bill also contained a bill of rights.[92]

While the bill was important in outlining the ANC's constitutional perspective in detail, it made certain provisions which were unpalatable to other parties. These included the suggestion that a new constitution could be adopted by a 51 % majority, failing a two-thirds majority.[93] Intensified bilateral meetings between Ramaphosa and Meyer bridged major differences between the ANC and the government, and paved the way for the signing of the Record of Understanding on 27 September 1992. The Record of Understanding was an important hallmark in that for the first time the government acceded to a major demand of the ANC. The government committed itself, more firmly than before, to the installation of an interim government, an elected constituent assembly, the release of the remaining political prisoners, the banning of the public display of dangerous weapons, including the cultural weapons often wielded by Inkatha members, and the fencing of hostels. While most of the issues, those dealing with violence in particular, had already been agreed to by the government without being implemented, the fact that the government began releasing political prisoners, including

MacBride and Mthetheleli Ncube, was a significant concession to the ANC.

The accord, however, which was branded by right-wing organisations as a major sell-out, backfired for the government on the very day it was announced. The IFP immediately announced that it was withdrawing from negotiations, with Buthelezi saying that "the KwaZulu government would reject as 'spurious and illegitimate' any laws passed by the South African parliament giving legal effect to such agreements". Reacting to the government's attempts to sideline him because of pressure from the ANC, Buthelezi quickly rallied Oupa Gqozo of Ciskei and Lucas Mangope of Bophuthatswana into an alliance with right-wing organisations, which came to be known as the Concerned South Africa Group (COSAG). A sense of frustration also seemed to overwhelm the government as it continued to make blunders. The deal with the ANC to release political prisoners saw it even opening prison doors to known psychopaths and criminals such as Lucky Malaza, much to the anger of the public. Furthermore, it also unsuccessfully attempted through parliament, and ultimately through the President's Council, to legislate the Further Indemnity Bill to indemnify from prosecution security officials who might have committed heinous crimes under apartheid.

Strategic self-analysis, the "sunset clause" and the new strategic perspective to power

The Record of Understanding and the extent to which the government was forced to accede to the ANC's demands prompted a major rethink within the ANC about giving back in kind to promote a smooth and speedy transitional process. This rethink also kindled what had become a dormant theoretical and confusing strategic perspective within the liberation movement on the approach to power. For years, the ANC and the SACP had adhered to the colonialism of a special type (CST) thesis, which gave rise to the adoption of militant strategies. Even when conditions favourable to peaceful negotiations emerged, the ANC continued to pledge its loyalty to this strategic perspective. Arguing in its Strategy and Tactics document adopted at the national conference in July 1991, and following the SACP's 1989 "Path to Power", the ANC stated that the fundamental essence of the crisis in the country had not changed. South Africa still exhibited the characteristics of "colonialism of a special type", which necessitated two broad approaches: the retention of the organisation as a broad liberation movement and the continuation of the four pillars of struggle – armed struggle, underground network, mass action and the mobilisation of the international community.

The organisation argued that it had to remain a liberation movement to represent a broad range of dominated class interests whose unity was essential in the dismantling of apartheid and the creation of a democratic state. Advancing this argument, Raymond Suttner stated in August 1991 that, as a national liberation movement, the ANC stood at the head of a whole range of organisations and social groupings which had struggled against apartheid.[94] He contended that, through appealing to the oppressed people as a whole and by carrying forward their aspirations as expressed in decades of struggle, the ANC was more than a single organisation made up of branches. It was not going to become a political party, and did not have to be one simply for the sake of negotiating and contesting elections. According to the ANC, remaining a liberation movement throughout the period of negotiations would allow it the leverage to use its liberation strategies to back up its negotiation efforts. These revolutionary strategies, it was contended, in no way contradicted or were irreconcilable with the discourse of negotiation. Instead, it was argued that the combination of the two could, in the South African conditions, secure the transfer of power to the majority.

Though adopted to justify the retention of existing liberation strategies such as mass action, the CST thesis suffered from significant weaknesses. The analysis of the South African state in the wake of negotiations, in particular, was poor. This weakness seems to have been caused by an overestimation of the achievements of the liberation movement. The ANC's guidelines on strategy and tactics entitled *Advance to national democracy*, which formed the basis of discussion at the national conference in July 1991, made wide claims that the changes introduced by the state constituted "a strategic defeat for the apartheid regime and an open admission on its part that all its counter-revolutionary efforts, both inside and outside the country have failed to suppress and crush the national liberation movement of our country …".[95] In his writings, Raymond Suttner also claimed that "the regime was forced to unban the ANC, SACP and other organisations because of our struggles inside and outside the country, using a variety of methods, legal and illegal, armed with military weapons and armed with the power of the people wherever they suffered oppression".[96]

While this analysis was important in providing the reasons for the ANC's spearheading of the negotiation process, its eulogy of the achievements of the movement presented an exaggerated picture of the balance of power. This basis weakened an understanding of state strategies, and in particular, an understanding of the growing predominance of violence alongside negotiations. It constrained an appropriate strategy, despite acknowledgement by the organisation of the potential inclination by the state and other reactionary forces to undo the advances of the struggle.[97] The theory was also weak because of its poor reading of the South African political situation. Combining liberation strategies with negotiation also proved to be difficult. In spite of its theoretical projections, the ANC came to discover that negotiating and continuing with other revolutionary strategies could not work as smoothly as it had hoped. Intensifying the armed struggle while a delicate understanding was developing with the government, proved to be unwise.

The difficulties of the CST thesis in accounting for the new challenges, in particular the path to power through negotiations, not only incited doubts about its relevance but also kindled a new search for alternative perspectives. The SACP's consultative conference held in Tongaat from 19–20 May 1990, sceptically but cautiously asked whether "our thesis on seizure of power had become irrelevant".[98] In his speech at the University of Western

Cape in July 1991, marking the 70th Anniversary of the SACP, Joe Slovo questioned the efficacy of the thesis in the rapidly changing conditions facing the country. He stated that "our Party is busy examining the impact of the changes that have taken place on some of our basic ideological concepts. It is clear that the thesis of colonialism of a special type needs to be looked at".[99] The basis of a full debate on the strategic perspective on power was laid by Jeremy Cronin, the SACP's Chief of Information and Publicity. Cronin argued that there were three strategic perspectives within the liberation movement:[100]

- The first was the "don't rock the boat" perspective, which promoted deals between elites and persuaded against mass action which was perceived to be antagonistic to the climate of negotiations.

- The second was the "turning on the tap" perspective which, while regarding negotiations as the viable route to power, also agitated for the use of mass action to bring the other party to adhere to the terms of negotiations. Mass struggles are primarily seen as a "tap" that could be turned on and off to suit the goal of negotiations.

- The third perspective was the "Leipzig way" which promoted insurrection. It saw mass action as essential in building dual power which would eventually lead to the overthrow of the incumbent regime.

After giving an incisive criticism of these perspectives, Jeremy Cronin considered the second perspective as the most viable, but only if it had three essential features. "It needs to be able to combine a *revolutionary* perspective and practice with an active and effective engagement on the terrain of *negotiations*; and it needs to orient us correctly in regard to our *organisational* tasks."[101]

In spite of his attempts to lay the foundation for a vigorous reassessment of the strategic perspective of the Tripartite Alliance, Cronin did not provide elaboration on how to deal with negotiations in a practicable way. It was Joe Slovo who made a bold attempt on this score. Justifying a compromise towards the NP government, Joe Slovo in his paper entitled *Negotiations: what room for compromise?* first argued that the ANC and the government were negotiating because of a stalemate in power relations. He argued that the immediate outcome of the negotiation process would inevitably be less than the long-term liberation objective of the ANC. "If such an outcome is unacceptable then we should cease raising false expectations by persisting with negotiations. On the other hand, if it is strategically acceptable then a degree of compromise will be unavoidable."[102] Distinguishing between quantitative and qualitative compromises, Slovo urged the ANC to clearly highlight its non-compromisable positions. These were agreement on a minority veto, compulsory power-sharing, giving the negotiating forum the power to determine the boundaries and powers of regions, and allowing the negotiating forum to bind a future government from being able to intervene and to redress the historical imbalances in the country.

However, while arguing for the need to pre-empt an apparent threat by counter-revolutionary forces and following the line of thinking earlier advanced by Soviet Union academics, Slovo suggested a series of compromises. These included a "sunset clause" in the new constitution, which would provide for compulsory power-sharing for a fixed number of years in the period immediately following the adoption of the new constitution. The ANC would also have to agree in advance with the government about regional boundaries and a general amnesty. It would also need to address the fears of the civil service, including the SADF and the SAP. Justifying these compromises, Slovo said that they were permissible because they would not permanently block the advance to real democracy. These compromises would induce a positive breakthrough in the negotiation process because they addressed, in a principled way, some of the basic and more immediate fears and insecurities of the regime and its constituency. "In particular, the prospect of a period of power-sharing, a shared vision of the future regional dispensation, some security for existing incumbents in the civil service, and undertakings which will promote reconciliation, will make it exceedingly difficult for the other side to continue blocking the transformation."[103] Slovo's suggestions were encapsulated in an ANC NWC paper entitled *Strategic perspective*, which was discussed during the last week of October 1992.

Slovo's "sunset clause" compromise was not entirely new in the ANC's strategies. During CODESA negotiations at the beginning of 1992, Thabo Mbeki had spoken about a "sunset clause" when proposing that the winner of the first election under the new constitution would appoint a coalition cabinet that included all major parties for a number of years.[104] The fact that the "sunset clause" was being advocated by Slovo, seen as more of a militant than Mbeki, a moderate and diplomat, appeared to be aimed at cementing its acceptance by ANC militants.[105] In a major debate that followed these proposals, Pallo Jordan, the ANC's Head of the Department of Information and Publicity, contended that the entire thesis of *Strategic perspective*, though not clearly pronounced, deviated from the strategic objectives of the ANC. He criticised the implicit assumption that the ANC and the government could cooperate, arguing that the relationship between the two was, on the contrary, conflicting.[106] He also contended that negotiation was not a strategy to replace the other four pillars of the struggle that had hitherto been pursued by the ANC. For Jordan negotiation was not a tactic, but part of a strategy. He criticised the thesis that the ANC had only opted for armed struggle because the possibility of negotiations had vanished. He pointed out that there was clearly a confusion of facts because the ANC only opted for the armed struggle when non-violent means of struggle were prohibited. At that time negotiation had not been on the agenda. He wrote that it was this confusion of non-violence with negotiations that the authors of *Strategic perspective* were using to justify the elevation of negotiation into a strategy. He argued that this constituted a major revision of the ANC's conception of the struggle. Contending that negotiation was only a key part of the strategy, Jordan stated that the ANC had not been defeated and therefore did not have to be lenient and make cowardly compromises to a government which was declaring war against it.

Apart from Pallo Jordan, Blade Nzimande of the SACP in Natal also criticised Slovo, although for a different reason. He argued that Slovo's proposed compromises were one-sided and lacked foundation in the broad mass struggles of the people. He argued that these compromises seemed to be made at the negotiating table, focusing on what should be given to the other side and what should be retained. "In his article he [Slovo] is primarily concerned with the freedom that should be given to negotiators to negotiate on and enter into agreements, without being concerned about the reverse process of accountability to the constituency and the role that our constituency should play."[107] Nzimande rejected Slovo's proposal for power-sharing, saying that should be determined by the balance of power at the time of reaching a settlement. "Our stance therefore should be to uncompromisingly and unashamedly aim at majority rule. If we decisively defeat the Nationalist Party and its surrogates in a democratic election, let them become the opposition or disappear from the face of a democratic South Africa."[108]

Harry Gwala also entered the debate to criticise Slovo's suggested compromises, their lack of mass action content and the dearth of class analysis. He did not understand how compromises would succeed which only addressed the fears of the regime and remained silent about the fears of the majority. In his words,

> ... it is not the good intentions of the negotiators and their ability to talk that will determine the fate of this country, important as this part of the struggle may be. But it will be the strength and ability of the contenders in the struggle that, in the final analysis, will determine the fate of this country. Any political expediency will lead to disaster.[109]

The ANC Youth League also criticised Slovo's compromises arguing, like Nzimande, that only the masses and not compromises would lead to democracy and would build a defence against counter-revolutionaries.[110]

Slovo's position had some support from Raymond Suttner and Jeremy Cronin. Unlike Slovo's critics, Suttner raised important questions about alternatives. Instead of compromising with the NP government and giving it credibility in the process, he raised the option of making a deal directly with the affected white constituency. He also urged for confidence in the power of the "masses" rather than in the notion of buying off counter-revolutionaries. Apart from supporting Slovo's temporary power-sharing deal, the thrust of his argument in the debate was the need to engage the people in the negotiation process through empowerment. To him, the attainment of freedom would not happen in a revolutionary "bang", as Nzimande and Gwala implicitly suggested. It would happen when the people themselves were "involved and empowered in the process".[111] Cronin's intervention in the debate was not only to back Slovo, but to confront the critics. He criticised them for not giving concrete details about attaining the objectives of the liberation struggle. He criticised Jordan's implied suggestion of political negotiation as a matter of all or nothing. Arguing that the existing situation was not a final showdown as implied by Jordan, Cronin wrote that "the all-or-nothing approach, when it is not an all-or-nothing moment, means that all you can offer is next to nothing".[112] In the end, the various contributions made in this debate were reflected in the ANC's NEC paper entitled *Negotiations: a strategic perspective*, which was adopted at a meeting in Durban from 23–25 November 1992. The major part of this paper included the postulations advanced by Slovo, but accommodating the contributions of his critics. The paper set out the ANC's strategy as

> ... a negotiation process combined with mass action and international pressure which takes into account the need to combat counter-revolutionary forces and at the same time uses phases in the transition to qualitatively change the balance of forces in order to secure a thorough-going democratic transformation.[113]

Five phases were elaborated:

- The first phase would be the period prior to the establishment of a transitional executive council. The aim here was to secure an agreement on free and fair elections, the interim government and a constituent assembly, as well as to stop unilateral restructuring, to broaden the space for free political activity and to address violence.

- The second phase would be the period from the establishment of the transitional executive council, leading up to the election of a constituent assembly and the establishment of an interim government of national unity.

- Phase three would be the period of the drafting and adoption of the new constitution by the constituent assembly. The aim would be to consolidate peace through joint control over all armed forces, ensuring free and fair elections, and mobilising for an election victory. The objective would be to establish an interim government in which the ANC would be a major player, to adopt a new democratic constitution and to start addressing the socio-economic problems facing the country.

- Phase four would comprise the phasing in of the new constitution, which would include the restructuring of the state machinery and the general dismantling of the system of apartheid.

- Finally, phase five would be the period of the consolidation of the process of democratic transformation.

The NEC paper argued that the process should be mass driven:

> The balance of forces, our specific objectives and our long-term goals would at each stage dictate the need to enter into specific, and perhaps changing alliances; and to make certain compromises in order to protect and advance this process.

Negotiation tactics were also seen as crucial to ensure a decisive leap forward. While Slovo's proposed compromises were accepted, it was underlined that such compromises should not be made unilaterally but be negotiated with the NP. The NEC paper was an important synthesis of the various contributions made in the debate. It failed, however, to give concrete elaboration on how the "masses" would drive the process. They remained, to use Cronin's words, "a tap to be turned on and off" to suit negotiations. Although in interviews ANC activists did not agree,[114] negotiations had, during this period, been elevated into the main theatre of the struggle by both subjective and objective conditions. Indeed, the suspension of the armed struggle and the redundancy of the political underground, together with the rapidly disintegrating sanctions campaign meant that the ANC was left with negotiation and mass action as the only workable vehicles to power. The obvious tensions between negotiations and mass action, however, meant that the two would not be employed simultaneously. Unavoidably, negotiations assumed pre-eminence, while mass action remained to be invoked in the event of problems in negotiations – the "don't rock the boat" scenario described by Cronin above.

The postulations advanced by the NEC's *Strategic perspective* clearly implied a break with the past and constituted a divergence from earlier ANC positions. While the movement initially talked about the transfer of power and majority government, the NEC's paper propounded the notion of a government of national unity, regardless of the verdict of elections. It envisaged a role for other defeated parties in the government of national unity and suggested ways of amicably carrying along the former instruments of repression – the army and the police. These postulations, which were bitterly debated, ultimately came to inform the ANC's strategic approach to power for the rest of 1992 and into 1993.

From *Strategic perspective* to the Negotiating Council and the passing of the transitional mechanisms bills

While the NP ceded much at the Record of Understanding in the following months and upon the resumption of multi-party negotiations in 1993, the ANC gave back in kind. Immediately after the NEC's adoption of Slovo's "sunset clause" and associated compromises in *Strategic perspective*, the ANC organised a string of bilateral meetings with the NP at which greater consensus was secured on a number of hitherto controversial issues. In their meeting held in December 1992 the ANC and the government established informal subcommittees to explore mutual agreement on a two-phased transition, including discussion on the elements, composition, structure, jurisdiction and actual character of an envisaged election commission, the role and control of electronic media, and the details of portfolios of law and order, defence and foreign affairs. In the subsequent bilateral meetings held for five days in January 1993 the two focused, in addition to the above, on state security and violence, as well as on constitutional principles. By the beginning of February major compromises were already emerging from these bilateral meetings. The ANC had offered the NP its compromises arising out of its NEC paper. The government abandoned its earlier insistence on entrenched power-sharing, arguing that this could be achieved by making binding constitutional principles which would be agreed upon before elections for a constituent assembly. Such constitutional principles would elaborate on the bill of rights, special majorities for certain decision making, and multi-party access to the branches of the state such as security forces and the civil service. The NP also dropped its earlier proposal for a rotating presidency, arguing that it was unworkable and had no justification because of the lack of precedent. Instead, it supported the leader of the majority party becoming state president, but acting on the approval of a cabinet. When President De Klerk opened parliament in February 1993 and presented a timetable for the transitional process which envisaged elections in early 1994, it was clear that significant compromises had been reached with the ANC during the bilateral meetings.

The endeavour to find common ground did not, however, end in these bilateral meetings. Both parties continued to woo other parties into negotiations, including the PAC and the CP, which were not party to the CODESA process. Attempts were also made to bring back the IFP which had withdrawn from the talks. However, such attempts to pull them into the process essentially meant their acceptance of what had already been agreed upon by the two parties. Important face-saving incentives were given to them to attract them into multi-party talks. For the PAC, the new talks would no longer be called CODESA nor would they be chaired by judges, as it had raised reservations about them. But the question of neutrality, which it had also raised, would not mean the holding of the new talks in Harare or anywhere else outside South Africa. For the IFP, not only would constitutional principles be discussed in the multi-party forum, but deliberation on the powers and functions of regions would also be placed on the forum's agenda to allay its fears which had led to its passing of a secessionist Natal/KwaZulu federal constitution in December 1992. The coming in of the CP was due more to the pressure put on it by its COSAG allies, than to any meaningful promise that the question of self-determination for Afrikaners would be discussed in the forum.

While the possibility of a deal between the ANC and the government sparked criticism by other parties and within the ANC itself, and despite their public denials of a power-sharing deal, this did not affect the momentum towards the resumption of negotiation. On 5 and 6 March 1993, a multi-party planning conference was held in Kempton Park, the venue of previous multi-party negotiations. In this meeting an agreement was reached that formal negotiations would begin on 5 April.[115] A Facilitating Committee was formed which comprised leaders of the 26 participating parties (initially CODESA had 19 parties). A ten-member subcommittee of the Facilitating Committee was also formed, consisting of Roelf Meyer, Cyril Ramaphosa, Joe Slovo, Natal Indian Congress' Pravin Gordhan, DP's Colin Eglin, IFP's Joe Matthews, Bophuthatswana Minister of State and Defence,

Rowan Cronje, Ciskei's Mike Webb and Transkei's Zam Titus. Issues to be discussed by this committee included the status of CODESA agreements, the participation of 11 groups which were given observer status at the planning conference, the chairmanship of the negotiation forum, the forum's name, as well as the role of the international community.

As illustrated in Figure 5, the new Multi-party Negotiating Forum was completely different from CODESA. It had a ten-member planning committee which planned and submitted recommendations on procedural and substantive issues to the Negotiating Council. The planning committee also comprised an administration committee, as well as technical committees, which effectively took over the work previously done by the working groups during CODESA. The Negotiating Council comprised two delegates and two advisers for each party. Extensive negotiations took place in the council. A Negotiating Forum comprising four delegates and two advisers was also set up but was later disbanded because it tended to replay what had been done in the Negotiating Council. A Plenary made up of ten delegates per party, a total of 260 people, was also set in place. Unlike CODESA, each delegation was compelled to include at least one female delegate. The question of naming the new multi-party talks was never resolved.

Having given in to the demand to discuss regional policy at the multi-party forum, the ANC convened its national consultative conference on regional policy on 20 March 1993. This conference, which was attended by more than 200 delegates from the organisation's 14 regions, adopted a new map with ten regions. It also decided that powers, functions and boundaries would be decided on by an elected constituent assembly.[116] However, developments in the following two months disrupted negotiations. The assassination of the ANC leader and SACP General Secretary, Chris Hani, on 10 April 1993, set in motion widespread mass action activities that diverted attention from negotiations.

The sudden death of Oliver Tambo, the ANC's National Chairman, two weeks after Hani's assassination, also dragged over the negotiation's timetable as the ANC was held up in weeks of mourning. The aftermath of the deaths of Hani and Tambo and the surging fears about Mandela's life, gave negotiations a sense of urgency. Mandela's courageous statesmanship during the crisis when De Klerk had lamely taken a back seat might have encouraged ANC leaders to speed up the negotiation process and herald the day of his inauguration as president. However, the anger demonstrated by ANC supporters and their vocal criticism of negotiations "that lead to hell" and "the organisation that has become an undertaker", prompted the demand for an election date. Notwithstanding a sense of urgency for the resumption of negotiations, the IFP and the CP continued to compel the forum to attend to their demands. At one stage the IFP threatened a walkout when it was prohibited from reading to the Negotiating Council its document on violence, which detailed cases of MK's killing of IFP leaders. Moreover, mass action outside the negotiation process occupied the political stage in May. The far right-wing political organisations organised themselves into the Afrikaner Volksunie (AVU) to mobilise and pursue the common goal of

Figure 5 Multi-party negotiating structure, 1993

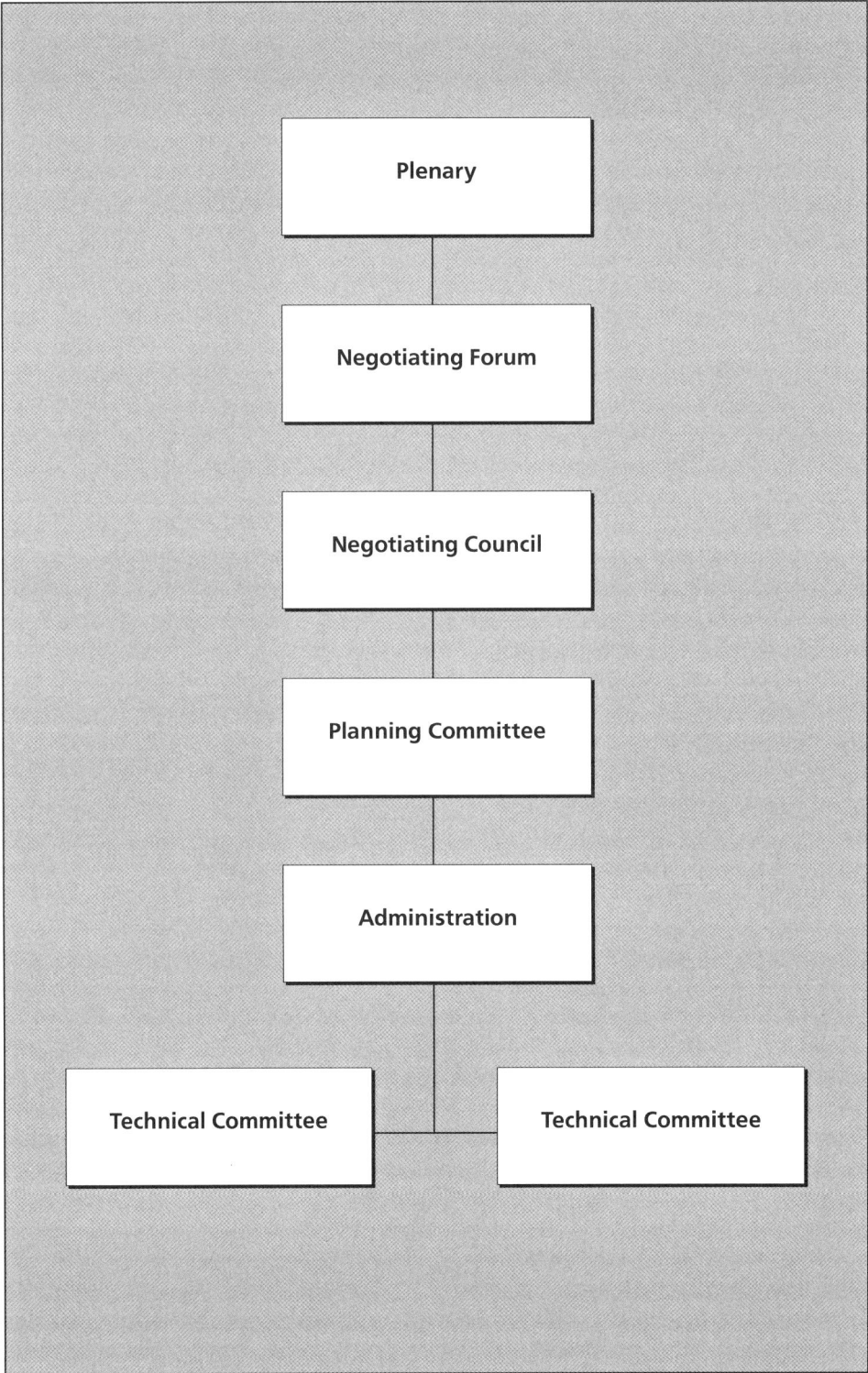

```
                    ┌─────────────────────┐
                    │      Plenary        │
                    └─────────────────────┘
                              │
                    ┌─────────────────────┐
                    │  Negotiating Forum  │
                    └─────────────────────┘
                              │
                    ┌─────────────────────┐
                    │ Negotiating Council │
                    └─────────────────────┘
                              │
                    ┌─────────────────────┐
                    │ Planning Committee  │
                    └─────────────────────┘
                              │
                    ┌─────────────────────┐
                    │   Administration    │
                    └─────────────────────┘
                              │
        ┌──────────────────┐  │  ┌──────────────────┐
        │ Technical        │──┴──│ Technical        │
        │ Committee        │     │ Committee        │
        └──────────────────┘     └──────────────────┘
```

self-determination. At the same time, education was in turmoil as teachers under the banner of the South African Democratic Teachers Union (SADTU) marched into the streets over insufficient pay increases. Students, under the banner of COSAS, opposed the Department of Education and Training's examination fee of R48. Alongside these events, fierce fighting broke out between IFP and ANC followers in the East Rand townships of Tokoza and Katlehong. Moreover, the killing of farmers, allegedly by APLA cadres, intensified with De Klerk threatening firm measures and a state of emergency against "radicals to the left and right" – a threat which was later effected by the arrest of 73 PAC leaders on 25 May 1993. In the midst of all these developments, sinister plans by right-wingers to assassinate SACP Chairman, Joe Slovo, and to destabilise the transitional process, were also uncovered.

These events did not, however, stop the negotiation process. By 1 June the Negotiating Council was able to announce a range of agreements.[117] These included a resolution which provided for a two-phased transition and an elected constitution-making body bound by agreed-on principles. The resolution also provided for interim regional governments and a transitional constitution. The two-phased transition comprised a transitional constitution to be drafted by the Negotiating Council, and the final constitution by an elected parliament. A technical committee on the constitution was mandated to make recommendations on the powers, structures and functions of regions during the transition. It would also look into the constitution-making process to be followed, the procedure to be followed in the drafting and adoption of a transitional constitution, and the procedure to be followed in the elected constitution-making body. On 3 June the Negotiating Council announced 27 April 1994 as the date for the country's first democratic elections. During these negotiations the ANC had also made an important shift in its regional policy. National, regional and local government would be democratically elected with legislative and executive powers and functions. This implied that regions would also have their own constitutions (as demanded by the IFP), and their powers, functions and duties would be entrenched in the national constitution. The organisation refused, however, to give in to the IFP's insistence that regional authorities have their own armed forces.

The announcement of an election date infuriated COSAG members. An upsurge of violence took a more vicious turn on the East Rand, spreading from Tokoza and Katlehong to Vosloorus, Daveyton and Tembisa, as well as to Wadeville. Sporadic incidents of racial attacks by right-wingers also increased. The mobilisation of the far right by the AVU, led by General Constand Viljoen and Dr Ferdie Hartzenberg, culminated in the siege of the World Trade Centre in Kempton Park on 25 June.

While the negotiators continued to maintain their cohesion and dedication, the tensions and hostility outside the forum grew. The apparent unwillingness of the government to take firm measures against right-wing organisations, the war talk by spokespersons of these organisations, including the IFP and APLA, with a continued offensive against white civilians in particular, heightened tensions and soured relations among parties. These tensions might not have been visible on the smiling faces of negotiators at Kempton Park, but they were glaringly apparent in Mandela's demeanour during his June and July tour of the United States to receive the Philadelphia Liberty Award with Mr De Klerk. Not only did Mandela avoid Mr De Klerk and cancel their joint photo session with American President Bill Clinton, he also sent a clear message of warning to foreign heads of state not to receive an "illegitimate white minority leader".

Hostility between Mandela and De Klerk was exacerbated by the latter's failure to end the violence on the East Rand. However, these events did not prevent negotiations at the World Trade Centre finally yielding results in September 1993. Four bills were passed: the Transitional Executive Council (TEC) Bill, the Independent Electoral Commission Bill, the Independent Media Commission Bill and the Independent Broadcasting Authority Bill. These bills were promulgated by a special session of parliament sitting from 13 September. The TEC Bill made provision for a multi-party body to monitor the actions of the government, homeland authorities and political parties during the election campaign. Aimed at levelling the playing field, the TEC's task was to remove any obstacle to legitimate political activity, to end intimidation, to ensure that political parties were free to canvass voters and hold meetings, and to stop any government body from using its powers in favour of, or against any political party. The TEC would not, however, have the powers of an interim cabinet. It would operate alongside the existing cabinet and other bodies and would take its decisions from 75 % of the members. Seven subcouncils were established: defence, intelligence, law and order, regional and local government, finance, foreign affairs and the status of women. The first three subcouncils would each have eight members making their decisions by an 80 % majority, while the latter four would each have six members taking their decisions by a two-thirds majority.

The task of the Independent Electoral Commission was to manage and monitor the first elections and any referendums that were conducted, and to decide if they had been free and fair. The Independent Media Commission was to ensure the equitable treatment of political parties by broadcasting services, state-financed publications and information services. The Independent Broadcasting Authority was to monitor radio and television broadcasting during the run-up to the elections, to ensure that they did not favour any party or organisation.

The promulgation of the transitional mechanisms was an important hallmark in the South African transitional process. In the words of political analyst Kaizer Nyatsumba, the establishment of the TEC meant that

> ... for the first time in our chequered history blacks will have a role in the running of the country, albeit on a limited scale and in specifically defined areas. It is an important stage in our transition since it clearly marks the interregnum: the end of the hideous past and the beginning of a new and hopefully democratic future.[118]

Mandela and De Klerk used the passing of the transitional mechanisms bills to drum up economic support and to ask the international community for the lifting of sanctions. Notwithstanding their common objectives, party political differences continued to hinder cooperation between them. While De Klerk was billed to address the World Economic Development Congress in the United States and to meet the United Nations Secretary General, Boutros Boutros Ghali, Mandela focused his attention on the United Nations and the heads of foreign governments.[119] On 24 September he addressed the UN Special Committee Against Apartheid and asked it to lift sanctions, except the arms embargo against South Africa.

Notwithstanding the euphoria around the passing of the TEC Bills, the road to the 1994 elections was bumpy. The TEC was important for its symbolic significance and the limited role blacks would play in influencing government decisions through a constitutional process. But it did not herald immediate freedom to the oppressed. After the passing of the transitional mechanisms bills, the Negotiation Council still had to finalise an interim constitution which would also elaborate on the bill of rights. Between then and the election date there was little time for transitional structures to be set up and to undertake their tasks. Ballot papers still had to be prepared and structures for the elections had to be established. Decisions about the number and spread of polling stations, and the training and coordination of independent monitors also had to be taken. A code of conduct for policing agencies still needed to be decided upon. A peacekeeping force also had to be established and trained. Voters had to be issued with identification documents and temporary documents had to be printed.[120] Moreover, all these would not be effected until the Negotiating Council wrapped up its negotiations on an interim constitution, including a human rights bill and the repeal of discriminatory legislation, as well as convening a planning meeting for the adoption of these agreements.

The passing of transitional mechanisms bills antagonised parties to the right and the left. COSAG members rejected the TEC, with the IFP and the CP saying that it meant a declaration of war. The IFP refused to be party to the joint force under the subcouncil on defence, contending that it would not collaborate with ''MK murderers''. Ciskei and Bophuthatswana reserved their positions on the TEC, saying that they wanted to see the outcome of the interim constitution before deciding on their next moves. Eventually all the COSAG members joined hands in September and formed the Freedom Alliance to pursue negotiations as a united bloc. The PAC, however, rejected the TEC because it did not see any need for it. The PAC believed that the supervision of the elections could have been handled fairly by the international community. The PAC was also opposed to the role of the TEC discussing constitutional principles at the multi-party forum which would bind an elected constitution-making body. AZAPO, too, while struggling to find a way to participate in the coming elections, did not greet the bills with enthusiasm.[121]

More significant, however, was the surfacing of differences within the ANC-led Tripartite Alliance. There had been simmering discontent since the

NEC's adoption of its *Strategic perspective*. Discontent about the movement's negotiation strategy had grown since Winnie Mandela's attack on ANC negotiators at the funeral of Helen Joseph in Alexandra in January 1993. She had warned against "a looming disaster from the distortion of the noble goal in favour of a short cut to parliament by a handful of individuals".[122] The ANC Natal Midlands region, led by Harry Gwala, had been at the forefront in making vocal opposition to the compromises made at the Negotiating Council. Gwala himself said that

> ... we find the agreement unacceptable. It is a drastic departure from what we have always known the ANC to stand for. This is indeed a strange way of appeasement. We are already setting down the rule of surrender before we meet the enemy. If we go out to negotiations with such terms of surrender where do we draw the line?[123]

Gwala's region had succeeded in pulling behind its banner of opposition the other two Natal regions (south and north), Allan Boesak's Western Cape region, the PWV region and Southern Natal structures of COSATU, the SACP and the Youth League, as well as the Marxist Workers' Tendency.[124] These dissenting voices were systematically silenced by the leadership. Mrs Mandela's statements were simply dismissed as the opinion of an individual, while the demand by some of these regions for a national conference to review the negotiation strategy was frustrated by a lack of response from headquarters. Carl Niehaus pointed out that a national conference was not possible without the support of 11 out of 14 ANC regions.[125]

Furthermore, the leadership responded to this crisis by means of steps aimed at suppressing differences. An ANC constitutional clause was invoked to remove Harry Gwala from the leadership of the Natal Midlands region on the pretext that he was also serving on the NEC.[126] This move failed when Gwala offered to resign from the NEC to retain his Natal leadership.[127] This attempted coup was not only informed by Gwala's opposition to the nego-tiation strategy. There had also been serious tensions between the ANC leadership in Johannesburg and two Natal regions, Natal Midlands and Northern Natal, over the question of violence and meetings with IFP leader, Mangosuthu Buthelezi. The two Natal regions had often resisted and ignored directives from headquarters to participate in joint committees with the IFP. They argued that the lack of consultation by the leadership in making decisions to appease Inkatha created a serious crisis on the ground. There were also bitter exchanges of words between headquarters and the Natal regions following the ANC's attempts to disown MK cadres who had been arrested with arms at the Swaziland border. The ANC had initially claimed that the men were a gang of criminal gun-runners, but later changed its position after protest by the Natal regions to say that it could not comment on whether the men were MK cadres until the government had allowed its senior official access to the men.

While the ANC had been content to press the lid on this simmering internal discontent, there was no guarantee that further compromises in negotiations or the occurrence of a major crisis, such as another assassination of a senior official, could stem the force of this potentially explosive anger. Until the passing of the TEC Bill, these differences within the rank and file remained invisible. However, the threat by COSATU in October 1993 to embark on a mass action programme which would culminate in a general strike, for the first time placed in public focus the strains on the unity of the alliance parties. COSATU had threatened mass action because of a clause in the interim constitution which was under discussion at the Negotiating Council, giving employers the right to lock out striking workers. In an attempt to mend public differences, both ANC and COSATU leaders argued that the issue was a matter of trivial misunderstanding which did not amount to serious tensions. ANC leaders particularly argued that they too were not happy with the clause. They had been silent on the clause because they believed that COSATU had agreed to the clause in the Constitutional Technical Committee. COSATU leaders, however, contended that their public outcry was not aimed at the ANC. While agreeing that they had been part of the constitutional discussions, they stated that the threat of mass action was aimed at preventing the Negotiating Council from adopting the clause as part of the interim constitution.[128]

Public statements by COSATU leaders that they were independent and that they could embark on mass action without consulting the ANC, clearly showed signs of strain between the two organisations. These strains were informed by what was becoming a pervasive feeling that ANC negotiators were compromising too much at the talks – a position also widely supported by ANC members. This was reflected in the decision by the PWV region to support COSATU's march to the Negotiation Forum. ANC negotiators apologised to COSATU marchers, with Joe Slovo ironically commenting that wearing a suit for too long can compromise one's ideological background. This indicated that without mass power constantly in view, negotiators were prone to make concessions on rights won through bitter struggles in the past decades. Overall, COSATU's threat of mass action and the dispute with the ANC over the timing of the strikes underlined the shallowness of the promise that the ANC would also articulate workers' interests at the multiparty talks – an argument which was used earlier to prevent COSATU's direct representation at the constitutional talks.

In spite of the euphoria trumpeted by the media about the achievements of the negotiation process, as well as the proximity of 27 April 1994, dubbed by Mandela as Freedom Day, there were few real gains. With a power-sharing deal for a fixed number of years, with attempts to secure the jobs of the current civil service, with the existing government disposing of state assets and with constitutional provisions which sanctioned the suppression of workers' strikes, it was questionable what meaningful gains had been negotiated for ordinary people during the interim period, apart from regaining their citizenship and going to the polling stations. Except for marking a historic moment of cheering, ululation and "sloganeering", Freedom Day appeared set to be a long sunset with little hope dawning for the black majority. It was in response to dissatisfaction within the ANC rank and file and COSATU, in particular, that subsequent developments demonstrated the ANC's attempts to mend these possible weaknesses. Balancing its intention to retain the existing civil service, the ANC also emphasised the need for restructuring with the aim of bringing black people into the field. Such a view also bolstered ongoing negotiations to integrate MK, the SADF and other military forces.

However, a bold move to water down internal criticism around transitional mechanisms came with the establishment of the TEC. On the day of its inauguration, ANC and allied members in the council were keen to ensure that the council took effective decisions on matters falling within its jurisdiction. Sitting for the first time on 7 December 1993, the TEC was made up of 19 members drawn from participating parties. Seven positions were reserved for the Freedom Alliance parties which had withdrawn from the negotiation process, and the PAC which had reserved its decision on participation. The council was co-chaired by Pravin Gordhan and Dawie de Villiers. Cyril Ramaphosa (ANC), Roelf Meyer (NP/government) and Joe Slovo (SACP) were among its members. Its seven subcouncils started sitting on 22 December 1993.[129] The first crucial decision of the TEC endorsed South Africa's application for an $850 million IMF loan, on condition that the future government abide by sound macroeconomic and monetary principles.[130] A decision was also taken to suspend a R216 million loan from the Development Bank of Southern Africa to Bophuthatswana on the basis that such an agreement, concluded after the establishment of the TEC, had not been submitted to it for consideration.

Following revelations by the Goldstone Commission about the existence of a hit squad within the KwaZulu Police, as uncovered by a snap commission authorised by the KwaZulu Commissioner, Lieutenant-General Roy During, the TEC ordered him to submit his evidence to them. In what was described by the media as a major test of its authority over recalcitrant homelands which boycotted participation in the TEC, the Lieutenant-General, on the instruction of the KwaZulu government, declined the TEC invitation. In an attempt to tighten its authority over this apparent resistance, the TEC decided on 9 December to call Lieutenant-General During to appear before it in his personal capacity as a citizen of South Africa. At the same time, the SAP was ordered to deploy its members in the violence-torn areas of KwaZulu over the Christmas period to "protect the lives and property of inhabitants of Empangeni, Nqutu, Dumbe and Newcastle".[131]

While decisions taken by the TEC during the few days of its sitting in the old President Council Building in Cape Town in December clearly marked the beginning of joint rule during the transitional period, the TEC continued to be opposed by the Freedom Alliance. During the first day of its sitting, 150 members of the Boerekommando mounted an abortive siege of the Schanskop Fort in Pretoria in protest against the new body. The siege was easily broken by the black-dominated 115 Battalion of the SADF.

The Independent Electoral Commission (IEC) was operationalised at the same time as the TEC. Sitting for the first time on 20 December 1993, the commission was charged with overseeing and certifying South Africa's first democratic elections. It also had to monitor voter education, the behaviour of political parties and their campaigns, and set up the elections. It was given substantial powers to act against individuals and parties that misbehaved in a manner calculated to disrupt the elections. These included fines, imprisonment, the deletion of candidates' names from party lists and party disqualification.[132] For its effective operation, the IEC was to establish central and regional offices before the end of January 1994. The commission was chaired by Judge Johan Kriegler and included the following members: Dikgang Moseneke, Frank Chikane, Oscar Dhlomo, Johan Heyns, Rosil Jager, Dawn Mokhobo, Charles Nupen, Helen Suzman, Ben van der Ross and Zach Yacoob. It worked closely with foreign advisers.

The interim constitution and the birth of South Africa's democratic dispensation

Apart from the establishment of the TEC and the IEC, the conclusion of negotiations on the interim constitution in November 1993 came as another breakthrough in South Africa's transitional process. The draft constitution was concluded against tight time schedules and intense debate on a variety of constitutional aspects, including the constituting of a constitutional court. It also happened in the midst of strenuous attempts to accommodate the demands of the Freedom Alliance. Other matters that were placed before the Negotiating Council such as the flag, symbols and the anthem, remained unresolved by the close of the multi-party negotiation on 5 November 1993.

While it was clear that the ANC and the NP dominated and dictated terms through their bilateral agreements, parties such as the DP challenged anti-democratic positions which were being foisted on the negotiating chamber. Against stern opposition by the ANC, the DP was able to win its demand that at least six out of the ten members of the constitutional court be nominated by the Judicial Services Commission. This was to avoid giving the ruling party an undue influence over the court through its unfettered presidential nominees. Notwithstanding the success of negotiating South Africa's new constitution and the celebrations of its birth (including the coincidental birthday of ANC Secretary-General Cyril Ramaphosa), negotiators were concerned about the need to include the views of the boycotting Freedom Alliance (FA). Continued efforts to negotiate with it were made, but these efforts failed to produce results even as late as the eve of the adoption of the constitution by parliament. The failure was caused by the fact that the ANC, NP and the FA were not willing to concede beyond certain points. The ANC and the NP were prepared to accommodate the demands of the FA provided that its members committed themselves to the process, participated in the TEC and in the elections, and accepted the election results. The FA promised to do so if its demands were accommodated and incorporated in the interim constitution. These demands included the right of regions to make and amend their own constitutions, fiscal autonomy for regions and a dual ballot system for local and national legislatures.[133] While both parties were keen to attend to each other's demands, the issue became a "chicken and egg" situation with each party demanding that the other act first.

It was evident on the basis of what the FA demanded, that parties such as the ANC would have serious difficulty in coming to terms with their demands. The FA, having failed to have their propositions accepted, let alone fully discussed at the Multi-party Negotiation Council, attempted to force their acceptance through the tactic of boycott and threat. The demand that regions have the right to write and review their constitutions, and have autonomy, clearly sought to pave the way for their complete autonomy, including secession from South Africa if they so wished. While the ANC and the NP were not against these demands, their insistence that they still go through multi-party negotiation and parliamentary processes before being included in the interim constitution demonstrated their unpronounced but firm resolve to have such demands whither away through democracy in these two political chambers.

The failure to reach agreement with the FA on the eve of the adoption of South Africa's new constitution also led to the cancellation of an accord, "The Memorandum of Agreement" between the ANC and the AVU in Johannesburg. In terms of this agreement, the AVU would have considered participating in the TEC and the April 1994 elections. This deal was not signed because of the lack of agreement between delegates of the NP, ANC and FA in Cape Town. In spite of the failure of these negotiations, a door was left open for possible future agreements. A task group was set up to explore this and to report back to the Negotiating Council by 24 January 1994. It was also conceded that in the event of such agreements, a special parliamentary session might be called to amend the interim constitution.

Called the new South Africa Constitution Act of 1993, the interim constitution was passed by parliament on Wednesday, 22 December 1993. A document of 150 pages, the interim constitution was a product of compromises agreed to at the multi-party negotiations. It did not represent the views of any one party although it contained democratic principles and provisions long advocated by organisations that had been outside the establishment. It was agreed that the transitional process would assume two phases. The first was the passing of the interim constitution through negotiations at the multi-party forum. The second was the drafting of the final constitution by an elected constituent assembly. The interim constitution would exist for five years and would provide for a multi-party government of national unity. The elected constitutional assembly, which would sit after the elections on 27 April 1994, would then write the final constitution within two years. It was also part of the agreement that the constitutional assembly would be bound by the constitutional principles agreed on and contained in the interim constitution. Any future violation of these principles by an elected constitutional assembly would be adjudicated by a constitutional court. The interim constitution provided for a social market economy; a unitary state with strong features of regionalism; national and provincial government; a multi-party cabinet; a president and deputy presidents; a bill of rights including a constitutional court; a decentralised police force and an integrated defence force. It was made up of 13 chapters, each dealing with key issues.[134]

As a product of negotiations, the interim constitution sought to promote the spirit of cooperation and consensus. It symbolised the dawn of a new South Africa, even though this still had to be demonstrated by its practical implementation. As Nelson Mandela commented, this phase represented an era for which many South Africans had struggled for years.

The new constitution emerged within a broader context of social transformation, ranging from the changing attitudes of the diverse sections of the population to the integration of what used to be predominantly white inhabited cities and towns. A majority of the population had already begun searching for, and had reached some degree of common understanding about each other's histories and aspirations. Important public decisions had begun to fall within the domain of relatively inclusive multi-party consensus. In essence, a degree of multi-party control took shape even before the conclusion of constitutional negotiations. Notwithstanding the government's public opposition to the introduction of an interim government by stealth, important multi-party forums at national, regional and local levels had taken shape during the transitional period, which to a great extent augmented initiatives taken at constitutional negotiations. Focusing on very sensitive issues such as the provision of housing to millions of homeless black South Africans, the installation of a non-racial local government system, the resolution of the education, economic, electrification, water and drought crises, these forums provided, for the first time, legitimate conduits through which communities through their representatives could have an impact on public policy. Moreover, they served as a meeting place where deep-rooted hostilities, anger and animosity could be resolved and harmonious relationships could be established. By 1993, a total of 22 national and regional forums focusing on a variety of aspects, had already been formed.[135] The most important ones at national level were the National Economic Forum, the National Housing Forum, the National Local Government Negotiating Forum, the National Electrification Forum and the Standing Committee on Water Supply and Sanitation, as well as the Education Forum. Despite the remnants of a white-dominated civil service, white minority rule was fundamentally effaced in key spheres of society well before the advent of formal institutions of democracy.

The conclusion of an inclusive settlement: popular uprising in Bophuthatswana, the fall of the Freedom Alliance and the succumbing of KwaZulu

The adoption of the interim constitution and the establishment of transitional mechanisms that would supervise South Africa's democratic elections were significant achievements. They nevertheless continued to suffer the problem of unacceptability by parties within the FA. Alongside the gathering momentum of electioneering at the beginning of 1994, significant attempts were made to draw these parties into the process. While initial talks with FA parties revolved around the question of powers for the regions and their fiscal autonomy,[136] the demands of the Zulu king also played an important role in the next round of talks. The difficult part, though, was that this occurred within an atmosphere of heightened tension which was also aggravated by what appeared to be concerted efforts by FA parties to hamper the election process. Not only were actions taken to undermine the authority of the TEC and its subsidiary structures such as the IEC, conditions were also created that made voter education and campaigning impossible in certain parts of the country. In other instances marches were organised that resulted in widespread intimidation and violence.[137]

In spite of earlier indications by Buthelezi that he would no longer entertain negotiations with the ANC and the government, a tripartite meeting was held between the ANC, the government and the FA on 19 and 25 January, to discuss the demand for a double ballot, provisions for provincial structures and the question of self-determination. These meetings were unsuccessful as the FA wanted the other parties to agree to its demands without an equal commitment to participate in the elections as requested. A stalemate was reached on 25 January because the IFP had raised a new demand, the constitutional recognition of the Zulu monarch in addition to the other demands. In this crisis, Mandela dismissed the Volksfront's demand for a *volkstaat* (nation state), an issue which resulted in Viljoen proclaiming the creation of an Afrikaner transitional authority. At the same time Buthelezi called upon his supporters to prepare to enter the politics of resistance. At a meeting on Monday, 31 January, FA parties again changed the focus of their demands. They demanded that regions be given the right to write their own constitutions subject to approval by the constitutional court, and without interference by central government. In essence, they rejected concurrent powers in favour of exclusive powers for regional functions, a demand that would have fundamentally transformed the constitution into a federal one. The shift in emphasis away from the demand for a double ballot paper was probably informed by the indications that the ANC and the government would concede to it. Already a number of parties such as the DP, PAC, the African Christian Democratic Party (ACDP), Dikwankwetla Party of South Africa, as well as business pressure groups, had joined the FA to demand a change from a single ballot. They feared that a single ballot would allow the dominant party a greater sway nationally, as well as in the regions.

The tripartite meeting of 3 February also ended in failure despite earlier indications by the ANC and the government that they would make concessions that the FA would find difficult to reject. The ANC and the government had made compromises in the hope that the FA would recognise the interim constitution and demonstrate flexibility in negotiations. It appeared during negotiations that the latter did not have a mandate to negotiate but rather to present demands – something that stalled the talks. Earlier, in a television interview, Buthelezi had indicated that concessions on the double ballot demand would make a big difference.[138] When this was conceded however, the FA argued that this had to be granted as a package, including agreement on powers and functions of the regions. It was because of this inflexibility that Thabo Mbeki retorted that

> ... we have been negotiating for a long time and we have put several proposals for the alliance to negotiate on and no agreement could be reached. One problem is that the alliance has been negotiating on the basis of demands that must be met and are non-negotiable, rather than looking for a negotiated settlement.

Even the meetings of 7 and 8 February (attended by FA leaders) did not make a difference. With the breakdown of talks, Volksfront leader General Constand Viljoen talked of embarking on passive resistance. On 12 February the IFP's Central Committee decided not to participate in elections but to call for international mediation to resolve the logjam. Addressing a rally at Empangeni on 13 February, and calling on all other ethnic groups to resist the ANC, Buthelezi listed the FA's minimum demands as the recognition of King Goodwill Zwelithini as the constitutional monarch of KwaZulu-Natal; a double ballot; regional taxation powers; entrenched regional constitutions; and a federal system of government.

The demand for the recognition of the Zulu king changed the focus of the political drama, as the ensuing crisis revolved around monarchical demands. On 14 February King Zwelithini, accompanied by 40 000 Zulus, met President De Klerk in Durban where he hinted at secession, saying that he was preparing to promulgate a constitution for KwaZulu and Natal to establish an autonomous monarchy. This pronouncement heightened tensions as ANC Natal regions countered it by organising strings of mass action campaigns to demonstrate that many Zulus opposed the King's secessionist intentions and wanted to participate in the elections. While De Klerk watered down the King's demands by mentioning that they were negotiable, the ANC leadership was worried about the potential conflict that could be triggered off by the demands which local ANC structures regarded as favouring the IFP.

It was against this background, and indeed because of the need for an inclusive settlement, that Mandela announced far-reaching compromises on 16 February to accommodate all the demands of the FA. Reaffirming that the election date of 27 April would not be postponed, and that the integrity and sovereignty of South Africa as defined in the interim constitution could not be tampered with, Mandela listed the ANC's compromises. These were the inclusion in the interim constitution of the principle of self-determination based on negotiations conducted with the Afrikaner Volksfront and others, as well as provisions for a mechanism and process for the consideration of the issue of a *volkstaat*. A concession, too, was the provision for voters to cast two votes. Furthermore, there was the agreement to amend the interim constitution to address a few concerns:

- The first was a constitutional provision for provincial finances based on agreement with the FA.

- The second was a constitutional provision allowing provinces in drafting provincial constitutions to determine their own legislative and executive structures.

- The third was the granting of greater security to newly elected democratic provincial governments and amendments to provisions of the interim constitution to ensure that powers granted were not substantially diminished when the constitutional assembly drafted the new constitution.

- The fourth and final one was the agreement that the democratically elected provincial legislatures would decide on names for their provinces and that in the interim constitution the province of Natal could be renamed KwaZulu-Natal.

Mandela also proposed the calling of a short session of parliament to effect these changes. However, the IFP rejected these concessions saying that they did not fully address the FA's demands. Buthelezi wanted firm agreement on the constitutional principle of self-determination. He also said that there had been no agreement on provincial finances. He expressed his dissatisfaction with the protection of provincial government powers which, he said, were inadequate. This position was repeated by the FA Executive Meeting of 21 February. On that day the Negotiating Council met and accepted Mandela's concessions. The council also agreed to amend the Electoral Act to extend the date for parties to register to midnight on 4 March, and to extend the date for submitting lists to 9 March. The council's concessions included the removal of "concurrent powers" in the interim constitution, thus allowing provincial legislatures more freedom from central government. Laws passed by provinces on those matters for which they would have competence, would prevail over Acts of parliament. This meant, in effect, that provinces would be granted exclusive powers as demanded by the FA. Despite these concessions and the invitation by the Negotiating Council to the FA to participate in discussions, the latter was non-committal with Buthelezi now posing the election date as a problem. He had earlier indicated that "even if all our demands were met we still will not participate because there is not sufficient time to campaign for the elections".

When parliament met on 28 February to effect changes agreed on at the Negotiating Council, the IFP submitted proposed amendments to the parliamentary constitutional subcommittee for the establishment of a KwaZulu-Natal monarchy. In these amendments, the IFP demanded the postponement of the elections in KwaZulu-Natal and the calling of a referendum on a provincial constitution which it would draft. These demands were rejected. On 1 March Mandela pleaded with Buthelezi to provisionally register for the elections. At the same time, agreement was reached to recognise the right of people to participate or not to participate in the elections. International mediators would also be called upon to help resolve the constitutional impasse. The call for international mediation was endorsed by the FA on 4 March. The IFP then began insisting that international mediation had to take place before its provisional registration.

It was clear at this point that the FA had adopted a stalling strategy. Notwithstanding all the concessions made to the IFP and its allies in the FA, the latter demonstrated an utter lack of will to make equal compromises or to show flexibility in reaching a settlement. The ANC's response was to find a means of creating a gap between Buthelezi and the King by attending to the latter's demands. A solution had to be found, as violence in Natal and the PWV was making it difficult to undertake election campaigns. Ultimately, it was the developments in Bophuthatswana which altered things.

The fall of the Mangope regime and the consequent disintegration of the FA precipitated a significant change of attitude in KwaZulu. The popular uprising in Bophuthatswana began with public and private sector strikes over pension payment. This gathered momentum between February and the middle of March as students, police and other workers joined demonstrations and marches. Originally, the main demand was for pension pay-outs and pay increases. This changed as the demand for free elections in Bophuthatswana and the reincorporation of the homeland into South Africa became predominant. The ANC initially held meetings with the Bophuthatswana government to reach agreement on free political activity. Despite the apparent obstinacy of the homeland leadership, the ANC avoided taking tough measures against the homeland for fear of wrecking its initiative to draw the FA into the election process. However, the brutal repression meted out to demonstrators and the detention and torture of ANC supporters by the police and soldiers propelled thousands of people into the streets. Further developments aggravated the situation. These included a Lawyers for Human Rights report released on 22 February, calling on the South African government to stop financial support to the homeland in protest against its repression of political activity. Hardening its attitude towards the homeland, the ANC called on President De Klerk to proclaim citizens of Bophuthatswana to be South African citizens in terms of the interim constitution. The organisation also called for the government to send in security forces to ensure free political activity.

On Monday, 7 March, strikes in the homeland spread to other sectors, including workers at the Bophuthatswana Broadcasting Corporation. The next day, Mangope announced his decision not to contest the elections until there was the intervention of international mediation. This led to widespread anger. Tension began in Mafikeng at the Garona government buildings after Mangope failed to address workers concerning their grievances. Clashes between demonstrators and the police also erupted in other parts of the homeland. Meanwhile, the TEC took a resolution asking Mangope to cooperate with the IEC in making preparations for the elections. Judge Johan Kriegler was also sent to the homeland to facilitate the implementation of this resolution. As it became clear that Mangope was intent on

denying Bophuthatswana citizens South African citizenship rights and participation in the elections, more and more people took to the streets. By
Thursday, 10 February, the homeland was engulfed by a violent uprising
which saw shops being attacked, looted and set alight. Mangope fled
Mmabatho. This sent waves of triumph all over the homeland. The police
and soldiers mutinied and sided with the people, and others took part in the
looting spree. Police still loyal to Mangope tried to quell the revolt and shot
people at random during the night. The AWB moved into the homeland on
Thursday night, shooting indiscriminately at people. Their crusade, however,
was halted when they were driven out by Bophuthatswana soldiers, with
three khaki-clad AWB members being slain in cold blood in front of the
media. On 12 February, Pik Botha, Minister of Foreign Affairs, and Mac
Maharaj flew to the homeland to inform President Mangope formally that
he had been ousted, and that two administrators would be appointed to run
the homeland until the elections.

Developments in Bophuthatswana were a warning to other homeland
leaders. Having won Bophuthatswana, the ANC and its supporters were
eager to see the same developments in KwaZulu. Already discontent had
surfaced within the KwaZulu civil service. While COSATU looked bent on
mobilising its members in the region to strike, the ANC leadership focused
on creating a wedge between the King and Buthelezi. A meeting between
Mandela and the King was arranged for 18 February, at which Mandela
would clarify the future status of the Zulu king. This meeting, which was
originally scheduled to take place in Durban did not take place for fear that
attempts would be made on Mandela's life. However, at the instance of the
IFP, the meeting place was changed to Ulundi before a gathering of Zulu
imbizo (the King's subjects). The meeting was aborted by the IFP who feared
that the ANC would create a wedge between the King and Buthelezi by
offering the former concessions that he would accept. The failure of this
meeting to take place aggravated what was an already tension-ridden
KwaZulu-Natal. King Zwelithini criticised Mandela's late withdrawal and
announced that he would not encourage his supporters to participate in
the elections. Moreover, the King suggested that the region was on the point
of a unilateral declaration of independence. He said: "We here today
proclaim before the world our freedom and sovereignty and our unwavering
will to defend it at all costs." Reacting to the King's pronouncements, ANC
Natal regions announced plans for marches to demonstrate that Zulus
opposed his declaration of sovereignty and that they wanted to participate
in the elections.

While these events occurred, the FA suffered further blows. The radical
AWB element which had called for war had already been marginalised
within the FA, following its role in the Bophuthatswana debacle. The
Volksfront had disintegrated when Viljoen opted for elections and registered
his new party, the Freedom Front. Moreover, those who still called for a
boycott of the elections, such as CP leader Ferdi Hartzenberg, were disap-
pointed when senior party members such as the Mulder brothers joined
Viljoen's Freedom Front. Added to this, Oupa Gqozo of the Ciskei, another

member of the FA, resigned after facing threats of public sector strikes and possible mutiny by his soldiers in Ciskei. In the wake of these developments, the FA no longer posed a threat to the democratic process. Only the IFP, and now the KwaZulu King, remained the major stumbling blocks towards an inclusive settlement.

Efforts at addressing the remaining stumbling blocks took a dual form. The TEC, on the one hand, took strong measures to ensure stability in KwaZulu-Natal, while Mandela, on the other hand, concentrated his efforts on wooing the King. Alongside these efforts, attempts were also made to consolidate the appointment of international mediators. These events occurred amidst the release of a Goldstone Commission report implicating senior SAP generals in the supply of arms to Inkatha. Moreover, the IEC had reported that the holding of elections in the area was impossible because of violence and intimidation. The TEC's task group had also reported widespread hit squad activities in the area. Judge Johan Kriegler, who had been sent to KwaZulu by the TEC to seek cooperation from the homeland's authorities about preparations for the elections, had been jeered at in the homeland's legislative assembly. By the end of March up to 120 people had been killed in violence in the province. It was against this background that calls to send in troops to KwaZulu-Natal and to impose a state of emergency were made by ANC representatives in the TEC. Aware of the likely outcome of the ANC lobby, De Klerk met Buthelezi in Durban on 26 March, where they agreed to create a mechanism to search for a solution to the practical problems relating to the holding of elections in KwaZulu. De Klerk had gone to Durban to help Buthelezi evade what were clear intentions by the ANC. Indeed, Mandela had pressured De Klerk during the week to take over KwaZulu and to impose a state of emergency.

In a move to shift attention away from KwaZulu-Natal, the IFP organised a mass march to central Johannesburg on Monday, 28 March, in support of the King's demand for sovereignty. Owing to what appeared to be a lack of organisation of and direction to the march, widespread intimidation occurred. About 53 people were killed. Fifteen of them were killed at the ANC headquarters at Shell House by security guards, others by unknown sharpshooters at the Library Gardens. Some people were killed in other parts of the city and surrounding townships. In the wake of this violence, a four-way summit, comprising Mandela, De Klerk, Buthelezi and King Goodwill Zwelithini, was organised to discuss the escalating violence, the creation of a climate for free and fair elections and the need to find a solution to political differences. This meeting did not take place, as the King asked for postponement until his deceased subjects had been buried. Unhappy with the King's decision, the TEC and the government decided to impose a state of emergency over KwaZulu-Natal on 29 March. The emergency was proclaimed by De Klerk on 2 April. Having been rejected from the beginning by the IFP, the state of emergency was not effective. A total of 101 people were killed in the first two weeks of its imposition.

The four-leader summit eventually took place at Skukuza in the Kruger National Park on 8 April. The ANC attended this meeting with the hope that it would grant significant concessions to the King, which would lead to a major constitutional breakthrough. Mandela had requested a private meeting with the King before the four leaders met, in order to make these concessions. Contrary to the expectations of this summit, it ended in failure with the only agreement reached being the setting up of a task group to pursue issues. Mandela's private meeting with the King did not proceed as he had thought. Instead of a private meeting, the King's indunas insisted on attending the meeting by virtue of protocol. The meeting between the two leaders also started on a bad note. Zwelithini started the meeting by reading a prepared speech in which he criticised the ANC. Notwithstanding, Mandela presented his proposals to the King, offering him constitutional provisions for the recognition of his monarchy in exchange for his support for peaceful elections in Natal. After a break in which consultations were held with Buthelezi, the King returned to Mandela saying that Mandela's concessions were not acceptable. Buthelezi had indicated to the King that Mandela's proposals would not be considered unless all the demands of the IFP were met. The leaders addressed the press with Mandela and Buthelezi disagreeing over their interpretation of the talks, as well as the issuing of separate press statements.

Because of the failure of the summit, the TEC and the ANC, in particular, began talking about a crackdown that would see the detention of IFP warlords in KwaZulu-Natal. The ANC leadership was no longer interested in further negotiations with the IFP and all efforts were geared towards elections. The IFP hoped that international mediators would assist in resolving the constitutional dispute. Mediation was the only vehicle left. An agreement was reached between the IFP and the ANC on the terms of reference, while the government jettisoned its oppositional stance and joined the process. The mediators, led by former American Secretary of State, Henry Kissinger, and former British Foreign Secretary, David Carrington, arrived in South Africa on 12 April.

However, the talks broke down even before the mediators could begin their work. The IFP bickered with the ANC and the government over the amendment of the terms of reference. In terms of the amendments, the question of the election date was not part of the mediation. With the breakdown of mediation and the departure of the mediators, the ANC ruled out further negotiations before the elections on 27 April. The IFP too, having been frustrated by the failure of mediation, intensified its opposition to the election process. Its Youth Brigade organised a week-long series of marches in central Johannesburg. However, with pressure having been exerted on the government and the Johannesburg authorities following the violence of the IFP's earlier march, De Klerk and the police were intent on halting the processions. The ANC called for further stringent measures against KwaZulu-Natal, as the death toll had reached 226 since the declaration of the emergency.

It was probably the realisation of the narrowing options before him that influenced Buthelezi to voluntarily consider participation in the elections, and to be more than predisposed to the advice of his friend, Professor

Washington Okumu, the only mediator who remained in the country when the others left. What Buthelezi agreed to at this point was little different from what he had been offered at the Skukuza Summit. According to press reports, Professor Okumu indicated to Buthelezi that if he did not enter into a settlement he would have no institutionalised power base to work from after the elections. He would be left with the option of waging a guerrilla warfare which he would not be able to sustain without outside support.[139] Faced with this prospect, Buthelezi arranged an urgent meeting with De Klerk and Ramaphosa in Pretoria, to strike a deal in which he would participate in the elections. Necessary changes would be made to the Electoral Act, and stickers bearing the IFP's name, logo and its leader's picture would be printed and inserted on ballot papers. The final constitutional settlement was reached on the following day, 19 April, in Pretoria, when Buthelezi, Mandela and De Klerk signed the "Memorandum of Agreement for Reconciliation and Peace". A few days later the ANC, the government and the Freedom Front signed an accord to set up a Volkstaat Council after the elections.

With the conclusion of these negotiations, violence subsided in KwaZulu-Natal as the IFP joined other parties in the election campaign a week before voting began. Despite the blasts that exploded in central Johannesburg near the ANC offices on 24 April and Jan Smuts Airport on 27 April, a major breakthrough had been made in constitutional negotiations that would pave South Africa's way to an inclusive democracy.

ENDNOTES

1. Harare Declaration, 1989, op cit.
2. The Pretoria Minute. See *South African Barometer*, 4(16), 27 August 1990, 240.
3. Suttner, R. *Progress in the talks*. Paper presented to the PWV Regional Workshop, 17 November, 1990, 1. See also Suttner, R. Do we continue the talks? *New Era*, 5(3), Summer, 1990, 5.
4. Speeches and resolutions. ANC Consultative Conference, 14–16 December 1991.
5. *Year of mass action for the transfer of power to the people.* Statement of the National Executive Committee on the occasion of the 79th anniversary of the African National Congress, 8 January 1991.
6. See also Rantete, J. *Room for compromise: the African National Congress and transitional mechanisms.* Centre for Policy Studies Transition Series, Johannesburg, February 1992.
7. Mandela, N. Out of strike. *South Africa in Exile*, 6(1), 1961, 22. This convention was different from the ones espoused by white liberal organisations, primarily because it sought representatives to a forum to be elected.
8. Phillips, I. Negotiation and armed struggle in contemporary South Africa. *Transformation*, 6, 1988, 44.
9. Ibid., 47.
10. Ibid., 47.
11. *The Star,* 20 July 1989.
12. *Resolution on the process of political settlement.* COSATU congress document, July 1989.
13. Phillips, M. & Coleman, C. *Another kind of war: strategies for transition in the era of negotiation.* Discussion paper prepared for publication, July 1989, 20. See also Niddrie, D. Negotiations: another site of struggle. *Work In Progress*, 60, August/September 1989, 8.
14. Ibid.
15. Raymond Suttner. Interview.
16. Harare Declaration, op cit.
17. Ibid. Expert advisers to the Inkatha Freedom Party obviously made more important decisions for the organisation than its elected representatives. During the December meetings of CODESA, an American IFP adviser, Prof. Albert Blaustein, persuaded the organisation (which had already

agreed in CODESA preparatory committees) not to sign the declaration of intent because it did not allow scope for federalism. See *Sunday Times*, 22 December 1991.

18. *Southern Africa Update*, 3(2), February 1991.

19. Hogan, B. Interview.

20. *Questions and answers on interim government*. An ANC information pamphlet. January 1991.

21. While originally the insistence that a majority party should have the right to write the constitution suggested the intention by the ANC to use a constituent assembly as a vehicle for majority domination, it now appears that its quest for a legitimate and popularly accepted constitution has forced it to accept the role of other parties, including minority ones.

22. De Waal, V. *The politics of reconciliation: Zimbabwe's first decade*. New Jersey: Africa World Press, 1990, 38; Astrow, A. *Zimbabwe: a revolution that lost its way?* London: Zed, 1983, 156–157.

23. Hudson, M. *Triumph or tragedy: Rhodesia to Zimbabwe*. London: Hamish Hamilton, 1981, 178–181, 184–186.

24. Marcum, J.A. *The Angolan revolution: exile politics and guerrilla warfare*. Cambridge: MIT, 1978, 258–263; Bhagavan, M.R. Establishing the conditions for socialism: the case of Angola. In Munslow, B. (Ed.), *Africa: problems in the transition to socialism*. London: Zed, 1986, 143.

25. Berger, L.P. & Godsell, B. (Eds). *A future South Africa: vision, strategies and realities*. Cape Town: Human & Rousseau/Tafelberg, 1988. See also Du Toit, A. *Applying the framework: South Africa as another case of transition from authoritarian rule?* Conference on South Africa's transition, Institute for a Democratic Alternative for South Africa (IDASA), Port Elizabeth, 21–23 June 1990.

26. See Van Niekerk, P. 'Giving flesh to an interim government'. Interview with Cyril Ramaphosa, the ANC's Secretary-General. *Weekly Mail*, 9–15 August 1991.

27. *Interim government*. Paper presented by Aziz Pahad to the ANC's PWV Regional Conference, 5, 6 & 10 October 1991.

28. 'Government in the interim'. *Mayibuye*, 1(2), September 1990, 30–31.

29. Ibid., 32.

30. 'Interim government: ideas from the ground'. *Mayibuye*, 2(4), May 1991, 22.

31. 'Beyond the deadline: on the political agenda'. Interview with Thabo Mbeki. *New Nation*, 617, 3–9 May 1991.

32. Thabo Mbeki's input to the workshop on interim government and a constituent assembly organised by the PWV Regional Political Education Committee, 17 August 1991.

33. Van Driel, M. Response to Suttner. Part 2. *New Nation*, 624, 21–27 June 1991.

34. Suttner, R. The debate on negotiations. *New Nation*, 625, 28 June – 4 July 1991.

35. Pillay, D. The patriotic front: can it prevent a constituent assembly compromise? *Work In Progress*, 74, May 1991.

36. *Reflections on interim government*. ANC discussion document distributed at the PWV Regional Workshop on Interim Government and a Constituent Assembly, 1 February 1992.

37. Ibid., 4.

38. Ibid., 5.

39. Raymond Suttner has in the past persistently argued that the present government should not only be de-legitimised, but should go beyond bearing the stigma of being a government and disappear. And if it returns to an interim government, it should return on a different basis.

40. *Reflections on interim government*, op cit., 3 & 5.

41. Ibid. See point 11, 3.

42. *Mayibuye*, 3(1), February 1992, 9.

43. Nelson Mandela, in his address to the Commemoration rally at Soccer City in Johannesburg on 16 June 1991, warned that his organisation would employ mass action if the demand for a constituent assembly was not met.

44. *Year of mass action for the transfer of power to the people*. Statement of the National Executive Committee on the occasion of the 79th Anniversary of the African National Congress, 8 January 1991.

45. *Notes on a constituent assembly*. Discussion paper distributed at the PWV Regional Workshop on an Interim Government and a Constituent Assembly, 1 February 1992.

46. Dikgang Moseneke, Second Deputy President of the PAC. Interview.

47. *Constituent assembly and interim government*. Discussion paper. ANC's Department of Political Education, 1991.

48. A simple majority means getting, say, 51 out of 100 votes, as opposed to demanding that decisions be taken by a two-thirds or three-quarter majority, that is 67 or 75 votes out of 100. In Namibia, SWAPO got 57 % of the seats, which meant that it could not automatically ensure that its views became decisions.

49. *Constituent assembly and interim government*, op cit.

50. *The Star*, 3 November 1990.

51. Friedman, S. The new National Party. *Monitor*, April 1990, 30. See also Dr Gerrit Viljoen's comments in *The Star*, 29 January 1990 and 6 February 1990. See also Mr Roelf Meyer's support for minority protection in *RSA Policy Review*, 4(1), January/February, 1991, 61.

52. *The Star*, 28 January 1992.

53. *Sowetan*, 9 March 1992.

54. Carl Niehaus, spokesperson for the ANC's Department of Information and Publicity. Interview.

55. *Weekly Mail*, 15–21 May 1992.

56. *The Star*, 29 May 1992.

57. Mandela (1994), op cit., 596.

58. The difficulties of the ANC's armed struggle are analysed by the author in an honours dissertation entitled *The ANC: from armed struggle to a negotiated transfer of power*, submitted to the University of the Witwatersrand, January 1990.

59. Mac Maharaj quoted in *New Nation*, 23–29 November 1990. For Siphiwe Nyanda see 'Operation Vula: the facts behind the fiction'. Interview with Siphiwe Nyanda. *Mayibuye*, 1(3), December 1990, 11.

60. Davies-Webb, W. *Umkhonto we Sizwe and the SACP: searching for a mission in the 1990s*. Special report of the International Freedom Foundation, June 1991, 13.

61. 'Vula and the men inside'. *New Nation*, 23–29 November 1990.

62. Davies-Webb, W., op cit., 14.

63. Mandela, op cit., 577.

64. 'Armed struggle'. *Mayibuye*, March 1991, 6.

65. See paragraph 5, point (ix) of the Report of the Working Group under Paragraph Three of the Pretoria Minute, 12 February 1991.

66. 'Waiting for the next order'. Interview with Chris Hani. *Mayibuye*, 3(2), April 1991, 12.

67. 'Umkhonto prepares for a future defence force'. *Submit or fight: 30 years of Umkhonto we Sizwe*. ANC's Department of Political Education, December 1991, 23.

68. *Let peace, freedom and justice prevail*. ANC National Conference Report, July 1991, 32.

69. Bulger, P. Self-defence booklet is written in red. *Business Day*, 23 April 1991.

70. *For the sake of our lives: guidelines for the creation of people's self defence units*, November 1990, 3.

71. Kasrils, R. The revolutionary army. *Sechaba*, September 1988, 5.

72. *The Star*, 31 January 1991; *Sunday Times*, 29 July 1990.

73. Mbulelo S. Defending townships: has the ANC done enough? *Work In Progress*, 75, June 1991, 20.

74. 'The traumas of coming home'. Interview with Mbulelo Mdledle, a returned exile. *Work In Progress*, 77, September 1991, 18.

75. Pillay, D. Sharpening the spear for peace, ibid., 14–15.

76. *Umkhonto we Sizwe: 30th anniversary, December 16, 1961 – December 16, 1991*. MK 30th Anniversary National Preparatory Committee. Mathibe Printers, December 1991, 11.

77. Jeremy Cronin of the SACP (see Mbulelo Siphetho above) ascribed the weakness of SDUs to a general perception within township communities that these structures were a narrow professional MK affair.

78. Suttner, R. *Negotiation, liberation and transformation*. Paper presented at the NUSAS July Festival, 4 July 1990, 1.

79. Kasrils, R. & Khuzwayo, M. Mass struggles and strategic initiative. *The Spark National*, 2(1), 1991. Also in *Work In Progress*, 72, January/February 1991.

80. See 'Campaigns report', *The Secretary-General's report*. ANC PWV Regional Congress, 5–6 October 1991, 2.

81. *The Secretary-General's report*. ANC National Conference, July 1991, 16.

82. Kasrils & Khuzwayo, op cit.

83. *Resolution on strategy and tactics*, ANC 48th National Conference, Durban, July 1991.

84. The ANC opts for mass action and mass mobilisation. *South African Update*, December, 1990, 5.

85. For more about power relations between the ANC and the state see Booysen, S. Transition, the state and relations of political power in South Africa. *Politikon*, 17(2), December 1990, 42.

86. *The Secretary-General's report*, op cit., 28.

87. This vindicated what Frederik van Zyl Slabbert conjectured in 1988, namely that De Klerk could exploit a more favourable international climate to marginalise his political opponents during the process of negotiations. See Van Zyl Slabbert, F. *The system and the struggle: reform, revolt and reaction in South Africa*. Johannesburg: Jonathan Ball, 1989, 218.

88. Jane Hunter, in *Understanding sanctions: Israel, the US and South Africa*, 1987, exposed military trade relations between South Africa and Israel amounting to $5000 million. Trade relations with Japan in 1987 involved $4,2 billion compared to America's $2,6 billion. In their thorough investigation, 'The asparagus connection', published in *City Press* in March 1988, Ian Walker and John Jones exposed a very sophisticated but clandestine undercutting of sanctions by South African agents operating under false identities. For more on sanctions, see Orkin, M. *Sanctions against apartheid*. Cape Town: David Philip, 1989.

89. 'The ANC opts for mass action and mass mobilisation'. *South African Update*, 2(16), December 1990, 4.

90. *Advance to national democracy*. Report of the ANC's National Consultative Conference, 14–16 December 1990, 20–21.

91. *The Secretary-General's report*, op cit., 28.

92. *Cape Times*, 4 September 1992.

93. *The Star*, 16 October 1992.

94. Suttner, R. *ANC: national liberation movement or political party?* Discussion paper. ANC's Department of Political Education, September 1991, 2.

95. *Advance to national democracy: guidelines on strategy*. ANC document, February 1991.

96. Suttner, R. *Where are we, where are we going from here and how do we get there? Current conditions and strategic priorities of the ANC.* Draft paper, November 1990, 2–3. This view is reflected in most of Suttner's analyses. See also Suttner, R. *Negotiation, liberation and transformation*, op cit., 2–3, and Suttner, R. *The road ahead: the character of our struggle.* Keynote address to the SANSCO/NUSAS National Workshop, 12 April 1990, 1–3.

97. *Advance to national democracy*, op cit. See points 5.0, 15.0 and 17.0 of the above strategy document. Point 5.0, in particular, outlines that despite the advances made by the liberation movement, the regime still retained the capacity to implement countermeasures on a whole range of fronts: ''The white ruling group has entered the negotiation process with its own agenda: a radically reformed system of apartheid which will retain the essentials of white domination of the economic, political and social institutions of our country.'' See also Kasrils, R. & Khuzwayo, M. *Some thoughts on advance to national democracy.* Unpublished paper, n.d., 2.

98. South African Communist Party Consultative Conference, Tongaat, 19–20 May 1990; Recommendations of the Consultative Conference. *History in the making*, 1(2), November 1990.

99. Slovo, J. Beyond the stereotype: the SACP in the past, present and future. *The African Communist*, Second Quarter, 1991, 9.

100. Cronin, J. The boat, the tap and the Leipzig way. *The African Communist*, Third Quarter, 1992, 41–54.

101. Ibid., 48–49.

102. Slovo, J. Negotiations: what room for compromise? *The African Communist*, Third Quarter, 1992, 37.

103. Ibid., 40.

104. *The Star*, 4 March 1992.

105. Friedman, S. *The long journey: South Africa's quest for a negotiated settlement.* Centre for Policy Studies. Johannesburg: Ravan, 1993, 161.

106. Jordan, P. Strategic debate in the ANC: a response to Joe Slovo. *The African Communist*, Fourth Quarter, 1992, 8–9.

107. Nzimande, B. Let us take the people with us: a reply to Joe Slovo. *The African Communist*, Fourth Quarter, 1992, 20.

108. Ibid., 22.

109. Gwala, H. Negotiations as presented by Joe Slovo. *The African Communist*, Fourth Quarter, 1992, 28.

110. 'ANC Youth League: summary of ideas on negotiations and the way forward'. *The African Communist*, Fourth Quarter, 1992, 45–47.

111. Suttner, R. Ensuring stable transition to democratic power. *The African Communist*, Fourth Quarter, 1992, 30–31, 1. See also his paper, *The deadlock and beyond: build organisation for people's power.* Presented at the ANC Western Cape Regional Seminar/Border Regional Workshop on 15/18 July 1992.

112. Cronin, J. Dreaming of the final showdown: a reply to Jordan and Nzimande. *The African Communist*, Fourth Quarter, 1992, 41.

113. *Negotiations: a strategic perspective.* ANC NEC paper. *The African Communist*, Fourth Quarter, 1992, 50.

114. Thabo Masebe, ANC Youth League member. Interview.

115. *The Star*, 9 March 1993.

116. *The Star*, 22 March 1993.

117. *The Star*, 2 June 1993.

118. *The Star*, 30 September 1993.

119. Not only did Mandela visit New York and Washington, he also proceeded to Lisbon, Brussels, Scotland and London.

120. *Weekly Mail and Guardian*, 10–16 September 1993.

121. Sello Rasethaba, AZAPO official. Interview.

122. *The Star*, 24 January 1993.

123. Gwala, quoted in Mkhondo, R. *Reporting South Africa.* London: James Currey, 1993, 162.

124. *City Press*, 21 February 1993.

125. Carl Niehaus. Interview.

126. *City Press*, 21 February 1993.

127. While the ANC's move against Gwala was informed by the organisation's constitutional provisions which prohibited a person holding regional leadership and an elected NEC position, the debacle was resolved when Gwala was re-elected chairman of the Natal Midlands region in late 1993.

128. Duma Nkosi, COSATU official and representative at the National Housing Forum. Interview.

129. Members of the TEC subcouncils were as follows: Regional and local government: M. Malatsi, G.S. Nota, Yacoob Mkada, Billy Cobbett, Tobie Meyer, J.S. Phathang; Intelligence: L. Landers, W.M. Ndzwayiba, B. Rogers, M.W. Mokoena, G.H. Rothman, A. Nzo, F. Schoeman, M. Shaik; Law and order: J. Nembambula, P. Gastrow, C. Bohlolo, L. Malan, S. Mufamadi, G. Myburgh, K. Naidoo, M. Gininda; Defence: D.M. Mahlangu, L. Bengu, G. Ramushwana, S.J. Maake, Joe Modise, W. Breytenbach, R. Kasrils; Foreign affairs: G.T. Hetisani, S. Sicqau, O. Ganie, C.J. Barratt, A. Pahad, Leon Wessels; Status of women: M.Y. Bassier, M.T. Moroke, N. Mtsweni, M. Manzini, T. King, E. Gandhi; Finance: J. Douw, J.N. Reddy, T. Alant, Tito Mboweni, T.J. Ndaba, S.O. Moji.

130. *Business Day/The Star,* 8 December 1992.

131. *The Star,* 22 December 1993.

132. *Business Day,* 21 December 1993.

133. *Business Day,* 20 December 1993.

134. See the 'Election 94' supplement, *The Star/Sowetan,* 10 December 1993. The interim constitution is summarised in Appendix B.

135. *South,* 3 July 1993. Other forums included: the Food Logistics Forum, Transport Forum, Vaal Forum, Durban Region Initiative, PWV Regional Economic and Development Forum, Orange Free State Regional Economic and Development Forum, Eastern Transvaal Regional Development Forum, Central Witwatersrand Metropolitan Chamber, Kosh 2000 Initiative, Port Elizabeth Single City Forum, Western Cape Economic Development Forum, Eastern Cape Regional Economic and Development Forum, Border-Kei Development Forum, Natal/Kwazulu Regional Economic Forum, the Northern Transvaal Development Forum and the National Consultative Forum on Drought.

136. *Sunday Times,* 20 February 1994. See the IFP's proposals outlined in the *Yellow Paper* of 19 December 1993. The demands made in this paper focused on granting more powers to provinces, giving them fiscal autonomy and a part in the deliberations on the role of the senate, provisions of rationalisation, a deadlock-breaking mechanism and matters relating to provincial civil service and the police, including the functions of local government.

137. *Sowetan,* 29 March 1994.

138. *The Star,* 4 February 1994.

139. *Sunday Times,* 24 April 1994.

Ke nako: the ANC's election campaign and victory of the elections

Preparations for democratic elections

In spite of the difficulty underlying the South African transitional process, the ANC had, with the negotiation process, begun to focus its attention on the elections. This started with the establishment of an organisational entity capable of organising members into branches and which was administratively efficient, both at office and at grass-roots levels, to mobilise people behind its banner. Given the concerns highlighted by Alfred Nzo at the national conference in 1991 about poor support within the non-African communities, initiatives were also taken to woo these communities. In public meetings, the media and interviews strenuous efforts were made by Mandela, in particular, to lessen the fears of these communities about the prospect of an ANC government. Minority parties were guaranteed involvement in the drafting of the constitution, including representation in parliament through an electoral system of proportional representation.

Crucial, though, was the initiative by the organisation to launch its election machine. The work of building the foundation for contesting elections began in earnest with the establishment of the National Election Committee headed by Popo Molefe. In this forum, an election strategy was devised to concretely outline the organisation's conceptual and practical approach to the elections. Broadly stated, the strategy envisaged the following:[1]

- Ensuring that people appreciated the importance of the elections
- Teaching people how to vote
- Encouraging them to go to the polls on election days
- Ensuring that they voted for the ANC

Furthermore, proposals were made for the creation of an electoral front to be headed by the ANC, with other parties coming under its banner. A Reconstruction Accord, particularly espousing COSATU's aspirations, was to be used to draw in the trade union federation. Already the SACP[2] and SANCO[3] had pledged their support for the ANC in the elections. The ANC also proposed that elections be conducted under two lists: national and regional. Structures of the electoral front would be set up at local level to prepare lists. All South African citizens above the age of 18, including the TBVC states, were to vote. An Independent Electoral Commission (IEC) consisting of 7 to 11 people and at least three international experts would be established to monitor the elections. An Electoral Act to govern the elections would also have to be agreed on at the multi-party talks. The organisation also proposed the setting up of a R400 million fund by the state, from which parties could draw on the basis of the percentage of votes they won.

In a more subtle way, the Department of Political Education asked ANC members to prepare for the likely challenges that would be produced by the election campaign[4]. It called for mass voter education and pleaded with ANC campaigners to educate people about basic issues such as the use of a ''cross'' and where it should be placed on a ballot paper. This particular point was raised against the background of the general perception that a cross represented anything negative. In practice there was the possibility of a person placing a cross against the party or individual that he or she opposed. Caution was also taken in the drawing up of lists. Popular and local leaders were to be given preference to war heroes, as examples in Nicaragua had shown that putting people on the election list simply on the basis of their role in the struggle was not effective. Furthermore, an election manifesto was to be drawn up around which people could rally.

Although poll after poll projected an ANC victory,[5] the organisation had to confront a number of problems before being assured of victory. As a liberation movement, the ANC had never contested national elections. The majority of the people from whom it drew support were unfamiliar with the voting process. Arguments about it sweeping the polls on the basis of its appeal as a liberation movement with a legendary heroic leader were not only simplistic, but also overrated the comparative aspect of the ANC to other liberation movements in Africa. Clearly, the coming into power of Zimbabwe African National Union (ZANU) in Zimbabwe and SWAPO in Namibia did not happen under conditions obtainable in South Africa. Unlike the ANC, these movements were not subjected to protracted negotiations after the signing of a ceasefire, and were therefore able to capitalise on the fresh memories of their struggles in the bush to win elections. In spite of the liberation dimension in the South African elections which continued to rally support behind the ANC, much still had to be done to mend the damage done by endless negotiations and widespread violence against the movement. The death of Chris Hani on the eve of a negotiated settlement was a major setback to the organisation's fledgling attempt to mobilise support for elections. The sudden death of Oliver Tambo, the organisation's National Chairman, the following week after Hani's funeral was an additional blow. It was against the background of this chain of events that the ANC's vociferous call for an election date gained impetus.

While an election date had to be secured to pacify what was an already angry and anxious following, ensuring that people voted for the ANC on the day of election was an entirely different matter. Its voter education campaign was not yet in full swing by the time the constitutional negotiations had been finalised in 1993. The rural population among whom illiteracy was high had not even been fully mobilised. In spite of large turnouts to rallies and demonstrations, there was an awareness within the ANC leadership that this was not easily translatable into votes. Without voter education, the likelihood of spoilt papers, violence and the complacency that the ANC would win, which could result in people staying away, became fears that increasingly filled the minds of ANC strategists. Other issues, such as the voting age of 18 which could cut a majority of its youthful supporters and the election strategy of bringing other parties under its electoral front and onto its list, carried equal critical challenges.

As part of its electoral strategy the ANC initiated a massive voter education campaign which started with the training of ANC education officers. Widespread publicity about the forthcoming elections was also undertaken. In all the major events and mass campaigns that were to follow, the ANC was quick to sometimes divert from the core issue to focus people's attention on the forthcoming elections. This was more apparent in the corruption scandals that rocked the government and was an important theme even in the aftermath of Chris Hani's assassination. The voter education programme bolstered initiatives taken by independent agencies. A concerted effort was also made to restructure the South African Broadcasting Corporation (SABC) and to make it more independent. The Campaign for Independent Broadcasting (CIB) was formed to coordinate the speedy transformation of the SABC. Negotiations were set up with the government to seek consensus on procedural matters relating to the appointment of an independent board which would govern the SABC when the term of the existing board expired at the end of March 1993. However, like the constitutional negotiations themselves, this was to prove to be a hotly contested issue. The expiry date came without agreement having been reached, and this prompted the extension of the date by two months. Even after a new board had been democratically selected, the alleged interference by President De Klerk in the selection process steeped the SABC in further controversy.

Devising an election strategy was one thing, but putting the strategy into practice was another. This was the daunting task which faced the ANC as it began to seek finance to foot its election campaign, let alone its mass voter education campaign. Already financial backing from foreign donors such as the Nordic countries was under severe pressure. It was against this background that the organisation proposed in its election strategy that a state fund of about R400 million be set up to assist parties during their campaigns. Much more crucial though, was its plea to the international community at the International Solidarity Conference held in Johannesburg from 19–21 February 1993 to foot its election campaign. The National Elections Commission Statement, which was read to 650 international participants and 260 South Africans, made it clear that a large sum of money would be needed to support the voter education initiative within the black communities.[6] This would pay for the training of 2700 national, regional and local election managers, including 140 trainers and organisers, 210 000 volunteers for voter education and 27 000 monitors. It would also cover the development of a communication system coordination network, the setting up of 94 fully equipped and efficient administrative subregional offices; research; transportation in the form of vehicles, motorbikes, bicycles, etcetera; sufficient first-aid kits and related equipment; and programmes geared towards ending or controlling violence during and after elections.

Estimating the costs of the campaign, the National Election Committee, in one of its glossy leaflets distributed at the conference under the heading "From anti-apartheid to pro-democracy", mentioned that the ANC would require more than R130 million ($43 million) to undertake this major task. Items ranging from computers, audio and video cassettes, as well as the relevant recorders, were listed as some of the things that would be required for the campaign. In summing up the ANC's attempts to woo the international community to continue its support for democratic change in South Africa, Oliver Tambo had stated in February 1993, "you are here today because by your actions you have brought the system of apartheid to its knees ... we must stand together in creating a new South Africa".[7] A resolution of the organisation's position on sanctions, which was reviewed three days before the conference, was also passed, promising the lifting of various sanctions in the event of the installation of a Transitional Executive Council, an Independent Electoral Commission and a Media Commission, as well as the enactment of a Transition to Democracy Act. However, it was Mandela's international fund-raising that was to bring hope to the ANC's prospects of raising money for the elections.

Towards the middle of 1993 the ANC released its comprehensive plan for the election campaign, which was to be implemented by its regions and branches[8] between June 1993 and April 1994. The plan had four broad objectives: setting up working structures at all levels; establishing human, physical and material infrastructures; putting in place a strategy and plans for the campaign at all levels; and talking to each of the 22,5 million voters at least once to motivate and educate them.

- The first phase from 1 June – 31 August 1993 would involve the setting up of preparatory committees for national, regional and local elections; and the training of volunteers, each having to mobilise a hundred voters through a door-to-door campaign. Training would be provided to volunteers, monitors, media officers and fund-raising coordinators. This would include training on the management data base and communications systems.

- The second phase from 1 September – 10 December 1993 would focus on talking to every voter for the second time; the consolidation and expansion of the infrastructures, both human and physical; consolidating the support of those who would still be undecided; challenging the opposition; and finalising the list and election manifesto.

- The third phase which would be called "mobilising for victory", would begin on 16 January and run to 31 March 1994. It would have six objectives: making a third contact with the voters; popularising the ANC manifesto and candidates; making sure that all ANC supporters knew how to vote; embarking on a media blitz; intensifying the challenge against opponents; and preparing the ground for the logistics of the election days.

- Phase four would be the election week in which ANC campaigners would: ensure that everybody knew where to vote and how; arrange security to ensure a free and fair election; and transport supporters to the polls.

Simultaneous with attempts by the ANC to create its election machine, was the need to develop an election manifesto.

The ANC election manifesto

The development of an election manifesto had to be based on policies. The ANC had already outlined its policies in *Ready to govern*, and these policies were further developed in the Reconstruction and Development Programme (RDP). The RDP policy proposals were simply summarised and included in the ANC manifesto for the election campaign. A vision of a future South Africa was shared in the manifesto and promises were made about the delivery of a range of outputs. Released at Nasrec in Johannesburg on 29 January 1994, the ANC's election manifesto was introduced by Nelson Mandela on a personal note, in which he stated that

> ... in 1986, when I suggested to the government that the time had come for us to resolve South Africa's problems through negotiations, I was confident that my endeavour to bring peace and democracy through dialogue would finally bear fruit... The ANC's vision of a South Africa in which people live in peace and with equal opportunities, is an ideal which sustained me during my 27 years in prison. It is an ideal for which I was prepared to sacrifice my life. An ideal which together we can realise on 27 April 1994.[9]

The manifesto stated that

> ... to build a better life for all requires clear goals and a workable plan. Any solution to the crisis of apartheid needs an approach which rises above narrow interests and harnesses all our country's resources. It requires a democratic society based on equality, non-racialism and non-sexism; a nation built by delivering our different cultures, beliefs and languages as a source of our common strength; an economy which grows through providing jobs, housing and education; and a peaceful and secure environment in which people can live without fear.

233

The manifesto focused on installing a government of the people, improving the quality of life, achieving peace and security for all, taking a rightful place in the world, and pledged to all South Africans to work together to build a new country.

The ANC manifesto outlined its basic democratic principles, including a constitution and a bill of rights. It called for the right of all people to elect a government of their choice in regular, free and fair elections in a multi-party democracy. Democratic government was also to be located at provincial and local levels. A judiciary and constitutional court would protect democracy from any government or party political interference. Fundamental to it was freedom from discrimination on the basis of race or gender or any other grounds, and freedom of association and the right to ownership. It empha-sised that the interim constitution was a beginning towards the realisation of these democratic goals, and mentioned that it would strive for an open society in which there would be vigorous debate, freedom of the media and freedom to criticise the government of the day. It promised diversity of language with none being accorded superiority over the other. Freedom of religion would be allowed and traditional leaders would be accorded their rightful status. A new style of people's involvement in government would be encouraged through an in-depth public protector who would investigate corruption by state officials, and through representative policy formulating forums and people's forums where ordinary people voice their opinions.

The ANC promised jobs and better incomes through a growing economy, a public works programme which would provide jobs for 2,5 million people over the next ten years, and opportunities for the small business sector. It committed itself to full rights for all workers, including the right to collective bargaining and the right to ensure the reduction of VAT on basic foodstuffs and the reduction of income tax to people earning less than R4000 a month. Rural poverty would be addressed through a rural development programme which would ensure the provision of water, clinics, schools, toilet facilities, electricity, telephones and roads. There would be a land reform programme which would encourage women's participation, bolster small farmers' access to training, credit and markets, and guarantee victims of forced removals restitution through a Land Claims Court. With regard to education, the manifesto promised a single education system that would provide ten years of free and compulsory education for children. A housing plan would address the plight of seven million squatters and the homeless, and the upgrading of townships would ensure the building of one million homes, would provide running water and flush toilets to over a million families, and would electrify 2,5 million rural and urban homes.

A health care programme would focus on immunisation, nutrition and free health care for children under five. It would direct resources to combat TB, AIDS, cancer, etcetera, and would facilitate the integration of traditional health practices. A welfare and pensions programme would be implemented to care for children, senior citizens, the disabled and victims of violence. Pensions and grants would be made available through accessible outlets such as post offices and banks. Achieving equality among all South Africans and eliminating discrimination would be done through affirmative action which would focus on training and upgrading those who were disadvantaged by apartheid laws.

The implementation of the programme set out in the manifesto would be achieved through the efficient use of resources, increasing public expenditure and encouraging the private sector to put money into productive ventures. A reconstruction fund would be established and beneficial international aid and loans would be sought. Promising peace and security for all, the manifesto committed itself to dealing firmly with crime and violence, promoting political tolerance, introducing a gun control programme and creating a police force accountable to the communities in which it would be based. A new security force would be created which would reflect the national and gender character of the country. It would be non-partisan, professional, uphold the constitution and respect human rights. There would be equality for all before the law, with no detention without trial. The system of justice would be made more accessible, cheap and fair to everyone.

Finally, the ANC manifesto committed South Africa to becoming involved in all international agreements which protect human rights in its clause "taking our rightful place in the world". It would interact with other countries on sport, culture and tourism. The country would take part in regional institutions such as the Southern African Development Conference. It would become a full member of the Organisation of African Unity, the United Nations, the Non-aligned Movement and the Commonwealth bodies.

The ANC manifesto was printed in all South African languages and some of its excerpts were printed in leaflet form for wider distribution. One such pamphlet, entitled "The future of youth is with the ANC", promised the participation of the youth in government and encouraged the creation of a national youth council to serve the interests of all the youth in the country.[10] The election manifesto played an important role during the election campaign, as ANC leaders rallied potential voters around job creation and the provision of housing. Rather than relying on people voting it into power on the basis of it being a liberation movement, the ANC focused people's attention on the basic needs which were of greater concern to them. Its promise to meet these needs was strengthened by the simplicity with which it articulated its commitment. At the various people's forums around the country people were able to question the way in which the organisation would meet these commitments. This also added an element of confidence in the RDP.

Nomination of election candidates

Alongside the process of drafting an election manifesto, the ANC started drafting lists of candidates who would represent the organisation in parliament. A List Committee comprising the ANC and representatives from allied organisations was formed to develop guidelines on the nomination process. The committee was mandated to provide all participating organisations with nomination forms, which would include an acceptance section to which a broad code of conduct would be attached. The committee would also help regions to run their nominations conferences which would include consolidating and submitting these lists to the National Executive Committee (NEC). In executing these tasks the committee produced guidelines in August 1993 which were then sent to regions. According to these guidelines, a nomination would be accepted if it was made by a constitutional structure of the participating organisations (ANC branches, regions and allied organisations), and by a given number of members of the various organisations. Popularity in a given area, honesty and integrity were some of the qualities expected of nominees.[11]

Regions were asked to produce these separate lists in compliance with these guidelines: a list for the national legislature, a regional list for the national legislature and a list for the provincial legislature. These lists would be submitted to a national nominations conference and finally be ratified or amended by the NEC. It was the early process of interaction between regions and branches and allied organisations that clearly demonstrated the diversity and the breadth of internal democratic exercise and transparency in the ANC. As in the field of policy formulation, ANC members were accorded an opportunity to express their wishes and to determine leaders who would represent them in parliament. These diverse wishes were displayed by the names that appeared on provisional lists. Names of highly regarded personalities such as sportsmen and -women, singers and academics were legion on the lists. The PWV list for the national assembly clearly captured this mixture. Its provisional list contained people like Miss South Africa, Jacqui Mofokeng, black business personalities like Sam Motsuenyane and Richard Maponya, Wits University sociologist Jacklyn Cock, television personality Felicia Mabuza-Suttle, Billy Modise of Matla Trust and many others. The release of this list without consulting nominees, most of whom were not aware of their nomination, drew criticism from the NP which accused the ANC of cheap opportunism. While this was a serious embarrassment to nominees who were often not members of the ANC, the list reflected the mood within the ANC constituency, which conveyed a greater sense of appreciation of the role of non-aligned figures. Of greater significance was the non-racial character of the list, with names cutting across the colour barrier.

A consolidated PWV list of nominations was released on 5 January 1994. On this list, Tokyo Sexwale was nominated, unopposed, as the PWV region's candidate for premier. Other regions also released their lists during the course of the same week, except the Western Cape which faced delays. The National Nominations Conference took place on 15 January in Johannesburg to consolidate and finalise the nominations list. It was attended by 500 delegates from the ANC and its allied organisations. Winnie Mandela, who did not appear on earlier lists, also appeared on the list submitted to the conference. Her non-appearance on earlier lists could have been caused by uncertainty about her criminal conviction. This, however, was clarified by the NEC on 14 January, a day before the conference. Her conviction for kidnapping would be treated as a political offence, thus opening a way for her to be nominated. Despite her late entry Winnie Mandela appeared at the top of all the women on the list. The production of the final list was delayed because of objections by Patriotic Front members who complained of under-representation. Moreover, a great deal of editing had to be done to remove the duplication of candidates' names on national and regional lists. This involved a painful process of contacting nominees to obtain their preferences. A committee was set up to work with the List Committee and ensure proper accommodation of members of the Patriotic Front. The NEC of the ANC met on 20 January to consider the final list, as well as to ensure the proper representation of women.

The list was officially released on Friday, 21 January. It contained the names of 200 candidates for the national assembly. At the top of the list was Nelson Mandela followed by Cyril Ramaphosa, Thabo Mbeki, Joe Slovo and Pallo Jordan.[12] Notable exclusions from the list were regional premier candidates such as Tokyo Sexwale (PWV), Patrick Lekota (OFS), Ngoako Ramathlodi (N. Tvl.), Matthews Phosa (E. Tvl.), Jacob Zuma (KwaZulu-Natal), Allan Boesak (W. Cape), Raymond Mhlaba (E. Cape) and Manne Dipico (N. Cape). Popo Molefe appeared on the list because his contest for premiership of the North-West Province came late, after the list had been released. Other ANC stalwarts excluded from the list either opted not to make themselves available (e.g. Walter Sisulu, Cheryl Carolus and Albie Sachs) or decided to be included on provincial lists for national assembly or on the lists for provincial legislatures.

The list reflected South African society as a whole. It included Robben Island prisoners, former exiles, former UDF activists, COSATU trade unionists, priests, former tricameral parliament MPs, homeland leaders and a policeman. It also contained a proportion of women, in fact the ANC had insisted that they have at least a one-third representation. There were enough whites, coloureds and Indians on the list in proportion to the country's racial population. Of the 11 COSATU names agreed on at the COSATU Congress in September 1993, nine were included on the ANC list. These were: Jay Naidoo at number 6, Moses Mayekiso (18), Chris Dlamini (19), Phillip Dexter (41), Alec Erwin (45), Marcel Golding (56), John Coperlyn (102), Duma Nkosi (110) and Don Gumede (151). Homeland leaders included Bantu Holomisa (13), KwaNdebele's Prince James Mahlangu (42), Venda's Brigadier Ramushwana (71), Lebowa's Nelson Ramodike (78) and Kangwane's Mangesi Zitha (104). Former tricameral parliament MPs on the list were J.N. Reddy (118) and D.S. Rajah (192). There was also Labour Party's Peter Hendrikse at number 106 and Llewellyn Landers (125). Former DP MPs who crossed the floor to join the ANC were included on the list. They were Jan van Eck (48), Dave Dalling (67), Jannie Momberg (80) and Rob Haswell (194). Singers included Jennifer Ferguson (114) and Miriam Makeba (129). A former policeman, Gregory Rockman, was also on the list at number 46. The SACP had a small but significant representation with 34 members on the list of 200 names.[13] Of the 34, only 29 stood a good chance of making it to parliament, with 16 of them featuring at the top 50.[14] Of the nine premiers, only two were SACP members: Raymond Mhlaba and Manne Dipico.

The NEC's amendment of the final list resulted in the inclusion of certain names which had not been nominated by regions and branches, and in the exclusion of others. Nominees who were felt to belong to impartial organisations were removed from the list. These included Enos Mabuza (member of the SABC), Sheila Sisulu, Zwelakhe Sisulu, Frank Chikane (IEC Commissioner), Franklin Sonn, Prof. Njabulo Ndebele, Billy Modise and Brigadier Gabriel Ramushwana and others.[15] New inclusions included Gazankulu's Chief Minister, Samuel Nxumalo, who was not even on the Northern Transvaal regional list. Winnie Mandela, who appeared top of all the women at number 9 on the earlier list, was dropped to position number 31. After the release of the list a number of nominees such as Alistair Sparks (142), J.N. Reddy and D.S. Rajah withdrew their candidacy. Others such as Nelson Ramodike were dropped from the list. Elijah Barayi and Elias Motsoaledi passed away. The removal of Ramodike and the withdrawal of Reddy and Rajah resulted from criticism by ANC branches and allies about the inclusion of people who had long been ''part of the oppressive system''. The final list was submitted to the IEC when the ANC registered to contest the elections.

The election campaign and the road to victory

The contest for the elections began as early as the commencement of constitutional negotiations. Notwithstanding the partnership which was emerging between the ANC and the NP, as demonstrated by the mutual working relationship between Cyril Ramaphosa and Roelf Meyer, the two major protagonists in negotiations were also simultaneously contesting for support. While the formation of the National Election Committee laid the ground for the ANC's election campaign through its massive voter education, the actual campaigning required more thorough strategic planning and execution. A committee led by Nelson Mandela and comprising Winnie Mandela, Cyril Ramaphosa, Thabo Mbeki, Jay Naidoo, Steve Tshwete, Joe Slovo and Bantu Holomisa, was formed to give political direction to the National Election Committee which was responsible for running the campaign. Extensive election machinery was then set in motion bringing together various researchers, experts and strategists. These included Stan Greenberg and Frank Greer who helped American Bill Clinton to win the United States presidency. Khetso Gordhan was also in the team. The Applied Marketing and Communication, headed by Julian Ovsiowitz and Louis Gavin and including Welcome Msomi and Ken Modise, was contracted to undertake the advertising campaign. The adoption of this political party strategy on election campaigning showed that the ANC, despite its insistence to remain a liberation movement during the period of transition, could not avoid operating like conventional political parties. There was a belief within the organisation that elections could not be easily won on a liberation ticket. Concerted efforts had to be made to canvass people to vote for the organisation.

The ANC formally registered on Wednesday, 9 February 1994, to contest the elections, a week after President De Klerk signed the election proclamation which required parties to register within the following ten days. By then, the campaign had already begun with Mandela addressing a number of people's forums (which had been running since November 1993) around the country. In a span of four months, including April, Nelson Mandela visited and addressed thousands of enthusiastic supporters in various places, including remote areas of the country. Emulating the American presidential campaign, the ANC campaign began with a train ride with Mandela to Nasrec in Johannesburg on Saturday, 29 January, to unveil the organisation's election manifesto. Simultaneous launches were also held in all the regions. A large part of the campaign focused on forums which the ANC was already addressing. People's forums, an assembly of people expressing their wishes and posing questions to ANC leaders, were seen as appropriate vehicles for participatory democracy. This initiative was started by Chris Hani before his death, when he visited and addressed groups of individuals to crowds of thousands in townships, towns, cities, villages and other places in remote areas. Mandela's publicised election campaign began in earnest with his tour of the Western Transvaal the day after the launch. During his tour, Mandela visited Boskop Training Centre in Potchefstroom and addressed a rally at Ikageng Stadium. He also went to Olympiad Stadium at Rustenburg, Stilfontein's Khuma township and Jouberton near Klerksdorp. He completed his tour by addressing businessmen in Potchefstroom's Banquet Hall.

Other ANC leaders also addressed various gatherings during this campaign. Ruth Mompati took the campaign into the black townships of the CP-controlled towns of Bloemberg, Schweizer-Reneke, Wolmaransstad, Christiana, Makwassie, Boskuil and Leeudooringstad. Essop Pahad went to the University of Bophuthatswana, while Thandi Modise visited Dinokana, Braklaagte and Leeufontein. De Klerk had been in some of these places a week before, including places such as Badplaas, the black townships of Witbank and Bethal, as well as Kwandebele, where he was dubbed an honorary Ndebele by the local King Makhosoke.

On 2 February Mandela went to Paarl where, together with other ex-prisoners, he lit the flame of freedom at Victor Verster Prison, where he had been released. On 6 February he concluded his tour of the Orange Free State by addressing a press briefing in Bloemfontein. His entry into Bophuthatswana in the Orange Free State was not without trouble. His entourage was stopped twice by Bophuthatswana police at a roadblock between Bloemfontein and Tweespruit, and also in Thaba Nchu where he intended laying a wreath at the grave of the late ANC leader, Dr Moroka.

The election boycott by FA parties and the threat of civil war had a negative effect on the election campaign, but could not stop it. On 12 March the ANC election campaign went to the Vaal townships. Unlike other forums where the central questions put to the ANC leadership concerned basic needs and violence, people at the Vaal forums were particularly concerned about developments in Bophuthatswana where a mass popular uprising had led to the fleeing of President Mangope. The fall of Mangope was particularly significant in opening a way for free political campaigning in the homeland. After the formal declaration of the termination of the homeland's independence by the South African government and the TEC, Mandela was very quick to enter Bophuthatswana. The rewards were in fact the product of a steadfast resistance and a grass-roots-orientated uprising by the people of Bophuthatswana. Notwithstanding this, Mandela was given a tumultuous reception and treated as a hero of the people's revolution. His tour to Bophuthatswana and the Western Transvaal also took him to the AWB-controlled town of Weselton. From here Mandela visited the Northern Transvaal, addressing rallies in Lebowa and Venda.

While the fall of Bophuthatswana allowed the ANC to campaign with renewed efforts, it was KwaZulu-Natal which remained a stumbling block to free electioneering. The IFP's refusal to participate in the elections and the ceaseless violence in the area had made it impossible even for local ANC members and supporters to undertake effective voter education, let alone electioneering. With the fall of Bophuthatswana, the ANC's three regions in KwaZulu-Natal were also eager to campaign for free elections in the area. However, their rallies continued to be disrupted by IFP supporters who blocked stadiums in Umlazi near Durban on Sunday, 13 March, and the Princess Magogo Stadium in Kwamashu on Sunday, 20 March. The failure by the police to stop this development made the ANC even more vociferous in its call for free political activity. The resignation of Oupa Gqozo in Ciskei also gave impetus to those in the ANC who were clamouring for the fall of the KwaZulu government. On Friday, 25 March, the ANC launched an 80 000 strong march in Durban. This happened simultaneously with other marches in Empangeni, Stanger and Pietermaritzburg under the banner "proud Zulus are not afraid of elections". With 120 people having been killed in six days towards the end of March, there were already numerous calls for a state of emergency in KwaZulu-Natal. The emergency, which was finally declared after the release of an IEC report saying that it was impossible to hold elections under existing conditions, was intended to end violence and to open a way for election campaigns. However, it tended to work against the objectives of free elections. The strict application of emergency regulations affected the holding of meetings, with parties being required to obtain permits for meeting places. Curfews inhibited the freedom of movement, as demonstrated by the arrest of ANC Regional Secretary, Sifiso Nkabinde. The rate of killings also rose dramatically, seemingly demonstrating the futility of the state of emergency. The IFP also launched a number of marches in Natal and Johannesburg in support of the King's call for self-determination. In a situation where the IFP was under extreme pressure, these marches also sought to demonstrate the party's capability to render the election process unworkable. It was only a week before the elections and after the IFP was persuaded to participate in elections that the terrain was opened in KwaZulu-Natal for free election campaigning. Mandela exploited this new opening when he addressed a large rally at the Kings Park Stadium in Durban.

While the entry of the IFP (the CP and AZAPO maintained their boycott) finally cleared the terrain for a vigorous election contest, considerable intimidation, dirty tricks and foul play continued to mar the election process to the final days of campaigning. ANC offices in the outlying towns and even in central Johannesburg, like those of the NP, were allegedly bombed by right-wingers. Most of the bombs exploded in the Western Transvaal and the Orange Free State. About 30 bomb explosions occurred between December 1993 and February 1994. Railway lines and power pylons were also blown up. Potential ANC voters in right-wing-controlled towns were systematically denied voter education and others had their identity documents confiscated by their employers to prevent them from voting. This practice was particularly rife on the farms. In other instances, farmworkers were told by their employers which party to vote for. This was the case in the Eastern Transvaal, Eastern Cape and the Orange Free State. It was against this background that COSATU lodged a complaint with the IEC and launched a campaign to force farmers to allow free political activity, voter education and election campaigning on their farms. In Johannesburg an ANC Youth League worker was savagely beaten for putting up ANC election posters.

Until the IFP's entry into the elections it was virtually impossible for the ANC to undertake its election campaign in Natal. Direct intimidation, violence and the killing of campaigners was widespread. Stadiums were blocked and public buildings were not made available. Voter education was also hampered with people being killed. The ANC's Deputy Secretary-General, Jacob Zuma, had his house set alight twice. These attacks were also directed at IEC officials. Other parties also faced similar problems which appeared to be linked to intimidation. Intimidation in various forms also came from ANC supporters. In February 1994 a woman was killed in Kimberley's Roodepan township in a clash between ANC and NP supporters. The meeting was supposed to have been addressed by President De Klerk. Following this incident the ANC and Mandela, in particular, were vociferous in calling upon their supporters to restrain themselves and to allow other parties to campaign for votes. The IEC's electoral code of conduct was also distributed to regions and branches to caution supporters about the implications of their actions on the organisation and the individuals concerned. Calls by ANC leaders were not, however, always heeded. In another meeting in Postdene, Northern Cape, President De Klerk was hit by a projectile hurled by ANC supporters. In early March, six NP electioneers were attacked by ANC supporters while putting up posters in preparation for De Klerk's visit to Natal. One of De Klerk's rallies in Venda was disrupted by ANC supporters. The DP's Tony Leon had to flee the campus of the University of Western Cape after being attacked by a crowd of ANC and PAC supporters. There were also reported fights between ANC and PAC supporters in the Transkei, which resulted in the killing of five people. Some ANC deserters whose names appeared on other parties' lists of candidates were also subjected to intimidation. There were also allegations of IEC monitors shouting ANC slogans at rallies.

From February to March 1994, there were already about 382 complaints relating to the violation of the electoral code of conduct. It was against this background that the IEC launched Operation Access to help parties reach areas which had been made "no-go areas". The operation began in the Northern Transvaal at the farm of Bertie van Zyl when IEC monitors, accompanied by the press, took various political party representatives to a group of about one thousand farmworkers. It also went to ANC-dominated Khanya village in Natal and Phola Park on the East Rand. The latter visit was, however, a failure, as IEC officials and party representatives were met by crowds chanting their loyalty to the ANC.

Dirty tricks abounded during the elections. A new party calling itself the African Moderates Congress (AMC) registered for elections. It was a completely unknown party, and the ANC objected to its registration saying that its abbreviation sounded very close to its own and accused the party of intending to confuse voters. Allegations and counter-allegations of foul play were also abundant. In one instance, the ANC's Western Cape premier candidate, Allan Boesak, alleged that R350 billion had been stolen from the government and that R70 million had disappeared into the pockets of cabinet ministers. The ANC's parliamentary candidate, Bantu Holomisa, former leader of the Transkei, alleged that the NP intended to rig votes through the National Intelligence System and the Department of Home Affairs. He also alleged that the NP was giving blacks *"pap en vleis"* laced with the invisible ink which would disqualify them from voting. The AWB also entered the field, spreading rumours which led to people in white suburbs stockpiling food in anticipation of "the worst scenario after the elections". The NP too, created a storm in the Western Cape through its distribution of a comic book entitled "Winds of change blow through South Africa – will you make it through the storm". Tapping the fears of the coloured community the book hinted that, among other things, people should expect slogans such as "kill a coloured, kill a farmer" after the elections. Although some copies had already been distributed, the ANC was able to halt further distribution through a court interdict. On making the application, the ANC argued that the comic book was "aimed at the coloured community and designed to promote tension, division and hatred between the coloured community and African community... the publication exudes racism, which could have very serious implications for free and fair elections in the Western Cape".[16]

Owing to alleged practices of intimidation by its supporters, the ANC began to face restrictions. It was fined R50 000 by the IEC for disrupting an NP rally in Venda which was supposed to have been addressed by De Klerk on 9 March. The fine had to be paid immediately. This judgement overruled an earlier suspended fine of R100 000, which had been imposed by a lower-ranking IEC tribunal. The ANC was also fined R10 000 for disrupting an NP meeting in Postmasburg in February. The fine was, however, suspended for two weeks. This was an overruling of an earlier decision which maintained that the ANC could not be held responsible for the disruption of the meeting. Bantu Holomisa also appeared before the IEC's tribunal and the ANC's disciplinary committee for his *"pap en vleis"* allegations against the NP.

In spite of intimidation and allegations of foul play, South Africa's first democratic elections were bitterly contested. There was a scramble for votes everywhere, ranging from the PAC's poorly attended rallies to the lobbying of South Africa's biggest church, the Zion Christian Church, the Muslim community and, indeed, the attempt by the IFP to exploit the powerful Zulu royalty for its own election ends. One of the most bitterly contested constituencies was the Western Cape coloured community. The NP was accused of racist practices and of turning coloured against African. The release of the comic book fostering racial animosity between the Africans and the coloureds was seen as the final blow which prompted the PAC's premier candidate, Patricia de Lille, to call for the NP and DP to be chased out of the townships.

The election campaign was also personalised, with much attention being focused on party leaders. De Klerk was eloquent and sharp but could not match Mandela's heroic attributes which saw thousands of people flocking and stampeding to most of the gatherings he attended. Young and old wanted to see with their own eyes a man whose reputation in contemporary world history could be compared to none. Since his release in February 1990 he had travelled to cities and towns around the globe, and had addressed millions of people over television, at conferences, rallies and in private meetings. He had met and shaken hands with world leaders in South Africa and abroad and had received numerous awards, including the prestigious Nobel Peace Prize which he shared with Mr De Klerk. Addressing multitudes of people on his campaign trail, Nelson Mandela was received with tumultuous applause, ululation and "toyi-toying", and was generally treated like a demi-god.[17]

The central issues in the election campaign were: who could best rule the country, who was responsible for violence and who could deliver jobs and houses? Another question that formed part of the contest was: who ended apartheid? While De Klerk contended that it was the NP, Mandela countered that it was the masses inside and outside South Africa. Cartoons showed Mandela knocking out apartheid and De Klerk jumping up outside the boxing ring declaring that he had done it. Election posters sprang up countrywide on poles and trees. ANC posters declared "Mandela for President", while NP posters projected its smiling President saying "De Klerk – the man who ended apartheid". The DP also entered the election poster contest with its "we did not kill people – only apartheid". These posters were later joined by the posters of other parties such as the Freedom Front, the Soccer Party, the ACDP, the PAC, Dikwankwetla and, in the dying days of the election contest, those of the IFP. At a time when it was clear that it would not be contesting the elections, the IFP had ironically released its posters in Durban declaring "vote IFP when the time comes". After its entry into the election contest, a week before voting began, IFP posters declared "South Africa we did it for you" and "So the last shall be the first". However, it was the ANC posters, some with Mandela's smiling face, which were everywhere – on buses, taxis, trains and private motor car windows. Others filled commercial advertising spaces. This contest was also captured in newspapers, with parties running full-page advertisements. Television and radio were also used to the full to convey the parties' policies.

On Thursday, 14 April, the climax of the election campaign went to television screens when Mandela and De Klerk had a live election debate. This was the battle of the titans. The two leaders started with bitter accusations. Mandela repeatedly accused De Klerk of not being frank, and his criticism of the NP was harsh. His criticism included the NP's inability to end violence, its uneven expenditure on black and white education and the fact that De Klerk, as President, did not pay tax. Mandela mentioned that they had been in close contact on a number of issues and had worked together to try to end violence, but that De Klerk had refused to show him the report upon which he dismissed senior policemen who were allegedly involved in instigating third-force violence. Mandela also accused the NP of racist tactics, quoting the NP's comic book which was banned by the IEC in the Western Cape. De Klerk hit back accusing the ANC of being party to violence, pointing to corrupt bantustan leaders on the ANC's list of candidates and criticising the ANC's RDP, which he estimated would cost up to R70 billion and would lead to tax increases.

The election campaign officially came to an end on the weekend of 23 and 24 April. Mandela wrapped up his campaign by addressing a *Siyanqoba* (We shall overcome) rally at the FNB Stadium in Soweto on 23 April.

Voting, the election results, victory celebrations and the installation of the Government of National Unity

According to the IEC's plan,[18] people would vote on the 26, 27 and 28 April at 9000 voting stations around the country. 26 April was earmarked for special votes. Only the aged, the sick, pregnant women, nurses, policemen and soldiers would vote on this day. Those outside the country would also cast votes in 76 countries. 27 April was the first day on which all South Africans would cast their votes and it was declared a public holiday. 28 April was an additional day for those who could not vote on 27 April.

The casting of the first votes on 26 April occurred in an atmosphere of jubilation as the aged and the sick, some carried in wheelbarrows, flocked to the voting stations. However, it was a fraudulent Nomaza Paintin, posing as Nelson Mandela's niece, who cast the first South African democratic vote at the Wellington booth in New Zealand, some time before South Africa woke up to vote. Nonetheless, high expectations, jubilation and pervasive feelings of the last ride to freedom marked the first day of the elections as people waited in queues to make, what was to them, the most important cross in their lifetimes. Nelson Mandela was the first to be shown on television screens casting his vote, followed by other party leaders at various voting stations. Mandela had decided to cast his vote in KwaZulu-Natal to encourage and show solidarity with the people of the province. His choice of Ohlonge High School in Inanda to cast his vote was symbolic, as it was there that the ANC's first President, John Dube, was buried. To Mandela the vote was a sentimental achievement of the course of freedom for which heroes such as Oliver Tambo, Chris Hani, Chief Albert Luthuli, Braam Fischer and others had paid the ultimate sacrifice.[19] Remarkable was the fact that for the first time in many years there was no official recording of violence or politically related killings on 27 April. Not a single case of intimidation was reported. The press reported on people waiting in queues, some impatiently, because of the logistical problems that cropped up at some voting stations. Even in places where there had been continued violence such as Natal, enemies queued together making jokes while preparing for their secret votes. The day was a triumph for *ubuntu* (kindness), as people needing advice were readily assisted, those who were thirsty were given water and those who were scorched by the sun were lent umbrellas by people of goodwill.

While these were the hallmarks of the day, problems were legion. These problems were logistical and to a certain degree a result of the inefficient preparation by the IEC. A number of stations did not open on time with some opening as late as 15:00 and others not opening at all. Some of those that opened did not have the required material to be able to begin the elections. Some stations did not have the IFP stickers which should have been stuck at the bottom of each ballot paper by IEC officials. Other stations such as those in Soweto and the Vaal ran out of the invisible ink, rubber stamps, and worse still, ballot papers. Notwithstanding these logistical problems, voting in a majority of stations ran smoothly.

Many of the problems that cropped up seemed to have been caused by a lack of proper coordination at the various IEC levels. The flow of information from polling stations to IEC centres seemed faulty in some cases, in spite of the sophisticated telecommunication technology installed by Telkom. Worse still, the various IEC directorates appeared to share little information with one another, some not fully understanding what was happening in the other directorates. This was particularly so between the administration and monitoring directorates. The responsibility for this lay with the administration directorate, as its task was to ensure that the voting stations and their equipment were set up and functioning. In some parts of the country no voting stations were ever set up. There were also no maps for voting stations in the rural areas, making it difficult for those transporting election materials. There was also a lack of accountability for the distribution of materials, resulting in some IEC officials at polling stations having to fetch the materials themselves. The issuing of voter cards was also not carried out quickly enough and people queued until late at night to obtain them before voting. The fact that one card-making machine was stolen also compounded problems and the suspicion of card racketeering. The working relationship between the IEC's commissioners and the heads of the directorates was not always good. The director of the administration, Piet Colyn, tendered his resignation over the interference by the commissioners, but was persuaded to stay. It would also appear that there was an element of sabotage. Large piles of boxes containing election material were found in warehouses on the East and the West Rand, and one was found in Pretoria. Five IEC officials, three of them seconded from the Department of Home Affairs, were subject to investigation. While election materials were delivered to most white suburbs in the PWV, large sections of the surrounding townships suffered a shortage, with some receiving nothing at all.

It was in response to this emerging crisis during the elections that voting was extended to 28 April, particularly to enable those in the former bantustans to exercise their votes. These changes implied additional costs. Seven hundred more stations were established in KwaZulu-Natal after the IFP had decided to contest the elections. More ballot papers were printed to cover the unexpectedly large turnout and to compensate for the papers that had disappeared. More pay had to be made available for the staff working during the extra days of the elections. While these factors raised the cost of organising the elections, they nevertheless fell within the IEC's budget of R1,5 billion – which was far larger than the officially announced budget of R700 million.[20]

Owing to these logistical problems and the decision by the IEC, TEC and the government to grant further days for voting, other problems arose. Allegations of rigged elections were reported in Port Elizabeth, KwaZulu-Natal and other parts of the country. Complaints and charges were laid about boxes that had been tampered with (30 of them were found opened at Lady Frere), boxes that had been filled with grass, and boxes that mysteriously disappeared empty and returned filled with ballot papers. Allegations and counter-allegations were rife in Natal, with the ANC accusing the IFP of taking voting stations to their bases and showing the elderly how to make their cross alongside their party. The IFP, in return, accused the ANC of giving voter cards to youth and children. By the conclusion of the elections, the IEC had received about 500 complaints related to voting. In spite of these voices of foul play, Kriegler dismissed these problems to circumvent discrediting the entire process. Indeed, the patience and sacrifice of the people to make use of their votes could not be frustrated by administrative hiccups and the apparent inability of the IEC's election machinery to contain irregularities.

Notwithstanding the IEC's bold attempt to downplay emerging problems, it was clear at the close of the elections that the birth of a new democracy in South Africa was not going to be easy. While the elections were free, as demonstrated by the absence of intimidation, a question was raised about the fairness of the process. The IEC was under pressure to assess the elections as fair. However, problems and hitches continued even during the counting of the votes which was initially delayed because of the extension of the voting. While results were initially fed to the media immediately they were made available, the release of the final results was halted as problems began to emerge. Most serious was the attempt to interfere with the IEC's computers to alter the tallies of certain minority parties, so that they could gain up to 3 % of the votes. Moreover, the reconciliation process was time-consuming, adding to the slow release of election results. This procedure was finally abandoned by the IEC, with Justice Johan Kriegler arguing that its importance was limited because voter registration did not exist to accurately reconcile the votes counted with the number of people who had voted. Most important in his and the IEC's view, was national reconciliation.

The final results were released on Friday, 6 May. By then, however, President De Klerk had already conceded defeat in view of the ANC's lead on Monday, 2 May. He said before his supporters that "Mandela deserves the congratulations, good wishes and prayers of all South Africans ... I look forward to working with him constructively within the government of national unity in our common effort to promote the well-being of all our people". Addressing a victory celebration party later in the evening at the Carlton Hotel in Johannesburg, Mandela joyfully said: "You can proclaim from the roof tops: free at last!" He congratulated the people for the ANC's victory, saying that

> ... this is one of the most important moments in the life of our country. I stand before you filled with deep pride and joy – pride in the ordinary, humble people of this country. You have shown such a calm, patient determination to reclaim this country as your own.

Mandela's victory speech and his dancing with the ANC choir set the pace for the countrywide celebrations that night as people went into the streets, "toyi-toying", dancing and ululating to mark the dawn of a new era. These celebrations were not, however, without incidents. In Sebokeng, a lone, frustrated and drunken driver ripped apart throngs of jubilant celebrators, killing 11 and injuring about 30 others.

Announcing the final election results at Gallagher Estates in Midrand, the IEC's Chairperson, Justice Johan Kriegler, declared the elections "substantially free and fair". He said that up to 19 726 579 votes had been counted. Of these, 19 533 498 had been accepted and 193 081 had been regarded as spoilt votes. On the announcement of the final results the ANC was ahead with 62,5 % of the votes, which entitled it to 112 seats in the national assembly. It also won seven of the nine regions – PWV, North West, Northern Transvaal, Eastern Transvaal, Orange Free State, Eastern Cape and Northern Cape. The other two were won by the NP (Western Cape) and the IFP (KwaZulu-Natal).[21] Successful premiers for the provincial governments were: Tokyo Sexwale (PWV), Popo Molefe (North West), Matthews Phosa (Eastern Transvaal), Ngoako Ramathlodi (Northern Transvaal), Patrick Lekota (Orange Free State), Frank Mdlalose (KwaZulu-Natal), Raymond Mhlaba (Eastern Cape), Hernus Kriel (Western Cape) and Manne Dipico (Northern Cape).

The ANC did not win the Western Cape, for a number of reasons. The organisation did not do enough preparatory work compared to the NP which had used every available opportunity, including demonising the ANC and stirring racial hatred between the coloureds and the Africans. There had, indeed, been tensions between the coloureds and the Africans in the Cape. On one occasion a group of African squatters invaded and occupied coloured houses – a move which the ANC was unable to deal with firmly. This had created deep-seated fears within the coloured community. Tensions had also been rising within the ANC region between the coloureds and the Africans. Mandela, in his bid to win over the coloured vote, persuaded the Western Cape Regional Conference to elect Allan Boesak as chairperson. The NP was also quick to exploit these tensions by trying to turn the coloured community against the ANC. Its comic book "The Wind of Change" only sought to foster racial hatred at the expense of the ANC. The coloured community, which constituted the majority in the Western Cape, also had a language and cultural affinity with the Afrikaner-dominated NP. Coloureds also had deep-rooted fears about a black government and were already having suspicions about the ANC's affirmative action policy, which they believed would be used against them. These issues and the ethnicity question, in particular, were not firmly addressed by the ANC leadership.

The loss of Natal came as a surprise to the ANC. At the time of writing, the reasons for its poor showing still await research, but one can make a preliminary assessment. The ANC in Natal faced numerous external and internal problems. Allegations of rigging of the polls cannot be ruled out, but await further analysis. However, opinion polls had shown significant ANC support in the region. Large numbers of people attended ANC rallies and the Sofasonke Festival, in particular, also demonstrated its support. Campaigning in Natal had been hampered by violence. Insufficient voter education, which had been hampered by the IFP's earlier decision not to participate in the elections, also played its part, as shown by the largest count of spoilt papers compared to other provinces. The ANC in Natal had not, however, taken adequate measures to ensure their success. In spite of good attendance at rallies, the ANC did not do enough groundwork in encouraging people to vote for it during the elections. The purpose of the rallies appeared to be to convey the message that the ANC were also proud Zulus who wanted the elections to go on in KwaZulu-Natal.

Internally, the ANC had to deal with political rivalries. The division of Natal into three ANC regions had divided loyalties behind three leaders. As only one premier candidate could be nominated from the three regions, this scaled down the enthusiasm of those who lost. The nomination of Jacob Zuma as the region's premier candidate was to avoid conflict. But this decision also created problems. Zuma, as Deputy Secretary-General of the ANC, had a weaker base compared to the other regional leaders in Natal. After losing the contest for premiership the other leaders no longer took responsibility for the election campaign. Lack of cooperation between the regions also contributed to the ANC's loss of Natal. Already there had been tensions in the region around negotiations with the KwaZulu government. There were clear divisions between radicals who aligned themselves with Harry Gwala and who were opposed to appeasement with Inkatha and moderates who favoured peaceful negotiations. The choice of Zuma could not bridge the gap, as he had already shown his inclination towards the moderate group through his appeasement meetings with the IFP. These internal problems probably accounted for the few ANC observers and assistants at polling stations during the elections. These issues, combined with alleged IFP rigging of the votes and the fear of violence, probably accounted for the ANC's failure to win the second most populous region in the country.

Following the election results, a series of events were planned to inaugurate the new democracy. On Saturday, 7 May, the various provincial legislatures were sworn in. On 9 May the national assembly met in Cape Town to elect Nelson Mandela as the first democratically elected State President. Frene Ginwala was elected Speaker. On 10 May Nelson Mandela was sworn in, in Pretoria, in front of a host of international heads of states, various dignitaries and thousands of South Africans who gathered on the lawns to celebrate.[22] To the thousands of people who celebrated and danced to music by numerous South African musicians, the thunderous gun salute and the aeronautic display of aeroplanes, helicopters and fighter jets brought the first true feeling of patriotism and freedom. Mandela's face appeared on a huge television screen flanked by white generals standing to attention beside him. People were filled with joy and pride as they could see the respect and honour granted to the first black president by the white establishment.

Soon after the ANC's victory Mandela announced the new cabinet of the Government of National Unity (GNU). Thabo Mbeki was given the first deputy presidency while the second deputy presidency went to Mr De Klerk.[23] It was probably the choice of Mbeki as First Deputy President, the allotment of the portfolio of Foreign Affairs to Alfred Nzo and the apparent exclusion of Cyril Ramaphosa from the cabinet that caused concern in the media. Mbeki had been in competition with Cyril Ramaphosa for the position of first deputy president. This was one of the most difficult choices that Mandela had to make. Already Ramaphosa had attained second position on the ANC's nominations list and with his organisational skills it was speculated that he would get the job. Mbeki, who had established his base in the ANC's International Affairs Department and was appointed the organisation's National Chairman after the death of Oliver Tambo, had not been a visible contender. Ramaphosa, the Secretary-General of the organisation, was also head of the negotiation team that successfully concluded the constitutional deal. He had also held a prominent position within the TEC and was prominent in the making of TEC decisions. The decision of the first deputy president was made by Mandela alone. His choice of Mbeki was probably influenced by the following factors: Mbeki was relatively older, 51 years of age and ten years older than Ramaphosa.[24] Apart from coming from one of the three most important dynasties within the ANC – the Mandela, Sisulu and Mbeki dynasties – he had a longer political history within the liberation movement than Ramaphosa who, though part of the internal mass democratic organisations, had been brought into the ANC's leadership less than four years earlier. Mbeki had worked in Oliver Tambo's presidential office during the period of exile and had the widest international experience. Most significantly, for the position of Deputy President Mbeki had the backing of the Youth League which had earlier engineered his appointment as National Chairman.

Ramaphosa did not have such a powerful constituency within the ANC to lobby for him. In spite of his reliance on the general will of ANC members who had placed him second on the ANC nominations list, he had no comparable strength to counter the Youth League's lobby. Moreover, a number of incidents also worked against him. There was an increasing feeling within the ANC that Ramaphosa was too omnipotent in the organisation. He used his power and position as Secretary-General with little restraint.[25] He had taken over the negotiation team originally headed by Thabo Mbeki. This reshuffling of positions had also seen Winnie Mandela being replaced by Cheryl Carolus, a move which Mandela overturned when he returned from his overseas trip. Notwithstanding the process of feeding information back to the ANC constituency, a number of constitutional decisions were taken within small caucuses, a style which was inherited from the clandestine operations of the UDF and COSATU era of the mid-1980s. Most crucially, when the media leaked a surreptitious plot to remove Mandela and to replace him with Ramaphosa as leader, the latter did not take sufficient steps to allay the suspicions – an omission which confirmed suspicions and annoyed Mandela. Indeed, allegations of cabals within the ANC were never thoroughly investigated or if investigated their reports were not made public. Despite the concern to maintain organisational homogeneity and to avoid splits, Ramaphosa, as the Secretary-General of the organisation, carried much responsibility with respect to these matters.

The power struggle between Ramaphosa and Winnie Mandela dating back to the cabal controversy might have worked against Ramaphosa. Although Winnie Mandela resigned her ANC positions because of pressures resulting from her conviction, her election as President of the Women's League might have given her room to challenge Ramaphosa. The controversy within the ANC about the appointment of a new cabinet might also have worked against Ramaphosa. An ANC meeting which discussed the RDP at Nasrec in Johannesburg had taken the decision that the task of appointing the new cabinet be made by the organisation's NEC. When this decision, which was taken by alliance organisations outside the NEC, was finally deliberated at an NEC meeting, the NEC maintained that the President of the ANC had the sole right of appointing the new cabinet. Ramaphosa was among those who defended the position taken by alliance formations. This incident might have swayed Mandela's choice of Mbeki.[26]

In the end the ANC projected a trouble-free face, saying that Ramaphosa had decided of his own volition not to take a cabinet post but to lead the ANC outside government. Notwithstanding, signs of unhappiness within the ANC were apparent. While the decision by Ramaphosa to stay outside the GNU and to strengthen the ANC in preparation for the next elections was congruent with the emerging consensus within the ANC to pursue this line, the move appeared to have other connotations. Ramaphosa's decision to remain outside could strengthen the ANC. It could also, however, be a vehicle to strengthen his base outside the GNU and parliament. Those in the GNU might find themselves alienated from the people through a lack of visible delivery of their promises. In this scenario it would more likely be those in government who would suffer popular indignation than those outside. The argument within the liberation movement that the ANC might mobilise against the GNU if it failed to deliver, could also present an opportunity for those outside to mobilise and win popular support for themselves. Indeed, the continued link with grass roots through the organisation's branches would allow extra-parliamentary leadership respect and support, while the new governing elite in government and parliament risked alienation from the people's grievances. The lack of accountability to constituencies inherent in the interim constitution also increased the risk of MPs being detached from their supporters. In these circumstances, patronage might become the solution to those in parliament.[27] Without constituencies, MPs would have to tow the line of the ANC party machine which would fall directly under Ramaphosa. Perhaps it was in an attempt to pre-empt this possibility that Ramaphosa was offered the key role of chairing the constitutional assembly. The constitutional assembly (made up of the national assembly with Frene Ginwala as Speaker and the senate chaired by Kobie Coetzee and Govan Mbeki as deputy) which would draft the country's democratic constitution, met on 24 May, when Cyril Ramaphosa was elected its chairman.

Mandela's new cabinet was one of national reconciliation and brought together leaders of the ANC, NP and IFP. All races and ethnic groups were significantly represented. However, women were glaringly underrepresented with only three out of 36. Mandela and his new cabinet met for the first time on Monday, 23 May. The installation of the GNU and the new democratic parliament presented the ANC with new challenges. Although it had won the elections, the ANC still set its eyes on the next elections. Party strategists contended that the 1999 elections were important because the party that would win would not be obliged to accommodate other parties, as required for the GNU. The objective of winning the next elections required the strengthening of the ANC outside the GNU, and the decision by Ramaphosa to stay outside the GNU to build the ANC was seen to be part of this strategy. The attainment of this objective was, however, questionable in the light of emerging challenges. Already a number of ANC leaders had been absorbed by the GNU, parliament and the provincial structures. The ANC had also trimmed its staff because of financial constraints and, indeed, because some of its major tasks had been taken up by the new government. Moreover, with democratic structures having been established, the relationship between the ANC, the GNU and parliament also posed its challenges. So too, the relationship between the ANC and its regions and branches.

ENDNOTES

1. '*Ke nako*: now is the time'. *Mayibuye*, March 1993, 14. See also an interview with Popo Molefe in *Learn and Teach*, February 1993, 4–5.
2. 'SACP will not contest elections'. Interview with Essop Pahad. *Barometer*, November 1992, 4.

3. Press statement of the South African National Civic Organisation on the forthcoming democratic and non-racial elections, 24 February 1993.

4. *Mass organisation is the key to victory: organising for elections and for government.* ANC's Department of Political Education, April 1992.

5. Research poll by the Centre for Policy Studies in *Sowetan,* 2 July 1991; Gallup poll in *The Star,* 3 July 1991, projections by Mr Logan Naidoo, a Durban professional consultant, see *The Star,* 20 December 1991. See also polls by the Human Science Research Council and Community Agency for Social Enquiry, *The Star,* 27 May 1992.

6. Statement of the Elections Commission to the International Solidarity Conference, 19–25 February 1993.

7. International Solidarity Conference Declaration, 19–25 February 1993.

8. Election campaign plan, June 1993 – April 1994.

9. 'A better life for all: working together for jobs, peace and freedom'. *ANC Election Manifesto,* 1994.

10. *The future of the youth is with ANC.* ANC election pamphlet. See other election pamphlets: *A message of the ANC to rural communities: A better life for all; Now is the time: Five reasons why you should vote ANC; Peace, freedom and a better life for all.*

11. 'Democracy all the way: ANC's list and manifesto process'. *Mayibuye,* November 1993, 26.

12. See Appendix C for names of candidates.

13. See Appendix D for the names of SACP members in the list.

14. *The Star,* 25 January 1994.

15. *Sunday Nation,* 22 January 1994.

16. *The Star,* 27 March 1994.

17. *City Press,* 13 February 1994.

18. In preparation for running the election the IEC unveiled a budget of R700 million. The administration directorate was apportioned R376 million, the monitoring directorate R163 million and the adjudication directorate R29 million. The rest of the money was reserved for voter education, salaries of commissioners who were to be paid R25 000 a month each (out of R5,5 million), cost for operation access, the daily operations of the IEC and the running of the international liaison office. For its part, the administration directorate would spend R182 million on salaries of the 9000 presiding officers and 270 000 voting and counting officers. The printing of ballot papers contracted to a British company would take up to R35 million, while R59 million would go to the purchase and installation of voting equipment. The installation of telecommunication network was budgeted at R18 million. Transporting material to voting stations would cost R9 million, and R23 million would be used to pay for the use of public and private transport by IEC officials. As for the monitoring division, R63 million would pay for 11 000 monitors and 4000 officers who would staff the IEC's operations offices. R12 million was set aside for monitors' transportation, while R74 million was budgeted for monitoring telecommunications operations. Back-up telecommunications was allocated R11 million. The adjudication division was allocated R29 million, most of which would go to the salaries of judicial officers and staff (*The Star,* 15 April 1994). A R6,5 million media centre was also built at the Gallagher Estate. The IEC also established an election fund to assist parties in the elections. The NP, ANC, DP, PAC and the Freedom Front each received R1,2 million to run their campaigns. Other parties could only be given money after submitting lists of signatures or a scientific opinion poll showing sufficient support. Parties competing at a national level had to submit an opinion poll indicating at least 2 % support to be able to obtain the full amount of R1,2 million, or 10 000 signatures to get half of that. Half of the money available in the electoral fund would be made available to parties after the elections. This fund was later increased to R44 million.

19. Mandela (1994), op cit., 610.

20. *Business Day,* 2 May 1994.

21. See Appendix E for the election results.

22. Apart from the more than 150 000 celebrators who gathered on the lawns, foreign dignitaries who attended Nelson Mandela's presidential inauguration included the American Vice-President Al Gore, accompanied by Bill Clinton's wife, Hillary Clinton; United Nations Secretary-General, Boutros Boutros Ghali; Commonwealth Secretary, Chief Ameka Anyouka; British Secretary for Foreign Affairs, Douglas Hurd; Prince Phillip (husband of Britain's Queen Elizabeth); Mozambican President Joaquim Chissano; Namibian President, Sam Nujoma; Zimbabwean President, Robert Mugabe; Cuban President, Fidel Castro; former Tanzanian president, Julius Nyerere; former Zambian president, Kenneth Kaunda; Palestinian Liberation Organisation leader, Yasser Arafat; Anti-Apartheid Movement leader, Trevor Huddleston; Benazir Bhutto, Pakistan Prime Minister; and many others, who came close to 5000.

23. See Appendix F for cabinet ministers.

24. See Lodge's analysis of the personal and political upbringing of the two leaders in an article, 'Thabo Mbeki and Cyril Ramaphosa, crown princes to Nelson Mandela's throne', *World Policy Journal*, 10(3), 1993, 65–71.

25. Peter Mokaba. Interview.

26. Peter Mokaba. Interview.

27. 'South Africa's election: the second struggle'. *The Economist*, 23 April 1994, 24.

9 Power positioning, negotiations and the making of South Africa's transition from apartheid

The road to South Africa's founding democratic elections was marked by two opposing strategic approaches to transition which were adopted by the country's two major political forces, the NP and the ANC. The former pursued a "transition-from-above" approach characterised by the desire to impose the terms of the transition with broadly outlined stages: liberalisation, democratisation and, possibly, the consolidation of the emerging democracy. The latter pursued a version of decolonisation with the emphasis on democratisation and the transfer of power from the incumbent regime. Within this version of decolonisation an interim government and a constituent assembly had to be established to oversee the birth of democracy and the transfer of power. The presence of these two divergent perspectives in the South African transition was a product of the intense conflict that had preceded negotiations. These differing perspectives were transplanted to the transitional process and manifested themselves in different forms. Before the conclusion of a settlement, the NP and the ANC sought to impose their own versions of transition. Efforts were also made to woo other parties behind these two blocs while simultaneously battling to undermine each other.

The NP's strategy was unambiguously apparent – an endeavour to rally support against the ANC and to dictate the terms of the transitional process, including the nature of the future polity. The strategy to rally support against the ANC began in the late 1980s. With the emergence of the first signs of anti-ANC resistance in the strife-torn areas of Natal and the threatened bantustans of Bophuthatswana and Ciskei, the NP had hoped that it could unite the homelands in a front against the ANC. However, this strategy did not evolve as expected. Only the IFP/KwaZulu government and the governments of Bophuthatswana and Ciskei moved into the informal NP alliance during the early 1990s. This alliance did not last, as it came to be fatally eroded by a string of incidents. The repression meted out to ANC supporters in the three bantustans antagonised ANC grass-roots members against the NP and fuelled mass action campaigns that undermined negotiations. The revelation of the Inkathagate scandal in July 1991 also strained relations between the NP and the IFP. The alliance formally died after the signing of the Record of Understanding in 1992 between the NP government and the ANC. This resulted in the IFP forging ties with the governments of Ciskei and Bophuthatswana, the CP and the AVU in a loose alliance, the Concerned South Africa Group (COSAG), which in late 1993 came to be known as the Freedom Alliance. Abandoned by its allies, the NP was left in the middle of the political spectrum with the DP, against an ANC-led alliance on the left and an IFP alliance on the right. While the NP was not seriously harmed by these developments, as its control of government enabled it to influence the negotiation process, the serious repercussions of an IFP-right-wing alliance and the defection of NP members of parliament to the IFP, gave parties to the right more clout to seek to undermine the transitional process.

Apart from its attempts to build a front against the ANC, the NP government through its cabinet ministers, took unilateral steps to either restructure state assets or to effect fundamental changes that required multi-party consensus. Although he was part of the National Economic Forum, the Minister of Mineral and Energy Affairs, George Bartlett, announced an increase of seven cents in the petrol price in mid-1993, without consulting the negotiation forum. In August of the same year, the Minister of Law and Order, Hernus Kriel, ordered without consultation with the Multi-party Negotiation Forum, the detention of senior PAC leaders. In October, the Minister of Defence, Kobie Coetzee, ordered the raid on an alleged APLA base in Umtata, Transkei, which resulted in the killing of five youths. During that month, the Minister of Housing, Louis Shill, violated an agreement with the National Housing Forum (NHF) and announced the extension of a R7500 capital subsidy on state rental housing stock acquired after 1984, which included arrears in service charges and serviced sites.[1] In spite of having struck a deal with the NHF which was passed into legislation on Interim Housing Arrangements for Housing, and in spite of an explicit agreement that there would be joint moves on this agreement in the future, Shill made another unilateral public announcement of the provisions of this agreement on 30 August 1993, without even mentioning the NHF. Notwithstanding existing negotiations with the NHF, on 23 September he announced in parliament the intention to introduce major policy changes in the safety net to enable the private sector to finance housing, develop equitable policy on rental payment, review the role and activities of government-sponsored organisations and non-governmental organisations, as well as to introduce incentives to promote the sale of existing housing stock.

At the same time, the state embarked on other unilateral actions which indicated its desperate desire to either control the transitional process or to undermine the capacity of a future government to use existing state resources in addressing the challenges of the day. These included the decision to issue identity documents for election purposes before agreement was reached in negotiations, secret attempts to destroy a significant quantity of identity documents belonging to potential black voters, the insistence that the SAP would maintain law and order during elections – a position taken without agreement at the talks, and the decision to go ahead in giving contracts for the distribution of cellular telephones irrespective of ongoing negotiations about the matter.[2] Furthermore, in a clear demonstration of partisanship, the NP government took over the financial administration of the Lebowa government (which had some leanings towards the ANC) after revelations of financial mismanagement, and besieged the Transkei, which openly identified with liberation movements, after a few incidents of attacks by APLA cadres on white civilians. While it had an obligation to take these steps as a government, these contrasted with its lack of action on similar financial mismanagement in other homelands and the brutal repression in homelands such as KwaZulu, Ciskei and Bophuthatswana. A state of emergency was declared in KwaZulu in 1994, only after severe pressure had been exerted on the government, while the dissolution of Bophuthatswana's independence occurred after mass uprising by the homeland's people. State corporations such as the railway, road transport and postal systems were commercialised in the name of economic efficiency, while land assets were disposed of to willing buyers.

This unilateralism demonstrated that, despite the momentum in constitutional negotiations, NP leaders were bent on effecting significant changes so that whatever democracy emerged at the end of the transitional process, it would not have the resources to exercise power. This two-pronged approach to negotiation, promoting a multi-party negotiated transition and taking steps that limited the fruition of democracy, was also prevalent at the multi-party negotiation forum.[3] It assumed different forms, however, and had a different emphasis. The NP sought to slow down the transition or to impose terms of transition, and took positions which sometimes amounted to electioneering. This was demonstrated by the unilateral referendum for whites only on 17 March 1991. Various stalling tactics were also used in the negotiation forum, including the tabling of a string of last-minute constitutional proposals which were rejected by a majority of the parties. This was probably done with a view to buying time to allow the party to maximise its support within the other non-white communities, in particular. Covert operations to destabilise the black communities with a view to undermining popular confidence in the ANC appeared to be condoned, whether or not they were blessed by party officials, primarily because of a lack of decisive action against culprits. Where a spirit of trust and cooperation was needed, some NP officials opted to demonise the ANC and its military wing and to blame it for the carnage in the townships. In this regard, the Ministers of Law and Order and Defence were often inclined to scourge the organisation's leadership as if they were not members of the party negotiating with the movement.

These attempts to rally support behind the NP by discrediting its main protagonist in negotiations were directed to a very restricted white public. This antagonised what was becoming a very sympathetic black audience. Playing to white interests became even more apparent during APLA attacks on whites and, indeed, during the aftermath of the assassination of Chris Hani. Unlike his attitude during the previous three years of his presidency in which thousands of blacks were killed and few culprits were apprehended, De Klerk showed a very strong military face in the wake of the killing of less than ten whites. All the alleged culprits in these cases were arrested. An army blockade was imposed on Transkei which was alleged to harbour APLA guerrillas, and schoolchildren in white suburbs were escorted to schools by military vehicles. In the wake of the assassination of Hani, instead of sympathetic gestures to blacks, more than 20 000 SADF and SAP personnel were deployed to protect what was seen by many to be white interests. In spite of scattered incidents of violence during the commemoration services in what was hailed by many as a week of peaceful mourning, the Ministry of Law and Order and the SABC chose to concentrate on these incidents to vilify the ANC and to repeat their fusillade against the organisation's inability to control its followers.

Against the NP's efforts to impose its version of transition and to rally support against its opponent, the ANC also embarked on counter-initiatives which were most visibly reflected by opposition mass action campaigns. These mobilisation efforts were not, however, without their own problems. While they were important in creating two blocs at the negotiating table which would facilitate speedy agreement on issues, they also created a basis for tensions between the major protagonists in negotiations and antagonised other parties.

Responding to government initiatives, the ANC resorted to mass action to enforce its version of decolonisation that would see transitional mechanisms set in place to oversee democratisation and the transfer of power. It moved outside its tripartite alliance with the SACP and COSATU to rally other organisations into a patriotic front alliance. In spite of its relative success, this alliance too was not as successful as the organisation had anticipated. While the aim of the alliance strategy was to unite as many anti-apartheid organisations as possible around common goals,[4] strains began developing as early as October 1991 before the convention of the Patriotic Front (PF) conference. This began with AZAPO, which was belatedly admitted into an ANC-PAC-led convening committee, calling on tricameral and bantustan parties within the alliance to renounce apartheid as a precondition to their participation in the front. This unilateral action antagonised AZAPO against the ANC and PAC, and ended in AZAPO's exclusion from the front.

However, further tensions developed between the ANC and the PAC which weakened the front. Problems began with the PAC accusing the ANC of violating the provisions of the PF agreement. The PAC accused the ANC of entering into secret undertakings with the government and arranging constitutional negotiations without consulting or informing its PF allies.[5] These alleged undertakings were revealed by Thabo Mbeki when he commented in Botswana on a document, the Declaration of Intent, which would form the basis for negotiations. The accusations and counter-accusations following the PAC's allegations resulted in the PAC walking out from the preparatory meeting of CODESA on 29 November 1991.[6] This was followed by its withdrawal from CODESA negotiations. While the PAC's allegations appeared to be vindicated by the ultimate existence of the

Declaration of Intent, its withdrawal from the initial CODESA negotiations was prompted more by dissension within its own ranks concerning the negotiations. This problem was resolved when the PAC leadership secured a mandate to negotiate at its conference in December 1991. The collapse of CODESA negotiations and the resumption of negotiations at the Negotiating Council eventually paved the way for PAC participation. This, however, did not lead to the resuscitation of the front with the ANC, even though the two parties shared common positions on some issues and sometimes pledged solidarity with each other. This was demonstrated after the detention of PAC leadership and the raid on its offices.

The meeting organised by Robert Mugabe of Zimbabwe in 1991 to reconcile the two movements into a front ended in failure without any clear commitment on the part of the ANC, in particular. While the ANC continued to work together with other PF parties during negotiations and continued to win the bantustans[7] of Transkei, Venda, Kwandebele, Kangwane, QwaQwa, Gazankulu, Lebowa and parliamentary parties, as well as defecting MPs behind it, it appeared reluctant to revive relations with the PAC, primarily because of what it perceived as the PAC's acts of subversion. The PAC's decision to go it alone in negotiating with the government and its particular insistence on the restructuring of CODESA negotiations were seen by the ANC as a direct assault on its initiative on negotiations. This feeling was clearly reflected in Mandela's opening address to the PF meeting of 29 October 1992, where he said that PF leaders should "resist with all the energy we can muster the notion that we should enter into protracted negotiations on a new negotiating forum in order to accommodate certain groupings which for reasons of myopia decided not to board the train when it left the station many months ago". It would appear that the ANC's anger with the PAC did not stem from the latter's actions, since calls for the revival of the front had been made long before the PAC's negotiation with the government. Rather, it was power politics that seemed to underline the squabbles between the two movements. ANC leaders particularly feared that the PAC sought to achieve equal control of the front. Moreover, the ANC did not want to be constrained by agreements with the PAC. It wanted to negotiate without having to consult and agree with the PAC on every issue, including procedural matters.

Apart from its attempt to cement an anti-apartheid front against the NP government, the ANC, though it sought to avoid a public showdown with the NP, eventually found itself dragged into acting like its rival. Despite its foresight in preparing for the elections, the organisation began by earnestly attempting to avoid antagonising its main opposition in the negotiations. From Mandela's description of De Klerk as "a man of integrity" to proposals of a government of national unity with the NP, the ANC even risked serious criticism by its militant supporters to smooth relations with its antagonist in negotiations. However, the continued failure of the government to stem the spiralling violence in the townships, allegations of it stalling the negotiation process, its calling for a white referendum and the corruption scandals created conditions in which the ANC began to nourish its electioneering machine. Inasmuch as the white referendum was a test of white support for De Klerk, the ANC's mass action campaigns which were invigorated in the aftermath of these events also sought to test popular support for its positions.

The intrinsic danger in this undeclared contest was its retarding effect on the process of negotiation, which still had to lay down the rules for electioneering.[8] The two parties sometimes embarked on party political contests that overshadowed achievements made in the talks. Thus talking and contesting became the major characteristic of South Africa's road to democracy, which undermined, to a great extent, the basis for unity and left the main parties vulnerable to the parties to the extreme right and left who were opposed to the conclusion of a settlement. This weakness was resolved after Cyril Ramaphosa and Roelf Meyer introduced a new style of political engagement, bilateral negotiation, which smoothed relations between the two parties. These new-found relations and the compromises reached in negotiations, as well as a number of intervening events, led to the conclusion of a settlement. The ANC and the NP refined their respective views of the South African transition with both moving towards an agreed-on centre stage. On the one hand, the NP abandoned its "transition-from-above" perspective in which it sought to determine the terms and the nature of the outcome of negotiations. On the other hand, the ANC departed from its "transfer of power" version in favour of "power-sharing". It successfully insisted on the installation of an interim government (the TEC) and the election of a constituent assembly as vehicles towards a new democratic dispensation.

The conclusion of a settlement was also heralded by mass action campaigns which were conditioned by the government's unilateral action during the period of transition and its failure to resolve the escalating violence. Mass action campaigns brought a sense of urgency to negotiations. Earlier, the anti-VAT mass action in 1991 demonstrated to the government the futility of unilateral action and conditioned it to multi-party decision making during the period of transition. Mass action campaigns at local level forced white municipalities into agreements with surrounding townships. The mass action campaign that followed the breakdown of CODESA negotiations in May 1992, as well as the Boipatong and Bisho massacres, produced the Record of Understanding in which the government fully committed itself to a democratic transition from apartheid. The demonstrations in April 1993 following the assassination of Chris Hani produced a commitment by parties to 27 April 1994 as the election date, while mass uprising in Bophuthatswana finally buried the myth of the independence of homelands. The latter also undermined the strength of the boycotting Freedom Alliance and allowed political freedom in Bophuthatswana.

Alongside compromises and mass action, calculations by the major parties' leadership were also significant in steering the country to the type of settlement it reached. In the midst of the uncertainty and insecurity that accompanied the transitional process there were no definite indications that South Africa could not revert to authoritarianism. Had it not been for the resolve and determination of De Klerk, no leader of a ruling party could have continued the transitional process against the storms of party-driven mass action campaigns and the ceaseless attacks on white civilians by APLA members. Against the option of reverting to authoritarian rule, De Klerk chose to press forward to negotiate a settlement at the expense of losing his traditional white support base. To him, an agreement on constitutional principles, a government of national unity and a guarantee for the security of civil service jobs was an adequate trade-off to the ANC's demand for an interim government and the election of a constituent assembly. Nelson Mandela's leadership was also important in securing the suspension of the armed struggle to boost negotiations. His conciliatory approach to De Klerk (which sometimes soured) and the white community in general was important in allaying fears of, and the lack of confidence in a future black-dominated government. Mandela exercised good judgement at crucial moments, which though not always well-received by ANC supporters, was important for the success of negotiations. Following the assassination of Hani and at a time when ANC supporters were calling for retaliation, Mandela appealed for calm and argued that the crisis called for an urgent decision on an election date. Furthermore, the compromises he made to the Freedom Alliance in 1994 were important in wooing these parties to a settlement.

Contrary to scepticism by theorists on transition to democracy who see liberation movements as antithetical to successful democracies, South Africa reached its founding democratic elections with the help of the ANC as a liberation movement. It was not simply its character as a liberation movement which mattered but its approach to the transitional process. The fact that it sought to represent everyone and the alliances it built with COSATU, the SACP, SANCO and a variety of civil society organisations were crucial in facilitating a common approach to negotiation. This made it easy for speedy and broadly acceptable agreements to be reached in negotiations.

ENDNOTES

1. National Housing Forum. Letter to the Minister of National Housing and Public Works, Louis Shill, 15 October 1993.
2. See the draft joint statement – ANC, COSATU and the South African government, 29 September 1993.
3. John Saul captured this simultaneity of the negotiation moment and the post-apartheid moment in a paper entitled *Structural reform: a model for the revolutionary transformation of South Africa*, presented at the Ruth First Memorial Colloquium, University of the Western Cape, 17–18 August 1992, 4.
4. For a further discussion of the ANC and alliance building see Cargill, J. Anti-apartheid alliance. *Work In Progress*, 65, April 1990, 16–19.
5. Gora Ebrahim. Interview. For a full discussion of this and the PAC's overall approach to negotiations see Rantete, J. *Liberation and negotiation: the PAC in the South African transition.* Centre for Policy Studies Transition Series, 5(2), 1992. See also Rantete, J. The non-CODESA wing of the Patriotic Front, the PAC and AZAPO. *South Africa Foundation Review*, December 1992. For another incisive analysis of the PAC, see Nyatsumba, K.M. AZAPO and the PAC: revolutionary watchdogs? *South African Review*, 6, Johannesburg: Ravan, 1992.
6. It is important to note that the PAC's allegation pertaining to minutes of the front-line states meeting of 20 November 1991, where Mbeki allegedly commented on the declaration of intent, was not only dismissed by the ANC (see ANC press statement on PAC statement and walkout, 1 December 1991), but also by the Chairman of the Front-line States Ambassadors, H.B. Lungu, in

the following words: "It has never been our practice to record minutes of such meetings. Therefore the so-called minutes cannot be of the Front-line States meeting referred to." Permanent Mission of Zambia to the United Nations Press Release, New York, 29 November 1991.

7. See Joint press release of ANC and homeland leaders, 15 March 1991. This statement was issued after the ANC's meeting with Kwandebele, Lebowa, Gazankulu, Kangwane and QwaQwa. Other separate meetings were held with these parties, such as the meeting with Intando Ye Sizwe on 18 January 1991.

8. Sparks, A. An election would ease the transition to democracy. *The Star,* 5 August 1992.

10 Conclusion

From apartheid to democracy: the ANC's road to power

While many African liberation movements attained power through a decolonisation process in which colonial regimes handed over power or facilitated democratic transfers, the ANC's road to power was relatively unique. Its return to the country after 30 years in exile was not a gateway to power. Owing to the internal nature of the colonial system pertaining to South Africa, the movement had to enter into a protracted negotiated transition to help transform the country from a white oligarchic apartheid system to a democratic dispensation. Majority rule was not a pre-given but a central aspect of the negotiations. Such negotiations had to be multipolar in nature, bringing into the theatre diverse political parties, some whose agenda was to frustrate the fruition of the democratic process. Moreover, the simultaneity of negotiating and building organisational structures posed their own unique challenges alongside the destabilising effects of violence. However, in spite of these relatively unique South African conditions, the ANC's organisational and strategic approach to power can be described as representing a significant achievement, but one set against weaknesses and limitations.

The ANC was able, despite problems in its recruitment campaign caused by objective (the spiralling violence) and subjective (e.g. poor planning) conditions, to create a mass-based organisation in South Africa. A relatively efficient bureaucracy made up of a head office, regions and branches was set up which, to a certain extent, allowed the participation of its membership. The convening of conferences and workshops at national, regional and local levels to deal with the myriad issues of the organisation, including negotiations and policy, served, in spite of certain limitations, to engender a culture of democracy unknown within a majority of South African parties. But organisational development within the context of a negotiated transition was not always unproblematic. Effecting democratic practice in an organisation with a million members was always contradicted by the vicissitude of negotiation which needed speedy decision making. Ebullient internal democracy was also undermined by the remnants of democratic centralism of exile leadership and the paternalistic semi-monarchic style of prison leadership. Democratic practice at grass-roots level was also not often successful in escaping tendencies by activists to mesmerise and dictate meetings. Moreover, seeking to effect organisational democracy against the background of revelations of past misdeeds and human rights' violations tended to impact negatively on existing innovations. Added to this, internal tensions, caused either by personality differences or differences over strategic issues, continued to hound the organisation both at national and local levels. Cooperation within the Tripartite Alliance and with other organisational formations falling within the ANC's sphere of influence, also came under strain as a result of the paternalistic tendency of the movement's leadership. Allied organisations were often informed about decisions on crucial strategic issues without being consulted, leading to parties such as SANCO and SASCO publicly defying instructions from headquarters. On the ground, a majority of branches had become paralysed by the intimidatory element of violence, while others were ailing or no longer operational because of poor attendance at meetings, ineffective branch executive committees and mismanagement of branch affairs. Notwithstanding these weaknesses, the ANC neither came close to splintering nor to degenerating into organisational paralysis. Its continued organisational homogeneity and the ability to go beyond potentially menacing crises were due to various factors.

The insistence on remaining a liberation movement representing all the people of South Africa was of utmost importance and played a pivotal role in sustaining the continued support of different class interests. Although apartheid had been significantly removed to justify this support, there was unanimity about the need to retain the liberation movement character of the organisation until the creation of democracy in the country. In this scenario, a number of policy positions deriving their principles from the Freedom Charter played a central unifying role with their universal provisions which catered for a variety of sectors.[1] The leadership of Nelson Mandela also played a crucial role in sustaining the unity of the organisation: as a living legend, an internationally respected father of the anti-apartheid movement and a man with exceptional leadership qualities,[2] he inspired a deep-rooted loyalty that overwhelmed internal divisions and hostilities. Notwithstanding some mistakes and the alleged attempts to sideline him, Nelson Mandela remained a father figure whose leadership of the organisation remained beyond challenge.

Organisational problems that almost weakened the organisation also received serious attention, with attempts being made to address them. Regional executive committees were strengthened with the creation of additional portfolios and the bringing in of new members. Several committees that focused on a diversity of topics – from organisational to policy-related matters – were created to cope with the immense challenges that were facing the organisation on a daily basis. Relations between regions and the national office on the one hand, and regions and branches on the other hand, were also remarkably improved. Members of the regions were allowed to sit in on National Executive Committee and National Working Committee meetings. NEC members were made responsible for regions on a rotational basis. In their relations with branches, regions facilitated the creation of subregions and zones for the efficient coordination of branches. Furthermore, subcommittees established at national level were replicated both at regional and branch levels.

Administrative hurdles that marred the organisation's reconstruction programme were also gradually overcome. Activists who had occupied positions because of their history in the struggle were included in an educative process to empower them with appropriate skills. A tendency also developed among ANC members to elect people to positions on merit rather than solely on the history of their role in the struggle. The overhauling of the administrative apparatus of the ANC saw headquarters and the office of the Secretary-General in particular, becoming more efficient. Branch membership lists were computerised, making it feasible to locate members and to know who had not renewed their membership. In the PWV region, the computerisation of these lists by Giles Mulholland made it possible to know, *inter alia*, how many men and women were in the ANC and which branches had the highest percentage of people with identity documents.

The ANC also succeeded because of its ability to address its shortcomings and to close obvious fissures. The appointment of a commission of inquiry into the treatment of prisoners in its camps, which was only conceded after strenuous pressure by human rights lobbyists, was an important example of this ability to be self-critical. Several commissions were also appointed to look into other organisational matters. A commission of inquiry was appointed after the suspension of the PWV Women's League, following a march by a group of women to the organisation's headquarters. The crisis with self-defence units in the Vaal also saw the appointment of a commission of inquiry headed by Chris Hani. Although it was difficult to enforce discipline against high-ranking officials, disciplinary measures were taken against certain individuals who violated the ANC's code of conduct. An example was the suspension for three months of the Western Cape Regional Committee member and Chairperson of the Kensington branch, Mr Dawood Khan, for allegedly shouting anti-Semitic statements during a demonstration outside the Israeli embassy in Cape Town on 19 March 1993.[3] ANC Eastern Transvaal Regional Secretary, Joe Nkuna, was expelled from office after numerous warnings for failing to perform his duties, suspicious dealings with the security forces and misconduct and corruption which involved soliciting thousands of rands from fraternal organisations and individuals.[4] As Lodge concluded in an article on the ANC, the renaissance of the ANC in South Africa was a story of mixed achievement.[5] The success of establishing organisational structures and sustaining their operation continued to be balanced against an unpleasant state of organisational problems produced by both objective and subjective reality.

While organisational reconstruction and mobilisation were important in positioning the ANC, it was its strategic approach to a negotiated transition to democracy which was even more crucial. The fact that the multi-party negotiations, bolstered by the bilateral agreement between the ANC and the government, were able to produce tangible products such as draft legislation on transitional mechanisms to prepare for elections and a fairly detailed interim constitution in the course of three years, was a significant break-through. The ANC's efforts to facilitate the re-acceptance of South Africa back into the international community by means of sport and the lifting of sanctions, were commendable. This also applied to the ANC's attempt to foster, alongside negotiations, the democratisation of the country in such areas as the composition of the broadcasting authority and the setting up of multi-party forums to deal with housing, local government, economy, education and the provision of different services.

In spite of these successes, certain weaknesses continued to mar the organisation's approach to power. It was clear immediately after its unban-ning that the ANC, notwithstanding the Harare Declaration, lacked a frame-work within which to confront the transitional process and the shrewd footwork of the government, as it sought to translate the dissolution of apartheid to its credit. This, in turn, produced different and sometimes inharmonious strategic perspectives within the movement. Although these perspectives cannot be neatly compartmentalised it appears that two broad schools of thought existed: the one was revolutionary and emphasised the centrality of the armed struggle and mass insurrection; the other was the negotiation school of thought, which saw negotiation as far more crucial than other forms of struggle. Different perspectives existed within the negotiation school of thought, which were informed to a considerable extent by the historical background of three segments of ANC leadership – prison, exile and internal. These elements of thought were not juxtaposed in a watertight fashion, but their presence within the ANC produced inconsistent and sometimes confusing approaches by the organisation. This lack of coherence was accounted for by the confusion between strategic man-oeuvres and compromises of fundamental importance in negotiations. Con-ventional wisdom within the organisation seemed to suggest that certain compromises such as the unilateral suspension of the armed struggle were strategically necessary. So too, were certain compromises made in relation to the evolution of the transitional process, particularly the installation of an interim government and elections to a constituent assembly, as well as certain compromises in relation to the interim constitution. Indeed, shifts in positions on the transitional mechanisms were informed by the fledgling understanding of the issues which were developing with the unfolding of the process.

The crucial question with respect to these strategic shifts, some of which amounted to misjudgements of capacity, was not whether they were neces-sary or not. Rather, the issue was whether they made a significant contribu-tion to the attainment of the objective of a democratic dispensation capable of extending, as speedily as possible, equality, empowerment and rewards to the majority of black South Africans. Although they were aimed at heralding a speedy movement towards a settlement, these shifts – in particular certain offers aimed at creating a fortress against future destabilisation by counter-revolutionaries – pessimistically indicated that the woes of apartheid inflicted on black South Africans would take time to be redressed. Agreeing to a power-sharing deal in which minority parties would be given a share in the running of the country for five years, appeared set to affect the speed and vigour needed to speedily redress past injustices.

Arguably, the ANC had to compromise on these matters because of the dictates of reality. However, there also seemed to be some degree of misjudgement of capacity – a level of sobriety which contrasted sharply with the mood of enthusiasm and preparedness by its supporters to bring change through their feet in the streets. Notwithstanding the limitations of an insurrectionary strategy on the eve of negotiation with the government, a significant degree of stalemate produced by the interplay of diverse forces, such as internal mass struggles and international solidarity, had been created that could have launched a bolder strategic encounter with the government on negotiations. Given the state of politics in 1989 and 1990 when the momentum towards democratic polities was at its apogee worldwide, there was little reason to shy away from insisting on the demilitarisation of the South African society as a precondition to negotiation. This could have contributed to the reduction of violence which came to inform some of the ANC's major compromises in negotiations.

The problem here appeared to lie in the ANC's weakened conceptualisation of negotiation, which tended to rely on the goodwill of the state. The road from the Harare Declaration to the Groote Schuur meeting appeared to have been travelled so fast so as to leave little room for ANC strategists to equip themselves with comparative literature on transitions and negotiations. The fact that negotiation is a terrain of struggle and not a gateway to freedom appeared to be taken for granted, in spite of contentions to the contrary by ANC leaders. The organisation was undoubtedly complacent that despite manifestations of resistance, world trends pointed to the imminent inevitable demise of apartheid and that the NP government would unavoidably negotiate itself out of power. This accounted for the strategy on negotiating with the NP, which tended to accentuate harmonious engagement. Hence Mandela's conciliatory remarks that De Klerk was a man of integrity, words which came to hound him.

It is arguably true that these positions were consciously taken to entice the government into negotiation and to give it confidence in the transitional process, so as to hasten the conclusion of a settlement. However, the consequence of a strategy that placed too much emphasis on negotiation and the politics of its give and take, was the dissipation of the significance of other forms of struggle. Not only were popular mass struggles or mass action activities left to degenerate into a "tap" that could be turned on and off at times congenial to the ANC. The armed struggle, too, whether due to logistical problems or not, no longer had room in this scenario. Admittedly, the impotence of these other forms of struggle was equally caused by existing reality and developments beyond the ANC's control. Armed struggle could not be contemplated when fruitful understanding was emerging among parties. Uncoordinated mass actions were also not perfectly congruous with the spirit of negotiation and thus had to be employed only at certain times. Organising the underground network had become purposeless in the event of legality, while sanctions began crumbling even before the ANC gave signals for their lifting.

Unlike the above, and in a more conspicuous way, the effects of a poor negotiation strategy were clearly evident in the ANC's difficulty to come to terms with the spiralling violence, which in all manifestations sought to destabilise the ANC's popular support base and undermine the democratic process. The challenge was not only to devise appropriate measures to stem the carnage wherever it happened. The state security apparatus, known for years for its repressive and counter-democratic practices, also demanded serious attention. Without having secured a mutually binding ceasefire with the government *de novo*, their complicity in the violence created a major headache for the ANC, as its countermeasures were always rendered ineffective. This was to be confirmed by Mandela in his autobiography when he wrote "of all the issues that hindered the peace process, none was more devastating and frustrating than the escalation of violence in the country".[6]

In conclusion, notwithstanding the zigzags of the transitional process, the ANC's decision to negotiate and to reach a settlement with the South African government within the span of three years was a historic achievement that not only put apartheid to rest, but firmly positioned the country and the rest of Southern Africa on the road to peace and democracy. The fact that this was achieved without foreign mediation after years of intense conflict in which the whole world took a stance against apartheid, created a precedent unknown in world history. The critical challenge to the ANC at the conclusion of the negotiated settlement did not, however, lie in winning South Africa's first democratic elections, important though this was. Rather, it lay in building democracy from the ashes of apartheid and in defying African precedents of neocolonialism, economic retrogression, corruption and nepotism past the day of the election victory.

ENDNOTES

1. Marais, H. Sticking together. *New Era,* Spring, 1991, 14.
2. Mandela, N. *No easy walk to freedom.* London: Heinemann, 1989. See the foreword by Walter Sisulu.
3. Disciplinary hearing by the Regional Committee of the ANC Western Cape in relation to the conduct of Mr Dawood Khan, 7 April 1993.
4. *The Star,* 14 December 1992. See *The Star,* 24 January 1992, where Mr Nkuna threatened in abusive language to "blow up" a garage owner who apparently discovered a gun in his car and reported the matter to the police.
5. Lodge, T. (1992), op cit., 73.
6. Mandela, N. (1994), op cit., 578.

Comrade Nelson Mandela, ANC President and South Africa's first
democratically elected president *(CDC Photo Unit)*

ANC PRESIDENTS

Albert Luthuli
(Mayibuye Centre)

Oliver Tambo
(ANC Dept. of Information & Publicity)

Nelson Mandela
(CDC Photo Unit)

Thabo Mbeki
(CDC Photo Unit)

Walter Sisulu, ANC veteran
(CDC Photo Unit)

Joe Slovo, SACP Chairman and ANC chief
strategist who coined the 'sunset clause'
(CDC Photo Unit)

Chris Hani, SACP Chairman and ANC
senior leader
(ANC Dept. of Information & Publicity)

Cyril Ramaphosa, ANC Secretary-General
and chief negotiator of the constitutional
negotiations *(CDC Photo Unit)*

Winnie Madikizela-Mandela, President of
the ANC Women's League
(CDC Photo Unit)

Harry Gwala, the lion of Natal Midlands and
Chairman of the ANC Natal Midlands
(CDC Photo Unit)

Joe Modise, Head of MK
(CDC Photo Unit)

Popo Molefe, UDF leader and later
Premier of North-West Province
(CDC Photo Unit)

Jay Naidoo, COSATU General Secretary
(CDC Photo Unit)

Raymond Suttner, ANC strategist and
political education coordinator
(CDC Photo Unit)

Tokyo Sexwale, Chairman of the ANC PWV
Region and later Premier of Gauteng
(CDC Photo Unit)

Ngoako Ramathlodi, Chairman of the ANC
Northern Transvaal Region and later
Premier of Northern Province
(ANC Dept. of Information & Publicity)

Oupa Gqozo, military leader of the Ciskei
(CDC Photo Unit)

Nelson Ramodike, leader of the Lebowa
government
(CDC Photo Unit)

Murphy Morobe, UDF activist and
Chairman of CODESA
(CDC Photo Unit)

Valli Moosa, UDF activist and ANC
constitutional negotiator
(CDC Photo Unit)

F.W. de Klerk, National Party leader and State President of South Africa up to April 1994 *(CDC Photo Unit)*

Tertius Delport, National Party negotiator at CODESA *(CDC Photo Unit)*

Judge Richard Goldstone, Chairman of the Goldstone Commission appointed to investigate causes of violence *(CDC Photo Unit)*

Mangosuthu Buthelezi, President of the Inkatha Freedom Party *(CDC Photo Unit)*

Leadership of the Tripartite Alliance represented here by
Joe Slovo (SACP), Alfred Nzo (ANC) and Jay Naidoo (COSATU)
(The Star)

A joyous moment as ANC President Nelson Mandela meets his
long-time friend and former ANC President, Oliver Tambo
(CDC Photo Unit)

Shell House — the ANC's headquarters in
Plein Street, Johannesburg
(The Star)

An impi of Inkatha Freedom Party supporters in fighting spirit
(CDC Photo Unit)

Peace summit between the ANC and the IFP on attempts to end the violence
(CDC Photo Unit)

A victim of train violence in Johannesburg
(CDC Photo Unit)

ANC Youth League President,
Peter Mokaba
(CDC Photo Unit)

Angry ANC supporters in Sebokeng calling
for vengeance against perpetrators of
violence following the Boipatong
massacre. Nelson Mandela addressed
this rally (CDC Photo Unit)

President of the ANC Women's League, Winnie Madikizela-Mandela,
addressing a meeting
(CDC Photo Unit)

Nelson Mandela at one of the many rallies he addressed after his release from prison
(CDC Photo Unit)

Mass mobilisation to demand the formation of a constituent assembly to
draft a democratic constitution for the country
(CDC Photo Unit)

Unions mobilising for change and speedy negotiations at CODESA
(*CDC Photo Unit*)

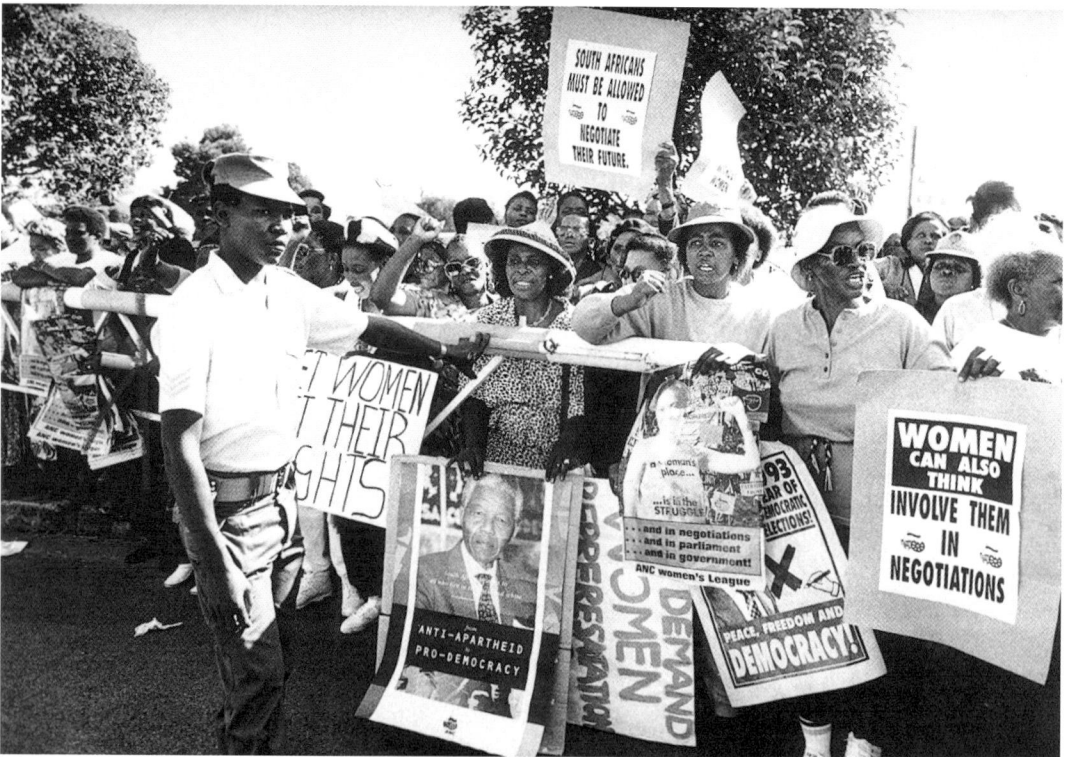

Women's groups demanding representation in negotiations
(*The Star*)

Chris Hani, 'the people's hero'
(*CDC Photo Unit*)

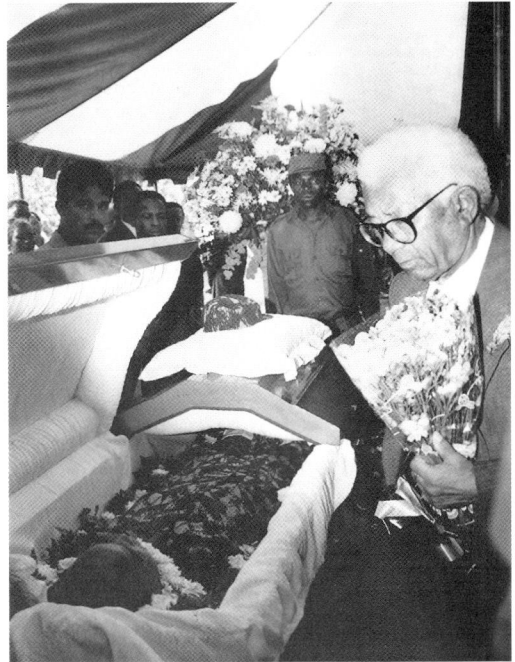

ANC veteran Walter Sisulu at the funeral of
Comrade Oliver Tambo (*CDC Photo Unit*)

Tokyo Sexwale attending the funeral of Chris Hani at the FNB Stadium, Soweto
(*CDC Photo Unit*)

Umkhonto we Sizwe's last march before integration into the South African National Defence Force (*CDC Photo Unit*)

IFP supporters wielding dangerous traditional weapons
(*Dynamic Images*)

Nelson Mandela at one of the election rallies
(CDC Photo Unit)

The first democratic elections on 27 April 1994
(CDC Photo Unit)

The ANC's election victory and the famous Madiba dance
(CDC Photo Unit)

A sitting of South Africa's first democratically elected parliament, Cape Town
(CDC Photo Unit)

Appendices

Appendix A

Members of the National Executive Committee of the African National Congress as at July 1991

1. Nelson Mandela: President **
2. Walter Sisulu: Deputy President **
3. Cyril Ramaphosa: Secretary-General**
4. Jacob Zuma: Deputy Secretary-General**
5. Oliver Tambo: National Chairman **
6. Thomas Nkobi: Treasurer-General **
7. Chris Hani * **
8. Thabo Mbeki **
9. Harry Gwala *
10. Kadar Asmal
11. Thozamile Botha
12. Cheryl Carolus *
13. Jeremy Cronin *
14. Ebrahim Ismail Ebrahim *
15. Pallo Jordan **
16. Ronnie Kasrils * **
17. Ahmed Kathrada *
18. Patrick Lekota **
19. Saki Macozoma
20. Mac Maharaj *
21. Rocky Malebane Metsing
22. Winnie Mandela
23. Trevor Manuel **
24. Gill Marcus *
25. Barbara Masekela **
26. Raymond Mhlaba *
27. Wilton Mkwayi
28. Andrew Mlangeni
29. Joe Modise **
30. Peter Mokaba
31. Popo Molefe **
32. Ruth Mompati
33. Billy Nair *
34. Joe Nhlanhla **
35. Mohammed Valli Moosa * **
36. Elias Motsoaledi *
37. Mendi Msimang
38. Sydney Mufamadi * **
39. Sister Bernard Ncube
40. Joel Netshitenzhe * **
41. John Nkadimeng * **
42. Siphiwe Nyanda *
43. Alfred Nzo **
44. Dullah Omar
45. Aziz Pahad
46. Albie Sachs
47. Reginald September *
48. Gertrude Shope
49. Albertina Sisulu
50. Zola Skweyiya **
51. Joe Slovo * **
52. Marion Sparg
53. Arnold Stofile
54. Raymond Suttner *
55. Steve Tshwete **
56. Mcwayiseni Zulu

*   Denotes SACP members
** Denotes members of the National Working Committee

With the untimely death of Chris Hani and Oliver Tambo in April 1993, the NEC decided in its meeting of 30 August 1993 to bring in Charles Ngqakula, Penuel Maduna and Josiah Jele to fill their vacancies. The NEC also co-opted Sankie Nkondo and Nkosazana Zuma. The vacant post of National Chairman was filled by Thabo Mbeki.

Appendix B

Summary of the 1993 interim constitution

Official language

The following were agreed as official languages: Afrikaans, English, Sindebele, Sipedi, Sesotho, Seswati, Xitsonga, Setswana, Luvenda, Sixhosa and Sizulu.

The right to vote

Read with the Electoral Act, this clause provided that any South African citizen over the age of 18 could vote unless he or she was of unsound mind or in jail for a serious crime.

Fundamental human rights

This provided for equality before the law regardless of race, gender, religion, belief, culture and language; the right to life; respect for human dignity; freedom and security of the person – no detention without trial and no torture; freedom of speech, of assembly, of association, of movement and the right to live anywhere; freedom of political activity; taking lawful action to protect one's rights; having the right, if arrested, to bail and to a lawyer and to challenge the arrest in court as well as have a fair and speedy trial; workers have the right to join trade unions, take part in collective bargaining and even strike; the right to property; children have the right to be cared for and not abused; the right to basic education and equal access to schools, technikons and universities.

Parliament

It would have two chambers – the national assembly and the senate. The national assembly would have 400 members made up of 200 national members (elected on proportional basis) and 200 provincial MPs drawn from the provinces they resided in. The national assembly would be presided over by a Speaker assisted by a Deputy Speaker. The Speaker would only vote (casting vote) if the numbers of those who support and oppose a particular decision were equal. If an MP resigned from a party, he would be obliged also to resign from parliament. The senate would be made up of 90 members, ten drawn from each of the nine provincial legislatures. Once elected to senate, these members were obliged to resign from the provincial legislature. The senate would be presided over by a president assisted by a deputy president. When the senate and the national assembly held joint meetings, the president of the senate would preside.

Adopting the final constitution

The constitutional assembly would be obliged to abide by constitutional principles contained in Schedule 4 of the interim constitution. The constitutional court would decide whether the new constitution complied with these principles. This chapter also deals with what should be done in the event of a deadlock in the constitution-making body.

The President and the cabinet

The first cabinet would be a government of national unity. There would be an executive president accompanied by deputies and cabinet ministers. The first president under the interim constitution would be elected by the national assembly, while future presidents would be elected by the national assembly and the senate sitting together. The President would be head of the state and government. While he would be given wide powers, he would take his decisions in consultation with the cabinet and his deputies. Every party with 80 or more seats in the national assembly would be entitled to appoint an executive deputy president. If no party had 80 or more seats, then the party with the highest number of seats and the one following it would each have a deputy president. The cabinet would include the President, his deputies and up to 27 ministers. It would take decisions by consensus. Every party with 20 or more seats would be entitled to a number of seats in the cabinet in the same proportion to the number of seats in the 400 seat national assembly. If parliament passed a vote of no confidence in the President, he should resign. If such motion was passed on both the President and the cabinet, a general election should be held. But if parliament passed a vote of no confidence in just the cabinet, the President could either form a new cabinet or call a general election.

Justice and the courts

The judiciary would be independent and no government would interfere with the judicial process. There would be a constitutional court presided over by a court president and ten judges who would serve terms not longer than seven years. This court would preside on all constitutional matters, including the legality of Acts of parliament. The president of the constitutional court would be appointed by the State President, with the advice of the Chief Justice. A Judicial Service Commission, headed by the Chief Justice and including the president of the constitutional court, provincial judge presidents, advocates, attorneys, senators and legal academics, would nominate six of the ten judges of the constitutional court. The rest would be nominated by the State President in consultation with the cabinet and the constitutional court.

The Public Protector and the Human Rights Commission

This would be a legal person who would investigate complaints regarding government maladministration, abuse of power by any official and corruption. He would make recommendations to the appropriate authorities. The

Human Rights Commission, made up of 11 people and approved by parliament, would promote respect for and recommend measures in favour of human rights. It would also investigate violations of such rights and help affected people.

Provincial governments

There would be nine provinces, namely Northern Transvaal, Pretoria-Witwatersrand-Vaal, Eastern Transvaal, North West, Northern Cape, Western Cape, Eastern Cape, the Orange Free State and KwaZulu-Natal. Provinces would have their own provincial legislatures and executive governments. The number of seats in each provincial legislature would be calculated by counting the total number of votes cast in the province and dividing them by 50 000. No provincial legislature would be allowed to have less than 30 or more than 100 seats. The Provincial Executive Council (provincial cabinet) would be made up of the Premier and ten members from the provincial legislature. Any party with ten or more seats in the provincial legislature would get seats in the council in proportion to the number of its provincial legislative MPs. Like the central cabinet, the Provincial Executive Councils would take decisions by consensus.

Provincial governments would exercise powers over the following matters: agriculture; casinos, including gambling and racing; cultural affairs; education; health services; housing; language policy; local government; nature conservation; police; provincial public media; public transport; regional planning and development; road traffic regulation; roads, including tourism, trade and industrial promotion; traditional authorities; urban and rural development; and welfare services.

With respect to the exercise of these powers by provincial governments, parliament reserved the right to make laws which these governments would be obliged to obey. Parliament could set national norms and standards, or make provinces conform to national economic policies. A provincial law could be overridden by a national law if it materially prejudiced the economic, health or security interests of the country or another province. A provincial legislature would be able to claim part of the income tax and VAT generated in its province, although the amount would be set by parliament, taking into account the national interest and balancing a particular province's needs against those of others. Provinces could also have their own constitutions, which nevertheless should not conflict with the South African constitution. Such provincial constitutions could only be approved by the constitutional assembly.

Local government and traditional authorities

Local government would be restructured in two phases:

- Phase one would begin in February 1994 and would be carried out in either one of the two options, namely a) existing racial councils would dissolve and form one new non-racial council with equal numbers of councillors chosen by statutory and non-statutory organisations, b) racial councils could remain in place and an overarching non-racial structure would be formed, also on a fifty-fifty basis, to gradually take over more and more functions.

- Phase two would begin with local elections. Sixty per cent of councillors would be chosen on a ward basis while 40 % would be chosen on proportional basis. Ward councillors would be divided in half: 30 % of the total would come from existing white, coloured and Indian communities and the rest from black areas.

Each province would have a provincial House of Traditional Leaders, which would advise and should be consulted by the provincial governments on matters concerning traditional authorities, indigenous laws and customs. The nine provincial houses would together elect 20 representatives to form a Council of Traditional Leaders, with similar powers to advise and be consulted by parliament.

Finance

This chapter provides for the setting up of a Financial and Fiscal Commission chaired by a presidential appointee, to advise parliament and the provinces on financial matters. It would include representatives of the provinces and seven people nominated by the President on the advice of the cabinet.

Public Service Commission and the public service

This body would recommend, direct and hold inquiries into how the public service and government departments should be run. It would set conditions of service for public servants and establish a code of conduct for the public service. Its members may not hold office in political parties. Provinces may have their own similar commissions. The public service, which should be broadly representative of the country, would be obliged to be impartial and to serve the government of the day loyally.

The police and army

There would be a national police force divided into nine provincial forces. The State President would appoint a Commissioner of Police. Provinces would approve or veto regional commissioners. The National Defence Force (NDF) would include all members of the SADF, the defence forces of the TBVC states and the armed forces of all the various political movements. The President would be the commander-in-chief of the NDF and would appoint the chief of the NDF. The NDF would have a permanent and a part-time reserve force. No permanent member of the NDF may hold any political party office.

Chapter 14

This chapter deals with transitional arrangements to ensure continuity in the various arms of the state as the old constitution is phased out and the new one introduced.

Appendix C

The ANC's nominations list for the national assembly

1. Nelson Mandela
2. Cyril Ramaphosa
3. Thabo Mbeki
4. Joe Slovo
5. Pallo Jordan
6. Jay Naidoo
7. Ahmed Kathrada
8. Ronnie Kasrils
9. Sydney Mufamadi
10. Albertina Sisulu
11. Thozamile Botha
12. Steve Tshwete
13. Bantu Holomisa
14. Jeff Radebe
15. Dullah Omar
16. Popo Molefe
17. Mac Maharaj
18. Moses Mayekiso
19. Chris Dlamini
20. Trevor Manuel
21. Zola Skweyiya
22. Gertrude Shope
23. Kadar Asmal
24. Joe Modise
25. Arnold Stofile
26. Mohammed Valli Moosa
27. Peter Mokaba
28. John Nkadimeng
29. Essop Pahad
30. Raymond Suttner
31. Winnie Mandela
32. Tito Mboweni
33. Thenjiwe Mthintso
34. Baleka Kgositsile
35. Blade Nzimande
36. Ruth Mompati
37. Aziz Pahad
38. Penuel Maduna
39. Billy Nair
40. Mavivi Manzini
41. Phillip Dexter
42. Prince James Mahlangu
43. Smangaliso Mkhatshwa
44. Alfred Nzo
45. Alec Erwin
46. Gregory Rockman
47. Gill Marcus
48. Jan van Eck
49. Thandi Modise
50. Shepard Mdladlana
51. Nkosazana Zuma
52. Nosiviwe Maphisa
53. Randell van der Heever
54. Frene Ginwala
55. Joe Nhlanhla
56. Marcel Golding
57. Pravin Gordhan
58. Max Sisulu
59. Saki Macozoma
60. Tony Yengeni
61. Geraldine Fraser
62. Jenny Schreiner
63. Reginald September
64. Patekile Holomisa
65. Thomas Nkobi
66. Bridgette Mabandla
67. Dave Dalling
68. Sister Bernard Ncube
69. Andrew Mlangeni
70. Ebrahim Ismail Ebrahim
71. Gabriel Ramushwana
72. Adelaide Tambo
73. Barbara Hogan
74. Sibusiso Bhengu
75. Rapulane Molekane
76. Kgabisi Mosunkutu
77. Nozizwe Madlala
78. Nelson Ramodike
79. Elijah Barayi
80. Jannie Momberg
81. Prince M. Zulu
82. Elias Motswaledi
83. Dorothy Nyembe
84. Derek Hanekom
85. Mbulelo Goniwe
86. Melanie Verwoerd
87. Sankie Nkondo
88. Pregs Govender
89. Lydia Kompe
90. Ivy Gcina
91. Ela Gandhi
92. Joyce Mashamba
93. Phumzile Nqcuka
94. Ellen Khuzwayo
95. Hilda Ndude
96. Zou Kota
97. Lindiwe Sisulu
98. Feroza Adams
99. James Stuart
100. Mnyamezeli Booi
101. K. Lekgoro
102. Lindiwe Mabuza

103. John Coperlyn	136. Curnick Ndlovu	169. Bathabile Dlamini
104. Mangesi Zitha	137. Willie Hofmeyr	170. Virginia Engel
105. Dipuo Peters	138. Josiah Jele	171. Danny Oliphant
106. Peter Hendrikse	139. Mzwai Piliso	172. Bheki Mkhize
107. Ismail Richards	140. Moss Chikane	173. Moosa Moola
108. Ntombi Shope	141. Aaron Motsoaledi	174. Ram Saloojee
109. S. Moeti	142. Alistair Sparks	175. Jackie Cock
110. Duma Nkosi	143. Mkhuseli Jack	176. Nomatyala Hangana
111. Thoko Msane	144. Firoz Cachalia	177. Sue van der Merwe
112. Zam Titus	145. Salie Manie	178. Lynne Brown
113. N.J. Mahlangu	146. Mewa Ramgobin	179. N. Bam
114. Jennifer Ferguson	147. Jackie Selebi	180. Gertrude Fester
115. M.J. Mahlangu	148. Stan Sangweni	181. Beatie Hofmeyr
116. Samuel Nxumalo	149. Henry Fazzie	182. Thandi Shabangu
117. Bongiwe Njobe	150. John Samuels	183. Thandi Zulu
118. J.N. Reddy	151. Don Gumede	184. Kamy Chetty
119. Thabang Makwetla	152. Mike Sutcliffe	185. Desiree Finca
120. Manto Tshabalala	153. Prince Madikizela	186. F.S. Baloyi
121. Nkosinathi Nhleko	154. Lechesa Tsenoli	187. Elizabeth Langa
122. S.S. Ripinga	155. Rob Davies	188. Farieda Mohamed
123. P.T. Shilubane	156. Essop Pahad	189. C.T.D. Marivate
124. James Maseko	157. Hassan Solomons	190. Nomsa S. Mtsweni
125. Llewellyn Landers	158. Makhosazana Njobe	191. Vusimuzi Mavimbela
126. Girlie Pikoli	159. Ismael Meer	192. D.S. Rajah
127. Brian Bunting	160. Samson Ndou	193. Doris Ngobeni
128. Diliza Mji	161. Christmas Tinto	194. Rob Haswell
129. Miriam Makeba	162. Lulu Xingwana	195. Jerry Ndou
130. Archie Gumede	163. Ebrahim Rasool	196. Dennis Nkosi
131. Cassim Saloojee	164. Amina Cachalia	197. Lillian Baqwa
132. Wally Serote	165. Tutor Ndamase	198. George Sewpersadh
133. Mendi Msimang	166. Colin Coleman	199. Lindelwa Mabandla
134. Max Coleman	167. Fatima Hajaij	200. Maite Mohale
135. Bulelani Nqcuka	168. Liz Abrahams	

Appendix D

SACP members in the ANC nominations list for the April 1994 elections

1. Joe Slovo	(4)	
2. Ronnie Kasrils	(8)	
3. Sydney Mufamadi	(9)	
4. Thozamile Botha	(11)	
5. Jeff Radebe	(14)	
6. Moses Mayekiso	(18)	
7. Chris Dlamini	(19)	
8. John Nkadimeng	(28)	
9. Aziz Pahad	(29)	
10. Raymond Suttner	(30)	
11. Thenjiwe Mthintso	(33)	
12. Blade Nzimande	(35)	
13. Billy Nair	(39)	
14. Phillip Dexter	(41)	
15. Alec Erwin	(45)	
16. Shepard Mdladlana	(50)	
17. Pravin Gordhan	(57)	
18. Tony Yengeni	(60)	
19. Geraldine Fraser	(61)	
20. Jenny Schreiner	(62)	
21. Reginald September	(63)	
22. Nozizwe Madlala	(77)	
23. Elias Motsoaledi	(82)	
24. Mbulelo Goniwe	(85)	
25. Joyce Mashamba	(92)	
26. Zou Kota	(96)	
27. Nkosinathi Nhleko	(121)	
28. James Maseko	(124)	
29. Brian Bunting	(127)	
30. Firoz Cachalia	(144)	
31. Rob Davies	(155)	
32. Liz Abrahams	(168)	
33. Bathabile Dlamini	(169)	
34. Dennis Nkosi	(196)	

Appendix E

Results of South Africa's first democratic elections, 26–29 April 1994

Table 1: Election results for the national assembly

Parties	Votes	Percentage	Seats
1. Pan Africanist Congress of Azania	243 478	1,2	5
2. Soccer Party	10 575	0,1	
3. Keep It Straight and Simple Party	5 916	0	
4. Freedom Front	424 555	2,2	9
5. Women's Rights Peace Party	6 434	0	
6. Workers' List Party	4 159	0	
7. Ximoko Progressive Party	6 320	0	
8. African Muslim Party	34 466	0,2	
9. African Christian Democratic Party	88 104	0,5	2
10. African Democratic Movement	9 886	0,1	
11. African Moderates Congress Party	27 690	0,1	
12. African National Congress	2 256 824	62,7	252
13. Democratic Party	338 426	1,7	7
14. Dikwankwetla Party of South Africa	19 451	0,1	
15. Federal Party	17 663	0,1	
16. Luso-South African Party	3 293	0	
17. Minority Front Party	13 433	0,1	
18. National Party	3 983 690	20,4	82
19. Inkatha Freedom Party	2 058 294	10,5	43
Spoilt ballot papers	193 081	100	400

Table 2: Results for the provincial legislatures (provinces according to the Interim Constitution)

Province	Parties	Votes	Percentage	Seats
PWV (Gauteng)	1. African National Congress	2 418 257	58	50
	2. National Party	1 002 540	24	21
	3. Freedom Front	258 935	6	5
	4. Democratic Party	223 548	5	5
	5. Inkatha Freedom Party	153 567	4	3
	6. Pan Africanist Congress	61 512	2	1
	7. African Christian Democratic Party			1
Northern Transvaal (Northern Province)	1. African National Congress	1 759 597	92	38
	2. National Party	62 745	3	1
	3. Freedom Front	41 193	2	1
	4. Democratic Party	4 021	0	
	5. Inkatha Freedom Party	2 233	0	
	6. Pan Africanist Congress	24 360	1	
Eastern Transvaal (Mpumalanga)	1. African National Congress	1 070 052	81	25
	2. National Party	119 311	9	3
	3. Freedom Front	75 120	6	2
	4. Democratic Party	7 437	1	
	5. Inkatha Freedom Party	20 147	2	
	6. Pan Africanist Congress	21 679	2	
North West	1. African National Congress	1 310 080	83	26
	2. National Party	138 986	9	3
	3. Freedom Front	5 948	0	1
	4. Democratic Party	7 894	1	
	5. Inkatha Freedom Party	72 821	5	
	6. Pan Africanist Congress	27 274	2	
Orange Free State (Free State)	1. African National Congress	1 037 998	77	24
	2. National Party	170 452	13	4
	3. Freedom Front	81 662	6	2
	4. Democratic Party	7 664	1	
	5. Inkatha Freedom Party	6 935	1	
	6. Pan Africanist Congress	24 451	2	
KwaZulu-Natal	1. Inkatha Freedom Party	1 844 070	50	41
	2. African National Congress	1 181 118	32	26
	3. National Party	410 710	11	9
	4. Freedom Front	18 625	1	1
	5. Democratic Party	78 910	2	2
	6. Pan Africanist Congress	26 601	1	
	7. African Christian Democratic Party			1
	8. Minority Front			1

297

Province	Parties		Votes	Percentage	Seats
Eastern Cape	1.	African National Congress	2 453 790	84	48
	2.	National Party	286 029	10	6
	3.	Freedom Front	23 167	1	
	4.	Democratic Party	59 644	2	1
	5.	Inkatha Freedom Party	5 050	0	
	6.	Pan Africanist Congress	59 475	2	1
Western Cape	1.	National Party	1 138 242	53	23
	2.	African National Congress	705 576	33	14
	3.	Democratic Party	141 970	7	3
	4.	Freedom Front	44 003	2	1
	5.	Inkatha Freedom Party	7 445	0	
	6.	Pan Africanist Congress	22 676	1	
	7.	African Christian Democratic Party			1
Northern Cape	1.	African National Congress	200 839	50	15
	2.	National Party	163 452	41	12
	3.	Democratic Party	7 567	2	1
	4.	Freedom Front	24 117	6	2
	5.	Inkatha Freedom Party	1 688	0	
	6.	Pan Africanist Congress	3 765	1	

Appendix F

The cabinet of South Africa's Government of National Unity, 1994

Position	Name	Department
Presidency	1. Nelson Mandela	President
	2. Thabo Mbeki	First Deputy President
	3. F.W. de Klerk	Second Deputy President
Ministers	4. Joe Slovo	Housing and Local Government
	5. Joe Modise	Defence
	6. Dullah Omar	Justice
	7. Sydney Mufamadi	Safety and Security
	8. Sibusiso Bhengu	Education
	9. Trevor Manuel	Trade and Industry
	10. Alfred Nzo	Foreign Affairs
	11. Tito Mboweni	Labour
	12. Pallo Jordan	Post, Telecommunication and Broadcasting
	13. Nkosazana Zuma	Health
	14. Mac Maharaj	Transport
	15. Roelf Meyer (NP)	Provincial Affairs and Constitutional Development
	16. Derek Hanekom	Land Affairs
	17. Stella Sigcau	Public Enterprise
	18. Zola Skweyiya	Public Service and Administration
	19. Jeff Radebe	Public Works
	20. Sipho Mzimela (IFP)	Correctional Services
	21. Derek Keys (NP)	Finance
	22. Kraai van Niekerk (NP)	Agriculture
	23. Steve Tshwete	Sports and Recreation
	24. Mangosuthu Buthelezi (IFP)	Home Affairs
	25. Kadar Asmal	Water Affairs and Forestry
	26. Dawie de Villiers (NP)	Environmental Affairs and Tourism
	27. Pik Botha (NP)	Mineral and Energy Affairs
	28. Abe Williams (NP)	Welfare and Population Development
	29. Ben Ngubane (IFP)	Arts, Culture, Science and Technology
	30. Jay Naidoo	Minister without Portfolio (RDP Implementation)
Deputy ministers	31. Aziz Pahad	Foreign Affairs
	32. Valli Moosa	Provincial Affairs
	33. Chris Fismer (NP)	Justice
	34. Penuel Maduna	Home Affairs

Position	Name	Department
	35. Winnie Mandela	Arts, Culture, Science and Technology
	36. Alec Erwin	Finance
	37. Sankie Nkondo	Welfare
	38. Bantu Holomisa	Environmental Affairs
	39. Tobie Meyer (NP)	Land Affairs
	40. Renier Schoeman (NP)	Education
	41. Joe Matthews (IFP)	Safety and Security
	42. Thoko Msane	Agriculture

Bibliography

Selected books

Asmal, K., Asmal, L. & Roberts, R. *Reconciliation through truth*. Cape Town: David Philip, 1996.

Astrow, A. *Zimbabwe: a revolution that lost its way?* London: Zed, 1983.

Berger, L.P. & Godsell, B. (Eds). *A future South Africa: vision, strategies and realities*. Cape Town: Human & Rousseau/Tafelberg, 1988.

Biko, S. *I write what I like*. London: Penguin, 1978.

Callinicos, A. *South Africa, between reform and revolution*. London: Bookmarks, 1988.

Callinicos, A. *Between apartheid and capitalism*. London: Bookmarks, 1992.

De Waal, V. *The politics of reconciliation: Zimbabwe's first decade*. New Jersey: Africa World Press, 1990.

Du Toit, A. (Ed.). *Towards democracy: building a culture of accountability in South Africa*. Cape Town: IDASA, 1991.

Ellis, S. & Sechaba, T. *Comrades against apartheid: the ANC and the SACP in exile*. London: Indiana University Press, 1990.

Frankel, P., Pines, N. & Swilling, M. (Eds). *State, resistance and change in South Africa*. Johannesburg: Southern, 1988.

Friedman, S. *The long journey: South Africa's quest for a negotiated settlement*. Centre for Policy Studies. Johannesburg: Ravan, 1993.

Gerhart, G.M. *Black power in South Africa: the evolution of an ideology*. Berkeley: University of California Press, 1978.

Gibson, R. *African liberation movements: contemporary struggles against white minority rule*. London: Oxford University Press, 1972.

Gifford, P. & Louis, R. (Eds). *Decolonisation and African independence: the transfers of power, 1960-1980*. New Haven/London: Yale University Press, 1988.

Giliomee, H. & Schlemmer, L. *From apartheid to nation-building*. Cape Town: Oxford University Press, 1989.

Gregory, J. *Goodbye bafana: Nelson Mandela, my prisoner, my friend*. London: Headline Books, 1995.

Holland, H. *The struggle: the history of the African National Congress*. London: Grafton, 1989.

Hudson, M. *Triumph or tragedy: Rhodesia to Zimbabwe*. London: Hamish Hamilton, 1981.

Huttington, S. *Political order in changing societies*. New Haven: Yale University Press, 1968.

Karis, T. & Carter, G. (Eds). *From protest to challenge: a documentary history of African politics in South Africa, 1882–1964*. 4 volumes. Standford: Hoover Institute, 1972.

Lee, R. & Schlemmer, L. *Transition to democracy, policy perspectives*. Cape Town: Oxford University Press, 1991.

Lenin, V. *After the seizure of power (1917-1918), Selected Works*. Vol. VII. Moscow: Marx-Engels-Lenin Institute, 1937.

Lodge, T. *Black politics in South Africa since 1945*. Johannesburg: Ravan, 1983.

Mandela, N. *Long walk to freedom*. Randburg: Macdonald Purnell, 1994.

Mandela, N. *No easy walk to freedom*. London: Heinemann, 1989.

Marcum, J.A. *The Angolan revolution: exile politics and guerrilla warfare*. Cambridge: MIT, 1978.

Meer, F. *Higher than hope: a biography of Nelson Mandela on his 70th birthday*. Braamfontein: Skotaville, 1988.

Meli, F. *South Africa belongs to us: a history of the African National Congress*. Harare: Zimbabwe Publishing House, 1988.

Merton, R. *Reader in bureaucracy*. Nw York: Free Press, 1952.

Miliband, R. *Marxism and politics*. London: Oxford University Press, 1977.

Mission to South Africa: the Commonwealth Report. Harmondsworth: Penguin, 1986.

Mkhondo, R. *Reporting South Africa*. London: James Currey, 1993.

Motlhabi, M. *The theory and practice of black resistance to apartheid*. Braamfontein: Skotaville, 1984.

Munslow, B. (Ed.). *Africa: problems in the transition to socialism*. London: Zed, 1986.

Murray, M. *South Africa time of agony, time of destiny: the upsurge of popular protest*. 1987.

Nedcor/Old Mutual. *South Africa: prospects for successful transition*. Cape Town: Juta, 1992.

Nolutshungu, S. *Changing South Africa*. Cape Town: David Philip, 1982.

O'Donnell, G. & Schmitter, P. *Transition from authoritarian rule: tentative conclusions about uncertain democracies*. Baltimore/London: John Hopkins University Press, 1986.

O'Donnell, G., Schmitter, P. & Whitehead, L. (Eds). *Transition from authoritarian rule: Latin America*. Baltimore/London: John Hopkins University Press, 1986.

O'Donnell, G., Schmitter, P. & Whitehead, L. (Eds). *Transition from authoritarian rule: Southern Europe*. Baltimore/London: John Hopkins University Press, 1986.

Orkin, M. *Sanctions against apartheid*. Cape Town: David Philip, 1989.

Pogrund, B. *How can a man die better: Sobukwe and apartheid*. London: Peter Halban, 1990.

Polley, A. (Ed.). *The Freedom Charter and the future*. IDASA publication, Johannesburg: A.D. Donker, 1988.

Rubin, L. & Weinstein, B. *Introduction to African politics: a continental approach*. New York: Praeger, 1974.

Sarkesian, S.C. *Revolutionary guerrilla warfare*. Chicago: President Publishing, 1975.

Slovo, J. *The unfinished autobiography*. Johannesburg: Ravan, 1995.

Stalin, J. *Leninism*. Moscow: Cooperative Publishing Society of Foreign Workers in the USSR, 1934.

Stoneman, C. & Cliffe, L. *Zimbabwe: politics, economics and society*. Marxist Regime Series. London: Printer Publishers, 1989.

Tambo, A. *Preparing for power: Oliver Tambo speaks*. London: Heinemann, 1987.

Tang, N.T. *A Vietcong memoir*. New York: Vintage, 1985.

Tordoff, W. *Government and politics in Africa*. Macmillan Education, 1984.

Turok, B. *Revolutionary thought in the 20th century*. London: Zed, 1980.

Uhlig, M. (Ed.). *Apartheid in crisis.*, Harmondsworth: Penguin, 1986.

Van Diepen, M. (Ed.). *The national question in South Africa*. London, 1988.

Van Zyl Slabbert, F. *The quest for democracy*. London: Penguin, 1992.

Van Zyl Slabbert, F. *The system and the struggle: reform, revolt and reaction in South Africa*. Johannesburg: Jonathan Ball, 1989.

Walshe, P. *The rise of African nationalism in South Africa: the African National Congress, 1912-1952.* Berkeley: University of California Press, 1971.

Selected articles

Anonymous. Bantustan leaders cosy up to ANC. *Work In Progress*, 80, 1992.

Anonymous. Colonialism of a special type. *Africa Perspective*, 23, 1983.

Anonymous. Homecoming hassles. *Enterprise*, March 1991.

Anonymous. South Africa: inside the Communist Party. *Africa Confidential*, 29(17), August 1988.

Bell, P. Feeling the way. *Leadership Magazine*, 8(9), November 1989.

Bell, P. Watershed. *Leadership Magazine*, 8(7), September 1989.

Berstein, H. The ANC seventy years on. *South*, March 1982.

Bhagavan, M.R. Establishing the conditions for socialism: the case of Angola. In Munslow, B. (Ed.), *Africa: problems in the transition to socialism*. London: Zed, 1986.

Bhagowat, C. After the Peace Accord: conflict continues in Kwa-Makhutha. *Work In Progress*, 73, 1991.

Booysen, S. Transition, the state and relations of political power in South Africa. *Politikon*, 17(2), December 1990.

Bundy, C. Around which corner? Revolutionary theory and contemporary South Africa. *Transformation*, 8, 1989.

Cargill, J. Anti-apartheid alliance. *Work In Progress*, 65, April 1990.

Cargill, J. Scoring points off Pretoria. *Work In Progress*, 61, September/October 1989.

Cargill, J. The same political home for hunter and the hunted. *Work In Progress*, 69, September 1990.

Cronin, J. Is the SACP traveling in the right direction? *Work In Progress*, 74, May 1991.

Cronin, J. Marxist Workers' Tendency: trying to change the ANC from within. *The African Communist*, Second Quarter, 1991, 22–25.

Cronin, J. National democratic struggle and the question of transformation. *Transformation*, 2, 1986.

Cronin, J. Preparing ourselves for permanent opposition? *South African Labour Bulletin*, 15(7), April 1991.

Cronin, J. The boat, the tap and the Leipzig way. *The African Communist*, Third Quarter, 1992.

Daniels, G. Fighting factionalism in the Western Cape. *Work In Progress*, 74, May 1991.

Daniels, G. Women chart the way forward. *Work In Progress*, 78, October/November 1991.

Davies, R. Rethinking socialist debate in South Africa. *The African Communist*, Second Quarter, 1991.

De Bragança, A. Independence without decolonisation: Mozambique, 1974–1975. In Gifford, P. & Louis, R. (Eds), *Decolonisation and African independence: the transfers of power, 1960–1980*. New Haven/London: Yale University Press, 1988.

Diamond, L. Beyond authoritarianism and totalitarianism: strategies for democratisation. *The Washington Quarterly*, Winter, 1989.

Du Toit, A. *Applying the framework: South Africa as another case of transition from authoritarian rule?* Conference on South Africa's transition, Institute for a Democratic Alternative for South Africa (IDASA), Port Elizabeth, 21–23 June 1990.

Egero, B. People's power: the case of Mozambique. In Munslow, B. (Ed.), *Africa: problems in transition to socialism*. London: Zed, 1986.

Farbian, J. The split in the ANC, 1958. *Searchlight South Africa*, 2(3), July 1991.

Fitzgerald, P. Democracy and civil society in South Africa: a response to Daryl Glaser. *Review of African Political Economy*, 49, Winter, 1990.

Fleisch, B. Inside the ANC Conference. *Searchlight South Africa*, 2(4), January 1992.

Francis, S. Communism, terrorism and the African National Congress. *Journal of Social, Political and Economic Studies*, 11(1), 1986.

Friedman, S. The new National Party. *Monitor*, April 1990.

Friedman, S. *The shapers of things to come? National Party choices in the South African transition*. Centre for Policy Studies Transition Series, February 1992.

Friedman, S & Narsoo, M. *A new mood in Moscow: Soviet attitudes to South Africa*. South African Institute of Race Relations, 1986.

Giliomee, H. & Rantete, J. Transition to democracy through transaction? Bilateral negotiations between the ANC and the NP in South Africa. *African Affairs*, 91, 1992.

Gwala, H. Negotiations as presented by Joe Slovo. *The African Communist*, Fourth Quarter, 1992.

Heymans, C. *Towards people's development? Civic associations and development in South Africa*. Paper presented to the Conference of the Development Society of South Africa, Grahamstown, 9–11 September 1992.

Horn, P. ANC women's quota debate continues. *Work In Progress*, 77, September 1991.

Hough, M. Revolutionary warfare in the Republic of South Africa. *ISSUP Strategic Review*. University of Pretoria: Institute for Strategic Studies, 1986.

Hudson, P. Images of the future and strategies in the present: the Freedom Charter and the South African left. In Frankel, P., Pines, N. & Swilling, M. (Eds), *State resistance and change in South Africa*. Johannesburg: Southern, 1988.

Hudson, P. The Freedom Charter and the theory of national democratic revolution. *Transformation*, 1, 1986.

Jordan, P. Strategic debate in the ANC: a response to Joe Slovo. *The African Communist*, Fourth Quarter, 1992.

Kasrils, R. The revolutionary army. *Sechaba*, September 1988.

Kasrils, R. & Khuzwayo, M. Mass struggles and strategic initiative. *The Spark National*, 2(1), 1991.

Ketelo, B., Maxongo, A., Tshona, Z., Masongo, R. & Mbengo, L. A miscarriage of democracy: the ANC security department in the 1984 mutiny in Umkhonto we Sizwe. *Searchlight South Africa*, 5, July 1990.

Kev (pseudonym). A contribution to the discussion on people's war. *The African Communist*, 115, Fourth Quarter, 1988.

Kitson, D. Marxism-Leninism and absolute truth. *Work In Progress*, 77, September 1991.

Lenin, V. Partisan warfare. In Sarkesian, S.C. *Revolutionary guerrilla warfare*. Chicago: President Publishing, 1975.

Lodge, T. Context of the policy guidelines. *Development and Democracy*, Development Strategy and Policy Unit of the Urban Foundation, 3 December 1992.

Lodge, T. State of exile: the African National Congress of South Africa, 1976–86. In Frankel, P., Pines, N. & Swilling, M. (Eds), *State resistance and change in South Africa*. Johannesburg: Southern, 1988.

Lodge, T. Thabo Mbeki and Cyril Ramaphosa, crown princes to Nelson Mandela's throne. *World Policy Journal*, 10(3), 1993.

Lodge, T. The African National Congress after Kabwe Conference. *South African Review*, 4, 1989.

Lodge, T. The African National Congress after Nkomati. *South African Institute of Race Relations Topical Opinion*, 16 September 1985.

Lodge, T. The African National Congress in the 1990s. *South African Review*, 6. Johannesburg: Ravan, 1992.

Mackintosh, P. Is the Communist Party programme still valid? *The African Communist*, Second Quarter, 1987.

Majola, S. The two stages of our revolution. *The African Communist*, 110, Third Quarter, 1987.

Mandela, N. Out of strike. *South Africa in Exile*, 6(1), 1961.

Marais, H. Sticking together. *New Era*, Spring, 1991.

Mashinini, A. People's war and negotiations: are they fire and water? *Sechaba*, August 1988.

Masondo, A. 'The autonomy debate rages on'. *Mayibuye*, June 1991.

Matthews, J. False theories and pessimism. In De Bragança, A. & Wallerstein, I. (Eds), *Africa Liberation Reader Document of the National Liberation Movements*, Vol. 3.

Mbulelo, S. Defending the townships: has the ANC done enough? *Work In Progress*, 75, June 1991.

Meintjes, S. Dilemmas of difference, the Women's National Coalition. *Work In Progress*, 81, April 1992.

Meli, F. South Africa and the rise of African nationalism. In Van Diepen, M. (Ed.), *The national question in South Africa*. London, 1988.

Michels, R. The bureaucratic tendency of political parties. In Merton, R., *Reader in bureaucracy*. New York: Free Press, 1952.

Morobe, M. Towards people's democracy. *South Africa International*, 18(1), 1987.

Mzansi, X. United front to end apartheid, the road to mass action in South Africa. *The African Communist*, 97, Second Quarter, 1984.

Ngoasheng, M. The ANC Conference: gearing to struggle for power. *South African Labour Bulletin*, 16(1), July/August 1991.

Niddrie, D. Negotiations: another site of struggle. *Work In Progress*, 60, August/September 1989.

Nyatsumba, K.M. AZAPO and the PAC: revolutionary watchdogs? *South African Review*, 6, Johannesburg: Ravan, 1992.

Nzimande, B. Let us take the people with us: a reply to Joe Slovo. *The African Communist*, Fourth Quarter, 1992.

Nzimande, B. & Skosana, M. Debating socialism. *The African Communist*, First Quarter, 1992.

Ottoway, M. Liberation movements and transition to democracy: the case of the ANC. *Journal of Modern African Studies*, 29(1), 1991.

Phillips, I. After Kabwe and the emergency, lessons of the 1980s. *Indicator South Africa, Issue Focus*, 1989.

Phillips, I. Negotiation and armed struggle in contemporary South Africa. *Transformation*, 6, 1988.

Phillips, M. Negotiations: it takes two to tango. *Work In Progress*, 60, August/September 1989.

Phillips, M. & Coleman, C. *Another kind of war: strategies for transition in the era of negotiation*. Draft paper, July 1989.

Pillay, D. Can the SACP change track? *Work In Progress*, 76, July/August 1991.

Pillay, D. The patriotic front: can it prevent a constituent assembly compromise? *Work In Progress*, 74, May 1991.

Pillay, D. & Webster, E. COSATU, the party and the future state. *Work In Progress*, 6, July/August 1991.

Powell, I. House cleaning. *New Era*, Spring, 1991.

Prior, A. South African exile politics: a case study of the ANC and the SACP. *Journal of Contemporary African Studies*, 3(1/2), October 1983 April 1984.

Ramadiro, S. & Vally, S. Now is the time. *Work In Progress*, 94, December 1993.

Rantete, J. The non-CODESA wing of the Patriotic Front, the PAC and AZAPO. *South Africa Foundation Review*, December 1992.

Reglar, S. & Young, G. Modern communist theory: Lenin and Mao Zedung. In Wintrop, N., *Liberal democratic theory and its critics*, 1983.

Saunders, C. Transformation in Namibia, 1989–1990, and the South African case. *Transformation*, 17, 1992.

Schlemmer, L. Between polarisation and pacts: what kind of transition does South Africa have? *Indicator South Africa*, 7(4), Spring, 1990.

Schlemmer, L. Negotiations in South Africa: a balance sheet of opportunities and constraints. Centre for Policy Studies "Negotiations Package", University of the Witwatersrand, 1989.

Seekings, J. Civic organisations in South African townships. *South African Review*, 6, Johannesburg: Ravan, 1992.

Slovo, J. Beyond the stereotype: the SACP in the past, present and future. *The African Communist*, Second Quarter, 1991.

Slovo, J. What room for compromise? *The African Communist*, Third Quarter, 1992.

Stalker, B. The crisis in our country: a realistic political solution. *Sechaba*, May 1988.

Steinberg, J. Leninist fantasies and SACP illusions. *Work In Progress*, 74, May 1991.

Strachan, G. Indecent obsession. *The African Communist*, Second Quarter, 1992.

Suttner, R. Do we continue the talks? *New Era*, 5(3), Summer, 1990.

Suttner, R. Ensuring stable transition to democratic power. *The African Communist*, Fourth Quarter, 1992.

Swilling, M. The politics of negotiations. *Work In Progress*, 50/51, October/November 1987.

Swilling, M. & Phillips, M. State power in the 1980s: from total strategy to counter-revolutionary warfare. In Cock, J. & Nathan, L. (Eds), *War and society: the militarisation of South Africa*, 1989.

Swilling, M. & Rantete, J. Organisation and strategies of the major resistance movements in the negotiation era. In Lee, R. & Schlemmer, L. (Eds), *Transition to democracy: policy perspectives*. Cape Town: Oxford University Press, 1991.

Swilling, M. & Van Zyl Slabbert, F. *Waiting for a negotiated settlement: South Africans in a changing world*. Centre for Policy Studies "Negotiations Package", University of the Witwatersrand, 1989.

Tjonneland, N.E. *Negotiating apartheid away? Constitution-making, transition politics and conditions for democracy in South Africa*. International Peace Research Institute, Oslo, 1990.

Trewhela, P. The ANC's prison camps: an audit of three years, 1990–1993. *Searchlight South Africa*, 10, April 1993.

Trewhela, P. The trial of Winnie Mandela. *Searchlight South Africa*, 2(3), July 1991.

Van Zyl Slabbert, F. *South Africa: beginning at the end of the road*. (Publisher unknown.) March 1990.

Vaughan, N. Consensus and contention: a note on the current state of land debate. *Transformation*, 13, 1990.

Zartman, W. Negotiations in South Africa. *The Washington Quarterly*, 11(4), Autumn, 1988.

Zuma, T. The surest way to people's power – a response to Brenda Stalker. *Sechaba*, February 1988.

Zumana, N. Revolution or negotiations? *Sechaba*, 23(4), April 1989.

Commissions of inquiry

Commission of inquiry into recent developments in the People's Republic of Angola. Stuart Commission, 14 March 1984.

Report of the commission of inquiry into certain allegations of cruelty and human rights abuses against ANC prisoners and detainees by ANC members. Motsuenyane Commission, 20 August 1993.

Report of the commission of inquiry into complaints by former ANC prisoners and detainees. Skweyiya Commission, Johannesburg, August 1992.

Report of the commission of inquiry set up in November 1989 by the National Working Committee of the National Executive Committee of the African National Congress to investigate the circumstances leading to the death of Mzwakhe Ngwenya (also known as Thami Zulu or TZ). Jobodwana Commission, n.d.

Report of the Douglas Commission, Durban, January 1993.

South Africa: torture, ill-treatment and executions in ANC camps. Amnesty International Report. London, December 1992.

Research reports

Cloete, F. *Comparative lessons for land reform in South Africa.* Centre for Policy Studies Comparative Perspectives, April 1992.

Davies-Webb, W. *Umkhonto we Sizwe and the SACP: searching for a mission in the 1990s.* Special Report of the International Freedom Foundation, June 1991.

Marcus, G. *The Freedom Charter: a blueprint for a democratic South Africa.* Occasional paper. University of the Witwatersrand: Centre for Applied Legal Studies, 9 June 1985.

Pierce, D. *Post-apartheid South Africa: lessons from Brazil's 'Nova Republica'.* Centre for Policy Studies Comparative Perspectives, February 1992.

Rantete, J. *Liberation and negotiation: the PAC in the South African transition.* Centre for Policy Studies Transition Series, 5(2), 1992.

Rantete, J. *Room for compromise: the African National Congress and transitional mechanisms.* Centre for Policy Studies Transition Series, Johannesburg, February 1992.

Suttner, R. *The Freedom Charter: the people's charter in the nineteen-eighties.* The 26th T.B. Davie Memorial Lecture delivered at the University of Cape Town, September 1984.

Official ANC publications

Published

African National Congress Constitution. As adopted at the ANC National Conference, June 1991.

African National Congress Youth League Constitution and Code of Conduct. 12 December 1991.

Declaration of the OAU Ad-hoc Committee on Southern Africa on the question of South Africa. Harare, Zimbabwe, 21 August 1989.

For the sake of our lives: guidelines for the creation of people's self defence units. November 1990.

From ungovernability to people's power. Statement of the National Executive Committee of the ANC, 1986.

Joining the ANC: an introductory handbook to the ANC. Johannesburg, May 1990.

Let peace, freedom and justice prevail. ANC National Conference Report, July 1991.

National Health Plan for South Africa. African National Congress, January 1994.

Negotiation as a terrain and method of struggle. Discussion paper for the Conference for a Democratic Future, issued by the Mass Democratic Movement, December 1989.

Negotiations: a strategic perspective. ANC NEC Paper. *The African Communist,* Fourth Quarter, 1992.

Opening statement of Comrade Oliver Tambo at the second ANC National Consultative Conference, 16–23 June, 1985.

Policy on farm-workers. August 1993.

Ready to govern: ANC policy guidelines for a democratic South Africa. Adopted at the National Policy Conference, 28–31 May 1992.

Reconstruction and Development Programme. African National Congress Policy Framework. Johannesburg: Umanyano, 1994.

Umkhonto prepares for a future defence force. *Submit or fight: 30 years of Umkhonto we Sizwe.* ANC's Department of Political Education, December 1991

Umkhonto we Sizwe: 30th anniversary, December 16, 1961 – December 16, 1991. MK 30th Anniversary National Preparatory Committee. Mathibe Printers, December 1991.

Year of mass action for the transfer of power to the people. Statement of the National Executive Committee on the occasion of the 79th anniversary of the African National Congress, 8 January 1991.

Unpublished

1987: What is to be done? Document distributed by the Politico-Military Council to Regional Command Centres, October 1986.

Advance to national democracy: guidelines on strategy. ANC document, February 1991.

ANC discussion paper on the issue of negotiations. 16 June 1989.

ANC Land Commission Workshop. Discussion document. Broederstroom, 14–21 October 1990.

ANC statement on negotiation. 9 October 1987.

Communiqué of the Second National Conference of the ANC. Presented by President Oliver Tambo at a press conference, Lusaka, Zambia, 25 June 1985.

'Conspiratorial cabal document'. Letter addressed to Walter Sisulu from the Release Mandela Committee, 6 June 1990.

Constituent assembly and interim government. Discussion paper. ANC's Department of Political Education, 1991.

Draft media policy. Department of Information and Publicity, 23 November 1991.

Interim government. Paper presented by Aziz Pahad to the ANC PWV Regional Conference, 5, 6 & 10 October 1991.

Inter-sectoral policy development: policy development in the PWV region. 1992.

Kasrils, R. & Khuzwayo, M. *Some thoughts on advance to national democracy.* Unpublished paper, no date.

Mass organisation is the key to victory: organising for elections and for government. ANC's Department of Political Education, April 1992.

Notes on a constituent assembly. ANC discussion paper distributed at the PWV Regional Workshop on Interim Government and a Constituent Assembly, 1 February 1992.

Organisational Report of the African National Congress Executive Committee. Presented by the Secretary-General CDE Alfred Nzo to the first legal National Conference of the African National Congress after 30 years of proscription. Durban, 26 July 1991.

Papers of the ANC National Workshop on the National Peace Accord. Johannesburger Hotel, 19 & 20 October 1991.

Questions and answers on interim government. ANC information pamphlet, January 1991.

Reflections on interim government. ANC discussion document distributed at the PWV Regional Workshop on Interim Government and a Constituent Assembly, 1 February 1992.

Report and resolutions from the Building the Organisation Commission. ANC National Conference, Durban, July 1991.

Report of the Office of the Treasurer-General. ANC National Conference, Durban, July 1991.

Report of the Violence Monitoring Committee. ANC PWV Regional Conference, 5–6 October 1991.

Report on the ANC National Consultative Conference on Local Government. Johannesburg, October 1990.

Resolutions of the Regional Policy Consultative Conference PWV region. 9–10 May 1992.

Skweyiya, Z. *The ANC constitutional guidelines: a vital contribution to the struggle against apartheid.* Paper presented at the Harare Conference of Lawyers, 31 January – 4 February 1989.

Speeches and resolutions. ANC Consultative Conference, 14–16 December 1991.

State of the nation negotiation: when and how? An anonymous ''cabal'' document which surfaced during July 1990.

Statement of the Elections Commission to the International Solidarity Conference, 19–25 February 1993.

Summary report: ANC Land Commission Workshop. Comparative Studies Workshop on Agrarian Restructuring, 14–21 October 1990.

Suttner, R. *ANC: national liberation movement or political party?* Discussion paper. ANC's Department of Political Education, September 1991.

Suttner, R. *Negotiation, liberation and transformation.* Paper presented at the NUSAS July Festival, 4 July 1990.

Suttner, R. *One year of an unbanned ANC: the road ahead.* Draft paper, February 1991.

Suttner, R. *Progress in the talks.* Paper presented to the PWV Regional Workshop, 17 November 1990.

Suttner, R. *The African National Congress and its relationship to civics.* Discussion paper no. 3, Department of Political Education, 1992.

Suttner, R. *The deadlock and beyond: build organisation for people's power.* Paper presented at the ANC Western Cape Regional Seminar/Border Regional Workshop on 15/18 July 1992.

Suttner, R. *The road ahead: the character of our struggle.* Keynote address to the SANSCO/NUSAS National Workshop, 12 April 1990.

Suttner, R. *Where are we, where are we going from here and how do we get there? Current conditions and strategic priorities of the ANC.* Draft paper, November 1990.

The spear of the nation (Umkhonto we Sizwe): armed struggle, strategy and tactics of the ANC. Address by President O.R. Tambo, Arusha, December 1987.

ANC press statements

ANC call to the people of South Africa: press home the attack! ANC statement, 22 August 1989.

ANC NEC response to the Motsuenyane Commission's Report, 29 August 1993.

ANC press statement about reports emanating from Beijing that ANC President Comrade Nelson Mandela sent a letter to the government of the People's Republic of China regarding future diplomatic relations with Taiwan, 18 August 1993.

ANC press statement about the controversy regarding the remarks made by the President of the ANCYL, Mr Peter Mokaba, 13 August 1993.

ANC press statement on Nomzamo Winnie Mandela's resignation, 10 September 1992.

ANC press statement on PAC statement and walkout, 1 December 1991.

ANC press statement on the position of the PWV Women's League, 15 June 1992.

ANC press statement on the Mazimbu handover, 10 July 1992.

ANC press statement on the restructuring of the department of the organisation and the allocation of portfolios to members of the National Working Committee of the ANC, 2 August 1991.

ANC statement on the alleged ANC-Miss South Africa secret deal, 10 September 1993.

ANC, SACP and COSATU joint media statement regarding the allegations in the *Sunday Star*, 22 February 1993.

Disciplinary hearing by the Regional Committee of the ANC Western Cape in relation to the conduct of Mr Dawood Khan, 7 April 1993.

Draft joint statement ANC, COSATU and the South African Government, 29 September 1993.

Joint press release of ANC and homeland leaders, 15 March 1991.

Joint press statement of the ANC Youth League and the ANC Secretary-General, Cyril Ramaphosa, 22 April 1993.

Letter sent to ANC branches by the PWV Regional Treasurer, Cassim Saloojee, entitled *Launching of an ANC hawkers scheme,* dated 24 June 1992.

Permanent Mission of Zambia to the United Nations press release, New York, 29 November 1991.

Statement by Nomzamo Winnie Mandela, 15 April 1992. Issued by the ANC Department of Information and Publicity.

Statement of the NEC of the ANC on the emancipation of women in South Africa, 2 May 1990.

Umkhonto We Sizwe: born of the people. Statement of the National Executive Committee of the African National Congress, delivered by President Oliver Tambo on Heroes Day, 16 December 1986.

Year of liberation for South Africans. Statement of the National Executive Committee on the occasion of the 82nd anniversary of the ANC, June 1994.

Periodicals

Africa Confidential
Bulletin of the National Commission for the Emancipation of Women
Enterprise
Finance Week
Financial Mail
Free Azania

Front File Bulletin
Horizon, the ANC Youth League's (ANCYL) magazine
Journal of Contemporary African Studies
Journal of Modern African Studies
Journal of Social, Political and Economic Studies
Leadership South Africa
Learn and Teach
Marxist Regime Series
Mayibuye, an ANC monthly magazine
Monitor, an ANC PWV weekly monitoring bulletin
New Era
Politikon, South African Journal of Political Science
Review of African Political Economy
RSA Policy Review
SASH, journal of the Black Sash
Searchlight South Africa
Sechaba, an ANC journal
South Africa International
South African Barometer
South African Foundation Review
South African Institute of Race Relations Survey
South African Labour Bulletin
South African Review
South African Update
Southern Africa Report
The African Communist, journal of the SACP
The Economist
The Rock, journal of the ANC Women's League
The Spark, a publication of the South African Student Press Union
Theoria
Transformation
Umsebenzi, an SACP magazine
United Democratic Front Publication
Work In Progress
World Policy Journal

Newspapers

Business Day
Cape Times
City Press
Congress Militants, a paper of the Marxist Workers Tendency of the ANC
New Nation/Sunday Nation
SASPU National
Sowetan
Sunday Times
The Citizen
The Star/Sunday Star
The Washington Quarterly
Vaal Vision
Weekly Mail/Weekly Mail and Guardian

General

Anonymous. A year of turmoil and change. *New Era*, 4(4), December 1989.

Anonymous. Negotiations: fighting with new weapons. *New Era*, 4(2), August 1989.

Anonymous. People's war and insurrection: the subjective factor. *Mayibuye*, 2, 1989.

Anonymous. Resurgence of the ANC, 1976–1988. *Indicator South Africa, Issue Focus*, 1989.

Anonymous. *The constitutional guidelines of the ANC: a Giddensian perspective.* 1988.

Cloete, F. *Prospects for a democratic process of political change in South Africa.* Paper presented at the Conference on Perspectives on the Contemporary South African State. Centre for Policy Studies, University of the Witwatersrand, 27–28 February 1989.

Costea, P. *Eastern Europe's relations with the insurgencies of Southern Africa (ANC and SWAPO).* Paper presented at the Bi-Annual Conference of Political Science Association of South Africa, Port Alfred.

Development and Democracy. Publication of the Development Strategy and Policy Unit, Urban Foundation, 3 December 1992.

Jordan, P. *The politics of the democratic movement in South Africa.* Draft paper, Lusaka, May 1989.

Lambert, R. *Political unionism in South Africa: the South African Congress of Trade Unions, 1955–1965.* Thesis, Faculty of Arts. Johannesburg: University of the Witwatersrand, 1988.

Lambert, R. *Trade unions and national liberation in South Africa: past perspective and current strategies.* Paper read at the Centre for Southern African Studies Conference, 1986.

Mandela, N. Speech delivered at the Rivonia Trial. A booklet of *Learn and Teach*. Published on the 70th birthday of Mandela, 18 July 1988.

Mission to South Africa: the Commonwealth Report, 1986.

National Housing Forum's letter to the Minister of National Housing and Public Works, Louis Shill, 15 October 1993.

National Peace Convention, 14 September 1991.

Pretoria Minute. *South African Barometer*, 4(16), 27 August 1990.

Rantete, J. *The African National Congress: from revolutionary armed seizure to a negotiated transfer of power.* Honours dissertation, Faculty of Arts. Johannesburg: University of the Witwatersrand, January 1990.

Rantete, J. *The Vaal uprising: rent increases, community resistance and the struggle against apartheid.* Unpublished manuscript, 1995.

Report of the International Conference held at the Foundation of Science and Politics (Stiftung für Wissenschaft und Politik). Ebenhausen, 10–12 December 1986.

Report to the ANC, COSATU and SANCO by a Mission sponsored by the International Development Research Centre, Canada, December 1992.

Resolution on the process of political settlement. COSATU congress document, July 1989.

Sarakinsky, I. *State strategy and the extra-parliamentary opposition in South Africa, 1983–1988.* Paper presented at the Political Studies Seminar, University of the Witwatersrand, 12 April 1989.

Saul, J. *Structural reform: a model for the revolutionary transformation of South Africa.* Paper presented to the Ruth First Memorial Colloquium, University of the Western Cape, 17–18 August 1992.

South African Communist Party: recommendations of the Consultative Conference, Tongaat, 19 & 20 May 1990. *History in the Making*, 1(2), November 1990.

South African National Civic Organisation press statement on the forthcoming democratic and non-racial elections, 24 February 1992.

Starushenko, G. *Problems of the struggle against racism, apartheid and colonialism in South Africa.* Paper presented to the second Soviet-Africa Conference for Peace, Cooperation and Social Progress. Moscow: USSR Academy of Science, African Institute, 1988.

Swilling, M. & Phillips, M. *The power and limits of the emergency state.* Paper presented at the African Studies Institute, University of the Witwatersrand, 14 August 1989.

'The politics of talking power'. *New Era,* 4(2), August 1989.

'The United Democratic Front statement on negotiations'. *Phambili,* 1, April 1988.

'The United Democratic Front today'. *United Democratic Front Publication,* September 1987.

Interviews

Cronin, Jeremy. Executive member of the South African Communist Party.

Ebrahim, Gora. Executive member of the Pan Africanist Congress.

Hogan, Barbara. Secretary-General of the ANC PWV region.

Javu, Pretty. Administrator of the ANC Border-Kei region.

Louw, Sam. Secretary of the ANC Western Transvaal region.

Macozoma, Saki. NEC member and spokesperson of the ANC's Department of Information and Publicity.

Makgabo, Thishang. MK cadre and ANC representative at the National Housing Forum.

Masebe, Thabo. ANC Youth League member.

Maselela, Chair. Secretary of the ANC Eastern Transvaal region.

Mayekiso, Vax. Deputy Secretary of the ANC Northern Orange Free State region

Mkwayi, Wilton. ANC Internal Leadership Core, Head of the Organising Department.

Mogale, Joas. Official of the Foundation for African Business and Consumer Services (FABCOS).

Mokaba, Peter, Executive member of the ANC National Executive Committee.

Moseneke, Dikgang. Second Deputy President of the PAC.

Netshitenzhe, Joel. NEC member and former Chairman of ANC Northern Transvaal region

Niehaus, Carl. Spokesperson for the ANC's Department of Information and Publicity.

Nkosi, Duma. COSATU official and representative at the National Housing Forum.

Ramathlodi, Ngoako. Chairman of the ANC Northern Transvaal region.

Rasethaba, Sello. AZAPO official.

Scott, Mpho. Deputy Secretary of the ANC Southern Natal region.

Sebothelo, Kaizer. Secretary of the ANC Southern Orange Free State region.

Suttner, Raymond. NEC member and Head of the ANC's Department of Political Education.

Tsenoli, Lechesa. President of the South African National Civic Organisation.

Index of persons, organisations and other bodies

(ff = and following pages)

A

Abrahams, Archie   186
African Christian Democratic Party
   (ACDP)   217
African Council of Hawkers and Infor-
   mation Business (ACHIB)   26
African Moderates Congress (AMC)   242
African National Congress (ANC)   3ff
African National Congress, departments
   Arts and Culture   8, 27
   Economic Planning   8, 11, 24
   Economic Policy   24, 67
   Education and Culture   4
   Finance   7, 24
   Health, Welfare and Human Re-
      sources   11
   Human Resource Development   43
   Information and Publicity   7, 8
   Information Systems   24
   Intelligence and Security   7
   International Affairs   8, 11
   Legal and Constitutional Affairs   8,
      11, 13
   National Organising   7, 8, 13, 18
   Personnel   4
   Political Education   7, 8, 13, 230
   Projects   24
   Security   57, 63
   Social Welfare   8, 24, 27, 41, 67, 72
   Special Projects (Military)   8
   Transport   7, 8
   Treasury   27
African National Congress Women's
   League (ANCWL)   19, 38ff
African National Congress Youth League
   (ANCYL)   32ff, 116
African Nationalists   68
Afrikaner Volksfront   217, 218, 221

Afrikaner Volksunie (AVU)   206, 208,
   215, 255
Afrikaner Weerstandbeweging (AWB)
   38, 180, 221, 242
Alexandra Peace Forum   104
Amnesty International   63
Anti-Apartheid Movement   194
Arts Foundation   27
Askaris   101
Association of Ex-Political Prisoners   24
Ayob, Ismail   129
Azanian People's Liberation Army
   (APLA)   110, 208, 256
Azanian People's Organisation
   (AZAPO)   46, 257
Azanian Student Organisation
   (AZASO)   32

B

Bahai of South Africa   43
Barayi, Elijah   70, 72, 238
Bartlett, George   255
Battalion 31   109
Battalion 32   101, 109
Bernstein, Ann   87
Bethel, Nicholas   129
Biko, Steve   32
Black Cats   17
Black Consciousness (BC)   32, 83
Black People's Convention   32
Black Sash   43
Boesak, Allan   71, 237, 242, 248
Botha, P.W.   129, 146, 150ff
Botha, Pik   109, 185, 221
Botha, Simon (Sindile Velem)   59
Bullet   60
Bunting, Brian   54
Burnham, Margaret   63
Buthelezi, Mangosuthu   38, 68, 99,
   107, 165, 198, 217, 219, 222

C

Cachalia, Azhar   70
Campaign for Independent Broadcasting
(CIB)   231
Cardoso, Silva   168
Carolus, Cheryl   9, 54, 67, 71, 73, 237,
250
Carrington, David   223
CCB   101
Chemical Workers Industrial Union
(CWIU)   50
Chiba, Lala   14
Chikane, Frank   62, 214, 238
Chissano, Joaquim   153
Civic Association of Southern Transvaal
(CAST)   105
Clinton, Bill   209
Cock, Jacklyn   236
Coetzee, Kobie   130, 251, 255
Cohen, Herman   135
Colyn, Piet   245
Commission on Development Finance
93
Committee of Ten   59
Communist Party of South Africa   53
Concerned South Africa Group
(COSAG)   198, 205, 208, 255
Congress of Democrats   116
Congress of South African Students
(COSAS)   32, 33, 208
Congress of South African Trade Unions
(COSATU)   6, 43, 50ff, 88, 89, 166,
184, 193, 212, 237
Congress of the People   116
Congress of Traditional Leaders of South
Africa (CONTRALESA)   16
Conservative Party (CP)   17, 38, 45,
154, 180, 205, 255
Constitutional Committee   147
Constitutional Technical Committee   212
Convention for a Democratic South
Africa (CODESA)   44, 45, 52, 107,
173ff, 183ff, 257
Coperlyn, John   237
Cronin, Jeremy   54, 89, 200, 202, 203
Cronje, Rowan   206

D

Dalling, Dave   237

Danjies, Peter   52
Dash, Samuel   129
Davis, Dennis   74, 93
De Klerk, F.W.   6, 70, 103, 107, 153ff,
180, 183, 188, 195, 209, 210, 218,
222, 239, 241, 243ff, 247, 249, 258,
260
De Lille, Patricia   243
De Villiers, Dawie   213
Debray   120
Delport, Tertius   180
Democratic Party (DP)   43, 154, 214
Development Bank of Southern Africa
(DBSA)   24, 93
Dexter, Phillip   237
Dhlomo, Oscar   214
Digital Equipment Corporation   26
Dikeledi, Paul   57
Dikwankwetla Party of South Africa   217
Dipico, Manne   237, 238, 247
Disabled People of South Africa   43
Dlamini, Chris   52, 237
Dos Santos, José Eduardo   135
Drake   58
Dube, John   244
Dumakude, Diliza   59
Durban Political Committee   186
During, Roy   213

E

Eagles Youth Group   102
Ebrahim, Ebrahim Ismail   9, 54
Ebrahim, Ismael   57
Education Forum   216
Eglin, Colin   205
Elmo de Witt Films   27
Eminent People's Group (EPG)   130,
143ff
Erwin, Alec   237
Essack, Farid   70
European Economic Community
(EEC)   196

F

Facilitating Committee   205
Fanaroff, Bernie   52
Fatima, Meer   70
Federal Independent Democratic
Alliance (FIDA)   102

316

Federation of South African Women
  (FEDSAW)   43
Federation of Transvaal Women (FED-
  TRAW)   39
Ferguson, Jennifer   237
Fihla, Benson   12
Film and Allied Workers Union
  (FAWO)   27
First, Ruth   57
Five Freedom Forum   131
Food and Allied Workers Union
  (FAWU)   50
Freedom Alliance (FA)   213, 214, 216ff
Freedom Front   222
Front de Libération Nationale
  (FLN)   xvi, xvii
Front for the Liberation of Mozambique
  (FRELIMO)   xvi, xvii, 143

G

Gavin, Louis   238
Gele, Grace   57
Gender Advisory Committee (GAC)   45
Ghali, Boutros Boutros   210
Gildenhuys, Antonie   105
Ginwala, Frene   43, 249, 251
Gogotya   102
Golding, Marcel   237
Gordhan, Khetso   238
Gordhan, Pravin   70, 73, 186, 205, 213
Gouvernement Provisoire de la Républi-
  que Algérienne   xvii
Government of National Unity
  (GNU)   244ff, 249ff
Gqozo, Oupa   198, 221, 240
Greenberg, Stan   238
Greer, Frank   238
Gumede, Archie   70, 72, 73
Gumede, Don   237
Gwala, Harry   12, 40, 54, 55, 68, 75, 76,
  202, 211, 248

H

Hani, Chris   9, 21, 36, 54, 55, 59, 62,
  75, 110, 181, 186, 189, 206, 230, 239,
  264
Harmel, Michael   118
Hartzenberg, Ferdi   38, 208, 221
Haswell, Rob   237

Hendrikse, Peter   237
Heyns, Johan   214
Hobo, Thembile   60
Hogan, Barbara   14
Holomisa, Bantu   106, 237, 238, 242
Human Rights Commission   192
Huna, Floyd   64
Hurley, Denis   104

I

Independent Broadcasting Authority
  209
Independent Development Trust (IDT)
  24, 93
Independent Electoral Commission (IEC)
  209, 213, 230, 232, 245
Independent Media Commission   209,
  232
Independent People's Republic of Ango-
  la   xvii
Inkatha Freedom Party (IFP)   17, 38,
  43, 99, 102, 173, 174, 205, 206, 210,
  211, 219, 223, 240, 246ff
Inkatha Institute for South Africa   70
Institute for a Democratic Alternative in
  South Africa (IDASA)   35
Institute of Contextual Theology   106
Intando Ye Sizwe   21
Interim Leadership Group (ILG)   47
Interim Regional Executive Committee
  14
Internal Leadership Core (ILC)   7, 12,
  69
International Freedom Foundation   63,
  70

J

Jager, Rosil   214
Jele, Josiah   70
Joint Working Committee   103
Jordan, Pallo   7, 8, 57, 61, 201, 237
Joseph, Helen   211

K

Kagiso Trust   93
Kashu, Jomo   12
Kasrils, Ronnie   9, 54, 63, 123, 186, 191
Kathrada, Ahmed   7, 8, 54

Kaunda, Kenneth 135, 154
Ketelo, Bandile 62
Kgositsile, Baleka 75
Khan, Dawood 264
Khanyile, Vusi 7, 72
Kheswa, Victor Khethisi 109
Khoza, Themba 107
Khumalo, Ernest 58
Khuzwayo, Mandla 191
Kilian, Johan 21
Kissinger, Henry 223
Koevoet 101, 107, 109
Kotze, Craig 107
Kriegler, Johan 214, 220, 222, 246,
    247
Kriel, Hernus 107, 247, 255
Kruger, Min. 128

L

Lala, Raymond 186
Landers, Llewellyn 237
Lekota, Patrick 7, 9, 12, 40, 42, 70, 72,
    237, 247
Lembede, Anton 32
Leon, Tony 241
List Committee 235, 237
Local Dispute Resolution Committee
    (LDRC) 103
Love, Janet 186
Luthuli Brigade 120

M

Mabhida, Moses 139
Mabuza, Enos 238
Mabuza-Suttle, Felicia 236
MacBride 198
Macmillan Publishers Ltd 26
Macozoma, Saki 7
Madlala, Nompumelelo 74, 75
Mahamba, Kenneth (Piper) 56
Maharaj, Mac 7, 54, 69, 71, 174, 186,
    187, 221
Mahero 60
Mahlangu, Gwen 75
Mahlangu, James 237
Makarov, A.A. 134
Make, Cassius 57
Makeba, Miriam 237
Makgale, Omry (see Sidwell, Moroka)

Makhosoke 239
Makunyane, Thabo 12
Malan, Magnus 100ff
Malaza, Lucky 198
Maledza, Zaba (see Nkondo, Ephraim)
Mandela, Nelson 7, 9, 32, 42, 50, 62,
    67ff, 90, 99, 128ff, 158ff, 188, 194,
    209, 210, 218, 221, 237ff, 243, 244,
    247, 249, 260, 263
Mandela, Winnie 8, 27, 40, 41, 62, 67,
    69, 71ff, 110, 187, 211, 236, 238, 250
Mandela Reception Committee 47
Mandela United Team 72
Mangope, Lucas 27, 198, 220, 221, 240
Manuel, Trevor 9, 12, 67
Maphetho, Andrew 42
Maponya, Richard 236
Marcus, Gill 7, 54
Marxist Workers' Tendency 68
Masekela, Barbara 8, 9
Mashatile, Paul 47, 48
Mason, Reg 105
Masondo, Jacob 61
Mass Democratic Movement (MDM) 6,
    7, 72, 137
Massango, Ronnie 62
Mathebula, Sipho (E. Mndebele) 59
Matlala, Terry 7
Matthews, Joe 205
Maxongo, Amos 62
Mayekiso, Moses 50, 51, 68, 237
Mayekiso, Mzwanele 49
Mayibuye, Peter (see Netshitenzhe, Joel)
Mbeki, Govan 7, 40, 251
Mbeki, Thabo 8, 9, 38, 171, 201, 237,
    238, 249
Mbengo, Luvo 62
Mbona, Dexter 64
Mboweni, Tito 93
Mchunu, Willis 12
McQueen, John J. 127
Mdlalose, Frank 68, 247
Meer, Farouk 73
Metsing, Rocky Malebane 27
Meyer, Roelf 197, 205, 213, 238, 259
Mhlaba, Raymond 7, 54, 237, 238, 247
Mhlongo, Kate (Nomfanelo Ntlokwana)
    59
Mkwayi, Wilton 7
Mlangeni 7, 8
Mlangeni, Babsy 59

Mndebele, E. (*see* Mathebula, Sipho)
Mnguni, Faith   74
Moabi, Max   57, 58
Modise, Billy   236, 238
Modise, Joe   8, 9, 57, 59, 64
Modise, Ken   238
Modise, Thandi   75, 239
Moeketsi, Stompie   69, 71, 73, 76
Mofokeng, Jacqui   236
Mofolo, Jabu   59
Mofolo, Titus   14
Mogotsi, Kediboni   75
Mohammed, Yunus   70
Mojapelo, Maria   74
Mokaba, Peter   27, 32, 36, 69, 70, 75,
   76, 110
Mokanyane, Nomvula   74
Mokhobo, Dawn   214
Moko, Thembi   75
Mokoena, Aaron   64
Mokoena, Aubrey   69, 70
Molefe, Popo   9, 47, 70, 71, 229, 237,
   247
Molekane, Zakes   12
Molobi, Eric   70
Momberg, Jannie   237
Mompati, Ruth   40, 239
Morake, Sello   21
Morena, Khotso (Mwezi Twala)   15
Morobe, Murphy   7, 70, 72, 174
Moroka, Sidwell (Omry Makgale)   59
Moseneke, Dikgang   214
Moses Kotane Self-Reliance Centre   5
Motaung, Grace   59
Motlante, Kgalema   12, 14, 51
Motsepe, Vincent   12
Motshabi, Caleb   12
Motsoahae, Lorna   75
Motsoaledi, Elias   54, 238
Motsuenyane, Sam   63, 236
Motwa, Bongani   59
Movement Enterprise   26, 27
Movemento Popular de Libertaçao de
   Angola (Popular Movement for the
   Liberation of Angola) (MPLA)   xvi,
   xvii, 59, 168
Mozambican National Resistance Move-
   ment (RENAMO)   134
Mpanza, Steven   7
Mpofu, Dali   27, 62, 71ff
Msomi, Ronald   60

Msomi, Welcome   238
Mthembu, Gabriel   64
Mufamadi, Sydney   9, 51, 54
Mugabe, Robert   259
Mulholland, Giles   264
Musi, Mbulelo (*see* Thema, Moses)
Muyeni, Musa   106
Mvelase, Catherine   186
Mzala   166

N

Naidoo, Jay   93, 237, 238
Nair, Billy   54, 70, 73, 186
National Campaigns Committee   192
National Commission for the Emancipa-
   tion of Women (NCEW)   43
National Council of Trade Unions
   (NACTU)   105
National Economic Forum   90, 216
National Education Coordination Com-
   mittee (NECC)   89
National Election Committee   229
National Electrification Forum   216
National Executive Committee (NEC)   6,
   7, 9, 37, 41, 54, 66, 128, 161ff, 197,
   203, 236, 238, 250, 264
National Film Trust of South Africa   27
National Forum   150
National Housing Forum (NHF)   90,
   216, 255
National Liberation Front of Angola
   (FNLA)   168
National Local Government Negotiating
   Forum   216
National Party (NP)   43, 129, 154, 179,
   180, 204ff, 214, 215, 242, 247, 248,
   254ff
National People's Tribunal   61
National Preparatory Committee   66
National Reception Committee (NRC)   7,
   68, 72
National Review Committee   61
National Statutory Council   150
National Steering Committee (NSC)   35
National Student Federation   102
National Union for the Total Indepen-
   dence of Angola (UNITA)   57, 134,
   168
National Union of Metalworkers of
   South Africa (NUMSA)   88, 184

National Union of Mineworkers (NUM) 16, 50, 88

National Union of South African Students (NUSAS) 32, 33

National Working Committee (NWC) 12, 54, 75

National Youth Organisation (NAYO) 32

Ncube, Mthetheleli 198

Ndebele, Njabulo 238

Ndlovu, Curnick 70, 73

Negotiating Council 45, 204, 219

Negotiating Forum 206

Netshitenzhe, Joel (Peter Mayibuye) 7, 9, 54

Ngungunyana, Solly 58

Ngwenya, Mzwakhe (Thami Zulu) 57, 61, 62

Nhlanhla, Joe 9, 62

Niehaus, Carl 7

Nkabinde, James 60

Nkabinde, Sifiso 240

Nkadimeng, John 8, 27, 54, 61, 69

Nkobi, Thomas 9

Nkomo, Maggie 74

Nkomo, Marjorie 75

Nkondo, Curtis 59

Nkondo, Ephraim (Zaba Maledza) 59

Nkosi, Duma 237

Nkuna, Joe 264

Ntile, Sakelo Llewellyn 27

Ntlokwana, Nomfanelo (see Mhlongo, Kate)

Nujoma, Sam 39

Nupen, Charles 104, 214

Nxumalo, Muntu 75

Nxumalo, Samuel 239

Nyanda, Siphiwe 54, 186

Nzimande, B. 49

Nzimande, Blade 202

Nzo, Alfred 9, 70, 72, 249

O

Okumu, Washington 224

Omar, Dullah 71

Omar, Obar 7

Ondala, Wandile 60

Operations Committee 103

Organisation of African Unity (OAU) 4, 108, 148, 184

Organisation of African Unity Ad Hoc Committee on Southern Africa 148

Ovsiowitz, Julian 238

P

Pahad, Essop 239

Paintin, Nomaza 244

Palestine Liberation Organisation (PLO) 20

Pan Africanist Congress (PAC) 43, 45, 68, 117, 178, 184, 205, 210, 257, 258

Pan Africanist Movement 46

Patel, Dipak 186

Patriotic Front (PF) 237, 257

People's Armed Forces for the Liberation of Angola (FAPLA) 59

Peterson, Sally 75

Phosa, Matthews 110, 237, 247

Pikoli, Girlie 75

Piliso, Mzwai 64, 70

Pillay, Ivan 186

Piper (see Mahamba, Kenneth)

Pityane, Barney 32

Plaatjie, Sol 40

Planned Parenthood Association 43

Political Military Council 58

Popular Movement for the Liberation of Angola (MPLA) xvi, xvii, 59, 168

Pretorius, M.C. 104

Provisional National Youth Secretariat (PNYS) 33

Provisional Regional Youth Committees (PRYC) 34

PWV Regional Women's League 40, 72ff

R

Rahupe, Golden 64

Rajah, D.S. 237, 238

Ramadiro, S. 88

Ramaphosa, Cyril 7ff, 51, 70ff, 197, 205, 213, 237, 238, 249ff, 259

Ramathlodi, Ngoako 237, 247

Rammego, Kgomotso 75

Ramodike, Nelson 237, 238

Ramushwana, Gabriel 237, 238

Reddy, J.N. 237, 238

Regional Dispute Resolution Committee (RDRC) 103

Regional Executive Committee
(REC)   74
Regional Political Committee (Tanzania)
61
Regional Political Military Committee   6
Release Mandela Committee   69
Relly, Gavin   131
Reserve Bank   94
Revolutionary Council   58
Rivers, Mrs   75
Rockman, Gregory   237
Roussos, Pete   26
Ruth First Centre   5

S

Sachs, Albie   57, 237
Saloojee, Cassim   70
Sankar, Amnesh Munessar   186
Schultz, George   132
self-defence unit (SDU)   100, 124, 189ff
Seme, Pixly Ka Isaka   115
September, Reginald   54
Serote, Wally   27
Serote, Wole   8
Sese Seko, Mobuto   153
Sexwale, Tokyo   37, 38, 110, 236, 237,
247
Shill, Louis   255
Shilowa, Sam   52
Shope, Gertrude   38ff
Shope, Ntombi   12
Sibeko, Solly   59
Sibiya, Messie   75
Sigxashe, Sizakhele   60, 64
Sihlangu, Zanempi   59
Simkins, Charles   87, 94
Simons, Jack   61
Sisulu, Albertina   39, 41
Sisulu, Max   8
Sisulu, Sheila   238
Sisulu, Walter   7, 9, 32, 116, 155, 237
Sisulu, Zwelakhe   238
Skosana, M.   49
Skotaville   26
Skweyiya, Thembile Louis   62
Skweyiya, Zola   8, 9, 61, 62
Slovo, Joe   8, 54ff, 63, 69, 110, 120,
136, 186, 200, 201, 205, 208, 213,
237, 238
Smith, Ian   167

Soames, Lord   167
Social Welfare Support Committee   74
Solomon Mahlangu Freedom College
(SOMAFCO)   4, 5
Sonn, Franklin   238
South African Broadcasting Corporation
(SABC)   231
South African Clothing and Textile
Workers Union (SACTWU)   50, 88,
184
South African Coloured People's
Organisation   116
South African Commercial Catering and
Allied Workers Union (SACCAWU)
50
South African Communist Party (SACP)
20, 37, 50, 52ff, 89, 117, 118, 120,
122, 135, 187, 198, 237
South African Congress of Trade Unions
(SACTU)   4
South African Council of Churches
(SACC)   7, 43
South African Defence Force (SADF)
101, 125, 188, 189
South African Democratic Teachers
Union (SADTU)   208
South African Indian Congress   116
South African National Civic Organisa-
tion (SANCO)   50, 68, 89, 93
South African National Student Con-
gress (SANSCO)   33
South African Police (SAP)   99, 101,
105, 109, 126, 189
South African Railways and Harbour
Workers Union (SARHWU)   184
South African Student Congress
(SASCO)   34, 68
South African Student Movement
(SASM)   32
South African Student Organisation
(SASO)   32
South African Youth Congress
(SAYCO)   21, 32
South West African People's Organisa-
tion (SWAPO)   39, 102, 230
Sparks, Alistair   238
Spoornet   106
Stalker, Brenda   137
Standing Committee on Water Supply
and Sanitation   216
Starushenko, Gleb   132, 133

Stofile, Arnold   12
Stopper   60
Stuart, James   60, 70
Students United for Christian Action
   (SUCA)   33
Sun International   27
Suttner, Raymond   7, 8, 49, 54, 55,
   171, 198, 199, 202
Suzman, Helen   214
Swedish Internal Development Agency
   (SIDA)   24

T

Tambo, Oliver   4, 9, 32, 33, 38, 39, 43,
   58, 61, 63, 124, 132, 134, 147, 159,
   186, 206, 230
Tennyson Makiwane faction   68
Terreblanche, Eugene   38
Thatcher, Margaret   154, 156
Thebe Investment Corporation
   (TIC)   26
Thema, Moses (Mbulelo Musi)   59
Titus, Zam   206
Tloome, Dan   61
Transitional Executive Council (TEC)
   182, 209, 210, 213, 222, 232
Tripartite Alliance (ANC, SACP and
   COSATU)   50ff, 89, 183, 193, 210
Tshabalala, Sussanna   186
Tshabalala, Trevor   109
Tshona, Zamxolo   62
Tshwete, Steve   8, 21, 48, 196, 238
Tutu, Desmond   62
Twala, Mwezi (*see* Morena, Khotso)

U

Umkhonto we Sizwe (MK)   5, 9, 53,
   100, 116ff, 122ff, 188ff
Union des Populations du Cameroun
   (UPC)   xvi
United Democratic Front (UDF)   6, 21,
   32, 45ff, 73, 84, 128, 129, 146
United Nations (UN)   4, 39, 108, 168
United Nations Security Council   184
United Nations Special Committee
   Against Apartheid   210
United Workers Union of South Africa
   (UWUSA)   102
Urban Foundation   87

V

Valli Moosa, Mohammed   7, 8, 54, 66,
   70, 71
Vally, S.   88
Van der Merwe, Fanie   174
Van der Merwe, H.   131
Van der Ross, Ben   214
Van Driel, Maria   171, 172
Van Eck, Jan   237
Van Zyl, Bertie   242
Vance, Cyrus   108, 185
Velem, Sindile (*see* Botha, Simon)
Viljoen, Constand   208, 217, 218, 221
Viljoen, Gerrit   155
Violence Monitoring Committee   104
Vlok, Adriaan   100, 101, 103
Volkstaat Council   224

W

Webb, Mike   206
Williams, Tim   64
Women of South Africa   43
Women's Bureau   43
Women's Legal Status   43
Women's National Coalition (WNC)   43
Workers Organisation for Socialist
   Action (WOSA)   88
World Apartheid Movement   109
World Council of Churches   24
World Economic Development Congress
   210
World University Services   24

X

Xobololo, Alfred   12

Y

Yacoob, Zach   214
Young Women's Christian Association
   43
Youth Christian Students (YCS)   33

Z

Z Squad   101
Zama, Linda   74
Zamchiya, David   63

Zimbabwe African National Union
(ZANU)   xvii, 230
Zimbabwe African People's Union
(ZAPU)   58, 121
Zitha, Mangesi   237

Zulu, Thami (*see* Ngwenya, Mzwakhe)

Zuma, Jacob   7ff, 62, 64, 68, 69, 237,
241, 248

Zwelithini, Goodwill   218, 220ff